# IN PLACE
# OF
# MOBILITY

**The David J. Weber Series in the New Borderlands History**

*Andrew R. Graybill and Benjamin H. Johnson, editors*

EDITORIAL BOARD

| | |
|---|---|
| Juliana Barr | Kelly Lytle Hernández |
| Sarah Carter | Cynthia Radding |
| Maurice Crandall | Samuel Truett |

The study of borderlands—places where different peoples meet and no one polity reigns supreme—is undergoing a renaissance. The David J. Weber Series in the New Borderlands History publishes works from both established and emerging scholars that examine borderlands from the precontact era to the present. The series explores contested boundaries and the intercultural dynamics surrounding them and includes projects covering a wide range of time and space within North America and beyond, including both Atlantic and Pacific worlds.

Published with support provided by the William P. Clements Center for Southwest Studies at Southern Methodist University in Dallas, Texas.

A complete list of books published in the David J. Weber Series in the New Borderlands History is available at https://uncpress.org/series/david-j-weber-series-in-the-new-borderlands-history.

# IN PLACE OF MOBILITY

Railroads, Rebels, and Migrants in
an Argentine-Chilean Borderland

# KYLE E. HARVEY

THE UNIVERSITY OF NORTH CAROLINA PRESS

*Chapel Hill*

© 2024 The University of North Carolina Press

*All rights reserved*

Designed by Jamison Cockerham
Set in Scala, Scala Sans, Libre Franklin, and Bleeker
By Jamie McKee, MacKey Composition

*Manufactured in the United States of America*

Chapter 2 appeared previously in somewhat different form as
Kyle E. Harvey, "'Because That's What His Consul Had Ordered':
The Chilean Consulate as a Labor Institution in Mendoza, Argentina
(1859–1869)," *Historia Crítica*, no. 80 (2021): 81–102.

Cover art: Entrance to Las Leñas lateral gallery, ca. 1900. Courtesy
of Alex Gulliver Papers, Archivo Nacional Histórico, Santiago.
Blueprint of the Transandine Railway, 1896. Courtesy of Protocolos
Notariales, no. 555, Archivo Histórico de Mendoza, Argentina.

Complete Cataloging-in-Publication Data for this title is available
from the Library of Congress at https://lccn.loc.gov/2024033121.

ISBN 978-1-4696-8225-9 (cloth: alk. paper)
ISBN 978-1-4696-8226-6 (pbk.: alk. paper)
ISBN 978-1-4696-8227-3 (epub)
ISBN 978-1-4696-8228-0 (pdf)

**To Susana and Matilda**

# CONTENTS

List of Illustrations   ix

Acknowledgments   xi

Introduction  MOBILITY AND HISTORY   1

**Chapter 1**  A TRANS-ANDEAN WORLD   13

Interlude 1  INFRASTRUCTURE AND GLOBAL SPACE   31

**Chapter 2**  THE STATE OF LABOR   37

Interlude 2  THE SHAPE OF LABOR   52

**Chapter 3**  PROPERTY AND EVERYDAY MOBILITY   57

Interlude 3  REENGINEERING THE TRANS-ANDEAN   82

**Chapter 4**  MANUFACTURING A REBELLION   91

*Interlude 4* ENGINEERS BETWEEN FRONTIERS   109

**Chapter 5** **KILLING THE TRANS-ANDEAN**   114

*Interlude 5* THE UNBUILT ENVIRONMENT AND GLOBAL SPACE   137

**Conclusion** **A HISTORY OF MOBILITY**   147


*Appendix A* DEMOGRAPHICS OF CHILEANS IN MENDOZA   153

*Appendix B* THEFT CASES IN MENDOZA   157

Notes   161

Bibliography   211

Index   239

# ILLUSTRATIONS

**Map**

Map of the Trans-Andean, ca. 1867   *xvi*

**Tables**

1.1. Chilean imports from Argentina, 1846–1862   *27*

3.1. Frequency of places mentioned in cases of transport animal theft in Mendoza, 1843–1872   *75*

A.1. Chileans in Mendoza by age, 1869   *154*

A.2. Chileans in Mendoza by gender, 1869   *155*

A.3. Chileans in Mendoza by occupation, 1869   *156*

B.1. Cases of animal theft reviewed, 1838–1872   *158*

# ACKNOWLEDGMENTS

There are many people to thank for helping this book come to fruition. From even before the beginning, Ray Craib has been enormously supportive and encouraged me to follow this direction. Without him, this book would not exist. Likewise, Ernesto Bassi has been a constant source of inspiration, particularly on questions of mobility. Sara Pritchard provided me with the kind of space and conversations on questions of technology that helped inspire this book and run throughout its entirety, even if not always present to casual observers. Mark Healey's insights and suggestions about turning this project into a book have been invaluable to making it what it is today. Without Josh Savala's early and continued encouragement and support, I would never have finished this project. Even before I conceived of this book, at the University of Michigan, many people inspired me to pursue history and to push myself, including Kathy Evaldson, Dario Gaggio, Jean Hébrard, Bruno Renero-Hannan, Rebecca Scott, and Ken Sylvester.

Throughout the development of this project and the research that has gone into it, many people and organizations have provided me with generous support and insights. Diego Escolar has inspired me and provided essential challenges to my ideas about the region. Early on, Ryan Edwards helped me get situated in the archives and made the initial research fruitful. Likewise, Alistair Hattingh aided in getting me situated in my early archival trips. Luis

Caballero lent me his insights, companionship, and help in getting sources on Casimiro Ferrari. Others have provided me with ideas, reading suggestions, and inspiration that run throughout this book: Nick Bujalski, Matthew Brashears, Tim Cresswell, Ariel de la Fuente, Tom Klubock, Max McComb, Ty McCulloch, Al Milian, Matt Minarchek, John Moran, Sharlene O'Donnell, José Ragas, Suman Seth, Jim Sweet, Chuck Walker, Eleanor Young, Jesse Zarley, and everyone who has participated in the New Research on Latin American Borderlands series and workshops. Portions of this book were also presented at the annual meetings of the American Historical Association and the Latin American Studies Association. I benefited from the feedback from the audience and fellow panelists. At the Social Science Research Council, Emily Carroll encouraged me to continue exploring the intersection of property and mobility, which provides the analytical and conceptual basis for much of this book. Funding for research has come from a number of sources: the SSRC, the Fulbright, and, at Cornell University, the Graduate School, the Latin American Studies Program (now Latin American and Caribbean Studies), the Society for the Humanities, the Atkinson Center for a Sustainable Future, and the Land Theme Project at the Institute for Social Sciences. Last, Josh Wilson, my graduate assistant in the History Department at Western Carolina University (with funds from the WCU Graduate School), provided much-needed assistance in compiling census data on Chileans in Argentina.

Archivists and librarians make everything possible. I relied on their support, help, and patience. In Argentina, I owe a great debt to Alicia Guevara and the other archivists at the Archivo Histórico de Mendoza. Although I was at the Archivo Histórico de San Juan only a short time, the archivists there made it possible for me to do an immense amount of research. In Buenos Aires, the archivists and staff of the Archivo General de la Nación, the Archivo Histórico de la Cancillería (especially Alba Lombardi), the Biblioteca Nacional, and the Sociedad Científica Argentina (especially Norma Sánchez) were amazing in helping me find what I did not even know I needed. In Santiago, José Fernández Pérez, Pedro González Cancino, Roberto Mercado Martinic, Pablo Muñoz, and the other archivists and staff at the Archivo Nacional Histórico, the Archivo Nacional de la Administración, the Biblioteca Nacional, and the Archivo de la Cancillería helped make this transnational project possible. In England, the staff and archivists at the National Archives and Archive of the Institute of Civil Engineers made short research trips enormously productive. Keiko Nishimoto, and the staff and archivists at the Harvard Botany Libraries helped me turn a one-day trip into a key part of my analysis in chapter 5. The staff at Cornell University's Olin Library were invaluable to the early stages of this book. Last, at Western Carolina University, Heidi Buchanan and Krista Schmidt, as well as everyone at Hunter Library, were enormously helpful as I revised and turned this work into a final book. I cannot express enough gratitude to all of those who make archives and libraries run.

Writing a book is not an easy task, but for me it has been made easier by those who have read pieces of it. Many people have read and commented on portions of this book, including Saheed Aderinto, Eddie Brudney, Amie Campos, Vera Candiani, Giuliana Chamedes, Javier Cikota, Youjin Chung, Rob Clines, Geraldine Davies Lenoble, Teresa Davis, Sebastián Díaz Ángel, David Dorondo, Mary Ella Engel, Jeff Erbig, Ben Fallaw, Rob Ferguson, José Andrés Fernández Montes de Oca, Sarah Foss, Ben Francis-Fallon, Pablo Gómez, Gael Graham, Hannah Greenwald, Elena Guzman, Emily Hong, Patrick Iber, Kathryn Lehman, Adrián Lerner, Christine Mathias, Nick Myers, Marcos Pérez Cañizares, Scott Philyaw, Angie Picone, Javier Puente, Lara Putnam, Daniela Samur, Osama Siddiqui, Adam Thomas, Barbara Weinstein, and Ray Craib's graduate seminar at Cornell University. Benjamin Hopkins and an anonymous reviewer provided some of the most insightful and thoughtful feedback I have ever received. This book is infinitely better for it. In the same vein, I thank Santiago Muñoz, Rachel Nolan, and Santiago Paredes, as well as the reviewers at *Historia Crítica*, who provided me with feedback on an earlier version of the second chapter. Rebecca Scheidt, Alex Macaulay, and my wonderful colleagues at Western Carolina University, especially in the History Department, have been very supportive in getting this book to publication. Ben Johnson not only read portions of this book and gave great feedback on it but also made its publication possible through his encouragement, patience, and shepherding of it through the review process. Andrew Graybill and Debbie Gershenowitz have been similarly fundamental to seeing this book come to fruition. I owe a huge debt of gratitude to Valerie Burton, whose tireless work has made this a much better book, as well as JessieAnne D'Amico, Alexis Dumain, Elizabeth Orange, Lindsay Starr, and everyone at UNC Press who has helped make the production of this book possible.

Someone wise once said, relationships matter. That has been especially true for my friends and family. He may not know it, but Tim inspired me early on, especially to be critical and pursue unconventional avenues of inquiry. As is sometimes the case with parents, mine deserve more recognition and gratitude than I could ever give. My in-laws have been enormously generous and supportive in providing me the space and resources to complete this book. My siblings have been very supportive throughout. Mario, Marcela, Lula, Karina, and others hosted me on various research trips. Cynthia Brock welcomed me into her home and provided a safe place throughout the research and writing of this book. Matilda has helped me remember what is important in life and how to say "no." Last and most important, Susan Romero Sánchez has provided unwavering support and intellectual inspiration for years and, I hope, for decades to come. To all whom I have not mentioned, thank you. Although many have made this book better, all errors belong to me.

# IN PLACE OF MOBILITY

**Map of the Trans-Andean (ca. 1867) as understood through the places and features mentioned in this book.** The map is based on Martin de Moussy's 1867 map of Argentina. As such, it is not fully accurate, particularly in regard to the exact location of borders. It is, therefore, a reflection of representations of space in formation. It features three of the mountain passes through which different railroad projects were to be built. The map also includes my own approximation of Indigenous-controlled territories and the Chilean military campaigns in the south. To provide an understanding of topography and to underscore that most of this history is told from lower and flatter ground than might be assumed from first glance, elevations in meters are included for some places and passes (based on Martin de Moussy's atlas in which the map appears). They are not always accurate and should be seen as approximations and reminders of spatial imprecision. Adapted from Victor Martin de Moussy's 1867 map of Argentina, *Carte de la Confédération argentine*. In *Description géographique et statistique de la Confédération argentine: Atlas de la Confédération argentine*, 2nd ed. (Paris: Librairie de Firmin Didot Frères, Fils et Cie, 1873), courtesy of the David Rumsey Map Collection at Stanford University Libraries, Stanford, California.

Introduction   **Mobility and History**

In the summer of 1869–70, in the mountains between Argentina and Chile, a migrant laborer, a rebel, and an engineer were crossing the Andes in different directions and for different purposes but with a shared historical meaning. The engineer, Emilio Rosetti, had been sent on a mission to expand state influence over the distant lands of what was becoming known as the Argentine Republic. The rebel, Casimiro Ferrari, and his Chilean companion, Tadeo Pavez, sought to escape that influence. Rosetti was surveying a route for a mountain-crossing railroad meant to connect the Atlantic and Pacific Oceans. Ferrari was a former rebel commander in Argentina turned fugitive, accused by Argentine officials of a gruesome murder. Pavez was a Chilean migrant who had served in Ferrari's rebel battalion years earlier.

This was not Ferrari's and Pavez's first time in the mountains. Years of political upheaval in western Argentina had familiarized Ferrari with an unsettled life. Swept out of Argentina with changing political tides, Ferrari became a rebel in exile in the early 1860s, returning to serve as a commander during a brief interregnum in 1866–67 when he and his fellow partisans reclaimed power.[1] After the rebellion ended in defeat, Ferrari resumed his exile in Chile, as political rebels of all stripes had done before him. He continued to draw on his rebel networks, employing the former rebel soldier and migrant Pavez as his right-hand man. Pavez, like thousands of other Chileans, had migrated to the province of Mendoza in western Argentina in the middle years of the nineteenth century. Along with many of his young male compatriots, he was conscripted into armed service while there, eventually parlaying his unwilling service under Ferrari into a seemingly regular job with the former rebel before both men found themselves the subjects of an international murder case. Despite the Argentine government's efforts to extradite the men, they remained in Chile. The only one to come back publicly from the mountains to Argentina was Rosetti, who returned to Buenos Aires months later in 1870 to present his railroad study.[2] Although Rosetti's work did not result in a railroad, forty years later in 1910 politicians and businessmen from the two countries inaugurated a different mountain-crossing railroad.[3] In the meantime, Rosetti returned to the University of Buenos Aires, where he led the newly established engineering program and trained the nation's first generation of engineers. That generation went on to be fundamental not only to the development of engineering in Argentina but also to the development of the nascent state. In conjunction with colleagues trained at other institutions in Europe, those young engineers became fundamental to the construction and functioning of the Argentine state at the turn of the twentieth century, specifically its public works bureaucracy.

The brief passage of those three men through the Andes that same summer in 1869–70 encapsulates a fundamental moment in Argentine and Latin American history. The state's pursuit of the former rebel commander and his exile and subsequent disappearance from the archival record represent the waning years of civil war and the onset of a centralized, nation-state order in Argentina. After Argentina declared independence from Spain in 1816, initial attempts at centralization and constitutionalism failed. Decades of conflicts between Federalist and Unitarian forces and geographical tensions between the interior provinces and Buenos Aires culminated in civil war and nation-state solidification in the 1850s and 1860s.[4] Although these conflicts were seemingly resolved with the Battle of Pavón in 1861, the creation of the Argentine Republic and the election in 1862 of the nation's first president, Bartolomé Mitre, holdouts like Casimiro Ferrari continued to agitate throughout the country. Elsewhere in Latin America, similar conflicts emerged. As in Argentina, those conflicts centered on contestations over and the consolidation of the postindependence political, social, and economic order.[5] If almost everywhere the stakes and meaning of independence were still open at midcentury, by the 1870s and 1880s, a sense of closure emerged.[6] Characterized by a rejection of political experimentation and an embrace of globalization and export-oriented capitalism that dominated by the last decades of the nineteenth century, the new order was a stark contrast to the varied republican experimentations still taking place at midcentury.[7] At the center of that transition to this new order were scientific, medical, and technological projects, specifically infrastructure ones brought about by engineers, such as railroads and telegraphs, which facilitated the creation of increasingly integrated national territories in Latin America, technocratic rule, and export-oriented economies.[8] That Ferrari seemed never to have returned to Argentina while Rosetti's influence only grew personifies this historical transition, which is the focus of *In Place of Mobility*.

## A Mid-Nineteenth-Century Trans-Andean

The transition from the postindependence period to the conservative liberal period around the mid-nineteenth century can be understood as much a place in space as a moment in time, one reflective of the tensions between the deterritorializing tendencies of capitalism and the territorializing tendencies of nation-state formation, where capitalism and the social changes tied to it moved faster than the always calcifying norms and institutions of the nation-state.[9] Indeed, this was the transitional place that Ferrari, Pavez, Rosetti, and others like them were making in the 1860s, a place that appeared at a moment of historical convulsions and then faded as so many places do. *In Place of Mobility* refers to this historical space as the Trans-Andean, understood here as a part of western Argentina—namely, part of the provinces of Cuyo (particularly Mendoza and, to a lesser extent, San Juan), in close relationship with neighboring Chile. The Trans-Andean was made from the intersection of historically particular social and political processes intimately connected to Chile in the mid-nineteenth century: Chilean migrations, cattle trading, Argentine rebellions, mining, and changing transportation technologies. In other words, it was a relational space, one founded on connections across (trans-) the Andes mountains (Andean).[10] Ultimately, these social and political processes made and unmade the Trans-Andean, momentarily revealing historical possibilities and uncharted paths too often foreclosed by historical hindsight.

To be clear, *this* Trans-Andean is not the *only* Trans-Andean borderland. The Trans-Andean examined in this book can be thought of as one of many Trans-Andeans that have existed and continue to exist, all comprising what could be called a Greater Trans-Andean, running from southern Bolivia and northern Argentina and Chile down to the southern tip of the continent.

All show how the mountains have been more of a conduit than a barrier to forging communities.[11] For millennia, people have made the Andes and crossing them a central part of forming community, creating economies, constructing culture, and building empires, including Tawantinsuyu (Inka Empire) from the fourteenth century and then the Spanish Empire beginning in the sixteenth century.[12] To the south beginning in the sixteenth and seventeenth centuries but drawing on existing connections between the western side of the Andes and the Pampas toward the Atlantic Ocean, the frontier between the Spanish Empire and Indigenous-controlled lands transformed into an interoceanic space based in the circulation of cattle, horses, salt, alcohol, textiles, weapons, and more among Huilliches, Mapuches, Pampas Indigenous peoples, Pehuenches, Spaniards, Tehuelches, and others.[13] Later, in the nineteenth century, mobility in the Greater Trans-Andean played an important role in political and economic developments, from independence in the first decades to the expansion of Indigenous power to the civil wars of midcentury to the territorial consolidation of the Argentine and Chilean nation-states in the latter part of the century.[14] Alongside the history explored in *In Place of Mobility* there exist several overlapping narratives unfolding in the Greater Trans-Andean, from Bolivia to Wallmapu (the ancestral lands of the Mapuche people, generally conceived of as comprising northern Patagonia and the Pampas, from the Pacific to the Atlantic), many connected by the same individuals and structural processes at the center of this book.[15] Indeed, some of the economic processes and the same Argentine rebels important to this study sit at the center of other histories of this period in the Greater Trans-Andean.[16] These connections among disparate parts of the Greater Trans-Andean are referenced at various points in the narrative, but *In Place of Mobility* focuses mostly on the dense Trans-Andean connections centered on Cuyo and, in particular, the province of Mendoza.

The timing of this Trans-Andean's unfolding in the 1850s and 1860s was linked to economic developments in the Pacific world and in Chile, along with foundational nation-state formation processes in Argentina. Rapidly expanding wheat production in central Chile and mining booms in the north (a region known as the Norte Chico) integrated the country into different markets through its Pacific ports, chiefly Valparaíso. The Trans-Andean became a space made through the crisscrossing of labor migrants and commodities across the Andes. As a result, Mendoza and the surrounding areas became integrated into Chilean markets over the mountains as Chile became integrated into global markets through the Pacific. At the same time, as the Argentine national state—centered on the capital and Atlantic port of Buenos Aires—was solidifying its power over the new republic in the 1860s, the Trans-Andean provided shelter for rebel holdouts against the ascendant conservative liberal order. In effect, the region was caught between a Pacific-oriented economic integration and an Atlantic-oriented political integration. Despite appearances, this space was not a mere mismatch of receding political ideas and advancing flows of capital and labor. Rather, it was one in which contested state sovereignty and capitalist expansion fed into one another as Chilean migrant laborers in Argentina challenged ideas of political community and emerging notions of nationhood; as mine owners in Chile financed Argentine rebels; and as mountain-crossing merchants navigated the perils and opportunities presented to them by rebellion. As rapidly shifting norms of state power failed to match economic and social changes in this turbulent period, people at different levels of society found extralegal activities, manipulation of evolving state institutions, and violence to be effective vehicles for social change and self-advancement.

Alongside the rebellious spirit of the 1860s in the Trans-Andean a different, more global history emerges throughout *In Place of Mobility*, one that foreshadows the coming late-century order. As a result of the intensification of economic connections between western Argentina and Chile, merchants, miners, financiers, and state officials became increasingly interested in building a railroad across the mountains. Although such a railroad was not completed until 1910, its emergence as a project in the 1850s and 1860s signaled a reckoning with the political and social turmoil born out of the same conditions that were birthing the railroad and thus embodied the period in the Trans-Andean and its relation to the world. As a project, it embodied the aspirations of its boosters; it inspired hope in national political leaders who wished to pacify the region; it drew on liberal educational reforms; it reflected the emerging marriage between global financial sectors and nascent nation-states; it found global relevance in the Anglo-settler boom of the time; it was in dialogue with struggles over Indigenous territory and economic activity in the mountains; and it even became connected to political rebellion when a project surveyor became a financial backer of Argentine rebels. Ultimately, these railroad projects were material manifestations of the world from the perspective of the Trans-Andean and help *In Place of Mobility* make localized social and political histories into stories of global change.

In line with other work that decenters Buenos Aires and traditional explanations of conflict in this period, *In Place of Mobility* makes the case for reframing this pivotal moment in Argentine history as more Chile- and Pacific-facing than previously understood.[17] By interweaving these narratives,

*In Place of Mobility* argues that through their mobility Trans-Andean actors—primarily, Chilean migrants and rebels from Argentina exiled in Chile—shaped state formation in Argentina at local, provincial, and national levels. In response, state institutions in Argentina attempted to develop stronger capacities to monitor, control, and punish contentious Trans-Andean actors. Although those attempts sometimes failed or were uneven in their effects, Argentine officials did create institutions and policies that fortified state control over the Argentine-Chilean border, often in conjunction with counterparts in Chile.[18] At the same time, statesmen, some of those very same contentious Trans-Andean people, and others who found themselves deeply involved with Trans-Andean commerce began to develop ideas and plans for a Trans-Andean railroad. Those border institutions helped increase national and binational sovereignty over the region while the railroad projects pulled the region into the orbit of Buenos Aires, the Argentine nation-state, and the global financial institutions that supported railroad projects, making the Trans-Andean increasingly connected to nation-state capitals and financial centers, thereby bisecting the region and revealing how mountains connected and railroads divided.

### Making a Railroad

This project began as a history of the railroad, not of a borderland. Even now, I hesitate to call it a borderlands history because the historiographical traditions and conceptual guideposts that informed the research and writing of this book were never founded in borderlands scholarship. Instead, the guiding questions that began this history had everything to do with the concept of mobility. How did people put themselves in motion over the Andes and across Argentina? What obstacles did they face? And if the modern state has been defined by its "monopolization of the legitimate means of movement," how did the state condition people's mobility and how did their mobility shape state formation?[19] In effect, what would a history of mobility in the nineteenth century look like? For the latter part of the century, the railroad represented a sea change in the practices of mobility and representations of space, and the Trans-Andean railroad's narrative within that historical shift is, to me, uniquely perplexing. For Argentina, the first age of railroad history (often defined by the creation and expansion of British-owned railroads in the country) often runs from the 1850s, when the first tracks were laid in the country, to the 1910s, when the first era of globalization ended.[20] The Trans-Andean as a project spanned this period. Conceived of in the 1860s and inaugurated in 1910, however, the Trans-Andean's history was one of waiting more than anything. Against the backdrop of a flurry of activity, with more than 16,000 kilometers of track built in Argentina by 1900, making it "one of the most extensive, integrated" railroad networks in Latin America, the mountain-crossing, bioceanic railroad was defined by inactivity.[21] Had its supporters been wrong about its importance? Could a non-railroad really belong to a transformative period for mobility?

Mobility lies at the foundation of what might be called "alternative geographies," the borderlands, transnational spaces, frontiers, places of "entangled" histories, Indigenous territories, and all sorts of worlds that are set apart from the national territories that provided the foundation for historiographical traditions in the nineteenth and twentieth centuries.[22] In contrast to the borders that shape national histories, routes define studies of these spaces.[23] Following the routes left by people's mobility in space, scholars have demonstrated how the borders that states have relied on as part of their claim to total territorial sovereignty have not determined people's "lived geographies" or erased those narratives that do not neatly conform to the ones nations have set up for themselves.[24] In effect, if nations have their origins in homogenizing narratives, borderlands have countered with the persistence of a multiplicity of narratives.[25] This is where *In Place of Mobility* and borderlands histories converge; the connection between routes in space and narratives in history turn historical space away from the primacy of idealizations and representations toward space as relationally produced by people's practices. This tendency toward multiplicity of narratives does not come without its problems, however. Bearers of this pluralistic tradition, borderlands histories have not only challenged the homogenizing claims of the nation but also its explanatory power. As much as the nation-state based its authority in visions of homogeneous territory and teleological narratives, it also gave scholars a stable unit of analysis with which to develop questions and explanations that could serve as the basis for a common conversation based in the unifying power of historical narratives (as opposed to ahistorical concepts or antiquarian fascination with descriptivism).[26]

The Trans-Andean railroad was *one* result of the development of the Trans-Andean borderland explored in this book, which was at its heart an *economic borderland*, connecting Cuyo in Argentina to the Central Valley, the Norte Chico, and the port of Valparaíso in Chile. My understanding of an economic borderland has emerged in dialogue with histories of colonial economic spaces in Latin America, specifically histories of the Andes and the Caribbean that foreground economic processes in the construction of those spaces, their influence on colonial and national state formation, and how the people who made those spaces ended up challenging claims of sovereignty by virtue of crossing imperial boundaries or subverting colonial control over trade.[27] An economic borderland can be understood, then, as an integrated economic space that covers territory in which there are multiple claims to sovereignty (not necessarily overlapping). The mid-nineteenth century offers fertile ground to see how economic borderlands confronted and challenged claims of state power. At a crucial moment in state formation in Latin America, economic borderlands existed across the region, some new and others long-standing.[28] In all these instances, as in the Greater Trans-Andean, those economic borderlands posed challenges to and opportunities for postindependence state formation, sometimes resulting in the rearranging of territory and fanning the flames of civil war in other cases. Wrestling with those economic borderlands and their refusal to adhere to aspirational borders became formative moments for many states. The result in the case of the Trans-Andean was twofold. On the one hand, state officials worked not only to exert control over the border and the people who crossed it but also to extend the spatial reach and coherence of the state. On the other hand, the development of this economic borderland made possible a project for a Trans-Andean railroad. In a sense, the railroad was this economic borderland "made durable."[29]

Infrastructure is the modern era made durable, bringing together the nation-state, capitalism, and globalization. For capitalists in the nineteenth century, infrastructure such as railroads not only brought sites of production and markets closer and expanded the possibilities of what could be shipped across long distances but also provided places for capital investment, which was important for avoiding crises of overproduction and overaccumulation of capital.[30] That drive to build infrastructure resulted in the vast proliferation of new spaces across the world (train stations, railroad cars, work camps, tracks, warehouses, and so on). For the state, that dynamic proliferated spaces through which power could be exercised in an impersonal way. Ports, sewage systems, roads, telegraph offices, traffic signals, and all the infrastructure of the modern state exercised power in society, conditioning how people moved in space and interacted with one another in a way that appeared deeply quotidian and impersonal.[31] Without displacing the human agency foundational to power, infrastructure helped create a new kind, one that naturalized itself in space and that was reflective of the underlying structures of the societies in which they were constructed.[32] As much as infrastructure exercised its influence on society through its immediate materiality, being seen, heard, smelled, and felt constantly, that appearance sometimes could hide as much as it revealed. Indeed, writers, politicians, and intellectuals from the nineteenth century onward made infrastructure, especially railroads, the conceptual manifestation of human progress, often in the process obscuring the human activity, social relationships, and historical conflicts that actually created the changes often placed under the banner of "progress."[33] What a railroad obscured is as important as how it appeared. In many ways, this history is the inverse of those railroad-as-progress narratives, highlighting the context in which a railroad could be made possible without ever touching on the physical railroad itself.[34]

When the Trans-Andean railroad was initially conceptualized by Juan and Mateo Clark, the main goal was to connect Mendoza with the Chilean port of Valparaíso, as the Trans-Andean made durable. As soon as the railroad could be conceived of as a useful thing, however, it had to be recognized as something else, a tool for the greater integration of not just an economic borderland but rather the world, analogous to interoceanic canals and intercontinental railroads elsewhere. The need to attract investors and support from the Chilean and Argentine states meant that the railroad needed to be seen as useful to representatives in Santiago and Buenos Aires, along with investors there and across the world, particularly in London.[35] In other words, the project was an abstracting out of space. Once a project to make the Trans-Andean durable, it then became *partially* divorced from that meaning and endowed with meaning from different places in the world, which in turn would help it become material reality through the capital provided by those distant states and investors. That process of abstracting out was also part of the work of railroad engineers as they made spaces in the Trans-Andean useful for (or impediments to) railroad construction and operation. This railroad was at once in place (part of the mountain environments it traversed) and out of place (part of capital accumulation and state making far removed from the Andes). It was, as most large-scale infrastructure projects of the modern era are, global space, pulling together nation-states and centers of capital accumulation into one place.

Mobility makes space and history and puts them together. The routes it creates, whether left in earth or constructed in steel, contain narratives of economic exchange, power struggles, and strategies for survival and advancement. They are the embodiments in space of the conflicts that drive history. Historian Ricardo Salvatore has reflected on the political meaningfulness of itinerant laborers' mobility in Buenos Aires province after independence, arguing that such mobility was an expression of laborers' attempting to forge

*Mobility and History*

their own histories different from the kinds that state officials would have wanted.³⁶ I share the perspective that mobility had overwhelming significance in the development of the state and of people's sense of political self in this period. The centrality of mobility in this period went beyond the conflicts between state officials and unruly subalterns. *In Place of Mobility* follows struggles over mobility in several cases: the mobility of labor (chapter 2), the mobility of transport animals (chapter 3), the mobility of capital in the form of cattle (chapter 4), the mobility of rebels and information (chapter 5), and of course the mobilities of engineers, boosters, and investors in the development of the various Trans-Andean infrastructure projects (interludes). The result is a collection of routes and the narratives of their making, which together reveal part of a Trans-Andean borderland. By tying together the routes of migrants and state officials, itinerants and capitalists, engineers and rebels, *In Place of Mobility* makes a case for seeing borderlands not as defined against the state or dominant narratives but rather as an alternative space through which to build explanatory narratives, where mobility (of state and nonstate actors) is the foundation on which to construct a different spatiohistorical paradigm, inclusive of but not reducible to the nation.

## Chapter Outline

This book is organized into five substantial chapters, each followed by an interlude. The five chapters focus on the social history of the Trans-Andean, exploring the lived geographies of the people who made the Trans-Andean in the mid-nineteenth century. The interludes, by contrast, focus on the infrastructure history of the Trans-Andean, chiefly the railroad. These short pieces connect the themes of the chapters and global processes occurring at the time. Readers should take them as experimental provocations and open invitations to discussion and contestation, not final declarations or exhaustive expositions.

In chapter 1, I outline the economic and social context in which the Trans-Andean emerged as a space in the mid-nineteenth century. The region experienced significant economic transformations from the 1830s to the 1860s: the expansion of Pacific markets and the development of wheat exports in Chile, along with mining booms in the country's north and the growing importance to the Chilean economy of western Argentina as an exporter of livestock, primarily cattle. These changes led Chileans to migrate to western Argentina, where they settled into various forms of employment. As a result, mobility—in terms of itinerancy, commerce, and migrations—ultimately came to define western Argentine society. The first interlude opens with the project for a Trans-Andean telegraph as a way to think about the problem of infrastructure and its role in globalization by following the family story of Juan and Mateo Clark, the Chilean brothers who headed up this project and who would become the main promoters of the only Trans-Andean railroad to be completed by 1910.

Chapter 2 (a revised version of an article published in *Historia Crítica*) focuses on the impact of labor migrations and itinerancy on state formation in western Argentina. I explore the meaningfulness of Chilean identity and demonstrate how laborers used the Chilean consulate there to take greater control over their own labor, which was under threat not only from abusive employers but, more important, from the state in two forms. The first was a labor institution known as the *papeleta de conchabo* (work papers), which in tying laborers to employers made labor an obligation to society rather than an individual's right. The second was military service. Mobile laborers in the Trans-Andean challenged these increasingly outmoded labor institutions, and the Chilean consulate helped them to advance those challenges. Drawing out from the focus on labor relationships in western Argentina, in the second interlude I describe how the Trans-Andean railroad project was connected to changing labor regimes across the world, making clear that changing spatial configurations across the world were intimately related to the problem of labor.

Chapter 3 analyzes people's everyday mobility. Horses and mules both facilitated and restricted mobility in rural Mendoza, not only as means of conveyance but also as pieces of property. In the context of increased labor itinerancy, laborers rode horses and mules as well as traded them as ways to move across space by garnering resources and fostering communities across vast distances. The propertiedness of animal mobility affected how laborers interacted with the environments that sustained animal mobility, such as pastures, and with the state authorities charged with protecting private property. In interlude 3 I focus on the geographies created by engineers. If the preceding chapter revealed how the Trans-Andean was situated in conflict with state spaces of western Argentina, this interlude underscores how mountain crossings, as in the case of an engineering survey, were part of a project to bind the Argentine nation. In both instances, property was central.

Chapter 4 examines how, in the context of Argentina's civil wars and the rebellions of the 1860s, the Trans-Andean played the role that it had for decades since independence: as a space of exile and refuge. Added to that were both the growth of new spaces of production and extraction in Chile (particularly in the mining districts of the north) and the increased economic circulation across the border to the service of these new spaces, leading to the curious partnership of Chilean mine operators and Argentine rebels in fostering greater conflict in Argentina. The next interlude reveals the double-sidedness of political conflict and emerging forms of global power in and around the 1860s. I examine how engineers became embroiled in a contradictory process of opening up politically and economically volatile and violent frontiers, as well as in creating the infrastructural power that turned frontiers into borders, and struggling nation-states into materially hardened hegemons, the subject of the final chapter.

In chapter 5, I explain how the Trans-Andean mobility of rebels encouraged greater and greater cooperation among local, provincial, and national authorities on both sides of the border, a process fraught with disagreements and failed attempts to control rebel movements, until the end of the 1860s. This process reveals not only how a Trans-Andean governance emerged but also how state authorities created distinctions between rebel or criminal mobility and neutral or commercial mobility even though many merchants participated in rebellion. The final interlude explores the effects of railroads on uniting the two institutions that would define global power in the following decades: the territorial nation-state and the global financial sector. Returning to the Clark brothers and their efforts to fund a Trans-Andean railroad project, I illustrate how railroads were meaningful chiefly in their capacity to bring a region such as the Trans-Andean to shareholders across the world, to discipline state fiscal policy, and to advance the profits of people such as the Clark brothers even as nothing was built for decades.

# 1 A Trans-Andean World

The nineteenth-century Trans-Andean at the center of this history formed out of the contending draws of two great oceans, between a Pacific-facing economic pull and an Atlantic-facing state-formation process. That was not always the case, however. In the fifteenth century, Tawantinsuyu (Inka Empire) expanded southward alongside the Andes into present-day Cuyo, in the process crisscrossing the mountains, which followed a long-standing trajectory of human mobility.[1] By the final decades of the fifteenth century, the present-day Uspallata Pass became the southernmost Trans-Andean passage of Tawantinsuyu and its extensive road network (Qhapaq Ñan).[2] Over the next century, the Uspallata Pass became part of the Spanish Empire, becoming a royal road and an important pivot point between the two oceans—Atlantic and Pacific—of that maritime empire. From the beginning of Spanish colonization in the sixteenth century until the early 1800s, the eastern side of the Andes in central Argentina found itself captured alternately between the Pacific and Atlantic Oceans in the course of changing colonial economies and administration.

Initially, Cuyo had a Pacific orientation. It was part of the Captaincy General of Chile, and some of the places with which it was most connected, such as Tucumán and Córdoba, had emerged in relation to silver production in present-day Peru and Bolivia. In what is now Argentina, those places thrived on producing for those mining centers or siphoning off contraband silver originally meant to leave through Lima to the Pacific, eventually developing their own internal markets.³ Rerouting silver to the Atlantic ran through Buenos Aires, which grew as a hub of contraband trade throughout the seventeenth and eighteenth centuries, leading to the establishment of the Viceroyalty of the Río de la Plata in 1776, with its capital in Buenos Aires.⁴ The new administrative unit was part of a growing Atlantic world, a space marked by the growth in the transatlantic slave trade and sugar production, the rise of the British Empire, and the development of European industry. The Atlantic and the Río de la Plata drew in Cuyo, as the region became part of the new administrative unit. In fact, as far back as 1707, regional elites had expressed their desire to be part of the colonial administration of present-day Argentina and not Chile.⁵ Nevertheless, the region remained part of different commercial orbits, to the north into northern Argentina, Bolivia, and Chile; to the east into the Pampas; to the south into Wallmapu; and of course to the west with Chile.⁶ In effect, at the turn of the nineteenth century, Cuyo sat at the intersection of several commercial circuits, situated in overlapping zones of influence and changing administrative jurisdiction. This situation would persist and intensify into the mid-nineteenth century as Pacific-oriented Trans-Andean economic and social connections conflicted with an Atlantic-centered Argentine nation-state formation after independence.

This chapter traces the emerging tension between the Pacific-facing economic and social life of the region and the political orientations of the emerging Argentine state (Atlantic-facing). In particular, it charts the expanded mobility of cattle, Chilean migrants, and laborers. Cattle from Argentina increasingly went to Chile in the mid-nineteenth century, and the province of Mendoza was a primary passage point. At the same time, agricultural changes in Chile led migrants from that side of the Andes to find their way to the province. Disproportionately, they worked as itinerant laborers. The mobility of things and animals, of migrants, and of laborers came to define the Trans-Andean centered on the province of Mendoza. The changes brought by the intensification of Trans-Andean mobility provide the context for chapters 2–5, as Chilean migrants challenged state institutions; as increased itinerancy and importance of animal property came into conflict; as capital from Chile supported rebellion in Argentina; and as those rebels became the target of binational governance across the border region.

## Postindependence Changes (1820s–1840s)

Independence movements in the 1810s and 1820s brought change, and a range of political experiments flourished in southern South America.[7] By the 1830s, political experimentation and the conflicts that came with it gave way to a push for what some perceived to be order and discipline in places that seemed to be reeling from conflict to conflict. In Argentina, this push led to the rise of Juan Manuel de Rosas, who wielded power for several decades from 1829 to 1852 mostly as governor of the province of Buenos Aires because there existed no centralized national government, making the province the preeminent power in the country.[8] His allies, known as Federalists, took power across the country in those years, including in the Cuyo provinces of Mendoza and San Juan, leading to the exile of several prominent figures in Mendoza, including the viticulturalists who had dominated the economy up to that point.[9] After his fall in 1852, state makers ratified a constitution in 1853 and civil war broke out to determine the stakes of this new political order, which culminated in the consolidation of power under the Argentine Republic, its first president, Bartolomé Mitre (1862–68), and its capital, Buenos Aires.[10] On the other side of the Andes, the Chilean constitution of 1833, ratified under the presidency of Joaquín Prieto Vial (1831–41), institutionalized what is called the Portalian state (1830–91). The period was defined by a centralized state with a strong executive and focused on "order" (despite intense civil wars in the 1850s).[11] Up to the 1850s, this system was dominated by Conservative politicians through the presidencies of Manuel Bulnes Prieto (1841–51) and Manuel Montt (1851–61), but the 1860s and the election of José Joaquín Pérez ushered in a period of Liberal rule and the effective marriage of Conservatives and Liberals.[12]

The conservative period from the end of the wars of independence to the midpoint of the century and the political economy it brought also represented a transformation of Cuyo's economy and of Trans-Andean commercial relationships. Centered on Mendoza, Cuyo's colonial economy had been based on viticulture and alcohol production. This continued into the 1820s, but it collapsed soon thereafter due to falling prices and foreign imports.[13] By the early 1830s, many elites in the region, including those tied to the viticulture sector, began to flee to Chile as they found themselves on the losing side of the political battles taking place during Rosas's ascent. In the process, the properties of those considered "adversaries were declared state property."[14] In a final effort to wrest control of the region back toward the viticulturalists in

Chile, exiles proposed that the Chilean state annex Mendoza and neighboring San Juan, a proposal that was eventually rejected.[15] Endemic warfare throughout the country between the wars of independence and the civil conflicts of the postindependence period took the lives of thousands of men and thus sapped the region of labor, further straining economic prospects there.[16] In effect, lack of labor, capital flight, and changing political tides crippled Cuyo's economy and hurt Trans-Andean commerce, which was further damaged by developments in Chile, as protectionism ruled the day throughout the 1830s, which notably affected the livestock trade.[17]

By the mid-1830s, however, there were attempts to recultivate trade across the Andes. In 1835, despite not being authorized to negotiate foreign treaties, a foreign policy role reserved for the province of Buenos Aires, the provincial government in Mendoza put into effect a commercial agreement with the Chilean government.[18] The treaty faced obstacles, not only from the government in Buenos Aires, which rejected the audacious display of autonomy by the provincial authorities in Mendoza, but also from the Chilean government's sense of obligation to Chileans who had taken up residence on the eastern side of the Andes.[19] Several unresolved conflicts and increasing complaints from Chileans facing military conscription reached a fever pitch by the early 1840s, which caused tensions between the two governments. In response to the deteriorating diplomatic situation, the Chilean government suspended trade with Mendoza.[20] The suspension of trade between 1842 and 1846 led to the increase in trade southward into Pehuenche-controlled lands, where Pehuenches, Mendocinos, and Chileans fed cattle on pastures there and traded them over the mountains.[21]

Although suspending trade was obviously as much a wishful idea as it was an enforceable policy, it opened up important debates in the following years on the meaning of the region. The initial impetus for suspending trade with the "provincias transandinas" (Trans-Andean provinces; meaning Argentine provinces) was, as Chile's minister of the interior articulated it, a matter of "national honor," but as time went on wounds faded more quickly for some than for others.[22] In the years following the suspension of trade, legislators and the press argued that commercial interests had been damaged due to the restrictive trade policy, leading to rising prices for certain goods and the inability of Chilean industry to export what it once did to the "provincias trasandinas."[23] One idea that emerged to critique both the policy and the protectionist justification of it was that of a "natural" division of labor in commodity production. Using the examples of livestock and the soap industry in Chile, one article in *El Mercurio*, one of the major newspapers in

Chile, argued against the idea that trade liberalization in the Trans-Andean would hurt the Chilean economy. In regards to livestock, the article claimed that because Chile did not have the "immense plains" that Argentina had, the country had to choose between land usage for livestock and agriculture. At the same time, soap, which was often imported from Argentina, had not been substituted by Chilean production after the suspension of trade. Rather, due to the lack of tallow in Chile for soap production and the demand from places such as the mining regions, prices had doubled.[24] Shortly after the Chilean government lifted the suspension of trade in 1846, Chile's economic ascent would connect newly reestablished Trans-Andean trade circuits to a rapidly expanding Pacific world.

## A Trans-Andean–Pacific World (1840s–1860s)

Although Chile had always been important to Cuyano society, the late 1840s to the early 1870s saw an intensification of Chilean influence on the eastern side of the Andes. The reasons were the expansion of wheat production in central Chile initially to feed the gold rushes in California and Australia, copper production in Chile's Norte Chico, and the cattle trade from Cuyo that fed both these growing sectors. The Chilean influences brought by these emerging connections revealed themselves early on to Benjamín Vicuña Mackenna, a liberal and prolific writer, who described them firsthand in the early 1850s. Traveling back to Chile after several years of exile, in 1855 he found himself in Mendoza and ended up staying nearly a month there due to a storm that delayed his trip.[25] As a Chilean, he found an unmistakable familiarity in Mendoza. Most notable families had spent at least some time in Chile, the elite women took their fashion cues from Chilean society, and many of the young elite men had studied in Chile's capital of Santiago.[26] It was not just high society, however, that bore this mark of Chilean influence. He noted that due to the abundance of cheap land in Mendoza and the high price that cattle could fetch (particularly in Chile), Chileans were beginning to invest their capital in the province. He worried, however, about the effect of this shift on the Chilean economy, since "this innovation, which is taking hold in ever greater proportions day by day, is going to spur a harmful emigration of hands and capital, particularly harmful to Chile."[27] Vicuña Mackenna thought that with the opportunities afforded to people in a place like Mendoza combined with "the misery and slavery in which the *inquilinaje* [tenant farmer class] live in Chile," laborers would leave for the eastern side of the Andes.[28]

Those opportunities that attracted laborers to Mendoza revolved around the cattle trade. As the province of Mendoza recovered in the mid-nineteenth century from the collapse of its colonial economy, it became the central pivot point for cattle coming from the east to Chile. It was not that Mendoza had great land for raising cattle. Indeed, the arid province offered little in the way of open pasture; most agricultural activities required at least some irrigation. Supplying that water were "oases," fed by rivers flowing down from the mountains and cutting through the province. The mountain snow that became these rivers was the primary obstacle to transporting cattle directly across the mountains in the winter from about May to November each year. During those months, cattle were fattened on winter pastures of cultivated alfalfa called *invernadas* before crossing the mountains to be sold in Chilean markets.[29] The various valleys and oases that could support alfalfa cultivation became the primary sites of production.[30] Merchants took advantage of the high price of cattle in Chile and made possible the commercialization of cattle and the financing of activities in Mendoza. This class of merchants was made up of local and Chilean actors; and many of those local actors had close connections to Chile, particularly Valparaíso.[31] As Chile was the ultimate destination for the cattle trade that went through Mendoza, it provided important components to sustaining and growing cattle production: market fluctuations, which conditioned prices, and capital to help finance productive activities, as well as advances on cattle purchases. All in all, the cattle trade was reflective of three interrelated processes: the influx of Chilean capital to Mendoza, the valorization of land in Mendoza, and the close connections between emerging elites on both sides of the mountains.

The cattle trade connected Mendoza to the agricultural boom in Chile taking place at the time, particularly in the Central Valley. If the postindependence period in Chile initially was marked by the collapse of its traditional colonial markets in Peru, by midcentury it not only had rekindled important commercial ties with Peru but also was beginning to connect with new markets. First, the gold rushes in California and Australia, beginning in 1848 and 1851, respectively, created a demand for wheat and flour that the areas surrounding the mining booms could not supply initially. Second, mining booms in the north of Chile created an internal market for Chilean agricultural products. Third, up to the last third of the nineteenth century, Chile supplied British, Argentine, and Brazilian markets with important agricultural staples.[32] In effect, in the mid-nineteenth century, Chilean agriculture was intensifying its connections with two major oceanic markets, the Pacific and the Atlantic. As urbanization increased and agricultural lands expanded, prices and demand surged and continued to rise to the end of the century.³³ Argentina met rising prices and demand by exporting tens of thousands of cattle annually throughout the second half of the century. Over that period, in Chile "the traditional extensive livestock was declining in favor of agriculture," with Argentina increasingly supplying livestock to the country.³⁴ Even toward the beginning of Chile's agricultural expansion in the 1840s, Chilean observers recognized the centrality of the vast tracts of land on the eastern side of the Andes to the country.³⁵

The expansion of agriculture in Chile pushed the country's frontier farther south into Indigenous territory on the western side of the Andes as efforts to colonize land accelerated. This increased the demand for cattle there, which was met by Pehuenches across the Andes on the frontier with the province of Mendoza between San Rafael and Malargüe, as well as farther south in Barrancas and Varvarco.³⁶ There, in Pehuenche-controlled areas, people raised and sold cattle, while *lonkos* or *caciques* (community heads) administered usufruct rights over pastures and access to mountain passes. Both Chilean and Mendocino traders took their cattle to feed on those pastures and bought cattle raised in Pehuenche lands. For the most part, cattle circulating in those trade networks were destined for Chile, but they also were sold for trade into the province of Mendoza, Ngulumapu, and the Pampas.³⁷ Thus, trade went not only east-west but also north-south, as the southern parts of the province of Mendoza were intimately connected with southern trading networks in the decades after independence into the mid-nineteenth century.³⁸ By the 1860s, however, Pehuenche and Mendocino economic integration slowed as frontier relations strained under the weight of the political upheaval and rebellions that dominated that decade.³⁹ One could speculate that the breakdown of these relationships might have aided in the development of the cattle economy in the north of the province of Mendoza, especially with cattle raising in San Carlos, which was the main location in the province where cattle raising took place outside the southern frontier around San Rafael, where the majority of cattle raising occurred.⁴⁰ In that sense, as Chile became increasingly intertwined with global markets through wheat and minerals, Mendoza went through a similar process of incorporation into Chilean markets, specifically through cattle.

The connections across the Andes that formed the Trans-Andean must be understood from the perspective of several broad processes, beginning with the expansion of Pacific markets. The gold rushes in California and Australia accelerated speculative booms already underway in those places as well as the need for commodities such as Chilean wheat.⁴¹ The gold rushes were part of an eastward drift in the center of gravity of an increasingly integrated Pacific world. From the second half of the eighteenth century up to the middle decades of the nineteenth century markets along the Pacific basin went through a double transformation. On the one hand, economic integration of the entire Pacific basin took place as linkages among ports in China, Japan, Southeast Asia, Australia, the western United States, Mexico, Peru, Chile, and Hawai'i and other Pacific islands became tighter, more sustained, and more interdependent than before. On the other hand, the center of commercial demand in this integrating Pacific shifted from China to the eastern shores of the Pacific (the Americas) and European markets throughout the Atlantic world.[42] This emergence of a Pacific world came with the increased desire to bridge the gap between the two great oceans of the Americas, seen in the fever for canal and interoceanic railroad projects in Nicaragua, Panama, Mexico, and the Andes.[43] Connections between Pacific and Atlantic were evident almost from the start. Indeed, as much as Chile's economic growth in the decades after independence tapped into this integrating Pacific, it engaged deeply with the Atlantic world, centered on the North Atlantic in "the global shift from polycentric commercial competition and integration to Anglo-centric industrial capitalism."[44] One of the commodities most important to that industrial-capitalist world system was copper, and Chile had lots of it. Copper mining did not begin with the Industrial Revolution, but it did accelerate with it. Copper mining in Chile increased in the second half of the eighteenth century in part as a result of demands from the Spanish metropole to feed its artillery.[45] It was not until the mid-nineteenth century, however, that Chilean copper mining reached its zenith. From 2,725 tons annually in the 1830s to 42,877 tons annually by the end of the 1860s, copper production in these decades soared and exports did, too, as Chile became a leading exporter of copper in the world by the early 1870s, much of it going to the British to feed the Industrial Revolution in different ways.[46]

Between copper and wheat, Chile's insertion into global markets conditioned the shape of Trans-Andean trade. For example, cattle products, such as "hides" and "jerky," supplied ships at Chilean ports.[47] Hide and leather manufacturers in Chile also likely relied on Argentine cattle. For example, driven by the importance of hides and leather in mining operations during the late colonial period, Coquimbo province in Chile became an important node in the trade of these materials as thousands of cattle were slaughtered annually there and used for the production of hides in nearby mines.[48] Coquimbo continued to be part of the leather and hide trade into the middle of the nineteenth century, and San Juan exported thousands of cattle annually to Coquimbo (as well as Copiapó at the center of the mining boom).[49] Connections between Mendoza and the Pacific world were not only mediated by Chilean merchants and ports. The establishment of commercial connections in Mendoza with California, as well as the presence of Californians in the province of Mendoza (in Junín, particularly), illustrate the extent to which the Pacific world penetrated daily life in Mendoza.[50]

Throughout the early redevelopment of Trans-Andean commerce in the 1840s and into the 1850s, Argentine liberals in exile used this trade to advance their cause against the Federalists in power in Argentina. There was perhaps no greater defender of Trans-Andean trade in Chile than Argentine author and political exile Domingo Faustino Sarmiento. Born in San Juan and exiled for his stance against the Federalist governor of Buenos Aires, Juan Manuel de Rosas, Sarmiento was both deeply familiar with the stakes of Trans-Andean trade and motivated to launch attacks on Rosas from Chile. In 1851, several articles on the issue of "comercio transandino" (Trans-Andean commerce) from one of Sarmiento's Chilean publications constructed a narrative of Argentina's Andean provinces as "naturally" Pacific in commercial orientation. For Sarmiento, the opening of land-based commercial relationships between Buenos Aires and the Pacific ports in the late colonial period had the effect of developing the Trans-Andean, economically and infrastructurally.[51] It was "the independence revolution," however, that "brought about a new revolution in the commercial routes of the Pacific," and "since then the commerce of the Trans-Andean provinces ... sought in Valparaíso [its] natural market."[52] Despite the historical evolution of those provinces toward "their natural market," "the civil war that happened suddenly in 1829, the destruction of wealth brought about by the caudillos, and the disorder and lack of a Constitution that secures the rights of all brought down Trans-Andean commerce, and with it the wealth of the cities of San Juan and Mendoza, so opulent before, and so miserable today."[53] Although trade had returned to the region by the time this article was published, it remained threatened by the machinations of Rosas's government in Buenos Aires, which sought to conjure up whatever excuse it could "to close the commerce of the Trans-Andean provinces with Chile."[54] The reason, to Sarmiento, was obvious. Rosas wanted to redirect all trade through Buenos Aires so that his government could siphon off customs duties levied in the port of Buenos Aires, thereby filling the coffers of his government and bolstering its control over the country.[55] In his lament of Rosas's stifling of Trans-Andean trade Sarmiento did not have to wait long. Only a year later, Rosas was ousted from power. Amid the construction of the republican order that followed, the Trans-Andean continued to exemplify liberalized commercial relations.

By 1869, Sarmiento had gone from exile to president and the Trans-Andean came to be a paragon of the modern liberal international order. That year the two countries negotiated a new commercial treaty, this time with the Chileans invoking the Trans-Andean to advance their goals of trade liberalization. The Chileans wanted to export wheat to the port of Buenos Aires freely. According to Félix Frías, the Argentine representative, allowing the free importation of Chilean wheat would necessitate by treaty the free importation of wheat from other countries, which would curtail state revenues. At that point in time, Frías argued, the Argentine state budget could not afford such a significant decrease in revenues, and therefore, the Chilean request for free importation should be denied.[56] By contrast, the Chilean argument rested on the Trans-Andean and its association with commerce and free trade. In effect, the Chileans wished to "extend the principle of free trade of both countries' production to maritime duties, which in the previous treaty only applied to terrestrial duties."[57] In other words, overland trade, or Trans-Andean trade, between Argentina and Chile was emblematic of free-trade principles, which the Chileans sought to apply to maritime trade. Indeed, even after the expiration of the previous commercial treaty in 1866, the Chilean government worked to craft legislation and regulations to continue those free-trade practices. Before negotiations began, the Chilean legislature had passed a law in October 1868 completely liberalizing certain imports from Argentina, such as livestock and minerals, as well as foreign goods going through Chile to western Argentina, important trade for Cuyo.[58]

By the 1860s, the Trans-Andean had emerged as a space of increasing commerce, tied to the integration of Chile into expanding global markets. Much as it had during the colonial period, when the fate of Cuyo oscillated between Pacific and Atlantic and between Indigenous communities to the south and colonial urban centers, the region sat at the intersection of several different gravitational pulls during the postindependence period into the mid-nineteenth century. Living in this Trans-Andean tension zone meant drastic changes, few of them more visible and consequential than transport labor, labor itinerancy, and labor migrations.

### Trans-Andean Chilean Communities

The Trans-Andean was a space of mobility. As livestock and other commodities traveled across the mountains, so, too, did people. Migrations across the mountains occurred in multiple directions, but most prominently from Chile to the provinces of Mendoza and to a lesser extent San Juan and from Argentina to northern Chile and the mines there. From the beginning, Chileans had been part of western Argentina. In Mendoza, after independence, there were around 1,500 Chileans (8.2 percent of the population).[59] As Chileans intermarried with Mendocinos and the foreign population dropped over the 1830s, official counts saw a reduction in the Chilean population into the hundreds, although officials likely undercounted Chileans.[60] By 1869, however, that number grew to about 6,000 Chileans (representing between 8.8 and 9.2 percent of the population).[61] In San Juan, where the Chilean population was less than in Mendoza, there were 2,059 Chileans (3.4 percent of the population), meaning that more than 71 percent of Chileans in Argentina lived in these two provinces.[62] Argentines, too, migrated to Chile, with a great number of them working in the silver and copper mines. Of the 8,423 Argentines in Chile, 7,184 (85.3 percent) resided in the province of Atacama, the center of mining.[63] These Trans-Andean migrants, then, directed themselves to two of the major centers of growth in the region, the cattle trading region of Cuyo, particularly Mendoza, and the Chilean mining province of Atacama.

Those migrations do not represent the full picture of Trans-Andean mobility. Though they are not central to this book, the Indigenous Huarpes and their descendants, centered on the area of the Lagunas de Guanacache in southern San Juan and northern Mendoza provinces, have structured themselves around mobility for centuries. For example, Huarpe *baqueanos* (guides) have used mobile knowledge to assert their authority and expertise not just over space but also over the cultural knowledge and history tied to those spaces, including in the mountains.[64] After the Spanish arrived in the mid-sixteenth century, Huarpe Trans-Andean mobility revolved around two issues. The first was their subjugation to encomienda labor demands in Chile.[65] The second were the cattle trade networks between the Pampas and Chile in which Laguneros (the people of the Lagunas de Guanacache) participated, which continued into the nineteenth and twentieth centuries.[66] Not just donning spatial authority onto Huarpe communities, mobility and livestock trading can be understood as part of long-standing marginalization. As anthropologist Diego Escolar notes, driving livestock and the nomadism it invokes are part of a "historic and political condition" connected to issues of land access, part of a "socioeconomic exile" that has made mobility paradoxically as much part of Huarpe survival as part of their erasure from mainstream historical memory.[67]

The migration of Chilean laborers over the mountains followed the flow of capital from Chile to Mendoza. The concentration of capital in Chile, particularly in the port of Valparaíso, aided by institutional reforms in the 1850s, paved the way for Chilean capital to become dominant in Mendoza in terms of both landownership and lending.[68] Chileans became investors in and administrators of estancias and haciendas, particularly in the Uco Valley (San Carlos and Tupungato Departments), and Chilean merchants became key to lending in the province, displacing in many ways ecclesiastical lending, which had been the dominant form of credit in Mendoza up to the 1850s.[69] Indeed, Chileans were disproportionately represented as merchants (*comerciantes*) in the province of Mendoza in the national census of 1869.[70] Aiding in the insertion of Chilean capital into Mendocino markets were the connections that some Mendocino elites had made with Chileans during the previous decades. In the 1850s, Vicuña Mackenna commented on these tight relationships, noting that there was a certain social and cultural fluidity among these parts of society, blurring the distinctions between Chileans and Mendocinos in the province.[71] Those relationships were in part the result of many being exiled from Argentina in the 1830s and 1840s to Chile, returning in the 1850s to participate in the consolidation of an economic and political elite in the province.[72] As a result, the circulation of capital and commodities in Mendoza was in many ways connected to Chilean merchants, whether directly or indirectly. If capital increasingly had a Chilean face by the 1860s, so, too, did labor.

Laborers migrated from Chile to Mendoza because of the expansion and intensification of wheat cultivation (and to a lesser extent alfalfa and clover) in Chile. By the late colonial period, a system characterized by hacendados commercializing the production of free peasants and residents of their haciendas had emerged in Chile.[73] However, the mid-nineteenth century saw the transformation of this system and the casting out of large numbers of laborers from haciendas, a process known as peonization. Agricultural intensification meant that the production of hacienda residents or "dependents" was insufficient to meet the rising demand. To meet demand, many large landowners—who increasingly belonged to the emerging merchant class instead of the traditional landowning class—began to prefer the *labor* rather than the production of "dependents."[74] Some became "stable peons," who still lived on the land like peasants or tenant farmers but were tied to the hacienda through labor rather than their own agricultural output. Others, however, recognized that the system was becoming untenable and undesirable, and these people circulated as free laborers in the countryside.[75] Some workers left the countryside, going to the cities, to the mines, and to work in new public works projects and railroad construction, sometimes leading to rural labor shortages.[76] Still others found themselves moving to the eastern side of the Andes, to places like Mendoza.

Chilean migrants in Mendoza could have come also from the south, to escape frontier conflicts, although that is less likely than them coming from the Central Valley, in the context of agricultural intensification. In the colonial period and well into the 1820s and 1830s, trading relationships in the southern portion of the province were closely linked to Chile and the Pehuenche lands.[77] Although cattle in Mendoza came east from the Pampas, connections with the south persisted into the 1840s and 1850s as Mendocino cattle herders continued to engage with Pehuenche lonkos to buy cattle, access pastures, and get permission to cross the low and wide passes in the south.[78] By the 1860s, as historian Geraldine Davies Lenoble explains, intensifying conflict in the frontier regions between Puhuenche lands and the province of Mendoza "pushed the frontier population to migrate to the center of the province," or deeper into Pehuenche territory.[79] In that context, Chileans in Mendoza may have migrated from the south as they too had used pastures and passes there for livestock.[80] Indeed, the exact places from which Chileans came do not appear in the 1869 census consistently, but when they do, places close to the Pehuenche-controlled Planchón and Pehuenche Passes, such as Linares, Curicó, and Talca, are among the most common.[81] It was not only Chileans who could have been part of this northward migration but also *indios amigos*, frontier Indigenous people who lived "under state jurisdiction," providing "military assistance" and getting "rations and goods," and who "settled in frontier spaces under state jurisdiction[,] lent military assistance . . . , and received rations and goods by the government."[82] During that turbulent decade of the 1860s some likely moved northward and "integrated into *criolla* society."[83] Part of that integration may have involved different social markers in official documents, such as the 1869 census, which did not tend to identify individuals as "indios," making reference to and counts of "indios" in frontier regions, or describing people's Indigenous ancestors in certain regions, such as Las Lagunas in Mendoza, where officials wrote of "indios guarpes, mestizados ya" (Huarpe Indians, already mixed).[84] Although "indio chileno" was a category already in use in different contexts (see chapter 2 for an examination of the meaning of "Chilean" as a category), one could speculate that "Chilean" was one of the identities available to "indios amigos" in Mendocino society.[85]

By the 1860s, Mendoza had become the Argentine province with the highest proportion of its labor force classified as *peones, gañanes, jornaleros,* and other common, mostly male laborers, which I will refer to collectively as peons.[86] In a province with such a high percentage of this class, Chilean men were even more likely than other men in the province to be listed as peons.[87] Generally, the terms *peón* and *gañán* were used to refer to manual laborers, with the latter being commonly used in Chile to refer in particular to manual rural laborers.[88] In Argentina, the "country peon class," as historian Ricardo Salvatore refers to them, broadly shared experiences of mobility and were not employed permanently but rather were often employed occasionally and left jobs with some regularity, pursuing as a complement to wages nonwage activities, such as small-scale vending, sharecropping, and others.[89] Although debt peonage prevailed to different degrees in other countries in nineteenth-century Latin America, peons in parts of Argentina were not often trapped and made subservient to *patrones* (bosses) by debt relationships (even if they were in debt).[90] Last, they had contentious relationships with the state. They routinely found themselves the targets of state harassment, often the subject of anxieties officials had over rural disorder and the main source of soldiers.[91]

As much as peon experiences changed from province to province, much of this characterization holds true for Chileans in Mendoza in the 1860s. In the following chapters, I will explore in greater depth their contentious relationships with the state, their engagement in nonwage economic activities, and their relationship to wages, but for now, it is enough to say that peons in Mendoza had a great deal of geographical mobility. For example, many likely worked seasonally in the burgeoning Trans-Andean transportation sector, which thrived from November to April when the summer weather allowed for crossing. The explosion in overland traffic between Argentina and Chile from the late 1840s into the 1860s (table 1.1) created an equally massive expansion in the need for labor devoted to carrying that traffic, which could reach a need for thousands of peons per season.[92] In highly mobile jobs, such as transportation or traveling east (or south) to buy cattle, peons had a great deal of independence vis-à-vis their bosses, to the point where one could renegotiate wage advances in the middle of a trip or leave altogether, putting a boss in a precarious position.[93] Transportation labor also increased the labor opportunities that peons had for work in both Chile and Argentina. Before the crossing season in the winters from May to October, if a migrant found himself in Mendoza he could have worked in various jobs, including

TABLE 1.1. Chilean imports from Argentina, 1846–1862

| YEAR | IMPORTS FROM ARGENTINA (IN CHILEAN PESOS) | IMPORTS FROM ARGENTINA THROUGH SANTA ROSA* | IMPORTS FROM ARGENTINA THROUGH SANTA ROSA (%) |
|---|---|---|---|
| 1846 | 32,193 | 30,823 | 95.7 |
| 1847 | 132,646 | 120,373 | 90.7 |
| 1850 | 182,145 | 155,381 | 85.3 |
| 1852 | 634,137 | 390,672 | 61.6 |
| 1853 | 94,212 | 0 | 0.0 |
| 1854 | 1,243,724 | 946,817 | 76.1 |
| 1855 | 920,220 | — | — |
| 1859 | 1,263,615 | — | — |
| 1860 | 1,569,695 | — | — |
| 1861 | 1,005,591 | — | — |
| 1862 | 978,910 | — | — |

*Source:* Chile, Oficina Central de Estadística, *Estadística comercial [. . .] año de 1846*, 77; Chile, Oficina Central de Estadística, *Estadística comercial [. . .] año de 1847*, 85; Chile, Oficina Central de Estadística, *Estadística comercial [. . .] primer trimestre del año 1850*, 54; Chile, Oficina Central de Estadística, *Estadística comercial [. . .] segundo trimestre del año 1850*, 57; Chile, Oficina Central de Estadística, *Estadística comercial [. . .] tercer trimestre del año 1850*, 59; Chile, Oficina Central de Estadística, *Estadística comercial [. . .] primer semestre del año 1852*, 66; Chile, Oficina Central de Estadística, *Estadística comercial [. . .] segundo semestre del año 1852*, 65; Chile, Oficina Central de Estadística, *Estadística comercial [. . .] primer semestre del año 1853*, 68; Chile, Oficina Central de Estadística, *Estadística comercial [. . .] segundo semestre del año 1853*, 66; Chile, Oficina Central de Estadística, *Estadística comercial [. . .] primer semestre del año 1854*, 65; Chile, Oficina Central de Estadística, *Estadística comercial [. . .] segundo semestre del año 1854*, 73; Chile, Oficina Central de Estadística, *Estadística comercial [. . .] segundo semestre del año 1855*, 100; Chile, Oficina Central de Estadística, *Anuario estadístico*, 5:377.

*Note:* Based on summaries of trade with Argentina provided on cited pages. For 1846–47, summaries are annual. For 1852–54, summaries are by semester, but figures provided are based on annual summaries in second semester volumes. For 1850, no annual summary is given, so figure is based on the three trimester summaries provided in each trimester volume. For 1855, data are presented differently from previous years, so the figure is based on the summary of trade with all countries in the second semester volume of 1855. For 1859–62, volume 5 of *Anuario estadístico* provides a summary of those four years of trade with all nations, including Argentina. The volumes of *Estadística comercial* also provide individual figures for different imports from countries, including cattle from Argentina. For a figure of cattle exported from Mendoza from the 1850s to the 1880s, see Richard-Jorba, *Poder, economía y espacio*, table 2.7, 100.

* Santa Rosa de Los Andes being the entrance point from Mendoza and southern San Juan.

*A Trans-Andean World*

ones related to the invernadas, the winter pastures on which cattle fed and fattened themselves in preparation for crossing the Andes once the passes were open.[94] If the cattle trade took Chileans back across to Chile in the summer months, there they might have found work in the summer wheat harvests or in infrastructure projects, such as the railroads.[95] Mobility was a defining feature of life for Chilean rural laborers in Mendoza.

As much as this mobility (and much of the mobility described in this book) presented itself as masculine—through male itinerant laborers, the targeting of them in criminal cases and through conscription, rebellions, cattle drives, and so on—women played a significant role in mobility. If Chilean men were disproportionately listed as peons, Chilean women were disproportionately listed in the 1869 census as textile workers—namely, *tejedoras* or *tejenderas* (weavers), *hilanderas* (spinners), and *costureras* (seamstresses).[96] Textile production was essential to the functioning of rural economy and mobility in the region. Ponchos and *chamantos* (common types of woolen garments in the region) gave protection against the elements, especially rain and even the sun. They could become a "blanket," a "tablecloth" for eating or playing cards, or protection in "knife fights."[97] Those textiles also became essential to mobility and the transportation sector, since to ride an animal required accessories such as spurs, hats, ponchos, and *mantas* (blankets), which created an essential part of the saddle and became a bed for sleeping at night. Textile production could, in some cases, become important beyond local communities. In Wallmapu, for example, Mapuche women earned a reputation by the nineteenth century as exceptional producers of woolen textiles, garnering the attention and praise of travelers.[98] Broadly, on the frontier, ponchos were one of "the most important products of indigenous commerce with hispanocriollos," along with salt and livestock.[99] Farther north, in the Chilean Central Valley in places such as Rancagua and Colchagua, hacienda and domestic production of ponchos, chamantos, and mantas had been part of rural life since the seventeenth century.[100] In Argentina, cottage industry and domestic production of textiles was also part of rural life, but by the 1860s with the importation of cheap wool and industrially produced textiles from Europe, women lost important markets in Buenos Aires, and over the following decades occupations such as weaving went into decline across the country.[101] For Chilean women in Mendoza, textile production continued to be an important activity in the 1860s, especially in the Uco Valley to the south of the capital and in the frontier settlement of San Rafael (table A.3). The prevalence of these activities should be understood not in terms of isolated, individual activities but rather as part of peasant family economies, which encompassed another aspect of Chilean communities in Mendoza.

Chileans were not only disproportionately classified as rural laborers and textile workers, but also disproportionately listed as *labradores* and *agricultores* with varying access to wealth and land, which I will call collectively peasant farmers.[102] Within the class of Chilean peasant farmers there was a great deal of diversity. Often occupying lands to the east of the capital, in departments such as Junín, or to the south in the Uco Valley, in departments such as San Carlos, some were small property owners and others were engaged in some form of tenancy.[103] For peasant farmers generally in Mendoza, the cattle trade loomed large. Alfalfa cultivation was an activity in which many participated, along with cattle herding.[104] However, whereas large-scale operations tended to devote most of their land and energies to alfalfa production, small-scale producers diversified their activities, including through small vineyards, orchards, wheat, and transport, as well as with nonbovine livestock, such as sheep, horses, and mules.[105] Chilean peasant farmers, peons, and textile workers could have tight connections and share many of the same spaces, particularly in the Uco Valley. Although the Uco Valley had a long history of connections with Chile, there had clearly been recent waves of Chilean migrants, indicated by the high percentage of Chilean children and adolescents living with their parents (table A.1). Those migrations also likely represented a displacement in the Uco Valley of Indigenous people, who had been part of a changing society there in the early nineteenth century.[106] In cases of family migrations, some Chilean women listed as textile workers were married to Chilean men listed as peasant farmers. Their daughters in many cases were also listed as some kind of textile worker, and their sons in some cases were listed as part of the peon class, indicating a generational component to occupational categories.[107] Of course, in other parts of the province, particularly in the central zone around the capital, the predominance of young Chilean men was in line with patterns of male-dominated migrations in and to Latin America (appendix A).[108]

In great part, the intensification of Trans-Andean commerce and migration brought Mendoza increasingly into contact with the Pacific world. The Chilean port of Valparaíso, in many ways, became Mendoza's port. In that sense, although eventually Mendoza would count as its port the Atlantic city of Buenos Aires, that was still decades off. Those connections between Mendoza and Valparaíso encouraged attempts by investors and statesmen to facilitate better communication across the mountains. Perhaps nobody represents these attempts better than the Clark brothers, Juan and Mateo, whose unrelenting zeal for Trans-Andean infrastructure resulted in the construction of the Trans-Andean telegraph and railroad. Their history and the history of their family reveals the personal stories of global and Trans-Andean exchange discussed at much more impersonal levels here. That family history and its relation to the construction of global space are the subjects of the following interlude.

Interlude One | Infrastructure and Global Space

On 27 November 1869, a group of men gathered in the Valparaíso Bolsa de Comercio building to celebrate the first shareholders' meeting of the Compañía del Telégrafo Trasandino (Trans-Andean Telegraph Company).[1] They aimed to build a telegraph across the Andes in order to "unite Valparaíso with the capital of the Argentine Republic," Buenos Aires, a goal that on its own would have been important enough but by then had taken on an air of global significance because the recently laid transatlantic telegraph cable would soon reach Buenos Aires and would thus give Valparaíso "instantaneous communications with the entire world."[2] They achieved that goal only a few short years later when the Trans-Andean telegraph finished in 1872 and the South Atlantic telegraph was inaugurated two years later in 1874.[3] At the center of this effort to connect these two countries "at the vanguard of [South America's] social and commercial progress" were Juan Clark and his younger brother, Mateo, who devoted their lives to building up communication across the mountains.[4] The telegraph, their first project to such an end, took fewer than four years to complete. Their second and final project, the Trans-Andean railroad, would take four decades.

The Clarks and the other nearly 200 investors in the telegraph project clearly understood the importance of linking to a rapidly globally connected world. Tapping into this system meant connecting with New York City, Lisbon, London, Paris, Shanghai, Hong Kong, and beyond.[5] By the end of the century, this network brought with it what historian Lila Caimari calls a "new global temporality" in which "instantaneity . . . emerged as a new conceptual horizon for the movement of information."[6] The reality was a "fractured temporality" of international news, ushering in a kaleidoscopic view of global society in which distant places sat oddly next to one another in newspapers while human interest stories and news of war gave a dizzying sense of a global world "radically decontextualized" and all at once.[7] The Trans-Andean telegraph conveyed those possibilities of disjointed temporalities and geographies, of shared spaces of community across the world.

That moment in 1869, when investors celebrated the coming Trans-Andean telegraph, provides a productive vantage point from which to observe the development of global space in the Trans-Andean. Looking backward from then reveals the building up of the Trans-Andean as a socially changing and politically conflictive space and how those localized processes appear when filtered through contemporaneous global changes. The Clark brothers' story offers an opening to think about the parallels between the formation of the Trans-Andean and the formation of the Trans-Andean telegraph project, as well as the connections between infrastructure and global space.

The Clarks' story begins in the 1830s before they were even born. Their mother, Tadea Torres y Quiroga, was a mountain crosser before them. In the turmoil of postindependence political conflict in the early 1830s, she fled western Argentina for Chile, where she would stay for most of her life. She had been born in San Juan in 1802 to one of the most established colonial families. Reared during independence struggles, she married a local independence leader, Francisco Javier Godoy.[8] The couple were on the wrong side of the political struggles that ensued when the Federalists took over the provincial government in San Juan. And so, like the viticulturalists of Mendoza and other Argentine political exiles, Torres y Quiroga left Argentina for Chile. Exile was almost a political rite of passage in those years. Many prominent political figures of nineteenth-century Argentina found themselves in exile at some point during the first five decades of independence: Juan Bautista Alberdi, political theorist and father of the Argentine Constitution of 1853; Mariquita Sánchez, a leading revolutionary during the wars of independence; and the first two presidents of the Argentine Republic, including perhaps the best known, Sarmiento, who like Torres y Quiroga was from San Juan, leaving ten years after her, in 1841.[9] As historian Edward Blumenthal illustrates, émigrés were important not only on their return but also during exile, where they served in key positions in different countries, building education systems, working at newspapers, and crafting legal codes.[10] For these exiles, Chile became one of the most popular destinations. They went to the capital, Santiago; they went to the port of Valparaíso; and, like Torres y Quiroga and Sarmiento, they went to the northern province of Atacama just as the mining boom was starting there.

Godoy and Torres y Quiroga went to live in a town called Huasco, the main port in the area, and the place through which minerals traveled down to Valparaíso to be exported out to the world. Like many of his contemporaries in exile, Godoy was a lawyer and worked in that capacity for a mining company there, Sewell and Patrickson (sometimes written in Spanish as Swell y Patrickson).[11] British merchants such as these were known for loaning capital to northern mining companies in exchange for cheap access to minerals. John Sewell came into his mining business when one such company, Rodríguez, Cea y Cía, went bankrupt in the early 1830s, leaving him with the mines and smelting infrastructure.[12] Sewell's acquisition of Rodríguez, Cea y Cía was no minor event: one of the partners, José Manuel Cea, was one of the first Chileans to introduce reverberatory smelting.[13] This process was developed with the help of Charles Lambert, an "Anglo-French mining engineer" who had befriended future Chilean president Francisco Antonio Pinto (1827–29).[14] Rodríguez, Cea y Cía's adoption of these techniques made the firm an early innovator in Chile's smelting industry. The problem with smelting in Chile was that it required fuel that simply was not available in abundance near the mines in the province of Atacama. The best source of fuel, firewood from the limited quantity of brush and trees in the arid region, was quickly depleted, and even as early as 1836 observers noted that the industry had slowed due to a lack of fuel.[15] This did not mean, however, that copper mining and smelting stopped altogether, as Sewell and other early investors well understood.

One of the representatives of Sewell and Patrickson in Chile was James Clark, originally from Scotland and the future father of Juan and Mateo. Clark came in 1827 with Samuel Lang, his cousin, a merchant and son of a shipowner in Liverpool. Lang himself had first arrived in Chile in 1822. His connections to Chile came through the independence leader Bernardo O'Higgins, whom he met while the two were studying in England.[16] Like Lambert's friendship with Pinto, Lang's connections with independence leaders gave him access to the merchant community in Chile. Other British merchants who also found their way to Valparaíso would help to establish firms that would substantially impact economic life in Chile, including those involved in the development of the mining boom in the north, where James Clark began working with Sewell and Patrickson in 1830.[17] Clark must have met Torres y Quiroga, still married to Godoy, while in Huasco working for Sewell and Patrickson. After Godoy died, Torres y Quiroga and Clark married, moving to Valparaíso in 1837, where Juan and Mateo Clark were born (1840 and 1843, respectively) and where James Clark died (1852).[18] It was there, in Valparaíso, that Juan and Mateo largely grew up and first experienced merchant life. During that time, they would have seen the radical changes taking place in the city. The first steamships arrived in the early 1840s, and the port was one of the primary destinations of the first major Pacific Ocean steamer service, William Wheelwright's Pacific Steam Navigation Company, established in 1838.[19] As teenagers in 1856, they might have seen the first gas streetlight on Valparaíso's streets, lit on Independence Day that year.[20] Then, later, in 1863, as they were beginning their careers in commerce, they would have seen the port connected with the capital, Santiago, via railroad.

To support these rapid infrastructural improvements, capital derived from mineral and merchant wealth came together with much-needed state support. For example, the Valparaíso-Santiago line relied on substantial investments from people in mining and agriculture such as Matías Cousiño, Custodio Gallo (on behalf of his mother, Candelaria Goyenechea de Gallo), and Joshua Waddington, an English merchant who came to Chile in 1817 as the country was breaking from Spanish rule and quickly became one of the most prominent merchants in Valparaíso.[21] Waddington's career shows how railroad, telegraph, and other infrastructure projects came to fruition in Chile at this time. Although Waddington arrived in Chile as a merchant, he quickly became involved in agriculture and mining, like Cousiño and Gallo. When the California gold rush created an intense demand for foodstuffs, Waddington attempted to insert himself into the flour trade.[22] The triangulation of agriculture, mining, and export commerce was central to forming the capital base required for these infrastructure projects, as well as to the formation of the Trans-Andean. Yet when it came to the Trans-Andean telegraph, Waddington's name was curiously absent from the shareholder list, even as it counted many of his fellow merchants in Valparaíso.[23] The exact reasons for this lie beyond our story, but it is possible that the unraveling of his waterworks project for Valparaíso, begun in 1855, in the same months that the telegraph project was being finalized played a part.[24]

Waddington's story, like that of the Clarks, did not stray far from the stories of other economic elites in Chile after independence who lent their names and capital to the great infrastructural projects of the time. Mineral and merchant wealth, accumulated in the context of Chile's integration into expanding Pacific markets in the mid-nineteenth century, provided the capital basis not just for infrastructure projects but for most economic endeavors. When the Clark brothers and others gathered in Valparaíso to celebrate the beginning of the Trans-Andean telegraph's construction, they were extending this Pacific world into the Andes and Mendoza, as so many had been doing in the years and decades leading up to that point. In wires and pulses, they were making "durable," to borrow Bruno Latour's characterization of how technology makes society materially present, those connections that had permeated the region up to then.[25]

The Trans-Andean telegraph, the later Trans-Andean railroad, and other modern infrastructure projects like them should be understood as global spaces. As material societal artifacts, they were global spaces not just because they connected disparate parts of the world but also because they acted as global centers. Beyond the Trans-Andean, infrastructure projects as global centers pull together information and "process it at a single location."[26] As infrastructure pulls together information, that information manifests as documentation: surveys, shareholder lists, technical reports, company minutes, legislative debates, government inspections, laws, newspaper articles, photographs, films, scientific studies, and receipts for construction materials. Those documents reflect and foster global connections as they represent how people from different places in the world invest in projects; help engineers make legible and commensurable diverse environments and topographies; allow governments to compare and evaluate modernizing technologies; and reveal how people participate in conversations about global "progress" and "civilization." In that way, infrastructure becomes an assemblage of the world's many and increasing fragments and a site for the production of information that shows how those fragments intersect and exist alongside and in relation to one another. This accumulation and materialization of the world's fragments and information are what give global spaces their materiality. In this way, infrastructure becomes a material center of a global society. Indeed, it is better to use infrastructure as centers of global society than nations, cultures, civilizations, or cities because infrastructures more accurately show *where* worldwide society and processes manifest materially. Infrastructure creates information that makes it legible to other places in the world. It attracts the attention of worldwide investors and becomes the priority of states. It gathers together capital, individual trajectories, political visions of the future, and

*Infrastructure and Global Space*

state-building projects from different places and then lays out a record of this assemblage of people and processes for historians to examine. It is the manifestation of a global historical narrative, which not only reveals the in-placeness of global society but also allows for the unfolding of other narratives within the same spaces in ways that nation-states and other cartographically territorialized spatiohistorical paradigms have not. As a result, infrastructure is global space (and history) made material.

## 2  The State of Labor

The young Andrés Lescano, faced with the prospect of military service to fight in South America's deadliest nineteenth-century war, the War of the Triple Alliance (1864–70), told the Argentine officer that "he didn't obey anyone because that's what his consul had ordered."[1] His consul, so he claimed, was that of the Chilean consulate, an institution that had gained a reputation among laborers for protecting people against military service in the Argentine province of Mendoza, as well as the province of San Juan. Lescano was well aware of that reputation when he claimed to be Chilean to avoid military service in 1868, a claim that Argentine officials would challenge, arguing that he was Argentine and thus obligated to serve.[2] It was not the first time that officials in Mendoza refused to believe someone's claim about being Chilean, and it was not the first time that the Chilean consulate defended these claimants. Indeed, over the 1860s, the Chilean consulate devoted enormous attention to handling the claims and cases of Chilean laborers looking for protection against military service and labor abuses, instead of the property claims and commercial issues traditionally handled by consulates.

There was a good reason for the somewhat unusual focus of the Chilean consulate on the workers' concerns: laborers in Mendoza came to see the consulate—and indeed the very notion of being Chilean—as the institution most closely representative of their experiences in the province. The Trans-Andean economic and social processes that surrounded worker migration and itinerancy outstripped state institutions formulated to address the problems of labor control in postindependence society, problems by the 1860s that were rapidly moving in different directions. That the term "Chilean" began to take on a class connotation for both workers (Argentines and Chileans alike) and state officials suggests that the stakes of conflict in the region were also rapidly changing. The Trans-Andean thus became the spatial locus for compelling state formation and giving rise to new stakes of conflict over the place of labor in society.

The disconnect between traditional ideas and institutions of labor and those experiences of migrants was itself part of a broader struggle over labor in Latin America. Revolution and independence in the early part of the century represented the destabilization of many finely tuned systems of labor control, leading to decades of struggle over those systems.[3] Struggles over labor in the mid-nineteenth century coincided not only with an emerging global and industrial capitalist order but also with the meaningfulness and ultimate legacy of the political changes brought about by the Age of Revolutions. In Latin America, the political openness and uncertainty of the decades after independence culminated from the 1850s into the 1870s in a struggle over the meaning and stakes of postindependence society, notions of political community, and governance in many countries.[4] By the 1880s, however, those struggles gave way to a system characterized by export-oriented economies, limitations on popular participation in politics, and a conservative liberalism that sought to reconcile the competing factions of intra-elite conflicts so prominent in the decades after independence.[5] Within this transition, transnational labor migrations and the institutions surrounding them were important to the development of national and ethnic identity, class consciousness, state formation, labor movements, and transnational revolutionary activity in the final decades of the nineteenth century and the beginning of the twentieth century.[6] As with the Chilean consulate, institutions based in nationality not only helped immigrants adapt to their host country but also shaped the "boundaries of civic inclusion" more broadly.[7] In the case of the Chilean consulate, those boundaries revolved around resetting the place of labor in Cuyo, with laborers (both Argentine and Chilean) at the forefront of making those demands.

## Being "Chilean" in Western Argentina and Beyond

Chileans migrated to western Argentina in the context of several processes, including increased commerce between Chile and western Argentina, changes in land tenure relationships in Chile, and emerging opportunities in the province of Mendoza. In that context, Chilean men were disproportionately visible as peons, which created a connection between the idea of being Chilean and that of being a laborer. In 1849, for example, traveler Isaac Strain noted the extent to which laboring and being Chilean were connected when he remarked, "So numerous are the Chilians at Mendoza and its vicinity, that any laborer is called Chilenoe whether he be a native of that country or not."[8] This association between laboring and being Chilean had connections with the early nineteenth century, when Chileans also made up an important number of rural peons.[9] More than Chilean, however, in the early part of the century, the rural peon class was classified in its greatest part as mixed-race.[10] Those rural areas were racially and ethnically heterogeneous, with about half of the population classified as white (*español, americano*, or *blanco*) and the other half as mixed-race (*mestizo, pardo*, and *mulato*), Indigenous (*indio*), and Black (*negro*), although there was significant variation depending both on the locale and the fact that counting and classifying people was far from a stable or reliable act.[11] This situation persisted into midcentury, and it is unlikely that increased Chilean migration significantly altered the racial and ethnic composition of rural Mendoza.[12] What did change was the disassociation between categories of class and categories of race or caste, which were in decline in state records, and as a result the increasing prominence of the category of Chilean nationality to identify the peon class.

The increasingly close association between Chileans and laborers came at a time when the norms and institutions surrounding labor were undergoing important changes. One prominent institution of labor control in the postindependence period was the *papeleta de conchabo* (work papers). Though this was notoriously difficult to enforce, laborers were required to carry a papeleta de conchabo, which confirmed that the carrier was employed. To echo Arturo Andrés Roig, this institution reflected long-standing ideas about labor as a social obligation.[13] By the 1860s the papeleta and the notion of labor as an obligation (rather than a right) were facing serious challenges, and in 1867 the provincial government attempted to abolish it.[14] Although the reasons for this institution's failures were many, one is that it did not match some of the changes brought about by Trans-Andean commerce, such as the increase in the physical mobility of labor. For example, in one instantiation of the papeleta laws in 1855, the provincial government alluded to the problem of transport peons, stating, "Having to be employed as soon as they arrive from a trip, peons of troops, carriages, and wagons will be considered vagrants, those who do not have the papeleta that verifies being employed in the present."[15] By singling out the problem of transportation labor, the provincial government acknowledged how particular aspects of transport labor—such as the transient nature of employment and the high degree of mobility that accompanied it—challenged this institution of labor control and how economic activities connected to Chile were at the center of changing labor relationships.

The rise of nation-states and transnational labor migrations also revealed a contradiction between traditional conceptualizations of the place of laborers in society and the growing need for a mobile labor force. This contradiction arose from the status of *transeúntes* (transients), particularly foreigners, and how that status's ambiguity intersected with civic obligations that defined being a resident or citizen, such as military service.[16] For "permanent" residents of a community, one important institution in the decades after independence was the local militia.[17] Although getting out of service had a class component to it, in the form of hiring replacements, for example, transients or migrants also could be exempted from that obligation, as long as they had work papers and were only seasonal or temporary laborers in the area.[18] After the Constitution of 1853 in Argentina, the national government wanted to centralize military command and thus reorganized the armed forces, creating the Guardia Nacional (National Guard) and the Ejército de línea (army), the former "made up of all [male] citizens" and the latter "composed of career officers and paid soldiers, 'recruited' voluntarily or conscripted by force."[19] Whereas noncitizen foreigners were exempt from military service, such exemptions could run afoul with notions of the tight connection between laborers and soldiers in places where laborers were overwhelmingly foreigners, such as Cuyo. Beyond Cuyo, this exemption caused problems across the Greater Trans-Andean: as one local official in northern Chile noted, foreigners had to serve in the military "because the workers that inhabit this department are, in their greater part, Argentines."[20] For those defending the exemption of foreigners from military service (often national representatives, such as consuls), the underlying point was to disconnect the relationship between soldiering and laborers by referring to the laborers' transient status.[21] In effect, transiency was being constructed as a semipermanent status, conferred by birth. Obviously, in places such as Mendoza, where a significant portion of its laboring classes was Chilean, this had the potential to create serious problems.

The meaningfulness of the category "Chilean" in the context of labor and military service coincided with similar processes revolving around the intersection of labor, identity, and military service going back to the early nineteenth century. For example, at the intersection of "racially discriminatory draft decrees" and soldiering expectations placed on the lower classes in Buenos Aires province, most Afro-Argentine men in the first half of the nineteenth century shared the experience of military service.[22] This common experience gave many an opportunity to advance their own interests. In Mendoza, for example, during the wars of independence, enslaved Afro-Cuyanos laid claim to their freedom as connected to fighting on behalf of the patriot cause, crafting a "situational identity" based in "the association between patriotism and civil liberty."[23] Although patriot forces, as well as postindependence ones, relied heavily on the labor of enslaved people, free people of African descent, and the rural poor, it did not mean that military leaders always accepted the claims to greater equality on the part of soldier laborers, often working to reinscribe racial and class hierarchies within military service, which created new arenas for contestation through acts of desertion and even mutiny.[24] In other contexts, such as in Brazil during the War of the Triple Alliance and afterward, impressment into military service represented a threat to honorable masculinity, forcing working men to highlight their patriarchal responsibilities as a way to avoid service, sometimes a difficult task for men who circulated far as traveling laborers to support their families.[25] In effect, military service provided a site for identity formation both as an imposition on laborers of different kinds and as an expression of political agency to gain more control over oneself and one's labor. In this context, the term "Chilean" fits well. Similar to claims to being an honorable patriarch in Brazil, the claim to being Chilean gave laborers a way to escape coercion.

As Chilean identity developed as a rejection of state control over laborers, its emergence coincided with the reconfiguration of categories of social differentiation in Argentina and Chile after independence. If the colonial period had no shortage of categories of social differentiation, state makers in the nineteenth century engaged in a project of actively erasing those categories. In Mendoza, by the mid-nineteenth century, officials had dropped racial and ethnic categories in many criminal records. Nationally, the first census in 1869 recorded categories for individuals such as occupation, nationality, and sex as the identities of social differentiation rather than race and ethnicity, emphasizing homogeneity through whitening via *mestizaje* (miscegenation), birthright citizenship, and defining Indigenous people as outside society.[26]

This coincided with parallel projects in Argentina to whiten the country and erase the presence of Afro-Argentines through a "deceptive use of official statistics" and the adoption of new categories to refer to skin color, such as *trigueño* (wheat-colored), which included people of African descent, as well as other mixed-race people and "swarthy-complexioned Europeans."[27] In Chile, the emphasis on nationality and omission of categories of race and ethnicity in censuses reflected a similar effort to create a homogeneous Chilean nation.[28] In both cases, attempting to homogenize society created categories of difference (in other words, nationality). In the Greater Trans-Andean, the ethnic and racial dynamics that underpinned the categories that marked Afro-Cuyanos and Indigenous people were far from irrelevant at this moment in time, particularly in the contexts of emancipation, Huarpe land conflicts, and changing relationships at the frontier with Pehuenches and others.[29] In a related context, Argentine officials deemed Mapuches to be *indios chilenos* (Chilean Indians), which allowed them to advance claims that they were an invading force, which paved the way for the invasion and occupation of Patagonia, known commonly as the Conquest of the Desert (1878–85).[30] Broadly, the imposition of nationality on Indigenous communities who did not conceptualize the mountains as a border in the same way that the Chilean and Argentine nation-states did was common.[31]

In the context of Chilean migrations not just to Argentina but also to other places, migrants constructed their identities along several axes, including nationality, class, masculinity, the Chilean consulate, and shifting notions of race and ethnicity. While Chileans were migrating to Mendoza and San Juan provinces, they also found themselves across the Pacific world in Peru, Bolivia, and California. In those cases, as in Argentina, Chilean men migrated often as labor peons. In the context of being foreign and targets of state officials, combined with being subject to strict labor relations, Chileans in these places developed a sense of identity that was closely tied to class and nationality (not always at the same time and sometimes in contradictory ways).[32] During the War of the Pacific (1879–83), in which Chile annexed Bolivian and Peruvian territory in a quest to control nitrate resources, nationalism intensified as conflicts between the Bolivian government and Chilean companies fueled conflict between Chileans and Bolivians generally, including workers of both nationalities.[33] In the throes of war, masculine virility and racializations of national difference also played important roles in identity construction.[34] If whiteness played a role in identity construction in Chile and vis-à-vis Bolivia and Peru during the War of the Pacific, in other places Chileans were denied whiteness. In California during the gold rush, Chilean miners' early successes made them the targets of resentful Anglo-Americans, leading to discriminatory nativist legislation against Chileans and violent attacks against Chilean communities. For white US Americans in California, Chileans and Mexicans "did not qualify... even as partially white."[35] In Argentina, the place of Chilean migrations in racial hierarchies and government programs was not clear. Immigration policies there with foundations in the 1850s privileged European immigrants to "whiten the population and build a prosperous, democratic society."[36] In Mendoza, for example, at the turn of the twentieth century, as the wine industry expanded, massive waves of Spanish and Italian migrants tended to receive preferential treatment in hiring.[37] Before those European migrations, provincial state officials expressed fears that Argentine laborers were falsifying Chilean identity to dodge military service, a practice that indicates that being Chilean was not something easily recognized externally. Nevertheless, for Chileans in Mendoza and elsewhere in the Pacific world, for whatever the malleability of their identity, the Chilean consulate was one constant. It played an important role in promoting the interests of Chilean workers abroad, a task that the consulate also performed in Mendoza and San Juan provinces.[38]

Ultimately, being Chilean became a way for laborers (whether Chilean or Argentine) to gain control over their own labor due to their ability to command the power of the consulate through that term. Being Chilean was a way to resist the state's attempts to control and condition their labor, not an uncommon component in the construction of peon identity in other places in Argentina.[39] This was not the only time that "Chilean" would be used against the state. For example, according to anthropologist Diego Escolar, the term "Chilean"—and later claims of indigeneity—informed collective identity construction in the intermontane region of Calingasta in San Juan, where state-formation processes found resistance from locals in the middle of the twentieth century when the Argentine national state embarked on a project of national incorporation of these border areas.[40] In the mid-nineteenth century, different from other contexts (Bolivia, Peru, and California) and closer to what Escolar describes for the twentieth century, being Chilean in Mendoza and San Juan was more likely to be a category of self-identification. Because it was a category of self-identification and not externalized easily, contestations between state officials and laborers over it meant that it was one expressed through institutional markers, such as the nationality papers and lists used by the Chilean consulate to identify Chileans. In this way, the term "Chilean" in this period can be thought of as a counterstate project, one in which laborers in Mendoza—Chileans and Argentines—attempted to construct identities and a state institution reflective of their experiences with the changing economy. For laborers, postindependence institutions and political discourse must have increasingly seemed unrelatable, making Chilean identity and the Chilean consulate attractive for expressing new experiences and addressing problems of a Trans-Andean work environment.

## The Chilean Consulate

By the 1860s in Mendoza, laborers began to embroil the Chilean consulate in a counterstate project. The consulate's ability to partake in this project relied on both its power to challenge the provincial government's authority and its uncertain mandate in Mendocino society, which allowed laborers to shape it. In the region broadly, there was a sense that the consulate would function as a commercial institution, charged with protecting and promoting the commerce of its mother nation in foreign territories. As the renowned jurist Andrés Bello articulated in the 1830s, "The consuls are agents that were sent to friendly nations with the task of protecting the rights and commercial interests of their homeland, and supporting their merchant compatriots in the difficulties that they encounter."[41] For Bello, one of the principal ways of accomplishing these tasks was through "observing if treaties are obeyed and upheld, or in what way they are broken or eschewed."[42] One implication of Bello's conceptualization of the consulate was that if it was the consulate's responsibility to ensure that international documents, such as treaties, were to be respected, consular officials were in a position to challenge the authority of local and provincial governments by asserting the supremacy of treaties as the law of the land. In Mendoza, this became a problem.

In 1859–60, a small crisis emerged between the Chilean consulate in Mendoza and the provincial government, revealing uncertainties over the consul's power. In the wake of a failed rebellion in Chile in 1859, Chilean rebels fled the country, some going to Mendoza.[43] Once there, Chilean exiles began to criticize the Chilean government, and in one instance the official newspaper of the government published an article against the Chilean president, Manuel Montt.[44] Seeing the accusations in the article as "very reckless and vulgar slander," the consul immediately wrote the government to express outrage.[45] The indignation expressed by the Chilean consul set off an intense debate over the nature of the consulate's role in the province and the extent of its power. The provincial government responded, claiming "it is not in a position to receive complaints from you [the consul] . . . because you . . . only have been recognized as a simple commercial agent."[46] The question of the extent of the consul's role as a "public official" with the right to petition, according to the government, came from Bello's description, which stated, "'The Consuls do not have a greater duty than that of protecting *the commercial rights and interests* of their *patria.*'"[47] If the government in Mendoza was working to keep this institution's power at bay, the consulate was going to fight to maintain its relevancy.

The consul responded to the provincial government's refutation of the consulate's power by correcting its understanding of Bello and the norms governing international relations. In a lengthy reply, the consul cited a litany of authorities on international relations, demonstrating along the way that he had the power of a foreign representative (that is to say, public official) and that, as Bello argued, "As responsible for safeguarding the observance of commercial treaties, it is incumbent upon the Consul to protest against all their infractions, addressing the authorities of the district in which they reside."[48] Ultimately, the Ministry of Foreign Affairs of the Argentine Confederation got involved and reprimanded the provincial government, rejecting its request that the government ask for the consul's dismissal and demanding that it not let Mendoza become "a center of permanent insurrection."[49] If the power of the Chilean consulate was saved for the moment, its specific role as a representative of the Chilean government was not much clearer than before.

Even by the mid-1860s, consular norms had not been established well enough to provide new consuls with a definite sense of their role as representatives not only of the national government but also of Chileans living in the province. Consul José de la Cruz Zenteno embodied the institutional flexibility of the consulate and the consul's role in shaping its direction. After the failure of the liberal rebellion of 1851 in Chile, many participants went into exile, some to Lima, others to Guayaquil, still others even to California, and some, like Zenteno, to Mendoza.[50] In Mendoza, he served different roles in the increasingly regularized judicial system, including as a state defender in criminal cases.[51] His tenure as Chilean consul in Mendoza began in late 1864 and continued until at least late 1867.[52] Early on, it was not punishing slander against the Chilean government or making commercial claims that attracted Zenteno; instead, he was most acutely concerned with impoverished and laboring Chileans in the province. A precise understanding of Chilean national policy toward emigrants abroad is still needed, particularly as countries such as France were simultaneously developing protective policies for emigrants.[53] It is worth noting here, however, the role that poor and laboring Chileans had in pushing for greater protection and assistance from the consulate, especially considering that Chilean representatives elsewhere had uneven and inconsistent responses to the demands from and conflicts involving Chilean laborers abroad.[54] In one of his first letters to the Chilean minister of foreign affairs, Zenteno wrote, "Since I arrived in this city I have seen on a daily basis so many poor and helpless Chileans knocking on the doors of this Consulate in search of assistance and alms for survival that my heart weeps.... To remedy these misfortunes I think it my duty to point out to you that it would be quite advisable to direct to these wretches all or part of the funds that are deposited in the coffers coming from alms distributed on behalf of Chileans for the unfortunate people of Mendoza."[55]

The funds to which Zenteno referred in his letter were for a major earthquake that had occurred in 1861, and it appears that people were still suffering greatly from it in 1864. His inclination to help "these wretches" was not limited to a single event. Only a few months after this letter, for example, Zenteno requested clarification on the limits of his power to represent "poor Chileans" in provincial courts. This request, however, was not necessarily out of his own desire, but rather proceeded from the constant requests made by "poor Chileans" themselves to have him "represent them or defend them... in their judicial proceedings."[56] He was advised against this, being told that he should help them understand the law but not go as far as representing them in court.[57] In effect, the unclear nature of the consulate's role in provincial society left open the question of what kind of institution it would be, a question increasingly answered by the demands of laborers against social obligations that no longer made sense for their changing context.

### Military Service and the Chilean Consulate

It was March 1865 when military authorities accused Juan Gonzales of lying about being Chilean to evade military service. The government's witnesses all said the same thing: Juan Gonzales was from Argentina, which was "known to the whole neighborhood."[58] Although he had lived in Argentina for most of his life, Gonzales was, at least according to his parents, born in Chile. They had moved from Chile when he was only three months old, and once Gonzales was old enough he, like his father (also Chilean), enrolled in the Guardia Nacional.[59] Whatever benefits father and son may have garnered from service, after the arrival of the Chilean consul Juan Godoy in the province, "they each got a Chilean certificate," which may have been a recently developed form of identification: nationality papers appear not to have existed in prior decades.[60] One of the first 800 persons to be registered as a Chilean national with the consulate, Juan Gonzales registered in July 1861 with witnesses to testify to the fact that he was Chilean.[61] Throughout the 1860s, the connection between Chileanness and military exemption grew, as did the institutional mechanisms to give Chileanness its power, such as the consular registry that Juan Gonzales used to claim Chilean nationality and thus exemption from military service.

Even as Zenteno solicited the government in Chile to find Juan's birth records, he defended the superiority of the registry over any claim the provincial government brought.[62] If taken too seriously, the rumors of Gonzales's Argentine nationality could risk delegitimizing the consulate's registry.[63] The stakes of defending the registry's trustworthiness, therefore, were high. Zenteno brought these to the fore when he reminded the provincial government that military officers lacked the power to arbitrarily question someone's nationality, as "the sole fact of an individual's registration in the Consular Registry means that his nationality has been verified with full knowledge.... The Chilean who obtains his respective certificate through these procedures should be respected for his nationality, *as long as the contrary is not justified with a greater proof.*"[64] Zenteno understood that for the consular registry to function, it needed to be respected in the face of spurious claims. The registry itself proved nationality, and therefore mere rumors were not enough to force the consulate to prove nationality again. For Zenteno, the stakes went beyond the registry and to the heart of international norms, as illustrated when he argued, "And if the government does not promptly enforce these rules, we will have advanced nothing in this matter with the consular registries nor with the existence of treaties."[65] Connecting the registry to the international treaties that sustained relations between "friendly nations," Zenteno put the consulate at the apex of the hierarchy of institutions in the province, as the preserver of the new inter*national* order.

Struggles between the provincial government and the Chilean consulate put the registry at the center of questions about state power. In Mendoza, as well as neighboring San Juan, consuls understood that the registry was useless without the consulates' ability to register people beyond the confines of their offices in the provincial capitals. Most Chileans lived outside the capital cities of Mendoza and San Juan, in places such as San Carlos, San Rafael, Jáchal, and Calingasta, far from the consulates, likely limiting their access to the registry.[66] The consul in San Juan was particularly concerned by the increase in the number of Chileans being forced into military service, arguing to the foreign minister that the problem was "due to the suppression of registration rights." To that end, he thought, "it would be convenient to establish consular agents in the villages of Jáchal, Valle Fértil, and in some mining areas so that they could register Chileans."67 By 1865, both consulates had ended up appointing representatives outside the provincial capitals, Benjamín Sánchez in southern Mendoza and Fabián Martínez in Jáchal.68 From their respective posts, both representatives could register Chileans and issue nationality papers. In that sense, registering people and issuing them nationality papers were parts of a process of bringing the registry to distant areas of the province and allowing "Chilean" as an institutional category to become as mobile as the people claiming that status.69

The stakes of the category "Chilean" were elevated in May 1865 when the Argentine Republic, Uruguay, and Brazil formed the so-called Triple Alliance to wage war against Paraguay, a war that would last until 1870, leave well over half of the Paraguayan population dead, and become enormously unpopular, particularly in provinces such as Mendoza, where a foreign war directed by the new national government in Buenos Aires not only threatened people's already precarious situations, especially soldiers expected to fight in the war, but also intersected with ongoing political tensions in Argentina.70 At the outset, far from the front in Mendoza in the patriotic fervor of a national war against Paraguay, people were rounded up against their will and incorporated into military units. For Chileans, the threat of conscription was particularly acute. In Mendoza, the Chilean consul reported in the early days of the war, "Armed parties have given rise to taking any Chilean whom they find without papers from their Consul," papers that protected them from being forced into service.71 The early days of the war in that sense were characterized by a patriotic zeal that left laborers susceptible to conscription.72 Sensing that the military already had conscripted a significant number of Chileans because they lacked the proper identification to prove their citizenship, the consulate began registering and issuing new nationality papers to Chileans to help get them released from service.73

Compared with earlier periods, rates of registration at the consulate reached a crescendo with the onset of the war in 1865, signifying the association that people had between being Chilean and military exemption.74 Laborers therefore likely saw appeals to the Chilean consulate as a way to resist military service and to exert more control over their own labor. If *Chilean* workers began to see the consulate in that light, then it is more than likely that other workers in Mendoza facing similar experiences did, too. Indeed, state officials were deeply suspicious of Chilean nationality claims, suspecting that Argentines were using the Chilean consulate to evade service.75 In Chile, too, there existed a difficulty in discerning nationality when it came to the obligations of military service.76 In that way, among state officials in different places, there was a generalized consternation about foreign labor migrations and their impact on state power, which in the case of the provincial government in Mendoza led officials to accuse Chileans of really being Argentines (as in the cases of Juan Gonzales and Andrés Lescano, the young man whose story opened this chapter) or, as some officials claimed, of using the consulate to back out of service after receiving wage advances.[77] In other words, officials in Mendoza sensed that the consulate was affording laborers in the province (Chileans and Argentines alike) too much control over their own labor, particularly vis-à-vis state institutions that relied on that labor. In the context of these struggles, the meaningfulness of being Chilean grew not merely as a marker of origins but as indicative of a relationship to oneself and to the state. For someone like Lescano, the significance of being Chilean was clear: "He didn't obey anyone because that's what his Consul had ordered."[78]

### Labor beyond Military Service

It was February 1865 when Cruz Galdames showed up at the consulate. He had traveled far, more than 100 kilometers, to seek the assistance of Consul Zenteno, to whom he explained what he had been facing over the preceding years. Years back, likely in 1862, a man named Francisco Guevara had hired him at an estancia in San Rafael. He was to tend to a sheepfold, for which he was to be paid 48 pesos per year, plus meat and wheat rations. In that role he served for twenty-eight months and twenty-four days, meaning that he should have been paid almost 116 pesos. For his work, however, he received only 29 pesos. That was not the end of it. Afterward, Guevara became the area's *subdelegado* (a local authority with broad powers, especially in rural areas) and demanded that Galdames return the 29 pesos.[79] Understandably, Galdames rejected Guevara's demand, prompting Guevara to bring a case against him.[80] During his imprisonment, Galdames told the commissary that he would pay Guevara back, but he needed to be released so that he could get the money; he never returned.[81] Instead, he went to Mendoza to seek the assistance of the Chilean consulate. Although the case remained inconclusive, it demonstrates how people constructed their Chileanness in connection to their sense of their labor and the institutions that conditioned it, such as the Chilean consulate and nationality papers.

Another institution related to labor control, and one that became entangled with notions of Chileanness and the introduction of nationality papers, was the papeleta de conchabo, or work papers. Chileans increasingly challenged this institution. In April 1863, for example, the provincial government in

Mendoza feared that Chilean laborers would participate in an impending invasion of the province by the Federalist rebel Francisco Clavero, from Curicó in Chile, across the mountains from southern Mendoza, where some of the highest concentrations of Chilean migrants lived.[82] Clavero's invasion seemed imminent, and it appeared to the government that substantial numbers of Chileans were ready to join his cause because of "the promise[s] that [Clavero] has made to them, of representing them in the future, abolishing the papeleta and conceding to them other false promises."[83] Fearing the worst, the government asked the Chilean consulate to plead with its compatriots in southern Mendoza not to join Clavero's forces.[84] Regardless of whether the government had access to Clavero's communications with potential soldiers, it clearly understood the problems it faced among Chileans in the province: the papeleta was worth fighting to abolish, and they clearly were not well enough represented. Whether only in the eyes of the state or in the eyes of laborers, incongruities between traditional conceptualizations of labor and experiences of it were diverging violently.

As the papeleta de conchabo faced challenges from different sectors of society, nationality papers could sometimes stand in for them. Reporting to the Chilean government in 1863, the Chilean consul noted that the jails always held a significant number of Chileans. Among the "infractions" that put them in jail was "the special demand that is made on them for nationality papers, without this widespread measure being made on foreigners of other nations."[85] The practice of arresting people who lacked nationality papers paralleled that of arresting laborers without the papeleta de conchabo, which itself was a way of controlling and reallocating labor, particularly to public works.[86] In that sense, nationality papers were a mechanism for harassing people, particularly Chileans, who made up a significant portion of the working classes in the province. For example, in late 1866, one man was arrested and placed in the service of the military for "nothing more than having been found once without the *papeleta de patrón*," meaning work papers.[87] The parallels between the papeleta and nationality papers are unmistakable. Only a year earlier Zenteno had noted that in the wake of the war with Paraguay "armed parties" were going around rural Mendoza rounding up anyone who did not have their nationality papers.[88] In effect, these different identification technologies became ways to control laborers. One can imagine that the only reason information from these Chileans exists is the Chilean consulate's ability to bring much of this to light. Indeed, as one consul reminds us, the administrative norms that governed the province could lead to "the frequent abuses that are committed against [Chileans'] rights by local authorities," who often left little evidence of these "abuses" because proceedings were usually handled through "verbal processing."[89] It is entirely likely, then, that these abuses were widespread for Chileans and non-Chileans alike.

If not having nationality papers presented a risk for Chileans, this did not mean that having papers automatically granted them protection. Throughout the 1860s, local authorities and military officers demonstrated disdain for nationality papers. In the early days of the war with Paraguay, for example, Zenteno reported that many Chileans had been forced into service "despite having shown their nationality papers."[90] In other cases, military officers were even harsher. In one instance, one man's use of nationality papers led to a violent confrontation, during which the officer wounded him and tore up his papers.[91] Thus, nationality papers had, in some sense, come to represent an affront to military power in the region by exempting the traditional soldiering classes from service. In ignoring and destroying these nationality papers, military officers were communicating their desire to reassert traditional notions of laborers as soldiers and labor as a community obligation.[92] Although nationality papers did help to liberate Chileans from these structures of traditional labor-state relations, it would be wrong to assert that they were simultaneously freeing Chileans from boss-peon relations.

In an interesting twist of fate, nationality papers ended up replacing the papeleta not only for questions of state harassment but also for reworking the power structures between bosses and peons because bosses had an interest in protecting their peons from military service.[93] Getting on the registry required the assistance of others. In the early days of the war with Paraguay, employers from across the province worked on behalf of their peons to free up their labor from military service.[94] In fact, laborers often had to rely on their bosses to get their nationality papers, especially if they had already been conscripted. In some ways, this allowed increased power of bosses over peons, thus fulfilling the goals of the papeleta in a different form.

These mechanisms of labor control developed during the mid-nineteenth century were by no means unique. Changing labor regimes across the world were intersecting with changing meanings of the Pacific world. The early promoters of the Trans-Andean railroad certainly saw their project as engaging with this new Pacific world.

Interlude Two | The Shape of Labor

Years after their telegraph project had finished, as the Clark brothers were attempting to sell their Trans-Andean railroad project to investors and to the Chilean and Argentine governments, they tapped into the very phenomenon that had birthed their project so many years before: the reorientation of Pacific commerce toward Europe and the Americas. In a report to the Chilean government in 1877, they claimed, "For the communication between Australia and England, transit between Valparaíso, Buenos Aires and Montevideo offers the quickest and most economical route of all known routes."[1] In their estimation, the traffic that normally went from England to Australia, passing through the newly built Suez Canal and the Indian Ocean, could actually be rerouted through South America and over the Andes. "Steamships from Australia," they stated, "would come loaded with products from that colony for England, passengers, suitcases, and treasure would disembark in Valparaíso, all of which would be taken over to Montevideo in forty-eight hours." "We have no doubts," they continued, "that the voyage from Melbourne to London could be made in forty days," which was five days shorter than the transcontinental route in the United States, nine days shorter than passing through the Suez Canal, and twenty days shorter than rounding South America.[2]

That the Clark brothers would invoke the image of Australia in selling their project is not surprising. As historian Pablo Lacoste puts it, "The idea of connecting Great Britain with its dominions in New Zealand and Australia" provided the "principal impulse" for projects such as the Trans-Andean railroad.[3] And yet, it bears remembering that the original project was never about connecting the two oceans or even the two nations but rather about better integrating a Trans-Andean market that centered on trade between Mendoza and Valparaíso. As Mateo Clark told his engineering peers in 1913, "The idea was not to make a line to Buenos Aires but solely unite the Province of Mendoza with Valparaiso on the Pacific," yet once the Argentine government expressed its own interest in uniting the Trans-Andean with Buenos Aires and the Atlantic, it became a transcontinental project to unify the Atlantic and Pacific Oceans.[4] Nevertheless, the connection with the England-Australia route had some sense to it. The centrality of Australia to the British Empire had grown in the mid-nineteenth century, along with the development of transpacific steamship services, and British trade had been central to the Chilean political-economic imaginary for some time.[5]

The reality is that the connection between Australia and the Trans-Andean railroad was about more than the colony's place in the British Empire by the 1870s. It was about labor and labor's changing relation to land and capital. Beginning around the second decade of the nineteenth century, according to historian James Belich, migrants from the British Isles fanned out west to create the Anglo-settler colonist world.[6] Although colonization in Australia began in the late 1700s, the first settler booms occurred in the 1830s. Later, one of the most explosive and sustained gold rushes in history led to another settler boom. Australia saw its greatest growth in population and economy, however, between 1870 and 1890.[7] New Zealand was also a site for settler colonialism. Beginning in the 1850s, white settlers began a sustained invasion of the islands, and between 1851 and 1886 the immigrant population grew from 26,000 to over half a million (580,000).[8] These settler migrations, of course, were not limited to Australia and New Zealand.

As the well-worn narrative goes, the steady march of settlers across the United States found inspiration in what was often called "manifest destiny," a process defined by a great deal of violence against Indigenous communities and against enslaved people dragged westward. This is not to forget Mexico, the country from which the greater part of the US West was taken in 1848 at the end of the Mexican-American War (1846–48). The term "manifest destiny" originated in the lead-up to the war as a justification for

*The Shape of Labor*

the annexation of Texas in 1845, the event that precipitated the war.[9] To the north, a similar process was taking place. The number of migrants heading to Indiana, Michigan, and Illinois, as well as Ohio and Wisconsin, was staggering in the first half of the nineteenth century. From 1810 to 1860, the combined populations of those states ballooned from about 250,000 to 7 million.[10] The most notable wave of this boom centered on Chicago.[11] Its growth from the 1830s onward came from its unique position as a changeover point in a number of different transportation systems. Shipping routes from the Hudson–Erie Canal–Great Lakes circuit, interior traffic brought by the Illinois and Michigan Canal, and eastern and western railroads all converged on the city.[12] In a way not too dissimilar from Chicago, Mendoza likewise had become part of a growth pattern based on pauses and interruptions in commodity circulations—in this case, seasonal ones devoted to feeding cattle. Later, in the 1850s, places such as Wisconsin, Iowa, and Minnesota would see their turn as destinations for settler migrations. In Minnesota, for example, the population grew from 4,000 in 1849 to 150,000 only eight years later in 1857. By the end of the 1860s, the population would be approaching half a million.[13] This growth would change "Minnesota from the 'American Siberia' into the 'New England of the West.'"[14]

The comparison between the western frontier in the United States and Argentina's southern frontier—often described as desert in need of the "civilizing" hand of (white) settlers—was not lost on people at the time (and has not been lost on scholars and commentators more recently).[15] In 1868, the Argentine minister of the interior, Guillermo Rawson, speculated on the potential impact of a Trans-Andean railroad built across Indigenous lands along the frontier on the republic. Such a technological crossing, Rawson proclaimed, would facilitate "the formation of cities and provinces whose names have yet to be made and . . . like the states of Illinois, Indiana, Michigan, and Jowa [sic] in the western United States, will show immense wealth."[16] Framing Trans-Andean railroad projects as existing within the same spaces as Anglo-settler migrations made it part of a substantial rearrangement of the Pacific economic geography, which over the nineteenth century shifted its center of gravity from the western Pacific based on Chinese demand eastward to the Americas and Europe.[17] By the 1850s and 1860s, when the Trans-Andean was becoming a feasible project, British industrial demand; US westward expansionism and an emerging Pacific presence in places such as Hawai'i; mineral booms in Chile, Australia, and California; declining demand of Spanish American silver in China; debates around transpacific steamship services; and mass migrations helped reorganize the Pacific economy and give it a more Anglophone character than it had before.[18]

Related to this reorientation of Pacific geographies was a reinscription of the practices and meaning of labor in the nineteenth century within and beyond this transoceanic space. If in the late eighteenth century slavery dominated the emerging capitalist global economy, by the time Rawson penned those words in 1868, slavery as a legal institution in the Atlantic world remained only in Brazil and the Spanish Empire, where at that very moment revolutionary and liberal theories on free association converged on the question of slavery and abolition.[19] Of course, the classic, but now discarded narrative of the decline in slavery as an institution and the rise of free, proletarian labor misses the fact that throughout this period there were various experiments with new coercive labor regimes. For example, in the aftermath of the 1857 mutiny in India, officials across the British Empire discussed plans to send disarmed soldiers to far-flung corners of the world, from British Guiana to Australia.[20] To be sure, these labor movements from South Asia to different parts of the British Empire were by no means disconnected from white settler colonialism. In fact, idealized narratives of free coolie labor "moving across the British Empire providing cheap labor free from exploitation while facilitating indigenous dispossession, was part of a broader cynical white imagination of free labor after the abolition of slavery."[21] Beginning in the second half of the nineteenth century, at the edges of the British Empire, in places including the North-West Frontier of British India, "economic dependence" forced people in these frontier areas into an "exploitative labor regime" defined by "military labor" and "migratory labor flows," a cornerstone of what historian Benjamin Hopkins calls "frontier governmentality."[22] In Australia, attempts to develop cotton and sugar industries amid the crisis of slavery in the Americas resulted in the kidnapping and enslavement of Melanesians, a process known as blackbirding.[23] And coolie labor from China going to Cuba and Peru, or the attempts by Peruvian and Chilean slavers to "recruit" and kidnap Pacific Islanders to feed Peru's guano and sugar industries, represented another set of heavily contested experiments meant to insert people into increasingly intense systems of production and extraction in the middle decades of the nineteenth century.[24] In Latin America these experiments represented a struggle over the ultimate meaning of the wars of independence that had at times resulted in the loosening of colonial systems of labor control as enslaved people, rural peons, peasants, and urban workers participated in (or refused participation in) these struggles as a way of laying claim to their

*The Shape of Labor*

own interests, often different from those of independence leaders, from emancipation to increased access to land.[25]

These struggles over the place of labor in society at midcentury embroiled as broad a swath of the globe as ever in history, including rural Mendoza. The shifting meaning of laboring and soldiering in western Argentina, the production of "Chilean" as a class category, and the place of identification papers (nationality papers and work papers alike) in those transformations, underscore the grounded meaningfulness embedded in global structural processes. These changes in the meaningfulness and practices of labor in the Pacific broadly undoubtedly changed the space itself. The orientation of the Pacific from its western rim to the eastern shores occurred in this period. This happened in conjunction, if not fully due to, changing labor patterns, both in terms of migratory patterns and in how that labor (settler, coolie, enslaved, proletarian) stood in relation to capital and land. This changing Pacific was what allowed the Trans-Andean railroad to take shape as a globally meaningful project. It became envisioned as part of the circulation of this labor, as well as the products of it. Not only that, but also in the context of the production of the Trans-Andean itself beginning in the 1850s, the railroad was part of a rearrangement of the meaningfulness and practices of labor. The original intention of the Clarks' railroad—to connect Mendoza and Valparaíso—arose with Chileans' migration to western Argentina, along with shifting patterns of capital migrations. These shifts themselves were in part a response to the changes in the Pacific, from the gold rushes in California and Australia to the silver and copper booms in Chile to the place of Valparaíso as one of the most important Pacific ports in the mid-nineteenth century. In this sense, the remaking of the Trans-Andean region in relation to the changes in labor was part and parcel to the creation of the Trans-Andean railroad as a project. If labor changes the production of space, it also allows for an understanding of the everyday experiences of it. The following chapter examines how these changes in labor and mobility became central to everyday life in the Trans-Andean.

## 3 Property and Everyday Mobility

José María Rojas was a Trans-Andean subject. When authorities in San Carlos, Mendoza, arrested him in November 1869 on suspicion of stealing a mule (the charge would later become two mules and a horse), his interrogation made this clear. His interrogator asked him the usual questions, such as what his profession was. "Gañán," he responded (later "peón" would be added).[1] The interrogator also inquired about his nationality. "Chilean," Rojas told him. He had left Chile at least three years earlier, perhaps with his wife and their newborn daughter.[2] As illustrated earlier, people such as Rojas embodied and took part in the changing social character of places such as the province of Mendoza in Argentina in the mid-nineteenth century. Chileans increasingly found themselves living in the province, and rates of itinerancy came to be the highest in the country. In the context of a changing society and intransigent state, migrants and itinerant laborers challenged established norms about the place of labor in postcolonial society, especially in the face of changing forms of employment and demands for soldiers to fight in the War of the Triple Alliance. They did this by appealing to the Chilean consulate, an institution with which Rojas was familiar. In fact, he was, according to his interrogation, in San Carlos "to get consul papers."[3] In regard to his occupation, he claimed to have "his fields here," in the area around the village of San Carlos.[4] Yet in his initial denial of the theft accusations, he claimed to have been hired to transport the supposedly stolen animals and sell them to a merchant who was traveling to Chile.[5] In sum, he was a Chilean migrant who tied himself to the land, transported animals and took odd jobs, engaged with merchants who transported goods between Mendoza and Chile, and was familiar with the Chilean consulate and likely the benefits it afforded him. In other words, he was a Trans-Andean subject, one who built up this mobile place that seemed to confront state-making projects almost constantly in this period.

This chapter follows Rojas's routes in space to reconstruct how he and others produced this mobile place. Specifically, it centers the transport animals that helped him and others like him move in, out of, and around the province of Mendoza in the mid-nineteenth century. For them, horses and mules were important not only as means of conveyance but also as pieces of property to be exchanged, which constituted one of the many survival strategies for people such as Rojas at the time. To ride and exchange those horses and mules, they needed access to places where they could feed animals, as well as places to exchange them. With that in mind, the two places most important to the mobility of people like Rojas were *potreros* (paddocks or pastures), where transport animals were fed and kept, and *casas* (houses), where people sometimes exchanged animals and sheltered. Rather than take them as neutral sites in the production of mobility, I focus on how pastures and houses, and how feeding and exchanging animals, were places and activities revelatory of the social dynamics surrounding mobility, from norms involved in what kinds of animals itinerant laborers were expected to have to processes of enclosure to peon-boss relationships.

If property was central to the production of everyday mobility, it is also the lens through which this narrative understands the effect that everyday mobility had on state formation. Animal property not only allowed people to move about but was also a cornerstone of political economy in the province of Mendoza. By moving about on animals and through animal exchanges, mobile people clashed with the political economic priorities of the state, leading to criminal cases over the provenance of transport animals in rural Mendoza.[6] Those cases constitute what I think of as an unintentional project for the spatialization of provincial state power in the mid-nineteenth century, as local and provincial authorities had to track people in space and connect officials in different parts of the province to procure testimony, processes that were reflective of long-standing attempts going back to the colonial era by governments in Mendoza to know and control rural areas.[7] Those cases also were part of a broader tension between city and countryside in postindependence

Latin America, as well as spatial projects taking place across the region to map, know, and tame spaces of new nation-states.[8] Ultimately, criminal cases open a window into the mobile, mostly rural, worlds of Trans-Andean subjects. Those worlds, in turn, show how spatial dimensions of state-making projects occurred within a context of the social transformations born out of the same processes examined in previous chapters.

### Animal Property and Provincial Justice

When José María Rojas went to Mendoza to face the provincial justice system, he was encountering the judicial wing of a provincial order that had developed with the goal of promoting and preserving the sanctity of animal property. The sanctity of animal property emerged in the context of an incipient livestock economy in the 1830s. As part of the collapse of the colonial viticultural sector and the rise of Federalism in Mendoza in the 1830s, animal property demarcated the boundaries of social inclusion and status. For examples, regulations crafted in 1834 and 1845 to address the emergent economy defined different classes tied to the economy not first through their access to land, which must have been assumed, but rather through their capitalization, as defined by a minimum number of animals.[9] If animals were at the center of delineating the economic order of the day, they were similarly fundamental to identifying social disorder from the state's perspective. Throughout the mid-nineteenth century, animals and specifically the lack of animal *property* came to be seen as important indicators of social disorder. Early in the construction of a system based on the sanctity of animal property, the provincial state associated unmarked, or *"animales desconocidos"* (unknown animals), with disorder. In 1830, for example, the provincial government lamented the problem of disorder in Las Lagunas de Guanacache by linking conflict to the prevalence of "unknown animals" in the area, where cattle trading had been an important part of the economy since at least the eighteenth century.[10] Its solution was to remove all unmarked animals from the area and ensure that all animals brought into the area were properly marked and identified by local authorities.[11] While unstated in government remarks on the area, conflicts in Guanacache were related to Indigenous land claims made by Huarpe descendants there, which found new life in the context of early postindependence political struggles in the province, illustrating the connection between animals and the spatialization of political power.[12]

In the context of postindependence state formation, the framework of animal property intersected with the construction of a number of institutions meant to safeguard order. Early in the provincial state's attempt to bolster the livestock economy, local rural officials were charged with protecting the economy through strict social discipline, as when the Reglamento de Estancias of 1834, which regulated estates and cattle ranches, began by affording local rural officials sweeping powers of social discipline, including "whipping," doing little to hide the connection between social control and economic development in rural Mendoza.[13] Perhaps the most important institution for the emerging cattle trade was the *subdelegacía* or *subdelegación*, an office developed in the 1810s and 1820s, then solidified in the 1830s, headed up by the subdelegado, a rural magistrate charged with keeping order in the countryside.[14] As guardians of the sanctity of animal property, institutions like the subdelegacía brought many rural people into contact with the state through severe judicial practices. In the 1830s and 1840s, another institution, the military commission, periodically replaced regular judicial institutions to confront perceptions of growing disorder. Composed of military judges with sweeping powers to expedite cases, the military commission became the judicial institution that enforced and handed out severe punishment to protect the sanctity of animal property. The state instituted this military tribunal in 1831 as a way of solving what was perceived to be a lack of order and the predominance of criminality.[15] Between 1831 and 1852, there were fourteen different iterations of the military commission, many lasting for only a few months.[16] Beyond its stated purposes, as historian Eugenia Molina notes, the military commission was part of a broad process of social control in the context of an economy coalescing around the cattle trade.[17] For anyone facing the military commission for violating the sanctity of animal property, for example by "stealing" horses and mules, the stakes were high. At the most extreme end, convicts of rustling could be sentenced to death if they were repeat offenders and had stolen a minimum value of animals.[18] Since punishment was a central component of completing a case, to be able to establish recidivism meant a sense of certainty as well as "a means of conveying authoritative messages to the lower class" through public execution.[19] Even for those who were spared execution, sentencing for stealing horses could be severe, from flogging to forced labor on the frontier.[20]

By the time Rojas was being interrogated by the judge in 1869 circumstances had changed, at least a little. The military commissions that had thrived under Federalist rule had given way to an ostensibly independent judiciary, although provincial and national penal codes would not come for several more years.[21] The punishments that had marked their rule, such as exile, lashings, and execution, became increasingly uncommon.[22] Of course, liberal judicial practices and institutions built on top of the judicial foundations laid under the Federalists, signaling important continuities between ostensibly starkly contrasted orders.23 For example, the subdelegado played an essential part in maintaining order in the countryside as well as in the province's "political administrative reorganization of territory and the development of rural villages" during the transition between the Federalist rule and liberal rule in Mendoza.24 The transition to a liberal justice system did not mean the end of concerns about animal property, either. Cases of animal theft were commonplace, particularly of transport animals such as the mules and horse state officials accused Rojas of stealing. For new judicial institutions and practices, the concern during this period became less about rural disorder itself and more about mobility. As with the papeleta de conchabo or Chilean nationality papers, theft cases reflected an emerging Trans-Andean social and economic space, one that overlapped in a conflicting way with state formation.

As much as Rojas fit the social profile of Trans-Andean subjects, he also fit the social profile of people arrested for the crime of stealing transport animals: Chilean, male, and peón gañán (or peón or gañán). Those descriptions characterized the majority of suspects in these cases. By the 1860s, in fact, nearly two-thirds of suspects in cases reviewed were identified as Chilean.25 This may say more about expectations of criminal mobility than anything, as categories such as peón gañán could be applied somewhat imprecisely (and sometimes professions changed to peón when someone became a suspect in a case) and categories such as Chilean could be adopted by people to protect themselves against military service. Nevertheless, it is clear that Trans-Andean mobility and mobile subjects became problematic for state formation in the 1850s and 1860s. In effect, if the sanctity of animal property came to define the provincial order in one way or another during the mid-nineteenth century, in the context of itinerant laborers the sanctity of animal property ran up against the different practices of mobility and rural-worker socialization in the Trans-Andean.

## Mobility Technological Systems

Being mobile was a social and material act. After nearly three months of interrogations, changing stories, various accusations, and direct confrontations among different suspects, Rojas finally "confessed" to stealing two mules and a horse from Dominga Ponce de Irusta (also spelled as Ponse at times).26 She was a widow merchant who lived in San Carlos with her six children, the oldest of which was sixteen or seventeen.[27] Paralleling gendered assumptions about mobility and professions related to them, the census taker initially wrote "costurera" (seamstress) as her profession—among the most common professions for women in rural Mendoza and across the Americas at the time—before crossing it out and writing in *"comercianta"* (merchant).[28] For a woman to be a merchant was uncommon in Mendoza, a place where if women were engaged in business it was almost exclusively in vineyards and operating *pulperías* (rural stores), not being a merchant.[29] Broadly, state officials did not expect women to be mobile actors, such as merchants, itinerant laborers, or criminal suspects. In some cases, as with Dominga Ponce de Irusta, women appeared in cases because they owned animals or pastures.[30] The only three women arrested in connection with the cases reviewed, Isabel Rojas, Josefa Arias, and Francisca Cornejo, drew the attention of authorities for being prostitutes, rather than taking part in the thefts.[31] In some ways, the low visibility of women in these cases reflects how masculine mobility could seem on the surface. Trading animals, theft, labor itinerancy, transportation labor, and labor migrations involved men more than women. However, it should be kept in mind that the prevalence of women in such domestic industries as weaving and spinning underpinned mobility through the importance of garments such as ponchos in being mobile.[32] When authorities encountered women merchants or mobile "concubines," their instinct might have been to "correct" or erase this reality to fit assumptions of masculine-presenting mobility.

The census taker listed Ponce de Irusta as being born in Córdoba in 1824. The only Ponce (or Ponze in this case) born there that year was Dominga Eulogia Ponze, born to Rumualda Ponze, who was listed as a "libre" (free) woman.[33] Throughout the late eighteenth and nineteenth centuries, women such as Rumualda Ponze, often in conjunction with emerging independent governments in the 1810s and 1820s, worked to remove the social stigma of Blackness from themselves and their children.[34] In whatever case, by the national census of 1869 racial categories had been dropped in favor of categories of nationality and occupation, part of the process of whitening the country, and Ponce de Irusta's racial identity was thus lost, at least in that record.[35] For whatever she might have faced in her journey from Córdoba to Mendoza, she ended up as a merchant and the widow of Tomás Aquino Irusta, a prominent military officer on the southern frontier, who had fought to halt rebellion and revolution in the province.[36] For Ponce de Irusta and other women across the Americas, being widowed was often what allowed them to go into business.[37] It may have been the wealth she had accumulated or her status as a widow that made her a target. For whatever reason, Rojas, along with his accomplices, Juan de Dios Arahuna and Toribio Villaseca, went to her *finca* (farm) and "took from her *potreros*" two mules and a horse.[38] Although it was seemingly obvious that they would steal animals from pastures because they were fundamental to animal mobility, the particularities of pasturage in the region conditioned the mobility of laborers well beyond animals' caloric demands.

Animal mobility was as much about taming animals as it was about taming land. One of the limiting factors in riding a horse or mule was feeding it, and in Mendoza, as well as San Juan, natural pastures could be hard to find. Throughout the mid-nineteenth century, observers noted the necessity of irrigation for cultivated alfalfa pastures and the region's "few natural pastures."[39] Those irrigated areas most fit for cultivation became central in the production of animal fodder, with up to 90 percent of cultivated land being devoted to alfalfa in the 1860s.[40] These areas were commonly referred to as the "oases" in contrast to the rest of the region's vast "deserts." Discourses juxtaposing "oases" and "deserts," however, were by no means neutral observations. Rather, they were part of a naturalization of political struggles, which pivoted on the association of "civilization" and whiteness against the "barbarism" caused by the deserts.[41] Such discourses would become central to twentieth-century conflicts over access to land, which worked to centralize water in wine-producing areas and led to the desiccation of Indigenous wetlands in northern Mendoza.[42] The combination of cultivated pastures and desert/oasis discourses illustrates the physical and cultural enclosure of land to forge an order based on the sanctity of animal property. For mobile workers, this process of enclosure affected the everyday production of mobility and shaped the terms of exchange.

Due to the paucity of natural pastures, feeding and resting transport animals often was tied to access to cultivated pastures, or at least enclosed ones. Access to those pastures could not have followed any singular trajectory, but if one sought to put a transport animal out to pasture in the 1860s, it likely would have cost roughly 2 reales per month (0.25 pesos).[43] To give a sense of what that meant relative to the animal itself, based on criminal records, a horse or mule sold by a laborer often went for 5–12 pesos.[44] By contrast, wages for laborers could have been around 4 pesos per month.[45] For rural laborers, however, remuneration for work was not just in wages but in both wages and food rations.[46] Wages, as one could suppose, did not always come to laborers.[47] Conversely, selling a horse could bring the equivalent of a month's wages or more. Not only that, but a laborer with a horse could find it difficult to maintain it for any lengthy period of time. Therefore, as much as horses offered laborers physical mobility, they also could give them the means of mobility that came from horses' exchangeability. For laborers, these tensions over transport animals' usefulness and their exchangeability conditioned their mobility and how that mobility intersected with how the state perceived it.

One way that feeding and caring for transport animals affected laborers' mobility was through perceptions about the relationship between the conditions of animals and class. A case from the same time that officials were interrogating Rojas demonstrates how animal conditions influenced laborers' mobility. In November 1869, officials in San Carlos detained three men for the theft of twelve animals and selling them to Santiago Medina, a young merchant.[48] Medina did not know the men. During the investigation, the interrogator asked why he "did not suspect that those mules were stolen," especially considering that the men were "peones gañanes."[49] He did not, Medina responded, "because the mules could not have been worth more, considering the state that the mules were in."[50] The relationship between price and social status was clear. An itinerant laborer selling a well-rested horse or mule was suspicious, but if he were selling a fatigued animal, it conformed to expectations. As part of the social norms and material necessities surrounding mobility, laborers rode and at times sold worn-out horses and mules.

As places where people stored and fed horses, pastures were workspaces for some day laborers as well as spaces of leisure and social interaction. For those who tended to pastured animals or set their own animals out to pasture, these places became sites in which people gathered to drink yerba mate, socialize, and occasionally fight. In one instance, a group of men were drinking yerba mate in a private pasture when a man appeared drunkenly riding a horse. After falling off, he attacked the men, cutting one of them.[51] Seemingly mundane, the event indicates the intersection between these spaces as ones of leisure and fighting, on the one hand, and as ones of the reproduction of mobility. The pasture was owned and was used as an enclosed piece of property for feeding animals. Within that space daily life transpired, revealing how private property and social life came together and structured the experiences of rural people. In that sense, the time it took to rejuvenate horses and mules paralleled leisure time, bringing together important forms of sociality with the everyday reproduction of mobility. When Rojas and his companions entered Ponce de Irusta's pastures, therefore, they were entering into one of the cornerstones of the production of everyday mobility in the sense not just of the animals' biological survival but also of mobility's social characteristics: the coming together of leisure, work, enclosure, and state discipline.

Other systems of rural movement reveal how these social aspects, particularly property, structured perceptions of space. Take the posthouses of the Pampas, a transportation system that connected the country through a series of small outposts, or posthouses, spaced several leagues apart that, for a price, furnished horses and postilions to travelers and provided overnight lodging. The posthouses were spaced out evenly and appeared frequently enough that travelers could maintain a gallop throughout their journey because fresh horses would be provided at each post.[52] This was, in effect, a technological system, a sprawling transportation system that was conditioned not so much by the innate *materiality* of the means of conveyance (in this case horses, in later cases steam power and railroad tracks) as by the different systems of property that undergirded them (from the posts' ownership over the animals and the travelers' renting of them to the norms of landed property and state regulation of these places). In allowing for a constant gallop, this system conditioned how people experienced the geography of the Pampas and affected their perceptions of space, leading some to complain of the Pampas's monotony as it fatigued the traveler to ride in such a way.[53] Again, this was due not to the natural or essential qualities of the Pampas but rather to how mobility was socially produced; in this case monotony was produced by the constant gallop allowed by the propertied aspects of mobility in the post system. Lucio V. Mansilla, Argentine writer, military officer, and politician, commented on the effects of traveling at a constant gallop on the rider's perceptions of space and time by recounting a gaucho story in which a man asked a gaucho how much farther it would be to arrive at his destination. The gaucho replied, "If you go on at a gallop . . . you'll get there tomorrow; if you go at a gentle trot, you'll be there in just a little while."[54] Mansilla was referring not just to overly fatiguing a horse but also to the perceptions of time shaped by traveling at a constant speed. "It is the same with traveling as with reading aloud," Mansilla wrote, "the longest readings are those in which there is no change in cadence or diction."[55] The parallels to the railroad were not lost on him, either. Reflecting on this new mobility technology, Mansilla said, "Traveling by rail, we experience the same phenomenon as when we hear someone reading aloud at excessive speed."[56] European travelers, too, were developing similar observations about railroad travel to ones made in Argentina about traveling by post on the Pampas.[57] Monotony brought together these seemingly different forms of mobility, and in the case of the post system it was a product of the propertied dimensions of that technological system.

Similar to the posthouse system, rural itinerants' technological system relied on particular social and environmental configurations regarding access to pasturage, ownership over animals, and feeding and resting animals, all of which structured everyday experiences. Therefore, as a concept for understanding technology, everyday mobility reveals how the environmental aspects of movement—for example, animal metabolisms—become intimately intertwined with the deeply social aspects of movement—for example, property relations—at the level of "lived geographies."[58] Indeed, as philosopher Henri Lefebvre points out, "In everyday life and in everyday life alone . . . *the natural and the biological are humanized* (become social), and, further, . . . *the human, the acquired, the cultivated, become natural.*"[59] For rural laborers, property conditioned how, when, and where they moved, as well as access to pasturage and patterns of fatiguing animals, making property a central technological component to everyday rural mobility. Indeed, property was critical for the transition at midcentury from the postindependence order to the late nineteenth-century order. In Argentina, the ability for the emerging liberal state and economic elites to create institutional stability and trustworthiness surrounding property diminished the need for the personalistic governing style that had dominated in the decades after independence.[60] Although this is an important perspective, what often gets overlooked in conversations about property as an institution is how it mediates the relationship between people and their material environments. How property shapes the material world and how people engage with it makes it a key part of understanding technology, the quintessential mediator of the relationship between people and their material environments.[61] In this light, the contestations over transport animals evident in cases of theft at this time can be understood not just as indications of rural disorder or state anxieties about rural people but as periodic breakdowns in the technological systems of everyday mobility, revealing in the process how the state worked to control and regulate rural mobility.[62] At the same time, these theft cases—as technological breakdowns—provide a window into how this rural technological system developed and maintained itself during these years.

To return to Rojas and his companions, their entrance into Ponce de Irusta's pastures was an intervention into the technological system of mobility formed by a tapestry of the places that held up the movement of people and things in Mendoza. The path that they took from those pastures, north to Cipriano Cabieres's house, reveals another element of this technological system, one that straddled the line between accepted practices of everyday mobility and dangerous criminality.

## Mobility in the Production of Social Life

As with pastures, houses were important to the mobility of rural laborers. After Rojas, Villaseca, and Arahuna took the animals from Ponce de Irusta's pastures in San Carlos, they headed north with them toward the city of Mendoza, later arriving at the house of Cipriano Cabieres, a Chilean cobbler.[63] Cabieres lived far north of San Carlos outside the city of Mendoza with his wife and four children, all likely recent arrivals, as the whole family was listed as Chilean.[64] However, this was not the first place that they lived in the province. The youngest son, Fabián de Carmen, was listed as Chilean but was born in San Carlos, indicating that the Cabieres family, like many Chileans, had lived in San Carlos, likely one of their first homes in Argentina.[65] The neighborhood where they found themselves now was quite cosmopolitan, with people from France, Spain, Chile, and other Argentine provinces living there.[66] This was the world in which rural laborers like Rojas circulated. Rurality, for them, did not mean parochial. Connected across substantial distances, their world was as expansive as the ocean.

What made this expansiveness possible were the kinds of small, common exchanges that had brought Rojas to Cabieres's house. At Cabieres's house, Rojas found two other travelers, José Dolores Fuensalida, a Chilean merchant, and his muleteer, Baldomero Roco, who were preparing for a trip to Chile in order to sell ostrich feathers. It was there, at Cabieres's house, that Rojas sold Fuensalida the animals that they had taken from Ponce de Irusta. The event would become a source of disagreement later when Rojas claimed that Fuensalida had known the animals were stolen, whereas Fuensalida denied this accusation.[67] Whatever the nature of this exchange, Fuensalida bought the animals, got the necessary customs documents to make his trip, and set off with Roco for Chile. After Fuensalida and Roco left for Chile, Rojas returned to San Carlos, where his troubles began. Apparently, before leaving, Rojas stole more animals to take back to San Carlos.[68] Along with his companions, he took two horses and a mule from one of Cabieres's neighbors, Vicente Molina, who, on learning that his animals were gone, went in search of them. On the road, he learned that José María Rojas took the animals to San Carlos. Not long after, Molina found himself in San Carlos. Needing to find Rojas and his animals, he asked the subdelegado of San Carlos for help in apprehending Rojas and recovering his animals.[69] The authorities sought him out and brought him in for questioning.[70] During his time in custody, he claimed that he had not acted alone in stealing Molina's animals. While at Cabieres's house, Rojas told the judge, Cabieres had proposed that Rojas take a few animals with him back to San Carlos to give to Manuel Fuensalida, suggesting that they steal the animals from Vicente Molina, his neighbor who lived alone and had no guns.[71] If Rojas had any doubts, Cabieres reassured him that if he got in trouble on the way to or in San Carlos, his patrón (who happened to be the judge presiding over the case) would make sure that he got off easy.[72] When the judge interrogated Cabieres about Rojas's version of the story, Cabieres denied everything.[73] Even when authorities interrogated both Rojas and Cabieres at the same time, Cabieres never budged in denying his involvement in the theft.[74] Despite repeated attempts by authorities to settle the inconsistencies among everyone's stories, no consensus was reached.

For whatever disagreements there were, they agreed that Cabieres's house was a site for selling and buying transportation animals. It was apparent that Rojas was familiar with the neighborhood—at least enough to know some of the figures within it—and with Fuensalida, since he had asked for him at Cabieres's house. These assumed aspects of the case reveal the fundamental components of mobility in the region. People such as Rojas, caught between different survival strategies, created a world based on their limited access to land and their peripatetic labor. Aimless roaming, however, it was not. It was a world that demanded social connections across distances, united by practices of selling and buying horses and mules. Joining these practices in space and making this world their home, if only for a moment, were the houses of people who likewise understood that their world consisted of a much larger swath of territory than the bounds of their property, the province, or the nation.

Like pastures, houses were significant as sites for stealing animals, a meaning that paralleled the meaning of houses as sites for mobility reproduction (through feeding, resting, and storing animals).[75] Having a safe, trusted place to stay was necessary for the reproduction of the kind of mobility on which thieves and rural laborers relied to reproduce their livelihoods.[76] As seen in Rojas's case, houses were also important sites of exchange. Typically, in historical writing on Argentina the pulpería has occupied the role of the place of exchange in rural society from the colonial period into the nineteenth century.[77] The pulpería sat at the intersection of commerce, vice, and gaucho sociality, housing gambling, drinking, fighting, and prostitution, as well as petty rural trade and more substantial commerce, which itself was not infrequently drawn from illicit activities.[78] In criminal cases of horse and mule theft, pulperías appear, but not nearly as frequently as potreros (pastures) and casas (houses), although it is likely the terms "casa" and "pulpería" were not mutually exclusive. Although pulperías have received much attention, alternative sites of exchange and social life did exist. The *almacén*, for example, was another rural store, although not often associated with the drinking of the pulpería. At a level even more related to this chapter, *sastres* (tailors) and *zapateros* (cobblers), such as Cabieres, had been part of networks of exchange since the colonial period, and it appears that these traditions continued in the case of Rojas, serving here as an example of places for people to buy and sell horses and mules.[79] One reason that rural laborers might have used alternative sites of exchange, such as Cabieres's house, over pulperías to engage in economic exchanges is that the pulpería had been a place that marginalized certain groups from participating in commercial life, such as Black and Indigenous traders in the colonial period, whose mere participation in selling "goods of a certain value" to a pulpería indicated criminality, making the pulpería a place that reinforced social stratification and expectations through prohibiting certain people from being commercial actors but potentially allowing them to engage in vice.[80] Broadly, exchange as the masculine realm, as anthropologist Marc Augé reminds us, traditionally stands in contrast to house and hearth, the feminine realm; but this divide has never been so black and white.[81] In fact, the house lies at the very heart of the history of capital exchange, as the term banking-*house* indicates. In London, from the eighteenth and into the nineteenth centuries, "purpose-built banks" did not exist (outside the Bank of England); bankers preferred the inconspicuousness of their Georgian townhouses, which created "a private landscape of capital," replete with "the aristocratic emphasis on privacy and discretion in financial matters."[82] In rural Mendoza, similar degrees of fluidity between feminine hearth and masculine threshold existed.

More than anything, the prevalence of houses in cases involving buying and selling transport animals reflects a tradition of small-scale commercial circuits in rural Mendoza, involving not just peons but also peasant farmers and others. From the early nineteenth century to the 1860s, if a peasant farmer or other person of modest means had any wealth measured in state records, it was at least in the form of a house.[83] Whether through renting or owning, the existence of houses does not say much about the kinds of activities carried out in those spaces, but other forms of wealth and common occupations can help fill in some gaps. Along with houses, those with very little wealth also counted as part of that wealth transport animals, sheep, and carriages and carts.[84] In addition, domestic industry that took place in houses, such as spinning and weaving, were prominent activities among women, particularly Chilean women, as were similar activities, such as cobbling, which Cabieres did.[85] Small-scale textile production and other economic activities in houses, transportation within the province, and small-scale dealing in horses and

*Property and Everyday Mobility*   69

mules must have played a role in the economic life of peons and peasant farmers.[86] The varied economic activities of laborers, networks of Chilean migrants, and family connections joined across space and through houses were central in putting people in motion. To return to the context of Rojas's case, if a laborer like Rojas wanted to buy or sell a horse or mule, they could search out individuals in different rural communities. Once buyers and sellers connected, the exchange often occurred at a house, whether of the buyer or the seller.[87] Arriving at a house with the intention to engage in an exchange did not guarantee one, and for that the key issue of trust had to be sorted out.

Trust was fundamental to making the house into a place of exchange, and it was forged in at least two ways. First, people tapped into their social networks to find partners for exchange. Intimate social ties—whether through friendship, coworker relationships, or boss-peon relationships—were an essential facilitator in the selling of horses and mules. In instances of exchange facilitated by social networks, trust was an obvious component to the exchange.[88] Second, when lacking the trust that social familiarity could provide, sellers and buyers sometimes relied on local mechanisms of governance to engender trust between people. Having the capacity to underwrite an exchange was one such mechanism. For example, in order to sell a horse to Cupertino Álvares at his house, Julián Salinas had Gregorio Banegas guarantee the sale (that is, he underwrote it by guaranteeing that if anything went wrong, he would be partially responsible). By the time Álvares had learned that the horse had been stolen, Salinas had disappeared, prompting Álvares to demand that Banegas pay him back, which he did in labor.[89] The house as a place of trust and exchange could also become expressed in language. When the authorities were interrogating Juan de Dios Romero in another case of theft, they asked whether he knew one of the other suspects, Fermín Prado. The question of "knowing" someone was common in criminal interrogations, expressed simply as "si conoce a [alguien]" (if he knows somebody). Normally, there were three answers: "no lo conoce" (I do not know him); "sí lo conoce" (yes I know him); and the intermediate, "lo conoce de vista" (I would recognize him or I know who he is).[90] Romero chose the first. When his interrogators discovered that he did know Prado, they asked him why he lied, to which he responded, "Porque no t[engo] relación con él, ni le cono[zco] casa" (Because [I] ha[ve] nothing to do with him, [I do] not even know where his house is).[91] While this may have been a clever response to being caught in a lie, it can also reveal the relationship between knowing someone and knowing their house and how long-distance rural social networks were built through houses and the exchanges that occurred in and around them.

At times, local officials undergirded the creation of trust. For example, when Melchor Troncoso went to Segundo Corvalán's house in 1858 to sell him a horse, Corvalán was inclined to buy it. However, not knowing Troncoso, he decided that they should go to the local judge to get his approval of the sale. Even though Troncoso met the judge's attempts to pin down the horse's origins with vague answers, the judge ultimately told Corvalán that he could buy it.[92] The role of local officials in the production of trust in cases like this was part of long-standing norms of local governance and mechanisms of social control in the context of both political upheaval and capital accumulation. In the context of the wars of independence and their aftermath, new institutions were created to forge some sense of social order. The people who were tasked with filling those institutions throughout the following decades were the face of the state for many people. They were in charge of monitoring local populations, maintaining sanitation, resolving petty disputes, and arresting and processing criminal suspects before sending them to the judge in the capital.[93] Undoubtedly, local officials had significant power at their discretion in the decades after independence, and despite attempts to transform the administrative order in the province in the 1850s, institutions developed during and after independence continued to play a vital role in the transition to liberal governance in the 1860s and 1870s.[94]

Although the role of local officials in imposing social order throughout significant historical transitions and processes—independence and the rise of the cattle trade—was important, order was not only about appeasing social and political elites. In fact, throughout the period in which local officials were charged with imposing the social order that could protect and foment the rise of the cattle trade, legislation signaled that they were not enforcing the very laws designed to impose a rigid order, indicating that local officials were not merely the handmaidens of capital accumulation for economic elites.[95] Instead, they were constantly attempting to negotiate a functional order in their communities, which at times meant jettisoning the laws and norms installed to create an idealized social order. Order for rural laborers and other nonelites was as much about establishing predictable and navigable norms for quotidian practices, such as exchange and mobility, as it was about having an elite order and ideology imposed on them. In that context, local institutions were mechanisms for facilitating exchanges, which, in the context of horses and mules, meant facilitating mobility, broadly. Horses and mules, then, were not mere means of conveyance; they were the bonds that held together in sociality members of the itinerant laboring class. These bonds brought these people together across distances, creating an expansive and mobile sense of

*Property and Everyday Mobility*

place. At the same time, however, built on the exchanges of privileged pieces of property (animals), these bonds confronted the emerging state apparatus and the sense of space that it produced in that confrontation.

## State Refractions of the Trans-Andean

Criminal investigations of this type were unintentional spatial projects of state construction, particularly in rural areas. Conflicting stories within Rojas's case certainly created confusion for the provincial state in Mendoza. Fortunately for state officials, they had ways of clarifying these details. After a second round of interrogations, Rojas began to revise parts of his story. Now, he knew that the animals had been stolen. He did not act alone, however. In fact, according to Rojas, everyone involved knew about the animals' provenance. One of the men at the center of this plan to steal and sell animals was Juan de Dios Arahuna, a Chilean muleteer who, as Rojas told them, was a "resident of San Carlos."[96] In order to interrogate Arahuna, state officials sent a request to the subdelegado of San Carlos, to which local officials in San Carlos responded by locating Arahuna and sending him to Mendoza to be interrogated.[97] It was seemingly a routine act: provincial officials interrogated someone; that person named someone and provided a place of residence; provincial officials, in turn, relied on local officials to root that person out and bring them in to affirm or contest the original interrogation. While its routineness is almost banal, it speaks to how the walls of a house contained much more than the elements of itinerant laborers' mobility and sociality. To live in a particular place meant to be familiar to the state, at least at a local level. In the same way that itinerant laborers used their knowledge of where people's houses were to move in and out of communities, so the state also used its knowledge of people's dwellings to track those people, particularly in the context of their "criminal" mobility. The house, in those moments, became a state space, refracting the expansive sense of rural laborers' mobile space. Even though the house was a place in which women were present, they appear infrequently as witnesses in theft cases. The reasons for this are many, but questions of property (in terms of both houses and the animals) and the gender norms associated with property played a role, from the tendency for a head of household to be a man to the suspicions raised with male cohabitation in the context of criminal investigations.[98] For judicial officials, women's witness testimony was relevant primarily when they owned or directly interacted with property implicated in cases (whether the horses and mules or the houses and pastures in which those animals could have been kept or sold).⁹⁹ Their status as witnesses because they inhabited and worked within houses seemed to be far less important to state officials.

The house as a space of state knowledge may have been produced in seemingly ordinary ways, but these mechanisms were, in fact, fairly recent developments for the judicial system in Mendoza. The institutionalization of rigid military justice during the 1830s and 1840s in Mendoza reflected the limitations of the state to impose an idealized social order. Brevity in cases of horse and mule theft, for example, was an effect of those limitations. Contrary to Rojas's case, which required several rounds of interrogations and witness statements over three months, cases were exceedingly brief during the military commissions. Most contained only one or two criminal interrogations.¹⁰⁰ Brevity, however, was not achieved merely by limiting written cases. Verbal declarations and confessions were also commonplace during the period, and it is likely that a significant number of cases were addressed in this manner.¹⁰¹ For example, during a twenty-month stretch in 1848–49, the military commission heard at least thirty-one verbal cases of horse and mule theft, representing over a third of the total verbal cases heard during that period.¹⁰² Verbal cases allowed for even greater expedience than fully written cases, with some lasting only two days before arriving at the desk of the military commission for a final decision.¹⁰³ Without a doubt, brevity was a fact of military justice in Mendoza, a fact often implied in the creation of military commissions and one made explicit in 1845 when the law instituting another commission stated, "The substantiation of these cases will be simple, rapid, and clear; in such a way as to shorten them as much as possible."¹⁰⁴

The self-conscious rejection of exhaustive judicial practices was partly a product of an increasing realization on the part of the state of its own limitations. Although in many cases the accused offered up no refutation or justification to allegations, when the military commission was prompted to investigate details of a case further, it was often unable to achieve much.¹⁰⁵ In cases in which the accused provided a justification for their possession of a stolen horse or mule, they relied on a number of different reasons, from having bought the animal to claiming that they had intended to return it or stole it out of necessity.¹⁰⁶ Often, when the military commission attempted to pursue cases further, it ran up against obstacles; local officials could not find witnesses or fugitive suspects remained on the run indefinitely, prompting officials to put the burden of proof on the suspects or ignore obvious follow-ups.¹⁰⁷ Brevity and judicial curtness affected how the state spatialized in this period. Aside from the particularities of justice in Mendoza, the juridical norms that accompanied the military commissions' inability and unwillingness to pursue cases are important for the analysis of space and mobility during the period. Those norms conditioned how space and mobility were expressed and made visible in the 1830s and 1840s. Since the essential questions of these cases were mostly about the act of theft in its most basic form, the places that tended to emerge were those of extraction—that is, those places from which the accused were alleged to have taken the horses or mules, such as casas (houses) and potreros (pastures) (see table 3.1).

By the time of Rojas's case, the state refracted a much broader and more specific sense of these spaces of laborers' mobility than during the military commissions. Towns and villages such as San Carlos, San Rafael, Lujan, and Uspallata became increasingly prevalent in the list of places that appeared in criminal interrogations. The provinces of San Juan and San Luis likewise came into relief during the 1850s and 1860s after the end of the military commissions. Without a doubt, one of the most prominent places to make its way into the shared sense of space between the provincial state and mobile people was Chile. Among all these places, what the state refracted was the Trans-Andean. These cartographies of criminal investigations created a distorted image of the Trans-Andean, with the provincial borders serving as the point at which the map became blurry and unfocused. Inside these borders, networks of houses, towns, and pastures came into stark relief to reveal not just the map of these mobile people's lives but also the social character of a space littered with houses and sites of social and economic exchange. Once outside that specificity, however, they collapsed into a vague sense of "Chile" or "San Juan."

As much as Trans-Andean subjects would have crossed them without losing their sense of place, they would have recognized those blurry edges of a refracted Trans-Andean, too. Rojas's and Arahuna's companion, Toribio Villaseca, likely recognized the provincial state's myopia and used it to his advantage. Local authorities in San Carlos must have ordered Villaseca's arrest along with Rojas in connection with the stolen animals.[108] Before the state could interrogate him, however, he escaped custody, likely fleeing to Chile.[109] There, provincial authorities could not reach him. Although virtually none of his background is known (he escaped before interrogation and no record of him appears in the census of 1869 in Mendoza), he had experiences in Chile, working for Arahuna and crossing the mountains to Chile the previous year with him.[110] Connected to those experiences, Villaseca likely had some familiarity with places in the country and knew people through whom he could establish his life there. In that sense, the provincial state's myopia fed

TABLE 3.1. Frequency of places mentioned in cases of
transport animal theft in Mendoza, 1843–1872

| PLACE | SEPTEMBER 1843 TO MAY 1852* (UNDER MILITARY COMMISSIONS)** | | JUNE 1852 TO JUNE 1872* (NO MILITARY COMMISSION)** | | CHANGE IN FREQUENCY (%) |
|---|---|---|---|---|---|
| | Number of cases | (%) | Number of cases | (%) | |
| Total number of cases sampled | 14 | — | 30 | — | — |
| Casa (house) | 9 | 64 | 25 | 83 | +19 |
| Luján | 0 | 0 | 5 | 17 | +17 |
| San Rafael | 0 | 0 | 4 | 13 | +13 |
| Chile | 1 | 7 | 11 | 37 | +30 |
| San Juan | 2 | 14 | 10 | 33 | +19 |
| Potrero (pasture) | 6 | 43 | 15 | 50 | +7 |
| Camino (road) | 2 | 14 | 13 | 43 | +29 |
| San Luis | 1 | 7 | 8 | 27 | +20 |
| San Carlos | 1 | 7 | 8 | 27 | +20 |
| Uspallata | 0 | 0 | 5 | 17 | +17 |

Source: Table B.1 (in appendix B).

* Cases represent a sample from the Archivo Histórico de Mendoza of criminal cases involving the theft of transport animals (horses and mules). In the archive, I favored cases that listed on the document cover that the case was about the theft of horses or mules but also selected several that just indicated theft of "cuatropea" (quadrupeds) or "animales" (animals). I selected an approximately even number of cases from the 1840s, 1850s, and 1860s, with a few cases from the late 1830s and early 1870s. I transcribed every witness, plaintiff, and defendant statement, then coded them for places. Then, I did network analysis on them to create spatial narratives for each statement. Although those networks do not appear here, the insights gained from creating them are foundational to my analysis. This table represents whether a place appears in any part of a case's statements.

** Some cases from table B.1 are not included in this analysis: O1/4, M3/7, R4/3, M5/25, P2/18, and J1/15. The first two cases (O1/4 and M3/7) did not take place during one of the military commissions, which changes how statements were taken and thus place frequency within them. For the remainder, they either do not include any statements from which spatial narratives could be constructed or are incomplete files. All cases, however, have informed my understanding of how theft cases of transport animals functioned, hence why they appear in table B.1.

into the construction of the Trans-Andean as people hid in the blurry edges of provincial state spaces.

Villaseca's escape to Chile, however, should not be read as an escape from state spaces altogether. If anything, he merely substituted one state for another. On the Chilean side, mobile Trans-Andean subjects faced similar conditions. Local officials in places such as San Felipe, Santa Rosa de Los Andes, and Putaendo (all just across the border from Mendoza) possessed their own anxieties about people like Villaseca—anxieties born in part out of the increased mobility of rural laborers—and developed mechanisms to assuage them.[111] In December 1874, for example, local officials in San Felipe arrested two men for stealing horses. Interestingly, the arresting officials did not have any firm evidence that the suspects had even stolen the horses in the first place. Rather, the men were itinerant, they fraternized with a suspicious person apparently known for stealing horses, and they were in possession of a horse that was in too good of a condition not to provoke suspicion.[112] In effect, although the Trans-Andean cut across many state jurisdictions, it was never a nonstate space.[113] It was in dialectical relationship with states, giving shape and direction to early state formation in the region.[114] A cornerstone of the state formation project, animal property made the Trans-Andean increasingly visible in the 1860s. It was at the heart of building up rural state institutions such as the subdelegacía. It was a key component to mobility technology for Trans-Andean subjects. It was a central concern for the provincial state in curbing rural disorder. As a result, increasingly liberal judicial norms—for example, recorded interrogations or resolving conflicting testimony—turned property into a lens through which to surveille and make known the routes and mobile geographies of itinerants and migrants, who often lived in rural areas. Those judicial norms centered on the capital city of Mendoza as information, witnesses, and suspects passed through the city and as orders and coordination of strategy in cases emanated out from there. As such, the propertied aspects of mobility helped in some ways the power of a capital city like Mendoza to dominate the countryside.

### The Labor of Theft

From a different angle, Rojas's case appears as a reflection of the tensions and potential uncertainties underlying Trans-Andean commerce. Not a story of laborers carving out autonomous spaces of sociality in a transnational region, Rojas's case reveals how laborers' Trans-Andean mobility, and that mobility's constant confrontation with the state, never escaped the looming force of capitalism's uneven geographies. If this chapter began with Rojas's capture by authorities in San Carlos, the actual case began earlier than his incarceration, in early November, when José Dolores Fuensalida was preparing to go to Chile. Before leaving, Fuensalida likely had a conversation with Juan de Dios Arahuna, a muleteer. He needed a few animals to make the trip and thought that Arahuna might be able to help him. He did not have the animals right then and there, but the understanding to which they came was that Fuensalida would hire him, along with two other men, Rojas and Arahuna's peon, Villaseca, to steal a few animals and bring them to Mendoza, where Fuensalida would wait. They parted ways. Fuensalida set off for Mendoza while the other three stayed behind.[115] Rojas, Arahuna, and Villaseca entered into Ponce de Irusta's pastures and stole two mules and a horse. Arahuna stayed back or had other business to attend to, so the other two set off for Mendoza. They arrived outside Mendoza and found Cabieres's house, where Fuensalida was waiting for Rojas. As planned, Rojas gave him the animals that they had stolen from Ponce de Irusta. Satisfied with the job that he had hired them to do, Fuensalida paid Rojas 10.5 pesos and set off with his muleteer for Chile.[116]

After being arrested, Rojas and Arahuna went through four months of interrogations, conflicting stories, and resigned confessions, at which time the case turned to the question of sentencing. Arahuna and Rojas initially faced a year of hard labor as their sentence, not an uncommon sentence for theft.[117] The *defensor de los pobres y menores* (public defender) took a different approach. He argued that Fuensalida was the true guilty party, invoking the defense of *complicidad* (complicity) for his defendants. As the argument went, Fuensalida had hired them and thus "instigated" them to steal. Apparently, this was not the first time that the defensor had used this line of reasoning. "In other occasions," he reminded the state, he "had the opportunity to exhibit the influence that the instigators of theft have on the perpetration of the crime."[118] In effect, being induced to steal through payment, Rojas and Arahuna were not fully culpable and therefore deserved lighter sentencing than would otherwise be given if they had stolen the animals unprompted by Fuensalida. This was not the only case in which someone used this line of reasoning.

Throughout the 1850s and 1860s, suspects of horse and mule theft began to pick up on these distinctions between knowing that animals were stolen and having stolen them, and between being induced to steal them and stealing them on one's own accord. The justification that Rojas provided, having been hired to transport stolen animals, was part of a trend that had developed since the late 1850s.[119] It even entered into suspects' language during interrogations. For example, around the same time that Rojas was being interrogated, another man, Rumualdo Pérez, also was being interrogated. According to him, authorities had arrested him "for having brought some eight mules to sell, mules that a Chilean, Manuel Reveco, gave him." Asked about the fact that they were stolen, Pérez responded that "he [knew] that in this he ha[d] done wrong and ha[d] become *complicit* in the theft."[120] Perhaps the scribe added this language, anticipating what had become a common defense, but it cannot be dismissed that people like Rojas and Pérez were aware of the implications of their plea. At the same time, the defense of complicity was tied into the labor and business dynamics of animal trading. For example, in 1866, Manuel Canales found himself accused of participating in the theft of eighteen animals in San Juan and bringing them to San Carlos to sell.[121] The defensor articulated an argument that made a suspect who was working as a "salaried peon" in the context of the crime inculpable. "A wage earner," he argued, was not guilty of being the "author of the deed," as they "[did] not know the secrets of a patrón, [as they] would know only in the case of a partnership."[122] In a way, much as with laborers and the Chilean consulate, judicial developments surrounding complicity as a defense against theft helped facilitate a class-based identity, one in which laborers intentionally invoked their subordinate status to bosses, bosses who were often at the center of networks of animal trade and theft.

Throughout this period, laborers came from Chile on behalf of their bosses to buy animals and bring them across the border, which may have been a profession in itself. For example, when Juan Antonio Hubilla came to Mendoza from Chile in 1853 to buy "horses or other animals," it was at the direction of his boss back in Chile.[123] It was, for Hubilla, a family profession; his father "had been employed in the same business" before him.[124] Of course, as Hubilla discovered, the risk associated with this was being accused of theft or, at the very least, of buying stolen animals. Other cases, too, indicate that buying animals to bring back to Chile was not an uncommon business.[125] It is difficult to know the extent of the business and its historical trajectory in the context of increased trade over the mountains in the 1850s and the expansion of Chilean agricultural production and need for animal power. Nevertheless, it is clear that people like Hubilla and the business in which they were involved had become a concern for the provincial state around that time. While cattle rustling was more concerning for state officials than the theft of transport animals, broadly the trafficking of stolen animals reached the point where the provincial state passed a law directed specifically at preventing the "illegal removal . . . of animals" from the province over the mountains to Chile.[126] The government lamented how the lack of "strict and stern observance of current regulation" by local officials had led to the repeated theft of animals.[127] This confluence of animal trading as a Trans-Andean business and local officials' inability to regulate the multitude of small exchanges generated anxiety on the part of provincial authorities about not just theft but also the business of theft. That business was what brought Rojas and Fuensalida into contact in the first place, and Fuensalida's role speaks to the place of animal theft in the development of Trans-Andean commerce.

When Fuensalida returned from Chile to San Carlos on 29 December 1869, someone told him that the animals he bought to go to Chile were stolen from Ponce de Irusta. Having learned about the suspicions now surrounding him, he went to the subdelegado in San Carlos to explain himself. Fuensalida knew the law well. To attest to the sale, he brought two witnesses before the judge.[128] The first witness, the muleteer, Baldomero Roco, explained that Fuensalida did not hire Rojas to bring him stolen animals. Rather, Rojas showed up while they were at Cabieres's house, trying to sell two horses and a mule, which Fuensalida agreed to buy for fifty pesos. Lacking funds, he asked Roco to loan him money. Fuensalida attempted to confirm the legitimacy of the animals, Roco assured the judge. He asked Rojas for the branding iron that would prove that the marks on the animals matched Rojas's mark. Rojas demurred, explaining that it was in Alto Verde, which was to the east of Mendoza, and would show it to Fuensalida once he returned from Chile. Apparently eager to continue their journey to Chile, Fuensalida and Roco left with the animals without receiving confirmation of their legitimacy, nor would they ever be able to make that confirmation. Roco explained to the judge that the animals arrived in Chile in very bad condition, which forced Fuensalida to attempt to sell them there. Unfortunately for Fuensalida, the mules were in such a state that he could not sell them, so he left them in Chile, presumably to use on his return. He was able to sell the horse for twelve pesos.[129]

For Fuensalida, his problems only mounted when Ponce de Irusta demanded restitution for the animals. His witnesses went a long way in convincing her that although he had failed to ensure their legitimacy, he had purchased the animals in good faith and had no knowledge that they were stolen when he bought them. She was convinced but not ready to let Fuensalida completely off. As a merchant, she understood the importance of her animals, as well as how to leverage her position to come out on top in a negotiation. They agreed that Fuensalida would replace the two mules he had left in Chile. As for the horse, Ponce de Irusta got twenty-five pesos, seven pesos more than Fuensalida had paid for it. On top of that, she demanded four pesos for the trouble that she experienced as a result of everything.[130] Despite these difficulties, Ponce de Irusta walked away from the case with twenty-nine pesos and two mules. For his part, Fuensalida ended up, according to his calculations, down thirty-five pesos and four mules, perhaps with the hope that the two mules in Chile would one day serve him again. For whatever he lost in money, however, he was able to gain back in freedom, at least temporarily.

Perhaps aware that his denial of participation in the theft would come under scrutiny, Fuensalida again left for Chile. His absence was to his benefit. In their confessions, both Arahuna and Rojas agreed that Fuensalida had hired them, compelling the judge to order his arrest. Local officials, however, reported that he had already left the province and was in Chile.[131] Apparently, his indirect role in the theft and his connections with Chile had given him just enough time to escape the justice that Arahuna and Rojas were now facing. The two bore the brunt of a fairly extensive plan to steal transport animals to the simultaneous benefit of and detriment to small-scale Trans-Andean commerce. In other words, this case can be seen as an expression of tensions and uncertainties surrounding Trans-Andean commerce. At its base, the case was one merchant stealing transport animals from another: one merchant taking away the mobility of another to make themselves mobile. Serving as intermediaries in this intraclass competition were the itinerant laborers hired to steal these animals. Theft, in that sense, was not opposed to or threatening to commerce from the outside but rather an internally generated threat. Although mobile laborers were perfectly capable of committing theft on their own, it is clear that during the intensification of Trans-Andean commercial activities, the labor of theft became increasingly necessary for aspiring merchants seeking to trade across the mountains.[132] That labor, at the same time, played into the place of horses and mules in the creation of a mobile Trans-Andean space built by laborers' mobility.

The construction of the Trans-Andean at this time by people such as Rojas reflected a place made through not just individual acts of mobility but also rural technological systems of mobility. These rural technological systems rested on a configuration of property rights, systems of land irrigation, and the social practices of everyday mobility in Mendoza. The Trans-Andean, to be sure, appears only as a fragment from this perspective, filtered through the provincial state's judicial apparatus. Nevertheless, what can be gleaned from this partial, distorted vision of the Trans-Andean by the 1860s reveals how itinerancy confronted the emerging provincial state in Mendoza. In the challenge presented by laborers' everyday production of mobility, the state struggled to keep aligned all the different pieces of its tenuous state apparatus. Local officials were certainly responsive to the demands of the central provincial government but always had to negotiate with the realities of governing local areas. The judicial system found itself constantly adapting to the new realities presented not only by labor itinerancy and the social networks underpinning it but also by the tensions born out of uncertainties in Trans-Andean commerce. All the while, mobile laborers circulated around, in, and out of the province, demonstrating almost incessantly the limitations of the state in Mendoza.

If this chapter has illustrated how the everyday mobility of itinerant laborers created the Trans-Andean, the next interlude reexamines the Trans-Andean through the practices of the new producers of mobility in this era: engineers. Using a railroad study conducted by engineer Emilio Rosetti for a Trans-Andean railroad in 1870, the interlude illustrates the meaningfulness of the reengineering of this Trans-Andean borderland in terms of tensions with Indigenous uses of mountain passes, liberal education and bureaucratic reforms that centered engineers and engineering in the construction of the nation-state's geography, and the curious intersection of engineering and poetry in the development of the Argentine nation as abstraction.

# Interlude Three | Reengineering the Trans-Andean

When Emilio Rosetti crossed the Andes in February 1870 to conduct a study for a mountain-crossing railroad at the same time that José María Rojas was being sentenced for stealing animals, he brought with him a different way of seeing the Trans-Andean than Rojas and others like him. An Italian-born engineer, Rosetti came to Buenos Aires in 1865 as part of a project by the rector of the University of Buenos Aires, Juan María Gutiérrez, to create the Departamento de Ciencias Exactas (literally, the Department of Exact Sciences), which included bringing three Italian academics to teach mathematics, natural history, and applied mathematics, which was taught by Rosetti.[1] The department was to be engaged in training young Argentines in key disciplines for national economic development, such as minerology and geology.[2] The most important of these, however, was engineering, and Rosetti trained the first generation of civil engineers in Argentina, known as los doce apóstoles (the twelve apostles) of Argentine engineering, the first of whom would defend their theses and obtain their degrees in the months after Rosetti's study for a Trans-Andean railroad.[3] In the years and decades that followed, these young engineers became integral members of the Argentine Republic's emerging state bureaucracy. Beyond Argentina, elites across Latin America and the world were embarking on similar projects to create a technical elite capable of embodying the ideals of the nation and of managing the rapidly growing state bureaucracies organizing it.[4] Indeed, Rosetti experienced these changes firsthand in Italy, where decades of reforms in engineering education and public works bureaucracies began to come together alongside and in conjunction with Italian national unification. He was one of the first engineering students educated after the Second War of Italian Independence in 1859 and trained at the Regia Scuola di Applicazione per gli Ingegneri (Royal Technical School for Engineers) in Turin, a place where he would have seen intimately the incorporation of engineering expertise into different levels of government, including municipal, in the context of national unification and liberal reform.[5] His expertise in railroads—he wrote his thesis on the freight locomotive— and his experience with engineering education in the context of national unification likely made him an ideal candidate for the new education of technical elites in the young Argentine Republic, which had unified after the Battle of Pavón in 1861. Engineering national unification was not just about administrative or professional aspects; it was also about changing national geography and representing it in new ways—namely, as an economic unit among many in a global economy. This interlude takes pieces of Rosetti's study to consider the processes and meanings of engineering to the service of creating the nation as a global economic unit.

In those early years of training Argentina's engineering class, culminating in 1870, when the first engineers began to graduate, Rosetti instilled in them a strong sense of the policy implications that engineering held for the nation, and as a result they spent a great deal of time considering means of transportation. Rosetti had ensured that their instruction would have transportation at its heart, and this choice was reflected in the theses his students wrote.[6] Focusing engineering instruction on transportation would make sense at any moment in a nation's history, but it was a topic especially pertinent in the late 1860s, when the railroad network was still in its formative years.[7] At the beginning of the decade, Argentina had a mere 39 kilometers of track.[8] By the end of the 1860s, that number would rise to over 600 kilometers, and by the close of 1875, Argentina's railroad network would stand at just shy of 2,000 kilometers.[9] This expansion was bolstered by the republic's second president, Domingo Faustino Sarmiento (1868–74), whose government laid some of the groundwork for a national railroad network, one that extended beyond Buenos Aires and the other centers of power in the east to the far northern and western reaches of the country and beyond.[10] Important to that national network were the various Trans-Andean railroad projects developing then.

An early debate on these Trans-Andean railroad projects concerned the one Rosetti was to study. It took place not in the national capital, as one would expect of an international railroad, but rather among the legislators of the provincial government of Buenos Aires. In 1868, provincial congressmen debated extending the provincial state–owned railroad, Ferrocarril Oeste de Buenos Aires (Buenos Aires Western Railroad), beyond the provincial borders, particularly whether to connect it to a route headed to the city of Mendoza or to extend it all the way to the border with Chile via a pass to the south of the province of Mendoza, the Planchón Pass.[11] The commission charged with studying the pros and cons of each option recommended the Planchón Pass, which would have put the port of Buenos Aires in contact with Chile and the Pacific Ocean, something that would have caused "an immense revolution," as one defender of the project put it, in "the paths of world commerce."[12] The debate on extending the provincial line outside the province, across the country, and to the border with Chile revolved around the financial cost of the line, commercial competition with the other port city in Argentina, Rosario, and the ultimate benefits of such a bold project. Rosetti's study echoed many of these debates, taking a tone indicative of an understanding of both the stakes of such a project and the financial implications of taking on such a large project for a state-owned line. The published study contained twenty-four pages of his observations of the Planchón Pass, its advantages and disadvantages, and basic comparisons with other potential passes. Several maps illustrated the railroad's elevation and slope at different places, along with its topographical path through the Andes.

In debates on the Planchón Pass, congressmen addressed the question of building a railroad across vast stretches of "desert," as some called these places.[13] Indeed, the route meant building a railroad through Indigenous-controlled territory and far from such population centers as Córdoba, San Luis, and Mendoza. Yet for some that was precisely the point. As one supporter put it, "This grandiose project would represent populating four-thousand leagues of desert."[14] The settlers, as stipulated in the proposed law, would help in the "common defense against invasions of barbaric Indians."[15] Echoing those sentiments, Rosetti emphasized the civilizing qualities of the railroad in his study. He repeated tropes about the unproductive nature of Indigenous people and how the railroad "would make the Argentine Republic gain an immense quantity of lands occupied by the barbarians," lands that due to their access to water "would be excellent for agriculture."[16] Rosetti was talking about conquest and erasure of the Indigenous peoples of the south. Such a process had already begun in Chile, called the Occupation of Araucanía (1861–83).[17] In Argentina, what is often referred as the Conquest of the Desert took place only a few years later.[18] Although Rosetti's railroad was never built, the project was certainly part of a mounting full-scale, zero-sum war against "barbarism," with the railroad serving as one of the chief weapons.[19]

Rosetti's language about "barbarians" may serve as an expected discursive shot, part of the all-too-common civilizing language of Argentine liberals, yet it is in the details of the study itself that the tactics of liberal conquest revealed themselves.[20] In particular, Rosetti's study shows how instrumentalism in engineering decontextualized landscapes from their social and historical moorings and ultimately naturalized the reappropriation of these landscapes for liberal nation-making. Take his overview of different valleys through which the railroad could pass. Each one offered a unique set of environmental limitations and technical opportunities. Central to evaluating the various advantages and disadvantages of the project was assessing the usefulness of the environment in terms of construction materials. As the Teno River valley became narrow and windy, for example, "the mountains begin to lose their scorched appearance to give way to arboreal vegetation," which "would provide materials for sleepers."[21] The marshy Azufre valley would necessitate drainage projects due to constant flooding, but those same damp pastures could "be converted into peat moss" and later used for fuel.[22] And in the Grande River valley, "There is no arboreal vegetation or stone for construction, but there are beautiful fields covered in excellent pastures and good land for making bricks."[23] Rosetti's resourceful eye allowed him to pick up on the ways in which mountain environments were not just impediments but could also prove useful in the construction of this difficult project.

Underneath Rosetti's emphasis on the usefulness of mountain environments lay the human element and the political conflicts underpinning that history. The usefulness of marshes, fields, and vegetation for Rosetti's railroad conflicted with how people were using those spaces. In the Valenzuela valley, for example, he noted, "There is also excellent grass here in some places, which in the summer Chilean herders take advantage of to raise livestock."[24] In another instance, he commented on how during the summer "one always finds many people; be they Chilean herders, who look after animals, be they muleteers who rest, [or] be they those who come to bathe in the sulfurous baths that are found around the Azufre River."[25] In the preceding decades, the pass through which Rosetti traveled and the pastures of which he took note sat at the center of political and economic life in the region as Pehuenches, whose influence dominated the eastern side of the Andes, came to take a central place in the cattle trade across the Andes beginning in the eighteenth century.[26] Irrigated by the snowmelt and rains of the spring and summer, pastures on the eastern side of the Andes and in passes such as the Planchón, as Rosetti observed, fed livestock coming over the mountains, the rights to which were often under the control of Indigenous Pehuenche lonkos, who granted access to pastures in exchange for money, goods, and animals.[27] These exchanges were deeply embedded in the political culture not just of Pehuenches but of the relationships developed in the region among people from different groups, and not just among individuals but also between Pehuenche lonkos and Spanish and later Argentine frontier authorities. Not merely one-time commercial exchanges, granting these rights implied the establishment of reciprocity relationships, inscribing in these spaces cultural and political meaning.[28] By the 1860s, the Planchón Pass in particular had become part of a larger contestation about control over these spaces. The Planchón sat in a frontier zone, south of which were Pehuenche lands (centered on Malargüe, Barrancas, and Varvarco) and north of which was the province of Mendoza (with the Atuel River, just north of the Planchón Pass, listed as its territorial limit in the census of 1869).[29] Up to that point, Pehuenches granted access to the Planchón, even if the provincial government in Mendoza attempted to establish guards there to regulate trade and pasture access.[30] After a turbulent decade in which warfare and rebellions turned the Planchón into a passage point for rebel invasions, control over the Planchón must have been unstable but was made clearer in the early 1870s when "Pehuenches recognized Argentine sovereignty over their territory."[31] In 1870, then, when Rosetti was completing his study, he passed through a significant turning point in the history of that space.

Rosetti's vision of emptying these spaces of their history and of the reciprocity relationships established through grazing and land rights to the end of reappropriating the material world to the service of the railroad was by no means unique. Scientific explorations into Patagonia, for example, permeated the emerging national imaginaries of both countries. These missions found refuge in emptying these spaces of human societies, and the cultural and political meaningfulness that accompanied them, and then filling them with visions of colonization and economic productivity. As cultural studies scholar Jens Andermann points out in his analysis of Manuel Olascoaga's map of La Pampa and Río Negro, made as part of the

Conquest of the Desert, it was part of a broad project of "de- and reterritorialization," which involved producing "abstract sovereignty," "empty space," and an "illegalization" of border-crossing frontier activities and histories.[32] Beyond southern South America, in northern Mexico and the Amazon, similar processes of environmental reappropriation were taking place, along with the familiar colonizer discourses of Indigenous idleness.[33] Of course, the knowledge that Rosetti and other engineers used to make their studies was Indigenous at its base; Rosetti credited a "vaqueano [sic]," or mountain guide, who would have undoubtedly been at least deeply familiar with Pehuenches who controlled the space, with providing him the knowledge of it.[34] Rosetti brought with him to the Andes that summer of 1870 a way of understanding space markedly different from that of the Pehuenches or, in a different space, of migrant and itinerant laborers, such as José María Rojas.

Ultimately, what Rosetti and others like him were doing was facilitating the reification of the "economy," disembedded from the social, political, and cultural practices that produced and continue to produce the so-called economy.[35] In that process of reification, resignification of the material world by engineers created a rift between the material and ideological worlds, between the economic and the cultural. That rift was fundamental to liberalism (and the railroad as property), demanding the alienation of the material world for capital accumulation and of the social world for political control. That "there are beautiful fields covered in excellent pastures and good land for making bricks," as Rosetti wrote of the Grande River valley, was one small moment in this liberal process of disembedding the material world from its social and historical context, universalizing and circumscribing it for capital.[36] In the end, erasing this context was necessary for creating the national economy that underpinned the next half century of liberal rule: autonomous, naturalized, existing in itself and for itself.

Emptying out the Andes in that way was a process of circumscribing the material world for not only capital but also the nation. Despite centuries of connections across the Andes and the reality that for most people in western Argentina Chile was an intimate partner and Buenos Aires often a distant stranger, writers constructed (and sometimes continue to construct) the Andes as a barrier rather than as a conduit.[37] Resembling Karl Marx's observation made twelve years earlier about "the annihilation of space by time" brought about by new transportation technology, Rosetti declared that the Trans-Andean railroad would not only shorten distance but annihilate the mountains themselves.[38] The destruction of the Andes would lift the great barrier that up to then "had divided two of the most important nations of South America."[39] This was not only a celebration of the awesome power of the railroad but also a process of naturalizing the border with Chile and thereby naturalizing the nation itself. Much as with the economy or the market, the nation as a socially constructed and socially maintained entity has a fragility often overcome by naturalizing it, a process helped along through promoting natural national borders, natural national parks and monuments, and natural national metaphors of the body politic.[40] Of course, the instituting of natural borders did not mean impermeable ones. In a system of international trade, natural borders were to be crossed only for the purpose of facilitating the orderly and legal flow of labor and goods on railcars and steamships. Ideals of ordered mobility never came true as disease, political radicals, social undesirables, and contraband moved along those same routes, presenting, however, an opportunity to strengthen the nation-state through hygienic programs for rearranging urban centers, political repression to root out (foreign) radicals, projects of othering and pathologizing social undesirables, and plans to fortify surveillance technologies along borders to crack down on untaxed trade.[41] In effect, Rosetti's study and his comments on the Andes as a barrier in particular represent the duality of nation-making projects in the mid-nineteenth century: on the one hand by creating natural borders and on the other by designing the technologies to cross them (and prevent unauthorized and undesirable crossings).

Rosetti was certainly not alone in embarking on a project to cross the Andes as a way to create the Argentine nation. One can hardly forget that the original crossing of the Andes to create the nation was General José de San Martín's in 1817 during the wars of independence.[42] Indeed, much of the construction of the nation, particularly in the nineteenth century, centered on the ritualistic national crossing of the Andes inaugurated by San Martín, including Sarmiento's *Facundo* (written in exile in Chile) and its opposite, José Hernández's epic nation-defining poem, *El Gaucho Martín Fierro*. New editions of the poem would not always reflect this, but the first edition came with an oddly situated ("interesante") appendix, "Memoria sobre el camino trasandino" (Report on the Trans-Andean route).[43] Josefina Ludmer, in her famous study of gauchesque poetry, remarks on this seemingly misplaced piece, pointing out how it reflects not just a particular manifestation of Hernández's liberalism but also a way of drawing the boundaries of the gauchesque genre.[44] Couched in a "learned written voice" indicative of the elite liberal class and opposite of the "oral" one used by the gaucho, which defines the *Martín Fierro* and gauchesque poetry, the *memoria* steps outside the gaucho's voice to contrast it with the very discourses of civilization and progress (particularly on the railroad) that embody the antagonist of the gaucho.[45] As Ludmer cleverly points out, the title itself is an allusion to a mix of nation-defining figures and objects—San Martín, railroads, and gauchos: "(San) Martín *and* (The transandean passage) *of* Fierro," a reference to the Spanish word for iron (*fierro*) and the French word for railroad (*chemin de fer* [*camino de fierro* in Spanish, or iron road in English]).[46]

Unbeknown to Hernández at the time, Martín Fierro, perhaps more than any other literary figure, has come to represent the Argentine nation.[47] As the popular personification of the nation, the poem marks another moment in national boundary construction, the literary body of the nation. Hernández and Rosetti, then, were bounding different versions of a similar body, the nation, albeit from *seemingly* opposite ends: one the universalizing, scientific, liberal version of Rosetti; the other the culturally particular, literary one of Hernández. In reality, the two emerge from a similar uniquely modern problem. As historian Andrew Sartori points out, liberal and culturalist approaches to the modern world are different responses to the problem presented by social abstraction, alienation, and the emergence of capital as the mediating force of all social relationships. Whereas the liberal response has involved a unique emphasis on the individual's "pursuit of private interests" as the primary reason for the interaction of humans and their material world to the end of creating the needs and wants of society, the culturalist response has seen these interactions as "the very substance of the social whole," as part of how the individual develops a sense of autonomy and subjectivity that is intimately connected to the collective.[48] In a way, capitalism's tendency toward an increasing division of labor and an increasing monetization of all social interactions has led simultaneously to a dependency of individuals on society for an ever-increasing list of needs and wants *and* to an alienation from society as getting those needs and contributing to society is an increasingly impersonal process. This duality between culturalist and liberal perspectives on these problems has parallels in the confrontation of the engineer Emilio Rosetti and the gaucho Martín Fierro: the engineer as the scientific embodiment of individual rationality and universality and the gaucho as the literary embodiment of individual autonomy and cultural uniqueness.

All these things—gaucho culture, technology, railroads, naturalized nations, neutralizing the material world as economy—must in the end be understood as the concepts and abstractions that necessarily obfuscated (and continue to cloud) what lies beneath: social conflict. The next chapter explores how social conflict born out of the mining industry in the north of Chile affected one of the last great battles in Argentina's nation-forming period, known as the Revolución de los Colorados (Revolution of the Reds).

## 4 Manufacturing a Rebellion

Nicolás Naranjo was not a typical Argentine caudillo. To begin, he was not even Argentine; he was Chilean. Beyond nationality, he defied many of the stereotypes classically associated with the caudillo, both in Argentina and in Latin America, more broadly. Emerging from the wars of independence and the power vacuum it left, as the traditional narrative goes, the caudillo was a military figure, a strongman whose charisma and man-of-the-people disposition solidified his cult of personality and lent credibility to his battle cries, which the rural popular classes heeded with some regularity in the decades after independence across the region.[1] For Argentina, perhaps no person has better embodied this stereotype than Juan Manuel de Rosas, at times seen as an avatar for a nation that seemed to replicate estancia life everywhere in those turbulent decades after independence.[2] Classically understood, the caudillo was a "warrior, regional chieftain, hacendado, and patrón."[3] His rise to prominence occurred in the context of "anarchy, institutional vacuum, ruralization of power, and armed competition."[4] Little of this conventional conceptualization of the caudillo defines Naranjo. He was not a member of the military or a large estate owner, and his place as a political leader can hardly be gleaned from the historical record. Rather, he was a Chilean mining engineer and capitalist, appearing more representative of the emerging order than of the receding postindependence one that caudillos sometimes are supposed to represent.[5]

In line with the traditional caudillo typology, if one were looking for one in western Argentina in the late 1860s, the obvious choice would be Felipe Varela. One of the last caudillos of the era, he took charge of the resistance to Buenos Aires's and the liberals' centralizing machinations after the capture and assassination of the legendary Ángel Vicente "Chacho" Peñaloza in 1863. The resistance mounted by Varela and Peñaloza to the new state-making project led by Buenos Aires found a receptive audience in western Argentina. Liberals waged campaigns against their enemies in the provinces, working to subdue unruly subjects and popular figures, many of whom fled the country or died resisting.[6] One of the last stands of the western provinces was the Revolución de los Colorados, which began in Mendoza on 9 November 1866. In short time, the rebellion grew and the governor of Mendoza, Melitón Arroyo, was toppled.[7] Shortly after the uprising in Mendoza, exiled rebels led by Varela returned to Argentina from the other side of the mountains in Chile. Their invasion of the republic was extensive. Beginning with their initial descent in December and in tandem with their allies in Mendoza, they invaded several provinces in western Argentina, including San Juan. Although the rebellion had many facets, this chapter focuses on Varela's invasion of San Juan from Chile, as well as the rebel preparations in San Juan for Varela's invasion of the northern provinces. Financing this rebellion was another "caudillo," Naranjo. Muffled in the historical record in many ways, Naranjo's role in Varela's invasion speaks to the importance of the Trans-Andean in Argentina's formative social and political conflicts at the time and suggests a different path for understanding the figure of the caudillo within them.[8]

Caudillismo aside, people like Varela and Naranjo seemed to stand on opposite ends of history. As a Federalist rebel commander from the western provinces of Argentina, Varela represented a political faction and style whose fortunes were waning, even if the image and grievances would remain potent for decades to come. The powerful caudillos who dominated the political landscape in the decades after independence—Facundo Quiroga, Juan Manuel de Rosas, Ángel Peñaloza—were giving way to a liberal order run by urbanites and technocrats engaged in managing the greatest era of globalization in the country's history. That "export age" defined not just Argentina's but also Latin America's economy at the time and the interests of those who most benefited from it defined its politics.[9] Although Naranjo was by no means a major figure in Chilean politics, he did represent the extractive industries that were central to the development of Chile in the nineteenth century and into the twentieth century. If Varela played the role of one of the last Federalist caudillos, then Naranjo stood his opposite as representative of the emerging export era. That era, however, required violence at its foundations.

The use of extreme violence at the inception of liberal hegemony over the nation is well known. Throughout the period of Federalist rule, liberals, often in exile, lamented excessive violent "barbarism" endemic to the country, laying the blame squarely at the feet of caudillos and their gaucho followers. Perhaps no thinker better embodies this criticism than Domingo Faustino Sarmiento, whose book *Facundo* (1845), examined the biography of Facundo Quiroga as an allegory and explanation of Argentina's postindependence history. Yet once in power, Sarmiento and other liberals practiced a particularly brutal approach to Federalist resistance. Most famously, in 1863, Peñaloza was "assassinated, drawn and quartered" by the government putting down his rebellion, an act seemingly justifiable for them despite their rhetoric about rule of law and due process (and even laws against execution for political crimes).[10] While these contradictions of the transition to late-century liberalism are well-rehearsed stories, this chapter focuses on violent rebellion as an economic activity—as a way not to rethink the figure of the caudillo so much as to cast a different light on the historical meaning of those rebellions and the meaningfulness of their defeat by tying them to different historical processes than is traditionally done: mining in Chile and the development of the Trans-Andean as an economic borderland.

This chapter contributes to a broader rethinking of the turbulent and formative decade of the 1860s in Argentina. Scholars have challenged the centrality of Buenos Aires in explanations of civil war in western Argentina by highlighting the place and interests of Indigenous communities and popular classes in the different uprisings of the decade.[11] Although a synthesis of these varied perspectives is beyond this book, they reveal that the political instability of the period created opportunities to reimagine political community, none of which pointed to an inevitability of nation-state dominance and centralization. If divergent interests of different actors and groups proliferated, they were connected across space through people such as Varela and the people who fought with them, running along the Andes from the Pehuenche and Ranquel lands in northern Patagonia and the Pampas through the Huarpe Lagunas de Guanacache in San Juan and Mendoza to northwestern Argentina. Added here is the interrogation of how that rebellious space was connected through not just the people who fought but also the money and resources required to maintain those struggles, demanding that capital, particularly Chilean

*Manufacturing a Rebellion*

capital, have a more central place in explaining those rebellions. Naranjo's history, though not a complete history of rebel financing, illustrates how that important financial component had little to do with Buenos Aires and much more to do with the instability of a rapidly changing economic situation in northern Chile and the Trans-Andean.[12]

## Financing a Rebellion

In early January 1867, a small citizens' expedition departed from San Juan, Argentina, to northern Chile in search of cattle stolen in the mountains by "rebel bandits." Those "rebel bandits" were Argentine exiles who were supporting the invasion of Argentina. What the expedition found when it arrived in Chile was a war machine of substantial proportions. From the port of Huasco to the towns of Vallenar and Carrizal, the expedition reported, the local economy was bustling with war-making activities. As rebels strutted about around town in their quintessential red shirts, people were manufacturing ammunition and sewing uniforms. Spurs, canvas, and other war articles were being purchased from local stores.[13] Without a doubt, manufacturing a rebellion was an economically intensive activity. This rebel war machine required someone to help underwrite it, and the expedition learned of the main financial backers of the Argentine rebels in Chile. One of the financers that the expedition identified was Nicolás Naranjo.[14] He appeared repeatedly in witness testimony, intercepted correspondence, and court cases after the rebellion.[15]

Naranjo's primary support of Argentine rebels came through his relationship with Felipe Varela. Their financial connections began years earlier when Varela went into exile to Chile in late 1863 and Naranjo gave him small loans to support him.[16] Small loans turned into large-scale financial support. By January 1867, Naranjo had financed Varela's operations to the tune of at least 8,255.27 pesos, and he provided another 3,955.24 pesos of support by 5 March of that year, a sum that would have bought almost 350 revolvers (to give a sense of the relative magnitude of these loans).[17] Varela's financial account with Naranjo included two additional points of interest. First, Naranjo charged the debts of other rebels to Varela's account; added to Varela's account was a payment order from another rebel exiled in Chile.[18] Although the payment was for a comparatively small amount (54 pesos), it indicates that Naranjo and Varela's relationship may have been financially important to the rebel cause in Chile, acting as a hub for procuring rebel credit. Second, Naranjo was not the sole financer of the rebels. Aside from the names that witnesses gave, it is clear that through Naranjo at least one "investor"—named only as

"Jorge G."—was buying portions of Varela's debt.[19] Again, although the sum was not significant (122.45 pesos in this case), it demonstrates that Naranjo was an intermediary between potential "investors" in Chile and the rebels.

Naranjo's experiences in Chile provided him with incentives to support Varela and the rebels. A mining engineer by training, he became involved in mining in the late 1840s and 1850s as a mine administrator and *cateador* (cateadores were "mine hunters," "discovering" mineral deposits and veins and securing rights to them).[20] By the late 1850s, Naranjo had begun his ascent within the mining world. In 1859, he went into business with two important mining entrepreneurs, José Tomás Urmeneta and Maximiano Errázuriz, acting as partial owner and administrator of six mines, as well as the representative of their mining interests in the province of Atacama.[21] Throughout the 1860s, he expanded his business interests and investments. In addition to the development of his mining interests, Naranjo diversified his investments through lending and buying property.[22] Due to the structures of the mining industry in Chile, diversification was an important mechanism employed by mining entrepreneurs for mitigating risk. In addition to unstable mineral markets, mining entrepreneurs faced constraints brought about through their relationships with merchants. Those relationships were based on the credit that mining entrepreneurs received from merchants, which worked to discourage them from reinvesting capital into their mining activities. Instead, they opted to reduce vulnerability through investing in landed property, loans, and various short-term ventures.[23] At the same time, Naranjo had experienced the impact of the market's vagaries on the Chilean mining sector and had experienced the economic uncertainties of mining operations firsthand.[24] From this perspective, Naranjo's financial participation in the rebellion appears as a short-term investment, meant to provide him with a different revenue stream from his mining interests.

The financial relationship between Naranjo and Varela affected rebel activities in Argentina as Varela and others worked to repay Naranjo. Naranjo's loans to Varela came not in the form of cash but rather arms, munitions, and other war materials, including cloth and buttons for uniforms, which he had bought in the province of Atacama and in Valparaíso.[25] Drawing on his experience in the mining economy, Naranjo appeared to be employing a system known to miners and merchants alike in which merchants provided "advanced leases of capital goods and the sale of consumable goods required for production" to miners in exchange for a portion of the sale of their mineral product.[26] Known as *habilitación,* it was a system with which Naranjo was familiar, but instead of capital goods for minerals, it was war materials for the spoils of war: cattle. The exact proportion of cattle guaranteed to Naranjo and his associates was based on established prices per head of cattle. In the case of oxen, the most expropriated type of cattle, the price was roughly between twenty and twenty-five pesos per head.[27] For each head of oxen, the price was discounted from Varela's account.[28] That price was lower than the market value of oxen at the time. Depending on the quality and weight of the oxen, prices fluctuated somewhere between thirty and forty-five pesos, giving Naranjo additional revenues derived from expropriated oxen.[29]

To provide Naranjo with cattle, rebels employed a system of expropriation. Expropriation came in different forms, but before Varela's invasion of Argentina, it relied on banditry. Soldiers in the mountains were employed to detain cattle drives crossing the mountains into Chile and to seize the animals in the drive. One area severely affected by banditry was the northern part of San Juan (Iglesia and San José de Jáchal), across the mountains from the rebels' base in northern Chile. This area was of great concern to Argentine officials. Before the invasion, Argentine consulates in Chile circulated reports about Varela's plans and correctly suspected that he would descend on Argentina after leaving from his base in the Chilean town of Vallenar through the mountain passes around Jáchal.[30] It was there that government forces had amassed to defend against Varela's invasion.[31] The government's maneuvers did little to protect the cattle trade, however. Beginning at least as early as December 1866, local and provincial governments had been getting wind of an increasingly volatile situation as reports continued about banditry in the mountains.[32] In the mountain passes leading to and from Vallenar and Copiapó, "pirates on land," as one official called them, preyed on cattle drives passing from Argentina to Chilean markets.[33] One of the valleys through which they passed in Chile was the Tránsito River valley, which was home to the Diaguita-descendent Huascoaltinos, who had been some of the only Diaguitas to retain control of their lands in the nineteenth century.[34] Rumors spread that these "pirates" were soldiers in Varela's army, holding up cattle drives and taking horses, mules, and cattle.[35] Although sources are not clear, it is likely that Varela's army kept the cattle taken from Argentina farther up the Tránsito River valley, around the mountain lakes.[36] Subsequently, cattle were taken down into Chile, where Naranjo would find a buyer. The system's impact on the pace of expropriation was significant. Estimates vary, but at least 500 cattle were taken as a direct result of Naranjo and Varela's partnership, with some estimates putting the number closer to 4,000. Even without exact numbers, it would be reasonable to estimate that the business generated tens of thousands of pesos.[37]

The profitability of cattle to the rebels was connected to the growth of the mining sector in Chile and the role played by cattle in that growth. Over the mountains from Argentina via the provinces of Catamarca, La Rioja, and San Juan, cattle came to the region to feed the mining boom in northern Chile, and from mine to port, in one form or another, cattle were present.[38] Even before extraction, mine workers had to prepare for laboring in the mines. To ensure good footing, particularly on their descents and ascents, miners used rawhide shoes.[39] Once in the mines, miners worked long hours in physically demanding labor. The caloric requirements to reproduce that labor were high, and cattle made up for that caloric want, whether directly or indirectly. Cattle may have supplied mining districts with much-needed caloric energy to fuel miners. However, despite casual observations about the importation of cattle to Atacama from San Juan for beef, it is unlikely that miners were eating meat regularly.[40] Instead, their diet likely consisted of "salted beans" and bread.[41] Nevertheless, to plow the fields to grow beans and wheat, oxen were likely needed. Sure footing and caloric energy, however, were not enough on their own to extract ore from mines. Mine shafts went well below the surface, thus preventing sunlight from entering the mines. Meeting the luminary requirements in mining operations were tallow candles, which likely came from cows.[42] After extraction, *apires* (a type of mining laborer) brought ore to the surface from the mines in rawhide sacks, called *capachos*. On average, an apire could carry roughly 90 kilos of ore each trip in his capacho. This process was still employed during the boom, thus increasing the need for rawhide to produce capachos.[43]

Once the ore was at the surface, it needed to be transported to foundries in commercial centers around the region. In the colonial era, roads were deficient or nonexistent, making oxcarts impossible. Instead, mules transported silver and gold to processing centers, while high-quality copper ores were smelted locally.[44] By the mid-nineteenth century, however, the expansion of mining allowed for greater investments in smelting operations, particularly for copper.[45] As these operations became capitalized over time, the need for road systems grew, too. Road construction in Chile during the 1840s and 1850s became important throughout the country, but Atacama received the greatest attention and by the 1860s had the longest road system in the country.[46] Populating those roads were carts driven by mules and oxen. Although mules were likely more prevalent than oxen in transporting ore, oxen were still required to fuel that transportation. Traversing arid environments with little food or water available on the road, transport animals required transportable food to sustain them on long, arduous journeys. To fill this need, agriculturalists converted crops to alfalfa, and aiding in the production of this fuel for transport animals were oxen for plowing fields.[47] Thus, in a number of ways, from the agricultural necessities of booming mining centers to the technologies of ore extraction and transportation, the mining boom relied heavily on the importation of cattle from Argentina. As a result, cattle had widespread and nearly universal value in the mining region and, through that universality, was a surrogate currency for rebels and their financial backers, allowing them to construct an effective business model for supporting their cause financially. Although that business model was an important force in the expropriation of cattle, it was not the only one compelling expropriation.

## Labor Interests in the Rebel Business Model

This was not the first time that Naranjo had taken part in violent confrontations with the state. In Chile, in 1850, while he was serving as the administrator of the Buena Esperanza mine near Copiapó, the government reviewed a civil case between that mine and a neighboring one in which the neighboring mine owners claimed part of the Buena Esperanza mine's land and therefore its minerals.[48] Ultimately, the state ruled in favor of the neighboring mine, but when a local official attempted to enforce the order, Naranjo led a group of about 200 men against him.[49] With "bullets, pistols, daggers, clubs, and crowbars" they confronted the subdelegado, and since he was outnumbered, he surrendered and obeyed Naranjo's orders.[50] The old stereotype of the Argentine caudillo was the estancia owner mobilizing labor for violent political confrontations. However limited this perspective has been, Naranjo's early experiences with violence in the context of mining reminds us of the blurred line between economic activities and political mobilizations. In a sense, they remind us that soldiering was labor.

As rebellion spread in San Juan, soldiers played a significant role in perpetuating expropriation. According to observers, the rebel takeover of San Juan unleashed a wave of social chaos. During the rebellion, the Chilean consulate in San Juan noted that rebel commanders were unable to control their soldiers, with the result that cattle were robbed almost daily by soldiers and eaten.[51] How true those claims were is difficult to discern, but there likely were expropriations in San Juan not authorized by military commanders. After the rebellion was put down, citizens in San Juan reported to the government what they had lost during the expropriations. For two departments in San Juan, citizens claimed 144 cattle stolen.[52] In those reports, government officials occasionally noted when the articles had been expropriated on the orders of military commanders, implying that at least some expropriations may have been carried out by soldiers alone.[53] The initiative of soldiers to expropriate (or at least threaten the expropriation of) cattle on their own terms was also fundamental to the development of labor relationships between soldiers and military commanders. The stakes of rebellion and warfare for many workers revolved around the question of their control over their own labor. Four years earlier, in 1863, provincial authorities in Mendoza acknowledged as much when they expressed concern over Chilean laborers and their opposition to the papeleta de conchabo when another rebel invasion threatened southern Mendoza, leading officials to speculate that Chilean workers hoped that the rebels were "abolishing the papeleta" (see chapter 2).[54] Clearly, rebellion gave laborers the opportunity to strike out against labor institutions. At the same time, workers treated the very process of rebellion as something on which to labor, to manufacture.

The need for capital to pay wages to soldiers contributed to the demand for expropriated cattle. Although details are scarce, it is clear that soldiers received wages in exchange for their services. By expropriating and selling cattle, military commanders could procure the capital necessary to pay wages.[55] Of course, expectations of wages and the inability of commanders to supply them consistently had the potential to boil over into labor disputes. In one dispute, military commanders in Jáchal promised a "pecuniary reward" to soldiers who had recently defected from the government. On sensing that their reward was going to go unfulfilled, soldiers became agitated, threatening to take action and "loot" the village. To prevent turmoil, the local government expropriated cattle from locals in order to pay the soldiers.[56] Soldiers' threats, therefore, acted as a negotiation tactic. That tenuous relationship between soldiers and commanders shows how strongly labor relationships and wages could shape the decisions of commanders and local governments. Soldiers clearly preferred money to whatever could be obtained through looting, and the expropriation of cattle was one way for rebel commanders and local governments to procure the capital necessary to pay soldiers.

The need for capital for the production of rebellion was also related to the gender roles soldiers played in their families as providers of money. In one revealing letter written during his preparations for invading the northern provinces, Felipe Varela reminded the governor of agreements stipulating that the state revenues collected in the Jáchal department were to be kept there to support the invasion, which included making "monthly payments to the women of soldiers."[57] Varela's need for capital to pay these women shows the economic demands that family structures put on the rebellion and the role that the rebel state played in meeting those demands. In a sense, therefore, rebellion for laborers linked up with and supported norms of family life, as well as supported broader demands for and modes of expression to gain greater control over their own labor.

## Commercializing Rebellion

When a group of Argentines went into Chile to track down "stolen" cattle, they discovered that Naranjo had taken at least 200 cattle to Copiapó and was looking for a buyer for the rest.[58] In order to turn expropriated cattle into capital, rebels and financiers needed to transport and commercialize the cattle. The efforts of Naranjo and others to traffic cattle across the mountains relied on legalization processes on both sides of the Andes. On the Argentine side, the rebels were able to legitimize the expropriation of cattle through their conquest of the state and the participation of key officials within it. Once the rebels took over the provincial state in San Juan, they institutionalized practices of expropriation through decrees, auctions, and notarial records. In one instance, a decree was issued on 3 February 1867, a month after the invasion, ordering the expropriation of cattle.[59] The cattle were then put up for auction. According to Varela, nobody bid on the cattle, and therefore 500 head were granted to him on 28 February. A week later, on 6 March, Varela and Fabián Martínez, another commander and partner in the expropriation business (also the Chilean consulate's representative in Jáchal, mentioned in chapter 2), documented the sale of those 500 cattle to Martínez before a notary public in the sum of 10,000 pesos, which Varela received "in money."[60] The participation of a notary public, the production of notarial records, and the use of auctions signaled that rebel economic practices penetrated traditional institutional mechanisms meant to legitimize and legalize property exchanges.

Legalizing rebel economic practices—namely, the expropriation of cattle—was central to ensuring that buyers would be able to sell livestock in Chilean markets. By legalizing those property exchanges, rebels and commercial actors alike were anticipating that eventually former owners of expropriated property might pose a threat since they could take buyers to court in Chile and dispute the legitimate ownership of the expropriated cattle. Witness accounts noted how rebels *consciously* used property records as a way of avoiding prosecution in Chilean courts.[61] Indeed, legalization was an effective way to cast doubt on property claims made in Chilean courts regarding transactions that occurred in Argentina. One Argentine official even complained that court cases in Chile against rebel economic practices went nowhere because of the uncertainties surrounding jurisdiction.[62] In effect, the Chilean courts became a force for legitimizing the commercialization of expropriated cattle, thereby offering protection to those who participated in commercialization. Although direct collusion with the rebels on the part of Chilean judges is possible, Chilean courts were unwilling to side officially with victims of expropriation because of the far-reaching implications this would have.

Chilean courts' reluctance to rule in favor of plaintiffs in civil and criminal cases arose from the deeply political nature of the cases. In one case, Francisco Tristán Coll went to Chile from San Juan, where he claimed that he was "robbed" during the rebellion of "a great quantity of animals," including horses, mules, and more than 200 oxen, all of which he valued at 20,000 pesos.[63] He accused Valentín González of buying a portion of those oxen and reselling them to a couple of Chileans. Coll's claim was true, but that did not make the original sale illegitimate. In fact, in order to prove that he was the rightful owner of the cattle, González showed the Chilean court that he had purchased the animals from a colonel in the revolutionary forces who had expropriated and sold the animals to pay soldiers in his regiment.[64] It would appear, therefore, that the practice of buying expropriated cattle required willing participation on the part of commercial actors to engage in exchanges with rebel forces. Despite that fact and even though the revolutionary government had been toppled by the time the case was going through the Chilean legal system, the court could not find a reason to rule in Coll's favor. In its ruling, the court argued that it lacked jurisdiction since it did not possess the "authority to qualify the legitimacy of acts executed by a de facto government in a foreign Republic."[65] In that sense, the Chilean courts deferred to the national government in Argentina to deal with property crimes within its borders executed under the revolutionary government, thereby offering de facto protection to commercial actors who had found their way into Chile with expropriated cattle. That protection, which was anticipated through the creation of institutional practices of legalization, helped to construct the business of expropriation as legitimate and profitable in the eyes of commercial actors.

If institutional legitimacy warded off legal problems in Chile, it also brought commercial actors into the fold. To procure capital for paying soldiers, obtaining capital goods, and bolstering the rebel government in San Juan, rebels sought to go beyond their financial backers and incorporate commercial actors into the business. One way of achieving that end was through selling expropriated cattle to commercial actors, occasionally through auctions. At least 12 commercial actors between January and April 1867 bought at least 883 head of expropriated cattle.[66] What they offered the rebels was important. Beyond the Varela-Naranjo partnership, rebel commanders required capital to continue their military plans and pay soldiers, and commercial actors provided not only that capital but also an important service. Expropriations and the Varela-Naranjo partnership had been a central component to procuring capital, especially early on, but those activities created the extra burden of having to transport cattle to Chile in order to realize their value. Trading directly with commercial actors in San Juan alleviated the burden of transportation, thereby giving rebel commanders speedy access to capital. Through their expertise with the cattle trade, therefore, commercial actors helped solve the problems of transportation and the work of commercialization. Outside of expropriation, the work of commercialization conditioned the experiences of commercial actors, and through those experiences they revealed the central tensions that drove the cattle trade: speculation and power.

A central constraint for commercial actors in the cattle trade was their lack of power in transporting cattle. Due to the difficulties and uncertainties of the journeys both from the provinces where cattle were raised to San Juan and from San Juan to Chile, cattle traders were often subservient to labor relationships. In addition to the cattle traders, cattle drives also consisted of muleteers and peons.[67] With respect to both of these professions, the cattle traders often depended on them more than they depended on him. In the Pampas of Argentina and the mountains of the Trans-Andean, muleteers were some of the most skilled people in navigating the vast stretches of unforgiving territory. Familiar with the various routes and survival techniques required to drive cattle, and helped by the social relationships that they developed across the land, muleteers were essential for cattle traders and were paid for those services.[68] Payment, however, did not indenture them to their "bosses." Throughout the nineteenth century, travelers commented on the tendency for muleteers to disregard the authority that travelers assumed they had over muleteers by hiring them.[69] Likewise, during the rebellion muleteers were confident enough in their independence to reject rebel requests to take expropriated cattle to Chile.[70] Muleteers, therefore, held their independence and power over their labor in high regard. Peons, too, were not in an absolutely subordinate position to their bosses. Like muleteers, peons had a great deal of independence within the cattle drive. They were needed to find cattle that had wandered from the herd. At times, trusted peons were also put in charge of finding cattle to purchase while the boss and others went to find cattle at other estancias. Mobility and independence within the cattle drive allowed peons some negotiating room, too. If bosses were too harsh or the drive became unbearable, simply leaving and finding work somewhere else was not out of the question.[71] Thus, cattle traders' power within the "work" of commercialization was negotiated and subject to the will of the laborers who worked cattle drives. Compounding those uncertainties were the uncertainties derived from the cattle trade's speculative nature.

For commercial actors the cattle trade was both an alluring endeavor, filled with potential profits, and a highly volatile one, often fraught with complications. The combination of those qualities of the cattle trade made it susceptible to speculation. Most cattle were not raised in the province of San Juan. Instead, cattle traders went to other provinces—especially Córdoba and Santiago del Estero—to find cattle to buy.[72] As a consequence, traders were at the mercy of price fluctuations from province to province; even within a province, moreover, prices could fluctuate drastically. For example, in Córdoba, one of the main providers of cattle to San Juan, between 1857 and 1867 cattle prices fluctuated between ten and twenty-seven pesos per head, depending on the type of cattle.[73] Of course, even within a given year, prices could swing from month to month and estancia to estancia, depending on demand and season. In response to those vagaries, some traders developed a practice of assembling a herd from cattle bought from several ranchers, rather than just one.[74] One of the effects of price uncertainties, therefore, was the piecemeal character of the accumulation of cattle by commercial actors. That practice of piecemeal accumulation influenced how and why commercial actors participated in the business of expropriation.

### The Boundaries of Property and Violence

In Naranjo's first violent confrontation with the state in 1850, he did something that revealed what was at stake not just in this attack but also in parts of the rebellions of the 1860s in the Trans-Andean. After storming the mine with his armed workers and confronting the state official, he went outside and "tore out and destroyed the boundary" that had marked the division between the two mines, effectively taking (or retaking, depending on one's perspective) the neighboring mine.[75] As a mining engineer trained in surveying and a cateador by practice, he would have understood the importance of those markers and the power they held to secure mineral wealth. For his role in this short-lived uprising, he was convicted of "resisting the authorities" and was sentenced to one year of exile, a sentence that he may have never served fully.[76] What was at stake were the boundaries of property.

In the following years, Naranjo learned an important lesson about boundaries. In 1859, he went into business with Urmeneta and Errázuriz in Chile, acting as partial owner and administrator of six mines, as well as the representative of their mining interests in the province of Atacama.[77] His partnership with them involved buying and selling minerals, landed properties, and representation in civil cases, one of which was over the boundary with a neighboring mine owned by Jorge Montt.[78] As part of the case, in 1865 Montt accused officials of, among other things, removing important boundary markers, going as far as to accuse one official involved in surveying the boundary, Miguel Callejas, of "malice or incompetence" and of being "an instrument of Naranjo."[79] Indeed, Naranjo and Callejas knew each other from having served together as state surveyors in Vallenar.[80] Montt's accusation points to what Naranjo understood: the importance, and mutability, of the boundaries between mines. Rather than being accused of violently moving property boundaries, now he was accused of having state officials do it for him. It would not have been the first time that Naranjo had worked to influence the government in a way that seemed unfair to others.

Only months before Montt's complaint, in May 1864, locals from Vallenar accused Naranjo and others of engaging in electoral fraud during the national legislative elections held in March.[81] Through their privileged position at the "polling station," they prevented people from voting and even allowed a noncitizen (Naranjo's own "bookkeeper") to vote to the end of electing Santiago Prado as Vallenar's and Freirina's deputy in the National Congress of Chile.[82] Despite the protestors' complaint to the local judge, Francisco Antonio Silva, it does not appear that Naranjo ever faced charges for electoral fraud, nor did Prado appear to have his position altered.[83] Later, in October 1865, after Naranjo had begun his engagement with Varela and only a year before the Revolución de los Colorados, officials again accused him of stirring up trouble, this time of "conato de motín" (attempting an uprising).[84] The motivations and character of this "scandalous attack," as one official described it, are not known, but the circumstances surrounding it are telling nonetheless.[85] About a month before Naranjo's "attack" in Vallenar, as Spain began an attempted blockade of Chile during the Chincha Islands War (a war between Spain and its former colonies along the Pacific Coast of South America over valuable guano islands), Spanish forces occupied several Chilean ports, including Caldera in northern Chile.[86] The effect on society across the north was drastic. "Several merchants," it was reported, had "extraordinarily raised the price of essential consumer goods."[87] The "high cost of staple goods" sent society into crisis: "In the town of Chañacal," for example, "the working classes [had] revolted."[88] In Vallenar, where Naranjo was, "hoarders of flour [were] hiding this product, motivated by the possibility of selling it at higher prices" later on.[89] Money, too, began to become scarce, so much so that even "individuals who own[ed] rich mines and valuable properties"—people such as Naranjo— couldn't "overcome the difficulty of accessing cash."[90]

Amid the turmoil, the governor of Vallenar, José B. Quesada, resigned his post.[91] Several weeks later, on 27 October, Francisco Antonio Silva was appointed governor, serving for the better part of the following fifteen months, during which time Naranjo and Varela planned and executed an invasion of Argentina from Vallenar.[92] On paper, Silva had left the governorship in January, only four days before the citizens' expedition from Argentina arrived in town, where they were detained by the government.[93] Although they did not identify the governor by name, he did warn them of "political enemies there."[94] It was entirely likely that Naranjo and Varela had allies there. Some witnesses reported that Chilean officials, including Silva, were helping Naranjo and his associates find safe passage into Chile, where they were able to sell expropriated cattle, even claiming that Naranjo was giving orders to the governor of Huasco, requesting protection for herds coming from Argentina.[95] The national government in Chile denied that local officials helped the rebels.[96]

Paralleling Naranjo's experiences were the cattle traders who participated in exchanges of expropriated cattle. Witnesses identified several commercial actors who participated in those exchanges, including José Ormaechea and Felipe Santiago Leguizamón. Reportedly, Ormaechea and Leguizamón were business partners in the trafficking of "stolen property" to Chile, including 60 oxen taken by Varela in San Juan.[97] Ormaechea and Leguizamón's partnership was not limited to trafficking in "stolen property" for the rebels. In fact, trafficking in "stolen property" was likely a mechanism to supplement their existing commercial interests. A year before the invasion of San Juan, in January 1866, Ormaechea came to San Juan from the northern province of Salta with a herd of cattle. Unable to take the herd to Chile at the time, he enlisted the help of Leguizamón to watch over it until they could take the cattle to Chile the following crossing season, some ten months later. In November, Ormaechea returned to San Juan, offering to take Leguizamón's cattle over the mountains along with his, to which Leguizamón agreed. It appears that afterward Ormaechea returned to San Juan. As the rebellion in Argentina was getting underway, Leguizamón and Ormaechea took the opportunity to do business with the rebels. In Copiapó and Ovalle, they sold 60 oxen that they had received from the rebels and perhaps another 87–147 oxen.[98] In that way, they used the rebels' sale of expropriated cattle to complement their existing cattle-trade business.

During their partnership to traffic expropriated cattle, Leguizamón ran into a civil case, one that revealed some of the underlying tensions that made violence and regional economy so interconnected. It was a year before the rebellion, in November 1865, when he entered into an agreement to sell over 200 head of cattle to Francisco Cortés Cumplido. After nearly a year, Cortés Cumplido still had not received the cattle. When he finally got them from Leguizamón, 4 had died and the remaining had all gained significant weight under Leguizamón's custody, leading both men to question the original price of the cattle. For interest, dead cattle, and other costs related to the case, Cortés Cumplido claimed that Leguizamón owed him 403.31 pesos. For his part, Leguizamón protested that the original price was too low; the cattle, after all, were worth closer to 45 pesos per head than the original 35 pesos per head, leading him to present a counterclaim of 1,063.99 pesos.[99] Those claims and counterclaims fluctuated throughout the case's evolution, representing anywhere from 6 to 15 percent of the total price of the cattle.[100] The case's potential financial ramifications, therefore, were significant. In the context of the struggles over those monetary implications, the problem of value and valorization emerged and, through its articulation, reveals the anxieties that lay at the heart of the cattle trade.

The case boiled down to the question of the cattle's value: who was responsible for its increase and who was entitled to those gains. Throughout the course of the civil dispute between Cortés Cumplido and Leguizamón, uncertainties arose around the nature of valorization and how the cattle's value was assessed. When Leguizamón presented his counterclaim, in which he asserted his right to the increased value of the cattle, Cortés Cumplido refuted the claim. He argued that Leguizamón was only entitled to part of the cattle's increased value—specifically, the value derived from the cattle's increased weight. The problem, according to Cortés Cumplido, was that the appraisal was based not only on the cattle's weight "but also on their increased age, on the abundance of plump cattle in the last summer season, on devaluation in Chilean markets, and on the necessity of slaughtering cattle so as not to fill them up on expensive pasture in the winter."[101] Among those factors, Cortés Cumplido made a distinction between different sources of value based on what he called "anexión natural" and "anexión artificial."[102] According to Cortés Cumplido, the former was the value added to a commodity due to "natural" forces, such as market fluctuations. By contrast, "anexión artificial" was the "material" value added due to intentional action, which in this case meant feeding the cattle. However, because the cattle's "material" value was measured in its weight, rather than the cost of pasture and labor needed to add that weight, "anexión artificial" was not equivalent to the cost of production (that is, the material inputs that went into fattening the cattle). Cortés Cumplido argued that since Leguizamón was not the owner of the cattle during the time in which the cattle gained weight, he was not entitled to the incidental increases in the cattle's value (due to market fluctuations and other "natural" processes, or "anexión natural"), nor, for that matter, was he entitled to the costs of feeding the cattle, since the original contract stipulated that Leguizamón would cover those costs.[103] In that sense, Cortés Cumplido was articulating a sense of value that neither originated in the cost of producing the cattle's weight (feeding costs) nor came about through market dynamics. Consequently, he left open the possibility for a third source of value, independent from both market forces and production costs: the intentional act of feeding. In a sense, Cortés Cumplido's argument differentiated between the part owed to Leguizamón for his "work" in sustaining the cattle and the part owed to him for his ownership of the cattle during their increase in value.

For the courts, these claims sparked a reassessment of how the cattle's value was determined. In response to Cortés Cumplido's argument, the court ordered another appraisal of the cattle in order to determine "the improvements . . . in the conditions of the oxen."[104] The new appraisers not only disputed Cortés Cumplido's evaluation of the value of the cattle's weight but also noted that the weight of the cattle's meat was not the sole consideration in determining its value. Rather, they argued that they had to account for the estimated weight of the cattle's hides and innards.[105] The appraisers, therefore, were anticipating the cattle's uses in order to determine the exact value of the "material" improvements on the cattle. The courts agreed with them, which allowed Leguizamón to recuperate at least a portion of the costs he had incurred during the dispute, although the court's decision was not reached until August 1867, almost a year after Leguizamón had turned over the cattle to Cortés Cumplido.[106]

Naranjo's and Leguizamón's struggles revolved intensely around the question of boundaries. The claims of different mines that led to Naranjo's invasion in 1850 of a neighboring mine and to the cases that dragged from 1859 to 1873 made abundantly clear to him that the central question of mining wealth was the question not just of habilitación—so often the story of miners' struggles and successes—but also of property boundaries and of the Chilean state's ability to determine property lines that could make or break a mine. Lines were crucial to Naranjo's life, and their seemingly weak state and the system that upheld them were a reminder of the importance of controlling them by violent force, as demonstrated by Naranjo's periodic threats of violence in the 1850s and 1860s. Leguizamón's case, albeit in a very different way, points to similar problems of boundaries. What is important about this case is not the value of the cattle but rather how the appraisers sought to determine what portion of it belonged to each party and why. Much like property markers, the process was about the property-creating capacity of the state at a moment in which these lines and the appraisals of value seemed to be unstable and in dispute. Varela's invasion, therefore, relied on these unstable senses of property boundaries for men such as Naranjo and Leguizamón, and how that instability encouraged violent means for stabilizing property boundaries, making the creation of property boundaries a fundamental stake in this rebellion.

Nicolás Naranjo was a typical caudillo. At least, he was if caudillos are understood as political and economic figures. In historian Jeremy Adelman's analysis of caudillismo and Juan Manuel de Rosas, he eschews the traditional emphasis on violent disorder and the caudillo, instead focusing on how Rosas came to be accepted as a figure who could mediate and distribute property rights, albeit imperfectly. In the absence of state institutions that could serve as "neutral" arbiters of conflicts over property, Rosas played a transitional role. He was a personal replacement for political and economic institutions that ideally were impersonal, and this produced in turn a kind of "cronyism" that would always work to undermine the long-term sustainability of his system.[107] Yet, in other accounts, the caudillo was not necessarily transitional but rather integral to so-called neutral state institutions. When writer Ezequiel Martínez Estrada wrote in the 1940s about the figure of the caudillo in his analysis of Sarmiento, he noted, "The caudillo hasn't disappeared, but rather has been reabsorbed in the civil servant and the magistrate."[108] Perhaps Naranjo sits somewhere between Adelman's Rosas and Martínez Estrada's thousand bureaucratic caudillos.

Through the lens of Naranjo, it becomes clear that caudillismo must also be understood as a process of enclosure, primitive accumulation, and the centrality of frontier economies to the establishment of late nineteenth-century liberalism on a national and global scale. To this end, the following interlude examines Naranjo not as caudillo but as engineer. The engineer here stands as the verso of the caudillo, two seeming opposites but really one and the same, a Janus-faced unity that sits at the heart of this period of historical transition.

Interlude Four | Engineers between Frontiers

When Nicolás Naranjo went into exile in 1854 due to his role in a violent confrontation with state officials, he changed. During his brief exile in Argentina, he likely was asked by William Wheelwright—the American capitalist who had been in charge of the first railroad in Chile (the Caldera-Copiapó line) and the forerunner of steamship traffic along the Pacific Coast—to help him conduct a survey for a new railroad, one that would extend from Wheelwright's railroad in the province of Atacama across the Andes and the Argentine interior to connect with the Argentine Central Railroad in Córdoba, which itself continued on to Rosario on the Paraná River.[1] Wheelwright's was an early concrete iteration of a Trans-Andean railroad, preceding the Clark brothers' and Rosetti's by a decade. In part based on Naranjo's notes, Wheelwright presented his preliminary project in January 1860 to the Royal Geographical Society in London.[2] After Naranjo returned to Chile, he continued his role as an instigator of violence, albeit in a very different way from his earlier confrontations. This interlude plots the parameters for understanding the dual role that engineers such as Naranjo played in the formation of the modern global order. They were at once violent figures confronting state power and harbingers of the impersonal power associated with the modern nation-state and turn-of-the-century liberalism. This interlude takes up this duality by examining the place of engineers in creating and closing frontiers.

The frontier, as Margarita Serje reminds us, "originate[d] with the history of capitalism."[3] It is best understood not in the outmoded framework of Frederick Jackson Turner—with its emphasis on "the battle between wilderness and rugged individualism"—but rather as a space "in which the conditions for new (but not necessarily originary) rounds of extractive accumulation are put in place," where "questions of law, order, rule, authority, profit, and property are all subject to intense forms of contestation and opposition."[4] In that sense, engineers do not need to be "explorers" or "pioneers" in the classical sense to be frontier creators; they need to be facilitators of extractivist economies and the kinds of political configurations that help those activities along. To be sure, the frontier is not a moment in time and space to be eventually "settled" and "domesticated"; rather, it is a particular configuration of social and political relationships, which can—and for capitalism must—be renewed periodically in all sorts of different spaces assumed to have already been "settled" and "domesticated."

Even before the Revolución de los Colorados, Naranjo was a facilitator of a frontier space, not by resisting the state, but rather by fulfilling its mission. After independence, the Chilean government began to assert its authority over the nation by taking possession of, measuring, and selling land. At one level, this involved dissolving the colonial Pueblos de Indios and declaring their "excess" lands public.[5] In the 1820s and 1830s, in the northern mining districts, Diaguita descendants in Huasco experienced this process, with only the Huascoaltinos managing to retain possession of their lands along the Tránsito River valley running up toward the border with Argentina, which likely became part of rebel geographies in the 1860s.[6] Across Latin America, the process of creating "empty" public land relied on surveying and measuring, which as in the case of Naranjo was not an impersonal, abstract process.[7] Of course, Naranjo did not survey the agriculture land often associated with that process but rather mineral veins in the mountains. Nevertheless, as a promoter of a "volatile and turbulent" place "associated with forced commercialization" in his cattle expropriation business with Varela and his mining activities in the previous years, Naranjo produced the kinds of "economies of violence" that characterize the frontier.[8] This should not be all that surprising either. What engineers quite often did was survey the prospects for accumulation in one form or another—surveying land for colonization, surveying mineral capacities of mining veins, surveying routes for canals and railroads. Like Naranjo, they understood both the importance of survey markers in capturing mineral rents, how deeply capricious those boundaries were, and how important violence was in either maintaining them or pushing them out of the way (whichever was necessary to perpetuate frontier forms of accumulation). In this way, engineers were frontier creators, pushing the limits of governability while also making legible these spaces for capitalist expansion. They facilitated the creation of a duality constitutive of those spaces, the "sovereignty of capital" and "state sovereignty," and embodied both the tensions between them and the fusion of them.9 Fundamentally, the "deterritorializing" logic of capital confronted and complemented nation-state fixity, particularly in the realm of the propertiedness of space (that is, land) and land titles, which could simultaneously provide the grounded legibility for nation-state fixity and circulate (not just confer ownership over land) in a deterritorialized way, allowing capitalists new places in which to invest and from which to draw capital.10

The place of the engineer in midcentury capitalist violence, particularly in the Americas, did not just revolve around measuring and surveying but was also tied to the military adventurism that proliferated at the time. The case of William Walker's filibustering expedition to Nicaragua in 1855 illustrates this well: not only did southern slaveholders promote the project but, oddly enough, so did European liberals escaping the repression unleashed after the uprisings of 1848, constituting, as Michel Gobat sees it, an episode in "liberal imperialism."11 This project, like others at the time, relied on engineers. In fact, some of the most important professionals to Walker's imperial project were the civil engineers who populated his Department of Colonization, including Maximilian von Sonnenstern and "his closest collaborators in Walker's Nicaragua," Eugene Hesse, Max Ströbel, and Adolph Schwartz, the first two having participated in surveys in the US West before their time in Nicaragua and all three, along with von Sonnenstern, having participated in the uprisings of 1848 in Germany.12 Other engineers found themselves drawn to filibustering in the 1850s, particularly military engineers who had gained glory in the Mexican-American War and in their masculine adventurism sought to release themselves from a world that could be "quiet, dull, & stupid," as one professor of engineering at West Point put it in reference to teaching cadets. This professor resigned in late 1854 and joined an eventually aborted filibustering mission to Cuba just months before Walker left for Nicaragua.13

Engineers were paradoxically also the very same agents who helped close these frontier spaces. Closure on the frontier (temporary as it might have been) was brought about by the rise of what can be thought of as

*Engineers between Frontiers*

"infrastructural power," an authority that expresses itself not through individuals or violence but rather through the persistence of state sovereignty in the material world: the impersonal, almost invisible power expressed in traffic signals, signage, and a whole tapestry of inanimate entities that make daily life and state power merge almost seamlessly.[14] Infrastructure appears at once a benign feature of everyday life and an overwhelming force that conditions society. It undergirds society almost invisibly, at least as long as it functions. Rather than being separate and autonomous from society, infrastructure is one with society. Produced as a "sociotechnical" assemblage, infrastructure constructs and maintains built environments, acting like "the connective tissues and circulatory systems of modernity."[15] The power of infrastructure has been central to the construction of the modern state. It has facilitated a modern "material" order. According to Chandra Mukerji, that order differs from the state's coercive characteristics insofar as it maintains control, not through its persistent threat of violence but rather through its penetration of society in the form of material infrastructures that reproduce the state through an "impersonal rule" that "can seem as inevitable as the natural order."[16] The infrastructural state, therefore, takes on an almost imperceptible palpability through the naturalization and materialization of its power and its imbrication in the practices of everyday life. The state manifests itself in materially impersonal and autonomous ways, and through that peculiar manifestation seems to be everywhere at once and nowhere in particular. The modern state, therefore, is one that relies on its own materiality.

In the decades from 1870 to 1910, infrastructural power seemed to be expanding everywhere. In Latin America, public works projects abounded: railroad networks, streetcars, waterworks, sewer systems and drainage projects, port building and expanding, and so on. Total railroad track built was greater than in any other forty-year period.[17] Public works budgets exploded, and the very administrations in charge of those projects came into being, quickly becoming some of the leaders in state expenditures.[18] Those railroad networks fortified the power of emerging states across Latin America, shrinking the travel distances between nation-states' capitals and their outer edges from weeks to hours. This helped end the era of civil wars and revolts, as illustrated in Argentina in 1874 when 2,600 soldiers were sent to Córdoba and arrived in one day to put down one such revolt.[19] Global powers such as France and Britain relied on infrastructural projects and expertise to spread their empires to all corners of the world.[20] Of course, as much as infrastructure extended state power, it created new problems.

Cholera outbreaks, for example, required state power in inspecting passengers during epidemics to minimize outbreaks across the increasingly well-connected nation, thus accelerating the dynamic between material change and expansion of state power.[21] By the turn of the century, as state power increasingly flowed through infrastructural networks, those networks became the site for political conflict. Railroad networks became grounds for labor action, such as strikes and sabotages, which were enormously effective in winning workers economic and political rights (as well as giving the state a greater role in mediating social conflict).[22] At the heart of this infrastructural power were the engineers who designed, promoted, built, and maintained these systems. Their privileged place in this new global order would elevate them above the stink of partisan politics and earn them a deceptively neutral place, giving rise to technopolitics, or "the kinds social and political practice that produce simultaneously the powers of science and the powers of modern states."[23] By the middle of the twentieth century in Latin America (and elsewhere) national and international struggles, such as the Cold War, "raised the stakes of expert knowledge," including the infrastructural systems that underpinned modern state power.[24]

The technopolitical order of the mid-twentieth century owed part of its existence to the thousands of Nicolás Naranjos of the previous century. Their role as engineers was to disrupt state power and open up new spaces of contestation as much as it was to bring the eventual closure of them through infrastructural power and the nation-state's increasingly visible materiality. As important as that state materiality and the place of the engineer in constructing it were, understanding the power of infrastructure in a region such as the Trans-Andean requires an examination of the social conflicts that preceded it and how states responded to them. The next chapter explores the history of how the Trans-Andean came to be subdued by state power on both sides of the mountains.

# 5 Killing the Trans-Andean

They came out with shotguns drawn and ordered the riders to dismount and surrender their weapons. The ringleader, Casimiro Ferrari, hung back, toting a double-barrel shotgun. As the highwaymen walked their captives down the road, several more came out to join them. They forced the captives off the mountain road that led to Chile and corralled them along the gorge's edge. As they removed the victims' watches and silver spurs, one of Ferrari's men began to tie them up. They berated their captives, accusing one of being "the reason that they were exiled in Chile and suffering so many losses."[1] Reading the writing on the wall, one of the captives, Tomás Jameson, leaped up and grabbed one of the shotguns on the ground. He aimed and pulled the trigger, but the gun would not fire. Someone charged him and grabbed the shotgun by the barrel. The two men struggled, but Jameson managed to throw his assailant down toward the river. He looked around and realized there was only one way out. So he jumped, plunging into the cold, springtime mountain river.[2]

Jameson survived his escape. As he floated down the river, Ferrari's gang attempted to cut him off. Frightened, Jameson needed to get out of the river, and after fighting the current, he managed to reach the opposite bank. Still attempting to impede his escape, the gang began throwing rocks down at him and shooting. Jameson threw himself back into the river, which whisked him far enough downstream to force Ferrari and his gang to break off their pursuit. Sensing that the current had delivered him from his captors, he wrested himself from the river. On the banks, distressed and soaked, he was overcome by exhaustion and fell asleep. Two hours later Jameson awoke and walked more than ten kilometers before coming across a group of muleteers, who were on their way to Argentina.[3]

Jameson's companions were not so lucky. The muleteers who found him had already stumbled across the murder scene. The group's leader, Pedro Antonio Espinosa, later testified that they had seen Ferrari and his men crossing into Argentina from Chile two days before the attack. On the day of the assault, 3 December 1869, Espinosa later told the guard at Uspallata that he had seen the same men returning to Chile. They must have just missed the attack, because not long after seeing Ferrari and his gang going back to Chile, they spotted a piece of leather off to the side of the road. One of Espinosa's peons, Juan José Gomes, went to inspect it. The scene that he found just beyond the leather was gruesome. There were two dead bodies covered in blood. One of the deceased had his "brains blown out." By the looks of them, they had faced their demise not long before Gomes discovered them.[4] Jameson's young hired hand witnessed some of the bloodshed. During the assault, he managed to untie his hands and, taking Jameson's lead, threw himself into the river, but not before he watched the gang shoot his uncle in the chest and head.[5] The other hired hand, Miguel Morales, faced a similar fate. One of the men struck his hand with an ax and then hacked his "head to bits." Jameson's friend Marco Antonio Bravo, another merchant from Argentina and the son of Desiderio Bravo, was also killed, his corpse thrown into the river, where it was later discovered facedown and half-submerged along the banks.[6] That was the scene that Gomes had discovered.

The murders appeared to be a robbery gone wrong. After things settled down, Espinosa and his men rounded up what was left at the scene. Ferrari's gang stole some items: they took the animals and mounts, along with some clothes and other travel effects. Yet the most valuable goods stayed in the mountains. Jameson had a considerable amount of silver with him when he was attacked, perhaps 20,000 pesos' worth.[7] Apparently, the gang attempted to take the silver but abandoned it farther down the road.[8] Perhaps the silver was more than Ferrari and his men had been expecting, and Jameson's unanticipated escape forced them to make a quick escape. Perhaps the target of the attack was not the silver but the men themselves.

Whatever the reasons for the murders, the case became one of international importance, setting off a monthslong extradition process. Beyond its diplomatic implications, the case involved high stakes. The fear sparked by the gruesome attacks on merchants threatened one of the main passes of the Trans-Andean commercial system. Underneath the case, too, lurked the specter of political rebellion—Ferrari and others had been rebels in the Revolución de los Colorados (see chapter 4). In a sense, this murder case embodied many Trans-Andean developments of the preceding decades: the construction of a space of commercial development and the unforeseen political and social consequences of that development, particularly challenging to liberal state building in Argentina. The case also signaled the beginning of a closure—partial, as all are—to the social and political challenges posed by the Trans-Andean throughout the preceding years. This onset of closure occurred through an erasure and criminalization of the sociopolitical stakes of commercial development in the region; a political neutralization of those developments and their agents, merchants; and most important, a construction of an assemblage of state institutions across the border meant to facilitate these processes of erasure and neutralization.

This final chapter highlights the role of the Trans-Andean in the construction of national policy and institutions in Argentina, as well as how the construction of binational governance on the border was based less in the partisan stakes of civil conflict in Argentina than in the material stakes of the region. It illustrates how foreign policy crafted to deal with outlaw rebels was developed not in the capital but rather in the Trans-Andean through the interaction of local and provincial governments in concert with officials charged with foreign policy in the region, such as the consulates and foreign ministry representatives. At the same time, this chapter shows how the stakes of this foreign policy revolved around deemphasizing the role of merchants in rebellion, turning the explanatory lens away from partisan stakes of political conflict. Ultimately, these contributions emerge out of this book's central understanding of borderlands and transnational spaces as the spatial expression of the unevenness between capitalism and territorial state formation. That unevenness, illustrated here, compelled new institutional arrangements that signaled the closure, however temporary and incomplete, of the Trans-Andean.

### "El italiano Ferrari"

News of the attack spread throughout the mountain in the following days. As Jameson was recovering from his near-death escape, two travelers named Pedro García and Manuel Betoño found him with Espinosa and offered assistance. Jameson told García and Betoño about the attack. He told them how he was ambushed and escaped. There were seven attackers, Jameson recalled: "One of them was a foreigner."[9] Tomás Jameson himself was a foreigner. Born in Ecuador, he was the son of the Scottish botanist William Jameson. At least seven years before the attack, Tomás left his home in Ecuador for Argentina. He was following his older brother, Guillermo, who was living in San Juan. Apparently, Guillermo was well connected in San Juan, which Tomás could use to establish himself.[10] Tomás's ambitions, however, were to create his own pot of wealth. In that respect, he did well for himself. Beginning as many aspiring merchants did, Tomás got involved in the cattle trade.[11] Through this activity and his brother's connections in Chile, he contacted merchants in Valparaíso, including Emilio Moyano, a close friend of his brother.[12] By 1869 Tomás had established commercial partnerships in the region, which his brother estimated would yield him great profits once finished.[13] In fact, when Tomás was attacked, he likely was going to Valparaíso to import goods into Argentina from Chile.[14] "One of them was a foreigner."[15] Jameson never gave a name, not even in Chile when he gave his testimony to the judge in San Felipe, but he knew that the attacker was foreign; that much he could tell by his accent.[16] After telling García and Betoño his story, he was taken over the mountains to Chile, leaving the two travelers to tell others about it. From there, word spread quickly.

On their way to the small mountain outpost of Uspallata, García and Betoño told at least three others in the mountains about the attack. In Chile at Guardia Vieja, one of the first outposts on the Chilean side of the summit, another person heard about the attack from Pepe León, who ran the outpost and must have learned of the attack when Jameson was being brought into Chile.[17] These mountain crossers, ten in total, including García, Betoño, and Espinosa, became the eyes and ears of a state investigation that would culminate in an international case to extradite the suspected attackers.

When García and Betoño arrived at Uspallata, they informed the guard about what Jameson had told them. They also shaped the tenor of the investigation that would follow; they not only brought Jameson's account of the story but added important details. They buttressed his observation that one of the attackers had a foreign accent by adding that the foreigner was "el italiano Ferrari." In their ascent of the Andes from Chile, they had recognized Ferrari descending into Chile, armed.[18] Jameson, however, did not recognize Ferrari. In his testimony in Chile three days after the attack, Jameson described what he could of his captors. Two of them, he later recalled to the judge, were not Chilean. He could not make a definitive judgment on where the first was from, but the second, who stayed back toting a double-barrel shotgun, was definitely either French or Italian; he could tell from the accent, he told the judge.[19] Apparently, two decades of living in Argentina had not washed away the Italian accent from Casimiro Ferrari's voice. After moving to Argentina in the 1830s, Ferrari settled in Mendoza likely in 1856. He wasted little time in becoming intimately acquainted with provincial social life, marrying Máxima Vargas in September 1857, only a year after his arrival.[20] In December 1857, Ferrari became an official in the provincial government, being named the administrator of the San Antonio Hospital.[21] The appointment could not have come at a more opportune time; Vargas was three months' pregnant with their daughter, Juana Guillerma.[22] If by the late 1850s his family and administrative career had helped Ferrari establish himself in Mendoza, the following years would uproot him from the province, both politically and literally.

In 1861, Ferrari began his descent into isolation and exile, one that in many ways paralleled the fate of the Federalists. It was April when the seismic shifts in Ferrari's life and the Federalists' fate in Mendoza erupted. Fewer than ten kilometers from the city an earthquake struck, razing almost the entire city to the ground, setting off fires, and leaving thousands dead or dying.[23] It is likely that both Máxima and Juana Guillerma survived the disaster, but Ferrari's attempts to rebuild their life in Mendoza afterward were frustrated at every turn.[24] Later in the year, as the city was being rebuilt, Ferrari filed a civil suit against the Masonic Society, which had been sending relief aid to Mendoza from Buenos Aires. He accused representatives of the society, of which he was a member, of refusing to distribute aid to him and of keeping it among "the people most connected to [them]."[25] For Ferrari, the case concerned not only his own interests but also those of society at large. In his deposition, Ferrari argued, "It is out of the question that a situation like this, aside from bringing unspeakable losses to a country so pained by misfortune, indicates the disastrous pattern that in the country there has been nothing but tribes of corrupt men."[26] In addition to being corrupt in their distribution of aid, Masonic Society members in charge of relief funds used their positions, Ferrari argued, to exert "a contemptible and mean pressure to ensure the new city be brought to where they possess property."[27] Ferrari's indictment of the corruptive influence of those who held power over the distribution of relief aid in the wake of a tragedy reflected a deep suspiciousness on his part. His charge against corruption, however, was unsuccessful. Unmoved by Ferrari's argument, the judge in the case ruled in favor of the Masonic Society, considering the matter to be of a purely private nature.[28] Ferrari's string of bad luck did not end there. In December 1861, liberals in the province overthrew the Federalist governor under whom Ferrari had served, marking the beginning of liberal rule in the province. By January 1862, there was a newly elected provincial government. Once formed, it decreed the exile of those people, particularly important members of the deposed government, whose presence in the province posed the risk of "perpetuating instability in the Province."[29] Ferrari was among those exiled, and although he was legally allowed to return to the province after a year, he remained relatively quiet for almost five years.

It is unclear whether Ferrari returned to the province in the first few years after his exile, but his return to Mendoza in late 1866 solidified both his fate as a mountain exile and his reputation as a dangerous rebel. The revolution in Mendoza that began in November 1866 catapulted Ferrari to a position of power once again. By December 1866, he took up the title of *comandante* (commander) in Tupungato, not far from San Carlos in the Uco Valley, the center of the Chilean community in Argentina.[30] He likely stayed in the province for the duration of the rebellion, commanding forces and eventually serving as military secretary.[31] During his time as comandante, he established relationships that became important in his second exile after the rebellion was quelled. When he returned to exile in Chile, he became acquainted with the officials at the mountain government outpost there. They referred to him as "el comandante Ferrari" and knew him as a frequent traveler of the mountains, always accompanied by his peon, Tadeo Pavez.[32] Pavez was not merely some hired hand but rather a former soldier in the rebel army. Whether Pavez joined voluntarily or was conscripted into the rebel forces is not known, but by March 1867 he apparently wanted out. During the rebellion, the Chilean consulate in Mendoza sent a letter to the rebel commanders regarding a list of "Chileans" serving in the rebel ranks.[33] The list included Pavez and a peon who before the rebellion was facing a possible death sentence for stealing transport animals and likely had escaped that fate by joining the rebel forces.[34] The consulate demanded their release from service because the treaty between Chile and Argentina prohibited the conscription of foreign nationals.[35] When the note came to Ferrari, his response was curt: "In the Squadron under my command, there exist no Chileans."[36] Whatever he meant by this blunt statement, Ferrari's service during the rebellion, as well as his prior exile, likely facilitated the social connections that would define his life after rebellion, as well as his status as comandante in the rebellion that followed him into the mountains. That reputation came to define the investigation into the attacks in the mountains.

Ferrari's reputation as a rebel commander and his refashioning of rebel personnel into a group of mountain marauders did not go unnoticed by the witnesses who gave testimony at Uspallata. After García and Betoño said that they had recognized Ferrari and others escaping back into Chile, Betoño told the guard, or perhaps reminded him, that Ferrari was a rebel from the "revolution of November," a reference to the Revolución de los Colorados.[37] It is uncertain the extent to which Betoño's invocation of Ferrari and the rebellion influenced how the guard at Uspallata questioned the witnesses who followed García and Betoño, but many of them told a similar story. They recounted how, too, they had seen Ferrari and others descending back into Chile in the immediate aftermath of the attack, armed and acting in suspicious ways. Many of them knew who Ferrari was, even if they had not seen him in a long time. According to witnesses, the other men with Ferrari were also known and feared in those parts, including Domingo Pastén, who had a history of attacking mountain crossers and robbing them.[38] If Ferrari was a known rebel, these other men were known bandits, and that triangulation among the murders, rebellion, and banditry became a common theme as the news spread among government officials in the region.

As word of the murders spread beyond the mountain passes, government officials in both Mendoza and San Juan began their criminal investigations, which highlighted not only the brutal nature of the crime but also the linkages among the murders, rebellion, and banditry implicit in the case. After interviewing travelers in the days following the murders, the guard at Uspallata, Cicerón Lemos, had collected enough information to satisfy him and informed his superiors in Mendoza and San Juan of the "horrible murder[s]" committed in the mountains.[39] In his note to San Juan, Lemos noted that three of the murderers—Ferrari, Pastén, and another man, Tomás Farías—were participants in the Revolución de los Colorados.[40] Witnesses, however, had identified only Ferrari as a rebel, accusing his accomplices of being criminals.[41] Nevertheless, word reached the provincial government in San Juan, which began inquiries into the matter, calling up witnesses and taking testimony. Only a week after the attack, the prosecutor in San Juan had heard enough; the highwaymen had not only committed a "horrible crime" but also "profoundly affected society."[42] For the prosecutor, the attack represented the intersection of the worst common criminality and the most dangerous political insubordination. On the one hand, he recommended that the government file an extradition request to the Chilean government because the treaty signed between the two nations permitted extradition for "crimes of all classes." On the other hand, the men were "famous bandits for their notorious villainy in the recent rebellion."[43] This was a refrain that had been voiced continuously in the aftermath of the rebellion: the rebels were politically dangerous and nothing more than common criminals. However, as important as that refrain had been in the region, the provincial government in Mendoza responded in a very different way.

When the government in Mendoza received news of the attacks, it began an investigation. Since Ferrari and the others had escaped to Chile, the investigation targeted other suspicious actors, including even some of the witnesses, whom the government suspected might have been involved in some way.[44] As the case dragged on, the inquiry focused on a destitute mountain crosser and his wife and the suspicious money they were throwing around in the mountains in the days after the attacks, effectively ending the Ferrari chapter of the case.[45] That chapter was left to the Argentine state representative in Chile, Félix Frías; the Chilean minister of foreign affairs; and the judges in San Felipe. Of course, Mendoza was responsible for bringing the case to the attention of those actors and initiating the process of extradition. Unlike the San Juan prosecutor's furious indictment of Ferrari and the others in his note to the provincial judge requesting extradition, the provincial government in Mendoza downplayed Ferrari's connections to rebellion. Officials there merely referred to his "notoriety" as a criminal in the mountains and surmised that the Chilean government would be more than sympathetic to assisting in the extradition of the suspects, as it, like the government in Mendoza, had a vested interest in keeping the mountains safe.[46] From that moment forward, references to Ferrari as a rebel all but disappeared. The provincial government's erasure of Ferrari's political rebelliousness reflected a decade-long struggle to depoliticize rebellion and criminalize rebels in the region. At the same time, depoliticization and criminalization of rebel politics such as Ferrari's demanded binational cooperation and communication, something mostly absent from state institutions across the Trans-Andean at the beginning of the decade.

## Rebellious Mobility and the Problem of Information

Almost immediately after Casimiro Ferrari and others were first exiled from the province in 1862, the provincial government and the Argentine consulate general in Chile, then headed up by Gregorio Beéche, kept tabs on their whereabouts.[47] As Beéche relayed news of their movements to the governor, he speculated that ultimately their goal was "to mount a campaign against Mendoza," stoking the fears of the new provincial government.[48] To neutralize

*Killing the Trans-Andean*

the threat, Beéche began petitioning the minister of foreign affairs in Chile, Manuel Alcalde, for the extradition of some of the most notable exiles.[49] Alcalde, though sympathetic to the severity of the accusations against the exiles, rejected the request for extradition, citing the need for documentation that proved the claims.[50] Beéche, frustrated by the Chileans' response, informed both the national government and the governor in Mendoza of the problems he was facing in Chile.[51] Beéche would become increasingly familiar with this frustration over the following years. Sharing in that frustration, and indeed learning from it, was the provincial government in Mendoza.

Frustrations about diplomatic requests were only compounded by the uncertainties surrounding the legitimacy of the new political order in Argentina. Ferrari and other exiles had hardly been in Chile a month when local Chilean officials in Santa Rosa de Los Andes, right over the border from Mendoza, detained a shipment of arms meant for the exiled former governor of Mendoza, Laureano Nazar. The government in Mendoza attempted to send its own officials to Chile to retrieve the arms.[52] Officials in Los Andes, however, demurred, citing the lack of authority that the province had to order such a diplomatic mission. According to them, there was no legitimate government in the province because of the uncertainties that civil war had provoked about state legitimacy in Argentina.[53] Problems of legitimacy were pervasive, even on the Argentine side of things. In his messages to the Chilean Ministry of Foreign Affairs throughout the initial months and years after the Federalist exodus, Beéche overcompensated for anxieties about legitimacy and its effect on establishing authority in the region by frequently reiterating, as he insisted in one letter, "There are no political parties in arms in the Argentine Republic, nor causes that justify them and the plots on the part of individuals who reside in Chile cannot be considered but common crimes."[54] For Beéche, then, the exiles were mere criminals who should not enjoy the rights of *political* exiles in Chile. Denying rebels their political legitimacy and the rights that came with it meant criminalizing them and erasing their political pasts, much in the way Mendoza did to Ferrari several years later.

Beéche continued to find his efforts to contain the Federalist exiles stifled by demands for documentation. As he warned the governor in Mendoza about the secret trips that the exiles had been making to the province, he asked Alcalde to assist in containing the exiles and preventing them from congregating at the border, arguing that they were abusing the hospitality of the Chileans.[55] It was a strategy that Beéche had communicated already to the national government in Argentina; if they could not extradite the exiles at that time, they would ask the Chileans to keep tabs on them, so that if and when documents for extradition became available, they would know where they were.[56] Alcalde once again sympathized with Beéche's predicament but reiterated the need for documentation proving the invasion plans of the exiles. He reminded Beéche that although the Chileans wanted to help, they had a duty to their constitution, which, he told Beéche, "guarantees to its inhabitants the freedom to remain in any part of its territory and that nobody can be imprisoned, detained or exiled but in the ways determined by law."[57] In accordance with those laws, Alcalde continued, the government would need to have "documents that will serve as a basis for criminal investigations and that prove the crime of which the emigrants are being accused."[58] The problem of documentation, as Beéche would learn, was also one of distance: receiving instructions and necessary documentation from the national government in Buenos Aires could take months.

That problem of distance conditioned foreign policy in those years. Although the Argentine national government in Buenos Aires was responsible for setting foreign policy, early on the provincial government in Mendoza and the Argentine consulate general often formulated foreign policy apart from the national government. For example, before the invasion of 1863, between January and May 1862, Beéche sent several messages to the minister of foreign affairs in Buenos Aires, communicating to him the movements of the exiles and the difficulties that he was experiencing with the Chilean government in extraditing them.[59] By the time the national government formulated a response to those messages in August 1862, the minister, while encouraging Beéche to continue his surveillance of the exiles, urged him not to worry too much about them.[60] Three months later, not necessarily knowing the national government's response, the provincial government in Mendoza countered the national government's lack of urgency, warning Beéche about rebel invasion plans.[61] The national government, however, was uncomfortable with the emerging relationship between Mendoza and the consulate general in Chile. When it learned that Mendoza had communicated its fears about the rebels' invasion in November 1862 directly to Beéche, it responded to both the governor and Beéche that the provincial governments were not to communicate with the consulates in Chile, unless on matters of urgent importance.[62] Despite these warnings, the two continued to communicate and influence foreign policy. It made sense, too. Even under the best of circumstances mail between the consulate general and the Foreign Affairs Ministry could take nearly a month to arrive, and from the provincial government in Mendoza it was two to three weeks to the national capital, meaning that setting policy could take months.[63] Meanwhile, mail between the consulate general and the provincial government took only about a week.[64] In the context of rebel threats and continued political instability, it made sense that neither the consulate general nor the provincial government wanted to wait for national policy to be dictated from Buenos Aires.

As Ferrari fled back to Chile in 1869 through the same pass that carried state correspondence between the two countries, the Chilean Congress was busy taking up the terms of a new extradition treaty between the two countries, a treaty meant, at least from the Argentine perspective, to stop rebels like him. Indeed, when the Ministry of Foreign Affairs in Argentina sent instructions to Félix Frías, who was negotiating the treaty on behalf of the government, it included the need "to introduce in said treaty an article, in which both [governments] are obligated to disarm and remove from their respective borders all political exiles, with the goal of impeding them from conspiring against the government."[65] Although Frías would have recognized the importance of the goal, he would also have understood the delicacy with which *political* crimes had been treated up to that point. The previous treaty had made specific exceptions for exiles accused of political crimes.[66] As a result, his predecessor, Gregorio Beéche, had labored tirelessly to uncouple the relationship between the Argentine exiles in Chile and their political projects, making them out to be common criminals much in the way the government in Mendoza did when sending its extradition recommendation for Ferrari. In effect, if the goal was to attack the rebels, Frías needed to moderate any suggestion that these figures or their crimes were in any way related to politics.[67]

To depoliticize the political crimes of political exiles, Frías developed an important phrasing of criminality, one that would broaden the crimes worthy of extradition. The phrasing was "asociación de malhechores y salteo" (criminal organization and banditry).[68] As Frías informed the minister in Buenos Aires, the phrase "is designated for the wicked men who in gangs would be able to cross the cordillera to steal and rob defenseless families, and who think themselves capable of making off with the fruit of their depredations."[69] Frías thought that such a phrase in the treaty would allow the government "to ask for the handing over of wicked men, like [Felipe] Varela; and the threat communicated against them in this pact would probably be enough to contain such wicked men."[70] In one confidential letter, he told the minister that Varela and the other rebels "should understand that the extradition treaty is aimed at them; and that they will not be able to make use of asylum like before."[71] In effect, the purpose of the extradition treaty was to create the scaffolding to restrict their freedom in Chile and signal to them that the Chilean government would cooperate in restricting their political activities in exile.

One problem that the Argentines had been facing was that rebels moved far faster than bureaucracy and the judicial system, and therefore they needed to create shortcuts that would permit rebels to be detained in Chile while proper documentation was produced in Argentina. One article of the new extradition treaty managed to do that, creating an exemption to the need for documents in order to *detain* the suspects and hold them for up to two months while the government requesting extradition put a case together.[72] The ability for the state, therefore, to be able to respond effectively to highly mobile and light-footed rebels relied to a certain extent on the suspension or at least softening of the very rights that the Chileans had invoked at the beginning of the decade. Of course, the ability for the liberal state to suspend liberal rights was a clear contradiction within the construction of liberal constitutional governance, broadly speaking, and it became the article that caused the most opposition to the passage of the treaty in the Chilean Congress.[73] Nevertheless, the treaty passed, including that article.

The lethargy of the state was addressed not only through tempering the obstacle of rights but also through the standardizing of the paths through which extradition requests would be made under the new treaty. After the treaty went into effect in 1870, the Argentine consulate general in Chile sent copies of the treaty and instructions for its implementation to all the consulates across the country. Embedded in those instructions was the standardization of the movement of information and the requesting of extradition. According to the instructions, state officials in Argentina—including provincial governments and judges—were to make extradition requests either to the consulate general or to the individual consulates across Chile. In cases in which one of the consulates received the request, the consulate was to relay the request, by telegraph, to the consulate general, which in turn would relay the request to the Chilean state. The Chilean state then was to order the arrest of the suspect by the relevant local authorities. In the event that the consulates judged that the flight risk of the suspect to another country was great, they were authorized to petition the local authorities directly for the immediate arrest of the suspect.[74] The standardization of these paths was not necessarily novel, and their effectiveness would take some time to gauge. Initially, the paths laid out were seemingly inefficient—provincial governments to consulates to consulate general to central state to local authorities. Efficiency at the level of state production, however, was far more about predictability and legitimacy than directness. Frías understood well the need for extradition requests to obey these hierarchies, remarking at one point during the negotiations that while provincial governments *could* request extradition, they would not, since if "requested by the provincial governments [extradition] could appear influenced more by partisan passions than by the desire to protect justice."[75] In other words, by their very nature, provincial governments could seem petty and partisan. Extradition, Frías thought, required a subordination of the provincial governments to the perceived political neutrality of the national government and its diplomatic representatives in Chile.

Unfortunately for the Argentine government, the new treaty could not be applied to the case. As Frías pointed out to the minister of foreign affairs, the crime took place before the new treaty had been approved in both countries, meaning that the case was still being prosecuted under the terms of the old treaty.[76] Nevertheless, Frías had been using the Ferrari case to hasten the passage of the treaty in the National Congress of Chile, where it was being held up despite having passed in Argentina in October 1869.[77] From the beginning of the case, he repeatedly told the Chilean minister of foreign affairs that the case demonstrated the need for the Chilean legislature to pass the treaty, which it did, but not until 1870.[78] Although the treaty could not be applied to the Ferrari case, the case and the treaty together signaled a further criminalization and depoliticization of rebels in the Trans-Andean and the solidification of binational Trans-Andean governance.

### "Security of Their Persons and Property"

As the government in Mendoza downplayed and even erased the political side of Casimiro Ferrari and his rebel past, it elevated and focused on a different aspect of the case: the threat to the Trans-Andean as a commercial space. Different from the initial notes that had emphasized the connections between the attack and political rebellion, when the governor sent a message to the Argentine foreign minister in Chile explaining the case to him, he warned the foreign minister, "The impunity of those crimes in this moment would give rise to the perpetration of new crimes, which would leave exposed the numerous travelers who circulate daily on that road."[79] The importance of those "travelers" and their safety could not be understated, according to the governor; their "security" was "indispensable" for commerce between the two countries, and without it the nations' mutual commerce would suffer "the most notable harm."[80] The following day, on 10 December, the provincial government sent another message about the attack to the Chilean consulate in Mendoza. Along with the copies of the testimonies taken in the mountains, he reminded the consulate of the importance of "commercial development" between the two countries, "for which the security of its means of communication is indispensable."[81] The government in Mendoza thus changed the stakes of the case from stopping rebels to the shared commercial interests between the two countries and the necessity for security in the mountains to ensure those interests.

As the case proceeded into the sphere of international relations, the issue of commerce became the common point of agreement between the two national governments. Félix Frías, the Argentine representative in Chile, sent a series of official extradition requests to the minister of foreign affairs of Chile. In his requests, he emphasized the terrible and brutal nature of the crime, but he did not neglect the case's greater importance. Frías reminded the foreign minister in Chile of the importance of the mountains, which "provide for the circulation of commerce between both countries."[82] It was not just him, either, he told the minister, but also the governor of Mendoza who wanted the mountain roads to "remain secure from such bandits" because "attacks of this kind would arouse so much more terror in travelers given that those places, already inhospitable, are often found unprotected."[83] The foreign minister of Chile assured Frías of his government's commitment to bringing swift justice to the case, especially considering the importance of "giving the traders through the Cordillera every kind of security in their persons and property."[84]

The Trans-Andean was therefore representative of years of international struggles over the shape and content of liberalized commerce and international relations between the two countries, which had begun to solidify by the late 1860s. Within that emerging commercial order, merchants occupied a key place not just in trade but also in the development of basic state functions. Nowhere was this more important than in the realm of circulating information. Despite attempts in the 1820s to establish regular mail service across the mountains and the existence of state mail carriers in the following decades, postal service was notoriously deficient.[85] Nothing evidenced this fact more than the issue of the contraband of letters and correspondence. In 1839, for example, one merchant in Chile complained that the government was levying fines against people for taking correspondence over the mountains outside the state system. According to the merchant, the prohibition of "the admittance of private correspondence by passengers" was a problem because "for months the post office hasn't dispatched any mail for the other side of the Andes; from Buenos Aires it doesn't come, either."[86] Apparently, this practice continued for years. As Domingo Faustino Sarmiento observed in 1851, "contraband of letters" was a widespread practice, with some people carrying up to fifty letters at a time to distribute in Chile. Those contrabandists, in Sarmiento's judgment, were not bad people; they meant "no bad intention, nor wish[ed] to defraud taxes" but did it "out of habit and the wish to serve." They were, according to Sarmiento, "delicate and decent people."[87] Whatever the reason for this "contraband of letters," mountain crossers, such as merchants and muleteers, were likely central to the circulation of information across the mountains.

After attempts in the 1820s to devise a national mail system faltered, building a national mail system did not get underway in earnest until midcentury. By the 1860s, with the institutionalization of the Argentine Republic, substantial steps were made to produce a mail system that could service the entire country.[88] Despite substantial changes to the mail system in the 1860s, even state officials were uncertain about how heavily they could rely on the effectiveness of those changes. For example, in the early 1860s, Gregorio Beéche repeatedly bemoaned that he was not receiving correspondence from the governor in Mendoza. In one instance, Beéche noted that he had not received several messages from the governor and asked him to look into "the cause of the loss of those communications."[89] To supplement the questionable mail system, state officials could lean on another mail system: merchants and muleteers. Although evidence is sparse, merchants did carry official state correspondence over the mountains. Specifically, in one instance, Beéche wrote to the governor of Mendoza in reference to a message that Beéche had sent him "under the care of the merchant, Don Máximo Viera."[90] How often merchants carried state correspondence across the mountains is unclear, but Beéche's insertion of Viera comes off as unremarkable, indicating that it was likely not the first time that merchants had facilitated state communication. The role that merchants played in handling state correspondence was due not just to their skills in mobility but also to their trusted status as *political intermediaries*.

During the rebel invasion of Mendoza in 1863, the provincial government and the Chilean consulate in Mendoza were attempting to discern the character and extent of Chilean participation in the invasion. According to the government's many accusations, Chileans were accompanying the rebels in their invasion. The minister of government recommended that the consulate send a note with Benjamín Sánchez, who could ensure that it got to those Chileans.[91] Sánchez had been appointed as a Chilean consular representative in the 1860s, helping Chileans in the south of Mendoza obtain nationality papers and exempt themselves from military service (see chapter 2).[92] Since at least the 1850s, Sánchez had been in the business of trading everything from cattle to nails over the mountains between Argentina and Chile. His commercial connections were born out of a business partnership with the outfit Ovalle Hermanos out of Valparaíso. The partnership was based on the development of the cattle trade in and around San Carlos in the south of Mendoza.[93] Ovalle Hermanos also had connections to other commercial interests in Chile, including mining in the north.[94] Their expansion into Mendoza's southern frontier represented another component of Valparaíso's expansion in the region, making mining possible in northern Chile and the cattle trade in western Argentina through access to credit and capital (see chapter 1). For Sánchez, the opportunity to develop his commercial prowess on the southern frontier put him in a position not only to become an expert in mobility in the region but also to make connections to local political figures. It is impossible to know for certain, but Sánchez's ability to go between the provincial government and the rebels was likely a product of his familiarity with the rebel leader, Francisco Clavero, who served as the commander of the southern frontier in the 1850s, his trusted status as a representative of the Chilean consulate, and his deep commercial experience in the region.

Thus, for all involved the stakes of ensuring justice were high. These were merchants, after all. As Frías put it in one letter, "The circumstance of having been committed on the road most frequented by merchants of both countries, and in places where, for the same reason, it is important to offer the greatest security to travelers; the indignation produced on both sides of the Andes, once the attack was learned of; all make desirable that justice is served . . . and that those responsible might be punished."[95] Securing the primary Trans-Andean road was paramount to the continued development of the region for all sides. Crimes of this nature, in the opinion of Trans-Andean officials, represented a danger to the commercial agents who traversed these mountain passes and depended on the governments on both sides of the mountain range to protect their activities. The attack on Tomás Jameson and Marco Antonio Bravo was emblematic of a particularly acute threat. The provincial government in San Juan was attentive to the danger its merchants faced and took care to make the governor in Mendoza aware of the request that Marco Antonio's father, Desiderio Bravo, had made on hearing of his son's murder.[96] In a sense, protecting the interests of people such as Desiderio Bravo held a privileged place in the hierarchy of concerns among government officials at different levels. And yet not even three years earlier, Bravo had found himself much closer to people such as Casimiro Ferrari than to the state officials now trying to bring him justice.

Before the Revolución de los Colorados, Bravo had established himself as a prominent merchant in San Juan. In the months before the rebellion, for example, he was importing about 20 percent of all the merchandise coming from Chile into the province.[97] When the rebellion began, he was appointed *inspector de policía*, a post that put him at the center of the collection and distribution of war materials on behalf of the rebel government.[98] In that capacity he organized donations for resources, such as tobacco and tea, and opened up funds for them in the absence of donations.[99] During the rebellion, Bravo also came to be in charge of the distribution of uniforms for rebel soldiers. With the help of Carlos León, he constructed a manufacturing and distribution operation, which relied on Bravo using his position of power to expropriate textile materials from a business in San Juan.[100] When the rebel state collapsed in April 1867, Bravo found himself in a difficult position. Initially, he fled the country along with other rebels, including Casimiro Ferrari, to Chile.[101] Apparently dissatisfied with his life in exile, he returned to San Juan to face prosecution. He faced not one but two charges. The first charge levied against him was for paying customs duties to the rebel government. Authorities had filed criminal charges against merchants who paid customs duties to the rebels in San Juan and Mendoza.[102] They claimed that those merchants needed to pay back customs duties that were originally intended for the national treasury.[103] The defendants, however, Bravo among them, rebuffed the national government's arguments, claiming that it was unreasonable to expect them to pay customs duties again. By letting the rebellion take place, they claimed, the government had not done enough to protect private property. Because the government was unable to protect private property, it lost the right to force merchants to pay taxes again. In other words, the merchants were doing what they could and, feeling threatened by the new rebel government, paid customs to it. Although the Supreme Court ultimately agreed and absolved Bravo and the other merchants of the charges, Bravo still had to answer for his role in the rebellion as a state official.[104]

Shortly after being absolved of charges on paying taxes to the rebel government, Bravo again faced the judge.[105] This time, the national government charged him with rebellion for the business enterprise that he and Carlos León had created during the rebellion. The government argued that the combination of providing war materials (considered to be food, uniforms, horses, arms, and anything that contributed to "maintaining the morale and lifting the spirit" of the soldiers) and using his power as a state official to profit from the situation meant that he was guilty of rebellion.[106] In this case, the judge agreed with the prosecution's argument and sentenced Bravo to pay a fine of 1,000 pesos or face four years in exile.[107] Whether Bravo had paid the government the fine or was given clemency, by 1868, he was back to importing goods from Chile.[108] At the same time, his rebelliousness had not reduced his good standing with the government, since the governor sent a specific request to Mendoza to investigate the murder of his son.[109] How Bravo was able to claim his innocence as a taxpaying merchant by invoking fear of the very rebel state for which he worked shows the duality of merchants in the region. On the one hand, he was an agent of neutral Trans-Andean commerce. Abiding by the "natural" evolution of the Trans-Andean and the highest commercial "law" of private property, his allegiance was not to any particular party but rather to the "state" of commerce and private property. On the other hand, as a merchant he was central to the construction of the state, even a rebel one, through his distribution expertise. Bravo thus bridged two sides of the merchant—politically volatile and firmly neutral. It was a duality that also helped construct a particular form of justice vis-à-vis the crime of rebellion.

The punishment of the rebels, from soldiers to government officials, reveals how a classed system of justice helped dissolve the cross-class alliances that had defined the Trans-Andean. For many rebels, the aftermath of the rebellion meant facing justice. Soldiers found fighting in the rebel ranks were summarily conscripted into the national forces even if military officers were nervous about the preponderance of former rebel soldiers in their ranks.[110] Many commanders, including Ferrari, and leaders, such as Varela, did not wait around for the national government to show them mercy. Memories of rebel leader Ángel Peñaloza's execution in 1863 must have weighed heavy on their minds and likely affected their decision to abandon the country and return to exile in Chile, despite the unconstitutionality of the death penalty for "political crimes."[111] Even if the Supreme Court ultimately showed leniency on rebels by overturning convictions, for soldiers such as Tadeo Pavez and commanders such as Ferrari the choice to go into exile appeared more appealing than whatever awaited them in the courts or elsewhere.[112] The same, however, could not be said for Bravo and others like him.

Freedom to cross the border with the approval of the Argentine state was crucial to the livelihood of people like Bravo. Punishments for crimes against the state—sedition, rebellion, treason, counterfeiting, and falsifying official documents—ranged from exile to imprisonment.[113] Bravo avoided all this through a built-in mechanism meant to address inequalities in the justice system. Bravo's punishment was that he had to pay damages to the private interests from whom he had taken the materials to make uniforms. In addition, the prosecutor recommended one of two sentences, either exile for four years or a fine of 1,000 pesos.[114] In general, rebels faced three kinds of sentences: a fine, exile, or military service, the fate many Chilean laborers, including Pavez, had been combating.[115] Those options represented the state's need for funds and labor in the form of soldiers but also bolstered and codified the class-based differences in Trans-Andean mobility, turning rebel soldiers and commanders into the marauding "bandits" who threatened the commercial interests of the merchants who depended on that space, even if those merchants had previously been rebels. It was a space on which both state and merchants depended and produced through their reciprocal relationship in maintaining it. Merchants needed the state to sanctify their activities and privilege them, whereas the state depended on merchants to move information and, of course, fill the state coffers with trade revenue.

The recommendation for extradition crafted by Mendoza and taken up by national representatives relied heavily on this privileged relationship between commercial agents and the state. Indeed, as much as erasing Ferrari's rebel past was part of depoliticizing the Trans-Andean, so too was erasing the past rebelliousness of merchants such as Desiderio Bravo—one criminalized, the other neutralized. By March 1870, the Chilean government agreed to proceed with the case for extradition. Almost as quickly as it started, however, the case seemed to fall apart. Not even all the suspects could be extradited. Whereas Pastén and Farías were Argentine and therefore eligible for extradition, Pavez was Chilean.[116] By law, he had the right to decide whether he would be tried in Argentina or Chile. Ultimately, he chose to be tried in Chile.[117] There is no way of knowing why Pavez decided to take his chances in Chilean courts, but he likely had experience with the judicial systems on both sides of the mountains.[118] The judge in San Felipe ultimately ruled against Pavez in the case of the murders in the mountains, sentencing him to death. As for Pastén and Farías, the judge was less than convinced of their culpability. Strong alibis and their continued denial of even the slightest involvement in the case cast enough doubt for the judge to rule in their favor and deny extradition to the Argentine government.[119] In the end, nobody was extradited. Ferrari escaped capture. After being sentenced, Pavez broke out of jail. Farías and Pastén were released. It would be another two years before the Argentines would have a chance at extradition, and that time the outcome was different.

## Extradition Revisited

On 9 April 1872, Santos Guayama led about twenty-five armed men up the eastern slopes of the Andes. He and his group were headed to the mountain town of Uspallata with plans to raid it. Like Ferrari, Guayama had participated in the Revolución de los Colorados, leading Laguneros from Guanacache into battle. Afterward, Guayama continued to champion the Lagunero cause, which revolved around political autonomy and land taxes for the Huarpe descendants of the area.[120] As with other rebel causes in western Argentina, Chile played an important role in Guayama's struggle into the 1870s; arms trafficking across the mountains likely benefited him, as well as other former rebels of the Revolución de los Colorados and Indigenous polities to the south.[121] The connections between Ferrari and Guayama may have been tighter than Trans-Andean associations and a shared rebellion. Among the men with Guayama was someone with the last name Farías, perhaps the same Farías who had escaped extradition two years before.[122] Whatever the case, the two shared a place in the development of extradition processes key to forging binational governance in the late 1860s and 1870s.

The following day, 10 April, the armed party approached Uspallata, and that night they assaulted the guardhouse. On finding and briefly detaining the guard as well as merchants, travelers, and a telegraph engineer working on the final stages of the Trans-Andean telegraph, the men took the money and arms of the guardhouse, along with forty mules and twelve horses.[123] Rather than admit to banditry, however, Guayama asserted, "This money is mine like everything that belongs to the national and provincial government."[124] His claim to legitimate state authority was reflective of what anthropologist Diego Escolar has called "the lost republic of Santos Guayama," a term that helps complicate the "anti-state character" often assigned to popular rebellions of this period, demonstrating that it is best to understand Guayama and the Lagunero uprisings as part of "a local political and juridical tradition that had organized government institutions, political representation, and local state mediation in a context of the absence or difficult construction of a organized and legitimate state."[125] This kind of construction of institutions and practices not conventionally understood as part of state formation projects of this period can also be seen in different contexts. Workers in Cuyo shaped the Chilean consulate in response to struggles over the place of their labor in the region, something in which Tadeo Pavez had participated when he and others petitioned the Chilean consulate to help get them released from Ferrari's command during the revolution.

After Guayama and the others left the guardhouse, they continued across the mountains to Chile.[126] The consulate in Santa Rosa de Los Andes, just over the border from Uspallata, sent word of the attacks to Félix Frías on April 13, and the provincial governments, too, learned of the events.[127] On 15 April, the governor of San Juan sent news of the attacks to the minister of foreign affairs in Buenos Aires. En route, the message was converted into a telegram and sent from Villa María near Córdoba.[128] The telegram hastened the delivery of the news to the national government, which relayed it on 17 April to Frías in Chile.[129] Frías, however, had already received word from the consulate in Santa Rosa de Los Andes.[130] By the time the national government was receiving the governor's telegram, Frías was writing to the minister of foreign affairs in Chile, informing him of the attack.[131] As the message from the Argentine minister of foreign affairs was making its way from one side of the continent to the other, the Chilean minister of foreign affairs was using the telegraph to alert the governments of Aconcagua, Coquimbo, Colchagua, Curicó, Santiago, Talca, and Valparaíso to be on the lookout for Guayama and his accomplices.[132] Even before the telegrams went out from the Ministry of Foreign Affairs, however, posses in Chile were in pursuit of them and eight of Guayama's accomplices were arrested around the time the telegrams left Santiago.[133] Four days later, the governor of Mendoza informed the minister of the attacks, the next day he sent a summary of the case in the hope that it would serve to extradite the suspects.[134] Meanwhile in Chile, Frías was requesting extradition under the crime of "asociación de malhechores."[135] By the time Frías received the national government's letter relaying the original telegram to him, the case already had been approved for extradition.[136] Extradition over the mountains, however, had to be delayed because of the coming winter in the cordillera. Not until January 1873 would the suspects be taken over the mountains to face trial in Argentina, marking the first successful rebel extradition case between the Argentine Republic and Chile.[137]

As the mountain passes were overwhelmed by winter conditions and the suspects awaited their passage across the mountains, the governments of Chile and Argentina celebrated another Trans-Andean success. As they were waiting, on 26 July 1872, President Sarmiento sent a message to the Chilean president, Federico Errázuriz. What was different about this message, and one apparently worth celebrating, was that no merchant took the message across. Neither did the mail carriers in the mountains touch the message in any way. Instead, copper wire was the conduit for the international message. Forgetting that the Andes never were a barrier, Sarmiento declared to Errázuriz in the message that with this work the mountains would no longer "be too high of a barrier" and that the two oceans would no longer "be separated by the continent."[138] The telegraph connecting the two countries was completed that year. The brothers who helped build it, Juan and Mateo Clark, would next spearhead the project for a Trans-Andean railroad.

By 1873, suspects were being extradited across the mountains at the same time that copper cables were beginning to take information from ocean to ocean. That simultaneity represented decades of developments in commerce, political conflict, and Trans-Andean governance. Seen from a different angle, however, it was nothing exceptional. There was no transformative moment. The fluidity of historical processes did not somehow culminate in the merging of an anecdote and a few electrical pulses. As much as a treaty's enactment or a trusted merchant moving mail or even the rejection of a policy request, it was but another moment in the meandering development of the Trans-Andean, no less impermanent than the others. Indeed, Guayama continued to agitate throughout the 1870s before being assassinated in 1879, ten years after Ferrari's case began.[139]

It is easy to forget the fragility, literally and figuratively, of something like the telegraph. Technological artifacts and systems, even those that have reached the historical status of transformative, can lie fallow and rot from underuse. Even when in use, the role of such systems and artifacts cannot always be assumed to be anything more than superficial. Perhaps this is the most interesting part of the Santos Guayama case: the telegraph was used but had almost no impact on the mobility of information, at least not in terms of affecting the development of the case. While the minister in Buenos Aires did find out within days, rather than weeks, of the events, the arrests and extradition requests had already been made by the time he could have had any input. At the same time, even though the minister in Santiago sent telegrams to seven provincial governments ordering the capture of the suspects, the messages had little effect on pursuing and detaining them. And yet, information appeared to move at lightning speed. The important institutions—the ministries and consulates in Chile, the local and provincial authorities on either side of the mountains—were the same as they had been for at least a decade. Their goals—control over the region, the protection of commerce—were the same, too. Even their methods for achieving those goals, such as the extradition of rebels, were familiar. Thus, the important shift was in how those goals, methods, and actors came together in time and space to engender state control. In other words, it was an expression of a well-oiled binational state. State activity in the form of telegrams flying across the Andes was the materialization of these less tangible social and institutional processes described in this book. Infrastructure was an artifact of historical change and a factor in that change, central to the state materiality of liberalism (see interlude 4).

As important as that state materiality is, however, it may obscure more than it reveals. In other words, it may be an effect that works to obscure its social origins, leading one to substitute the centrality of the *physical*-material for that of the *social*-material. For example, the telegraph's late (and somewhat irrelevant) arrival in this chapter's narrative illustrates how the *social*-material processes undergirding the construction of information pathways across the Andes preceded the *physical*-material. At the same time, however, the demands of the physical artifacts of state building may engender changes in social relationships. This is precisely what happened in the Trans-Andean. The railroad that ended up traversing the mountains ushered in a transformation in the sociomaterial relationships governing that space. An infrastructural project such the Trans-Andean railroad, as the final interlude of this book will illustrate, marked a shift in those relationships and a marriage that would come to define the period and make global social space out of the Trans-Andean: the union of finance capital and the nation-state.

## Interlude Five

# The Unbuilt Environment and Global Space

After the extradition of Santos Guayama's accomplices and the first Trans-Andean telegram in 1872, Juan and Mateo Clark set out on a different Trans-Andean project: a railroad. It took nearly four decades to complete, and by the time it was inaugurated in 1910, Juan had died.[1] Mateo got to see his family's life project completed, an endeavor that in many ways began even before he was born. Years later, as he sat in the Institution of Civil Engineers in London in 1913 during a paper presentation on his railroad, he reflected on those early years.[2] Although many engineers had worked on the project over those four decades, perhaps no one had devoted as much time as Mateo Clark, who had been, after all, a member of the institution since 1879.[3] Even before then, he studied the mountain passes through which the train would run, through which the last rebels in western Argentina escaped, and in which Casimiro Ferrari came to be noticed almost as quickly as he was then erased from the historical record.

Perhaps unsurprisingly, the national government in Argentina had similar dreams of filling those same passes with ferrous currents to connect the two great oceans, the Atlantic and the Pacific. To that end, the legislature authorized President Sarmiento in 1872 to entertain proposals for the construction of a Trans-Andean railroad, offering some 33,000 Argentine pesos per kilometer in guarantees to concessionaires to build the railroad over the Andes.[4] Those guarantees were central to the construction of railroads because they mitigated the risks associated with building capital-intensive infrastructure projects that took years, and sometimes decades, to see returns. They attracted investors by requiring governments to assure concessionaires annually a certain percentage of costs incurred by building the railroad. In Argentina, guarantees were one of several strategies for facilitating construction during the early years of the railroad (circa 1850s–70s).[5]

Although those guarantees were by no means the only strategy for railroad construction (indeed, early construction in Argentina in the 1850s and 1860s often required local merchants to spur building and raise funds), they offer a window into the important connections between nation-states and finance capital in the emerging liberal global order. Those guarantees—not unique to Argentine public works' projects—and other construction strategies, including direct state construction, relied heavily on the state's creditworthiness. Large infrastructure projects such as railroads were much too expensive, took far too long to build, and posed too great a risk to be built by private capital alone. At the same time, states such as Argentina did not have budgets large enough to finance those projects alone.[6] And yet, both capitalists and state officials wanted them. Hence, a marriage between the nation-state and finance capital took place. The state would borrow from those finance capitalists the funds to guarantee such projects as the Trans-Andean railroad, which, in turn, would attract investment from some of the same finance capitalists. What state bonds and state guarantees did for capital was to give it perhaps some of the most secure investments one could have. The growth of those agreements between state and capital coincided with a similar growth in capital accumulation and concentration in such financial centers as London and Paris, along with the development of mechanisms to channel those stores of wealth, such as joint-stock banks.[7] In that context, state bonds and massive infrastructure projects (often backed by state bonds) were beginning to serve a central role in the development of the global financial sector. The result was the establishment of a close interdependency between nation-states and finance capital.

Despite the Argentine government's guarantees, the initial concession awarded to the Clarks in 1874 could not have come at a worse time. In 1873, on the heels of changes in monetary policy in various nations and massive financial speculation across the world, the global economy experienced a crippling financial crisis, leading to a severe depression throughout the decade. Although the Argentine economy was not hit as hard as it would be by later financial crises, lending in London slowed, leaving the Trans-Andean railroad in a financially precarious position.[8] As a result, the project lie fallow for several years. For everyone involved, waiting for financial markets to recover to the point of capitalizing the project was likely less than desirable. To remedy the problem, the government approved modifications to the original concession in 1877. One of the most important components to these modifications was an article that gave the government "the right to order the construction, by means it deems convenient, the section from Villa de Mercedes [in San Luis Province to the east] to Villa de la Paz, or to Mendoza," and in return the Clarks were obligated to buy the line after it reached San Juan.[9] Obviously, the government was concerned that the contract with the Clarks might end up serving as "an impediment" to having a railroad to Mendoza "as soon as possible."[10] The article therefore allowed the Argentine state to advance the extension of the national network without having to incur the costs of the line. For potential investors, it provided greater security for the railroad project by effectively guaranteeing that it would be built up to the Andes before any private capital was advanced.[11]

It would be another three years before the government had the resources to begin construction on the railroad. Once started, however, construction progressed relatively quickly. The Villa Mercedes–Mendoza–San Juan section of the Ferrocarril Andino (FCA), the state line covering this space, began in 1879–80, reached the province of Mendoza in August 1883, and finished in San Juan in April 1885.[12] Assisting in the line's construction was a loan provided to the national government with the help of French capital.[13] In some ways, this loan kicked off a "bonanza" of foreign loans and infrastructure building in Argentina, a trend that seemed to resonate across Latin America; the number of loans to nation-states in the region in that decade totaled roughly the same as the previous half century, and the amount of track built nearly quadrupled the existing network across the region in one decade (the greatest percentage increase in a decade).[14] That loan in 1881, made explicitly for the purposes of building infrastructure in the country, was worth £2,450,000 at 6 percent interest.[15]

Interest was and is the only reason loans exist, and yet we often forget what interest means to our modern world and what it has represented. The problem of interest, as one of capitalism's strongest defenders, economist Eugen von Böhm-Bawerk, described, was that it appeared to be a source of income that "owe[d] its existence to no personal activity of the capitalist . . . a lifeless thing producing an everlasting and inexhaustible supply of goods."[16] It was the embodiment of a system that seemed to expand and multiply wealth naturally as a function of time; and the dream it conjured up became one of sitting idly by while accumulating wealth. Wealth expansion as a function of time was precisely the problem that capitalism presented to people in its early development. Up to about the nineteenth century, it is safe to say that for the most part wealth did not seem to be *produced* at all but merely existed since growth was fairly flat for most of human history. That changed in the nineteenth century. The same economic growth produced over centuries was now being produced in decades, even years.[17] People saw and felt economic growth happening in their lifetimes, and the visibility of growth provoked new ways of seeing the world. For example, one trope for discussing the changes brought about in the nineteenth century is that of the transformation of time. Railroads, telegraphs, steamships, and other communication and transportation technologies brought about "the annihilation of space by time," in Karl Marx's famous words.[18] At the literary level, too, there seemed to be something to that concept. By the late nineteenth century, the idea of time travel came to the literary world through works such as H. G. Wells's now famous novella *The Time Machine* (1895). If the technology and science of time travel was odd, even more bizarre was the idea that by traveling in time one would be traveling to a materially different world. One would stay in place, but everything would change. For the longest time, if one wanted to travel to a different world fictionally, it would have been by traveling in space, sailing to a distant land.[19]

Similar to the transformation of geographical travel to time travel, capital saw a transformation from wealth produced geographically to wealth produced temporally. Throughout the age of sail, the conquest of the Americas, and the creation of global empires between the fifteenth and eighteenth centuries, if one wanted to change their wealth significantly, one would move (or move things) in space. Merchants bought low and sold high in part by taking goods from a place of abundance to a place of scarcity or from a place in which they could pillage to another. Finance capital was different. Whereas merchant capital produced wealth by moving things in *space*, finance capital did so by moving things in *time*, with interest as its means of conveyance.[20] Perhaps few institutions gave interest the appearance of solidity more than the nation-state with its control over wealth distribution through its capacity for public borrowing, pacification of territory, and taxation. When the state used those interest-bearing loans to support public works, it was erecting its own power materially and thus was borrowing in time from the future to build up its spaces of power in the present.

That was what the FCA built across Argentina to the base of the Andes did: it built up the national state and made it material. Having places such as Mendoza connected directly with the port of Buenos Aires meant a shift in the orientation of national space. If, as Sarmiento once said, the western Argentine provinces, particularly Mendoza and San Juan, had once "sought in Valparaíso their natural market," in the lead-up to and aftermath of the FCA's construction, the province of Mendoza became much more tightly connected to Buenos Aires and the Atlantic.[21] The wine industry revived in the final decades of the nineteenth century, and Mendoza integrated into national markets through it.[22] Along with the other major trunk lines built in the 1860s–80s in Argentina, the FCA was key to creating a national space over which the nation-state governed. But the FCA as a state-owned line was never meant to last. The article that permitted the state to build the line instead of the Clarks also demanded that they buy it on completion. In January 1887, they did. They bought the line for 12,312,000 Argentine pesos, representing 24,000 Argentine pesos per kilometer of track plus 6 percent annual interest.[23] The Clarks, for their part, were now in possession of 513 kilometers of track and a monopoly on railroad transportation in the region of Cuyo.

Almost immediately after receiving the rights to the FCA, the Clarks sold the line to a newly formed London-based railroad company, the Argentine Great Western. The company was created less than a month before the sale with the explicit purpose of purchasing the line from the Clark brothers.[24] In return, the Clarks were able to pay the government to purchase the line, plus they received additional funds destined for a number of things, chief among them £100,000 to begin construction on the Trans-Andean line (called the Transandine Railway).[25] In effect, by waiting for a decade, the Clarks were able to advance their project and begin construction on the mountain section of the Trans-Andean. That was where the story of the Trans-Andean railroad's physical construction began. Within months of having sold the FCA in Argentina, in May 1887 the Clarks finally secured a concession from the Chilean government.[26] That year, both sections of the Trans-Andean railroad, Argentine and Chilean, began.

Despite the common assumption that the technical and physical-material considerations of railroad construction represent the bulk of the construction process, railroads were never just about material construction. For capitalists, railroads were perhaps most important for their nonsensuous qualities. When the fictional Great South Central Pacific and Mexican

Railway Company was formed in the novelist Anthony Trollope's book *The Way We Live Now* (1875), the board of directors understood that their wealth "was to be made not by the construction of the railway, but by the floating of the railway shares," a reality that was muffled under the discourses of "humanity at large and of the coming harmony of nations."[27] Beyond the pages of Victorian novels (some of which were in dialogue with finance capital's peculiar temporality), railroad shares were a kind of capital that Marx referred to as "fictitious capital," which represented "claims" on "future production."[28] Shares, bonds, and debt papers were all different forms of fictitious capital, and although optimism about projects such as railroads was important, what gave fictitious capital its verisimilitude in many respects were governments, whose debt provided the foundation for sustaining a future-oriented global economy. Decades later, in the 1930s, Argentine writer Ezequiel Martínez Estrada echoed the same fictious aspects of the railroad, noting that many lines (supported by the state) did not even meet a need, running empty cars or cars full of passengers riding with state-subsidized passes. "An empty car," he remarked, "is a lie on wheels, and the people who travel inside with official passes are phantoms set in a fiction," invoking what one could only describe as the spectral railroad geographies of finance capital.[29]

Fictitious or otherwise, capital is difficult to follow in historical records. When investors in the Argentine Great Western, for example, bought and sold shares in the company, when they received their dividends, they rarely left a record of exactly where that specific money was coming from and where it was going to. Numbers have a way of obscuring truth. The investors themselves, the capitalists or the "bearers of capital," as it were, can certainly assist in the task of following the obscure serpentine path of capital to help answer questions about the place of such projects as the Argentine Great Western or the Trans-Andean railroad in the global economy. Jérôme Du Mont, for example, was an early investor in the Argentine Great Western, 1 of almost 200.[30] The owner of 250 shares of ordinary stock in 1887 (1 percent of the total 25,000 ordinary shares emitted from the initial offering), Du Mont had interests in other parts of the world. For example, he was on the board of directors of the Spes Bona Bultfontein Diamond Mining Company, which sought to conglomerate various mining groups in Griqualand West, South Africa.[31] As Du Mont's investments make clear, the place of finance capital in the emerging global economy was not just about production but also about rent speculation, from mining to transportation lanes such as railroads. In this system, the nation-state organized these rents, manifested in things like mining and railroad concessions, state guarantees, and of course the state bonds underpinning all this.

Ultimately, Du Mont ended up cashing out only a few months before the famous Baring Crisis of November 1890, a calamity emblematic of the overenthusiasm for fictitious capital, caused by the overzealousness of financial investors and the overissuance of state bonds by the Argentine government as part of the railroad "bonanza" of the 1880s, in which financial investors speculated on state guarantees made to encourage the construction of railroads and other public works projects in the country. Had Du Mont stayed on as an investor into the crisis, he might have gotten a firsthand look at how the Argentine government handled the fallout of the crisis, revoking state guarantees from lines and implementing a series of reforms meant to better regulate the railroads.[32] Among the effects of these reforms in Argentina (although one can see this trend elsewhere in Latin America and the world) was the ascension of engineers as central agents in the development and implementation of policy.[33] In particular, engineers became important to managing the relations between nation-states and capital, as they assessed concessions, freight rates, and the viability of projects not only in their technical dimensions but also in their economic and financial ones, making engineers key actors in the curious nexus of rents, financial speculation, nation-states, mining, state bonds, and railroads.[34] All in all, these developments could not avoid a partial reliance on the state, as an abstraction and as particular governments in Latin America not merely in the way that all social things in the modern era have been connected to the state but also as a source of secure investment. As that self-referential objectification of human society's productive capacities, the state was and is where fictions about social progress congealed and congeal into state bonds and other forms of fictitious capital to construct an inflated reality embodied in those material infrastructures that would and still go on to puncture those fictions periodically.

The connections reveal something else more immediate to the question of this book. In planning and building infrastructure in the Trans-Andean, the state and capital began in some ways to dismantle it. Bits and pieces of the physical environment in the Trans-Andean (in the telegraph and the railroad) were now part of social processes taking place across the world, and many lacked awareness of the others, obscured by the numbers. Physical aspects of the region now owed their existence to and promoted the existence of other railroad projects, mining projects, and financial speculation at large. In this way, the building up of environments, as with the railroad in the Trans-Andean, required a simultaneous dismantling of the connections between physical and social space, as well as subsequent dispersals of the social relationships that shaped that space across the globe. As much as infrastructure projects are a key part of the built environment, they also seem to be connected to a counterprocess, the *unbuilt* environment: a parallel process that helps understand how infrastructure could simultaneously reify the nation-state in physical space *and* disperse the social relationships undergirding that spatial production across the world, creating, in effect, global space.

In this new world, the border took on a quite different meaning. When rebels, migrants, merchants, and muleteers crossed the Argentina-Chile "border" in the 1860s, it appeared as a vague and inexact thing, more important in its implications—customs, criminal jurisdictions, and so on—than as a point located in space on the ground.[35] But with the Trans-Andean railroad, the border became measurable in the grams of material and precise monetary amounts embedded in railroad tracks: the respective states granted concessions to the constructors with state-backed guarantees for returns to be based on a precise number of kilometers of track, which required state backing derived from state bonds sold in international markets and revenues derived from taxes on international trade. Those guarantees, in turn, became the basis for attracting investors hailing from all corners of the financial world and whose interests in the projects were often less in the railroad itself than in what state-backed guarantees meant to their portfolios.[36] This chain, from the material laid in the mountains through to markets for state bonds and infrastructure shares, illustrates how the building up of spaces throughout Latin America at the turn of the century could strengthen the nation-state as material reality (embedded in rails, ports, sewage systems, and so on) and as meaningful abstraction (as an entity that bounded world geography for financial investments) while also dispersing the social production of space across the globe (from the cooks and workers in the Trans-Andean who built the railroad to investors in London to other places in the world built up in the same way as the Trans-Andean railroad), revealing that these borders were hardened first not in the imaginings of statesmen but as a material necessity. The nation-state was a financial unit and finance capital a product of the speculation made possible by the territorial nation-state.

Mediated by engineers, this relation between state and capital should provide a distinct perspective on borders, borderlands, and transnational spaces and their meaningfulness and place in global historical narratives.

Hardly just the coming together and division of varied people and polities, the modern border and the existence of transnational spaces should be understood as the manifestations of the unevenness of capitalist development and state sovereignty—not just as a disciplinary institution regulating global systems but also as the evidence of an inability to regulate that system. The modern system characterized by intensifying change must be read from places like the Trans-Andean—transnational and bifurcated by a border—as a spatiotemporal paradigm in which nation-states are not the sole unit of analysis (a trivial point by now) and transnational spaces have not been just counternational or nation-complicating spaces. Rather, this spatiotemporal paradigm demands an understanding of these national and nonnational spaces as outgrowths of a global system whose material contradictions have demanded a making of abstractions (such as the nation-state) that have required an unmaking of the contradictions' own product (transnational spaces and borderlands). The Trans-Andean is one of those places whose history is the history of its unmaking.

## Conclusion  A History of Mobility

This book has traced the history of a Trans-Andean borderland in the mid-nineteenth century through the development of trade across the mountains; Chilean migrations to the province of Mendoza; the circulation of laborers and transport animals; the movement of Argentine rebels into and out of exile; the attempts by state officials to track and control the mobility of labor migrants, itinerants, and rebels; and the various trajectories of engineers, boosters, and investors in the development of varied Trans-Andean infrastructure projects. In narrating those histories of the Trans-Andean, I have been concerned with two broad lines of inquiry. The first has involved the place of this historical space at a significant moment in the formation of Argentina. The mid-nineteenth century represents the consolidation of not just the national state in Argentina but also power at local and provincial levels. That political consolidation came on the eve of the first era of globalization, which signaled radical transformations in the country from the development of various export industries to the construction of a national railroad network to urban reforms of the capital and to the expansion of the national territory—namely, with the occupation of Patagonia through the so-called Conquest of the Desert. The contribution of this book has been to situate the Trans-Andean in this pivotal moment in Argentine history and in the process center actors, places, and processes normally underaccounted for. The second line of inquiry has been to understand mobility as a historical object of study, method, and conceptual framing in histories of borderlands, transnational spaces, and other non-state-centric geographies. The border-defying mobility of people has been at the heart of studies of those historical geographies. This book's contribution to them has been to develop methods, framings, and provocations for the problematization of mobility.

To the first line of inquiry, *In Place of Mobility* tracks the clash between the Trans-Andean as an economic borderland and state-formation processes in Argentina, examining the effect of the former on the latter. Important to the formation of the Trans-Andean were several developments in Chile: the expansion of agricultural production in the Central Valley and the mining booms in the Norte Chico. The development of those two export activities caused the accumulation and concentration of capital, the rise in demand for cattle, and the increased outmigration of people from the Central Valley. At the same time, across the Andes in Cuyo, the collapse of viticulture by the 1830s allowed for people to redirect land use and capital toward livestock. By the late 1840s and 1850s, those changes provided the conditions for the acceleration of Trans-Andean trade and the expansion of land use for cattle in Cuyo, financed partly by Chilean capital and worked by Chilean laborers. Those broad changes, well known to historians of nineteenth-century Argentina and Chile, had important effects on state formation at local, provincial, and national levels in Argentina, the subject of the bulk of the book. I have focused heavily on two often connected groups to explore those effects: laborers (often Chilean migrants) and Argentine rebels. The effects that I have explored have been primarily on the spatialization of state formation in two broad ways: the effects of migrant itinerants on provincial and local spaces of state formation and the effects of rebels on border governance.

As the rapidly changing economic situation put laborers increasingly in motion over the mountains and within places such as the province of Mendoza, they found themselves seeking out ways to adjust to their mobile lives often in manners that challenged state notions about such matters as labor and animals, developed in the decades after independence. Through their use of the Chilean consulate to evade military service, Chilean migrants (and Argentine laborers pretending to be Chilean) encouraged the consulate to appoint representatives in different parts of the provinces of Mendoza and San Juan and to issue nationality papers. Those developments not only created new institutions of power in rural areas, whose geography followed Chilean laborers' mobility, but also challenged the entrenched ideas about the connection between laborers and military service, making the mobility of Chilean laborers an important site of state formation. To put themselves in motion itinerant laborers used not only the Chilean consulate but also transport animals, particularly horses and mules. As laborers engaged in small-scale trading of those animals across Mendoza and San Juan and into Chile, they not only challenged the institution of animal property so important to the provincial state in Mendoza but also encouraged the integration of rural areas into provincial state authority in Mendoza because judges in animal theft cases had to get local officials from across the province to seek out rural people and bring them in to give testimony. In the cases of migrants and itinerants, their effect on state formation was not about large-scale shifts or revolutions but rather the quotidian conditioning of state officials to find new strategies for controlling labor or to routinely activate networks of state institutions across the province.

Conversely, Argentine rebels posed a more immediate and existential threat to the Argentine state and the provincial governments along the border with Chile than migrants and itinerants. By focusing on the financial support rebels received in Chile, this narrative has not merely expounded on the actors in those struggles but also considered the stakes of these contests, which in the case of Nicolás Naranjo appears to have been related more to the mining economy in Chile than anything else. The mobility of rebels across the mountains also provoked the new Argentine Republic throughout the 1860s to seek out ways to better control and stop those movements, especially through extradition. Those efforts involved the strengthening and regularizing of networks across the border and at different scales of government, from local and provincial authorities to consulates to officials in foreign ministries. In that way, this book has shown how rebel mobility helped strengthen important relationships not just between the two national governments but also among the various institutions that made up the network responsible for effective border governance. As such, this book has shown how rebels and their relationships with Chileans helped state officials on both sides of the mountains govern the Trans-Andean increasingly as a binational space.

Together, those histories of laborers and rebels have underscored the meaningfulness of the Trans-Andean as an economic borderland that complicated the processes of state formation occurring in mid-nineteenth-century Argentina at different levels. *In Place of Mobility* understands economic borderlands such as the Trans-Andean as spatial expressions of the tensions between capitalism and territorial state formation. Although the nation-state and capitalism have been complementary in many ways for modern history, this has not been only because of how the capitalist class has influenced and often controlled nation-state institutions. Rather, the two have been coconstitutive through their different spatial tendencies and temporalities. On the one hand, capital has a tendency toward deterritorialization, whereas nation-states have a tendency toward territorialization. On the other hand, the rapidity with which capitalism has brought disruption over time to the world has often challenged the nation-state's claim to order and stability. Between the two, capitalism and state formation have developed dialectically with each other, with capitalism's disruptive deterritorialization in time providing the nation-state with opportunities for expanding its reach in an effort to bring order and stability to this ever-changing world, which in turn has created new opportunities for capitalist disruptiveness. Economic borderlands can be understood as products of that dynamic. In the case of the Trans-Andean, expanding Pacific markets brought Cuyo into the orbit of Valparaíso and capital accumulation elsewhere in Chile. In response, local, provincial, and national state institutions in Argentina attempted to control the social and political effects of that Pacific-facing economic integration. Conceiving of borderlands in this way can help bring other borderlands, particularly of the mid-nineteenth century in Latin America and across the world, into conversation with one another to understand a key moment in global history.

For the second line of inquiry, mobility, this book has conceived of it as a way of studying the construction of historical space. Rather than centering borders, *In Place of Mobility* has centered the routes of laborers, rebels, merchants, engineers, animals, and others in space as a way to develop a historical geography not left on maps of the time. The construction of those routes and how they became interwoven has been about understanding not just space but also the histories embedded in those routes. Narrating the construction of those routes, I have sought to develop ways to study mobility as a historical object. Foundationally, I have attempted to make the social and material relationships undergirding that mobility central. How people formed social relationships and relations with their material world to put themselves in motion across the mountains and within western Argentina can tell us a lot about the meaningfulness of space and how mobility was central to conflicts over the uses and interpretations of those spaces. Although each chapter has been founded in these basic questions about mobility, chapter 3 makes the most overt attempt at demonstrating the kinds of methodologies and approaches I see as important to creating a history of mobility. In that chapter, there are several interconnected components of a history of mobility to keep in mind: institutions, social relationships, environments, and technologies. People interact with their environments to move. They require calories, water, and shelter (including clothing) at the most basic level. Of course, those needs are mediated by social relationships and expectations. As shown throughout this book, a number of relationships and expectations have conditioned how people moved to create the Trans-Andean: boss-peon relationships; exchanges among different people of horses, mules, cattle, and pasturage; expectations about criminality, laborers' place in society, and itinerancy; rebel leaders and their relationships with soldiers in terms of wages; and norms in the flow of information. As those relationships and expectations developed in space, they expressed themselves through institutions that provided the terms on which conflicts produced by those social and material relationships would take place. Importantly, they also left historical records for us to analyze.

Although nationality papers, consular registries, ministries of foreign affairs, treaties, courts, and other government organizations have provided a documentary basis for understanding how those institutions filtered the social and material relationships underpinning mobility, the most important one has been property. Property was as foundational to mobility in the production of the Trans-Andean as anything. It conditioned people's access to pastures and animals; it conditioned how people used animals, not just as means of conveyance but also objects of exchange to procure money; it conditioned the stakes of rebel mobility; and it provided the baseline for mediating all the relationships that put people into motion at this time. Property can be thought of as an institution, but I have seen it as so important to the conditioning of people's mobility in material space that I have thought it better to conceptualize it as a technology. If, to summarize Marx, technology is the mediating force between people and their environments, then it seems appropriate to consider property as a technology. In the context of this book, property not only conferred ownership over cattle, horses, mules, pastures, and all the objects involved in mobility but actively shaped their material attributes and their relations to society. Although *In Place of Mobility* has not been able to systematize property as a technology in making a history of mobility, I am convinced that property as technology must be at the heart of modern histories of mobility, broadly conceived. It brings together the social and the environmental in space and time in a way and with records as few other things can.

Last, *In Place of Mobility* has worked to inject the railroad into the history of this Trans-Andean economic borderland as one route among many, similar to the other histories contained within this book. Three different Trans-Andean railroad projects were treated throughout the course of this book: the northern route going from the Norte Chico in Chile to central Argentina and then the Atlantic; the southern route passing through the Planchón Pass to Buenos

Aires; and the one that was eventually built through the Uspallata Pass, originally intended to integrate Cuyo with Chilean markets and later part of an interoceanic railroad between Valparaíso and Buenos Aires, between the Pacific and the Atlantic. Seeing them as both the material manifestations of this Trans-Andean economic borderland and as projects that needed to attract the attention of global investors and distant nation-states, I have constructed narratives of them that have connected processes happening in the Trans-Andean to ones taking place across the world. Those Trans-Andean railroad projects were routes (or routes-in-formation) that embodied seemingly disparate histories. In a borderlands sense, then, they were not routes of conquest necessarily but rather ones that I have used to make sense of the connections between local and global without recourse to spatial hierarchies. In my conceptualization of a history of mobility, property has also been central to my understanding of the railroad as a transformative mobility technology (especially evident in interludes 3, 4, and 5). Although the railroad's physical qualities were undoubtedly important, I have centered the formation of the railroad as a piece of property, from how the railroad transformed notions of use in the mountains to the formation of railroads as concessions and bonds.

In constructing those narratives, two things have become clear. First, the histories of the railroad in this book have made clear the centrality of engineers and engineering in the transformation of geography in the second half of the nineteenth century. Engineers were fundamental to the construction of the railroad as property and to the creation of nation-states in the development of railroads not just as physical infrastructures but as entities that needed the financial support of states. Second, in conceiving of property as a mediator of physical and social worlds of mobility, I have worked to develop a conceptualization of the railroad and infrastructure generally as global space. In its construction as property, the railroad pulled together people and processes taking place across the world. Yet, as part of the Trans-Andean environment, it existed as at once in-place and out-of-place, a condition that is fundamental to understanding global space. It is a material space, not a scale. It is one route in space among many, with a narrative that can be interwoven with others in the same geography. That last point can help us understand borderlands histories beyond histories that complicate national narratives. Instead, we should see them as histories that provide us room to construct the many routes of historical narratives in space to conceptualize a spatiohistorical paradigm that is at once more grounded in space and more global in scope, inclusive of scales not as hierarchies but rather as network configurations in the production of the routes that make history and put history in motion.

# APPENDIX A
# DEMOGRAPHICS OF CHILEANS IN MENDOZA

TABLE A.1. Chileans in Mendoza by age, 1869

| PLACE | 0–5 | 6–10 | 11–15 | 16–20 | 21–30 | 31–40 | 41–50 | 51–60 | 61–70 | 71–80 | 81–90 | 91–100 | 101 | TOTAL |
|---|---|---|---|---|---|---|---|---|---|---|---|---|---|---|
| Depts. 1 and 2 | 42 | 65 | 59 | 100 | 243 | 131 | 73 | 35 | 19 | 8 | 2 | 2 | 0 | 779 |
| Guaymallén | 14 | 20 | 29 | 39 | 131 | 118 | 62 | 35 | 9 | 5 | 4 | 0 | 1 | 467 |
| Junín | 13 | 33 | 29 | 39 | 128 | 86 | 61 | 55 | 32 | 8 | 3 | 0 | 2 | 489 |
| La Paz | 1 | 7 | 6 | 7 | 27 | 19 | 8 | 6 | 3 | 0 | 0 | 0 | 0 | 84 |
| Luján | 28 | 41 | 38 | 42 | 142 | 83 | 42 | 28 | 10 | 3 | 5 | 0 | 0 | 462 |
| Maipú | 13 | 32 | 31 | 27 | 74 | 50 | 37 | 35 | 10 | 4 | 3 | 0 | 0 | 316 |
| Mendoza (Ciudad) | 18 | 45 | 47 | 78 | 237 | 147 | 59 | 15 | 8 | 6 | 4 | 0 | 0 | 664 |
| Rosario | 0 | 0 | 0 | 3 | 8 | 2 | 2 | 2 | 0 | 0 | 0 | 0 | 0 | 17 |
| San Carlos | 47 | 95 | 96 | 84 | 219 | 173 | 118 | 63 | 41 | 9 | 8 | 6 | 1 | 960 |
| San Martín | 38 | 65 | 66 | 70 | 158 | 156 | 51 | 45 | 18 | 10 | 7 | 1 | 0 | 685 |
| San Miguel del Rosario | 0 | 0 | 0 | 0 | 0 | 0 | 0 | 0 | 0 | 0 | 0 | 0 | 0 | 0 |
| San Rafael | 11 | 25 | 34 | 42 | 102 | 65 | 30 | 19 | 7 | 3 | 0 | 0 | 0 | 338 |
| San Vicente | 2 | 7 | 8 | 14 | 65 | 36 | 29 | 16 | 16 | 4 | 1 | 0 | 0 | 198 |
| Tulumaya | 0 | 0 | 0 | 0 | 10 | 5 | 4 | 2 | 2 | 1 | 0 | 0 | 0 | 24 |
| Tupungato | 50 | 56 | 42 | 65 | 123 | 83 | 48 | 37 | 19 | 9 | 9 | 0 | 0 | 541 |
| Total | 277 | 491 | 485 | 610 | 1,667 | 1,154 | 624 | 393 | 194 | 70 | 46 | 9 | 4 | 6,024 |

*Source:* Archivo General de la Nación, Buenos Aires. Data compiled with familysearch.org. Assistance in compiling data provided by Josh Wilson.

*Note:* Based on survey of individuals listed as Chilean in Mendoza from the Argentine Republic's National Census in 1869. Total Chileans here differ from official count in the published census. Additionally, because data here are based on hand counts from *libretos de censo* (census schedules) place categorizations are reflective of those schedules and do not always conform to *agrupaciones* (provincial subgeographies) in the published census. For comparisons with the published census, see Argentina, Comisión Directiva del Censo, *Primer censo de la República Argentina*, 350.

TABLE A.2. Chileans in Mendoza by gender, 1869

| PLACE | MALE | | FEMALE | | UNDISCLOSED | | TOTAL |
|---|---|---|---|---|---|---|---|
| | Number | (%) | Number | (%) | Number | (%) | |
| Depts. 1 and 2 | 537 | 68.9 | 242 | 31.1 | 0 | 0 | 779 |
| Guaymallén | 333 | 71.3 | 134 | 28.7 | 0 | 0 | 467 |
| Junín | 338 | 69.1 | 151 | 30.9 | 0 | 0 | 489 |
| La Paz | 59 | 70.2 | 25 | 29.8 | 0 | 0 | 84 |
| Luján | 302 | 65.4 | 160 | 34.6 | 0 | 0 | 462 |
| Maipú | 187 | 59.2 | 128 | 40.5 | 1 | 0.3 | 316 |
| Mendoza (Ciudad) | 440 | 66.3 | 224 | 33.7 | 0 | 0 | 664 |
| Rosario | 16 | 94.1 | 1 | 5.9 | 0 | 0 | 17 |
| San Carlos | 527 | 54.9 | 433 | 45.1 | 0 | 0 | 960 |
| San Martín | 451 | 65.8 | 234 | 34.2 | 0 | 0 | 685 |
| San Miguel del Rosario | 0 | 0 | 0 | 0 | 0 | 0 | 0 |
| San Rafael | 183 | 54.1 | 155 | 45.9 | 0 | 0 | 338 |
| San Vicente | 142 | 71.7 | 56 | 28.3 | 0 | 0 | 198 |
| Tulumaya | 19 | 79.2 | 5 | 20.8 | 0 | 0 | 24 |
| Tupungato | 331 | 61.2 | 210 | 38.8 | 0 | 0 | 541 |
| **Total** | **3,865** | **64.2** | **2,158** | **35.8** | **1** | **0.02** | **6,024** |

*Source:* Archivo General de la Nación, Buenos Aires. Data compiled with familysearch.org. Assistance in compiling data provided by Josh Wilson.

*Note:* Based on survey of individuals listed as Chilean in Mendoza from the Argentine Republic's National Census in 1869. Total Chileans here differ from official count in the published census. Additionally, because data here are based on hand counts from *libretos de censo* (census schedules) place categorizations are reflective of those schedules and do not always conform to *agrupaciones* (provincial subgeographies) in the published census. For comparisons with the published census, see Argentina, Comisión Directiva del Censo, *Primer censo de la República Argentina*, 350.

TABLE A.3. Chileans in Mendoza by occupation, 1869

| PLACE | AGRICULTOR | ARRIERO | CARPINTERO | COCINERA | COMERCIANTE | COSTURERA | HILANDERA/ TEJEDORA | LABRADOR | LAVANDERA | NO ANSWER | PEÓN/GAÑÁN JORNALERO |
|---|---|---|---|---|---|---|---|---|---|---|---|
| Depts. 1 and 2 | 1 | 22 | 9 | 16 | 11 | 79 | 13 | 20 | 14 | 150 | 310 |
| Guaymallén | 12 | 6 | 18 | 8 | 10 | 21 | 12 | 11 | 15 | 58 | 195 |
| Junín | 5 | 1 | 5 | 4 | 6 | 31 | 11 | 42 | 10 | 111 | 191 |
| La Paz | 0 | 4 | 0 | 0 | 4 | 0 | 0 | 13 | 0 | 30 | 7 |
| Luján | 0 | 6 | 9 | 9 | 2 | 23 | 10 | 17 | 14 | 139 | 154 |
| Maipú | 5 | 4 | 17 | 2 | 1 | 4 | 11 | 20 | 7 | 132 | 71 |
| Mendoza (Ciudad) | 3 | 1 | 17 | 19 | 17 | 32 | 3 | 4 | 25 | 155 | 210 |
| Rosario | 0 | 0 | 0 | 0 | 0 | 0 | 0 | 4 | 0 | 2 | 8 |
| San Carlos | 45 | 15 | 10 | 13 | 20 | 119 | 144 | 78 | 30 | 183 | 218 |
| San Martín | 10 | 10 | 10 | 6 | 6 | 6 | 24 | 30 | 4 | 269 | 246 |
| San Miguel del Rosario | 0 | 0 | 0 | 0 | 0 | 0 | 0 | 0 | 0 | 0 | 0 |
| San Rafael | 0 | 0 | 2 | 2 | 12 | 17 | 55 | 37 | 6 | 99 | 75 |
| San Vicente | 1 | 6 | 1 | 2 | 2 | 4 | 12 | 16 | 4 | 28 | 77 |
| Tulumaya | 0 | 1 | 0 | 0 | 0 | 0 | 1 | 1 | 0 | 7 | 14 |
| Tupungato | 0 | 12 | 3 | 11 | 7 | 36 | 78 | 38 | 10 | 140 | 164 |
| Total | 82 | 88 | 101 | 92 | 98 | 372 | 374 | 331 | 139 | 1,503 | 1,940 |

Source: Archivo General de la Nación, Buenos Aires. Data compiled with familysearch.org. Assistance in compiling data provided by Josh Wilson.

Note: Based on survey of individuals listed as Chilean in Mendoza from the Argentine Republic's National Census in 1869. Total Chileans here differ from official count in the published census. Additionally, because data here are based on hand counts from *libretos de censo* (census schedules) place categorizations are reflective of those schedules and do not always conform to *agrupaciones* (provincial subgeographies) in the published census. For comparisons with the published census, see Argentina, Comisión Directiva del Censo, *Primer censo de la República Argentina*, 350.

# APPENDIX B
# THEFT CASES IN MENDOZA

TABLE B.1. Cases of animal theft reviewed, 1838–1872

| MILITARY COMMISSION (Y/N) | CASE | DATE | DEFENDANT |
|---|---|---|---|
| N | O1/4 | 9/8/1838 | Juan Ocaña |
| N | M3/7 | 7/1/1839 | Santos Mesa |
| Y | R4/3 | 17/3/1839 | José Manuel Rodríguez |
| Y | R3/25 | 22/9/1843 | Cipriano Rodríguez |
| Y | P2/28 | 29/9/1843 | Mariano Pereira, Manuel Mayorga, Bautista Rojas |
| Y | C2/12 | 26/9/1843 | Agustín Cardoso |
| Y | M5/25 | 30/7/1844 | Eugenio Moreno, Mercedes Salinas |
| Y | T2/15 | 8/7/1845 | Tomás Torres |
| Y | M3/28 | 7/8/1845 | Abelino Miranda |
| Y | R1/9 | 6/9/1845 | Lorenzo Ramos |
| Y | S4/7 | 11/9/1845 | Juan Sevilla |
| Y | AHM, SMC/449/17 | 30/1/1846 | Juan Ocaña, José María Pérez |
| Y | P2/18 | 18/2/1846 | Mariano Peralta |
| Y | G4/12 | 1/4/1846 | José González |
| Y | M5/5 | 15/4/1846 | Cesario Morales |
| Y | T2/8 | 17/9/1846 | Luca Torres, José Arias |
| Y | M3/5 | 17/11/1846 | José Guzmán Medina |
| Y | S4/6 | 9/1/1847 | Juan Sevilla |
| Y | S1/22 | 15/2/1852 | Juan de Dios Salinas |
| N | B3/1 | 16/11/1852 | José Bergara |
| N | R4/25 | 11/12/1852 | Pascual Rojas, Basilio González, Francisco Monserrat |
| N | H1/25 | 5/1/1853 | Juan Antonio Hubilla |
| N | M3/6 | 28/3/1853 | Mariano Medina |
| N | M5/28 | 10/4/1853 | José Eugenio Moreno, Pedro Ferreyra |
| N | T2/4 | 27/9/1853 | José María Torres |
| N | S1/24 | 1/4/1853 | Julián Salinas |
| N | Z1/15 | 20/6/1854 | José Mercedes Zárate |
| N | G4/5 | 30/3/1855 | Vicente Gómez |
| N | T2/23 | 27/8/1855 | Melchor Troncoso |
| N | M3/10 | 6/3/1856 | Cecilio Méndez |
| N | M3/16 | 15/4/1857 | Pedro Meneses |
| N | T2/24 | 12/6/1858 | Melchor Troncoso |
| N | G1/10 | 9/11/1858 | José Gallardo, Santiago Alcaras |
| N | S4/24 | 5/2/1859 | Tadeo Silva, Juan Abarca |
| N | M3/13 | 7/9/1861 | Marín Méndez |
| N | S6/19 | 1/3/1862 | Serapio Suárez |

TABLE B.1 *(continued)*

| MILITARY COMMISSION (Y/N) | CASE | DATE | DEFENDANT |
|---|---|---|---|
| N | M1/11 | 17/5/1862 | Aniceto Maona |
| N | G4/24 | 9/3/1864 | Juan José González |
| N | Z1/17 | 25/6/1864 | José Zenteno, José Figueroa |
| N | P2/27 | 13/1/1866 | Juan de Dios Pereira |
| N | R5/9 | 7/3/1866 | Juan de Dios Romero, José Canales |
| N | N1/11 | 26/4/1866 | Miguel Navarro |
| N | S4/19 | 1/8/1867 | Juan Silva |
| N | J1/15 | 21/9/1869 | Salvador Jofre, Exequiel Guzmán, Secundino Pérez |
| N | O1/10 | 15/10/1869 | Agustín Olivera |
| N | R4/20 | 11/11/1869 | José María Rojas, Juan de Díos Arauna |
| N | L3/20 | 13/11/1869 | Francisco Lucero, Rumaldo Pérez, Manuel Rebeco |
| N | M3/15 | 31/8/1870 | Vicente Mendoza |
| N | C2/16 | 31/12/1870 | José Carmen Garrido, Andrés Garrido, Eujenio Calderón |
| N | Ch1/14 | 10/6/1872 | Carlos Chaqary |

*Source:* Archivo Histórico de Mendoza, Época Independiente, Sección Judicial Criminal and Sección Sumarios Civil y Militares.

*Note:* The cases reviewed in this table are discussed in chapter 3.

# NOTES

**Abbreviations**

AHCA  Archivo Histórico de la Cancillería Argentina, Buenos Aires
AHM   Archivo Histórico de Mendoza, Mendoza, Argentina
AHSJ  Archivo Histórico de San Juan, San Juan, Argentina
ANH   Archivo Nacional Histórico, Santiago
EI    Época Independiente
FG    Fondo Gobierno
FSL   FamilySearch Library
MREL  Fondo Ministerio de Relaciones Exteriores
SDC   Serie Diplomática y Consular
SE    Sección Exteriores
SJC   Sección Judicial Criminal
TC    Tratados y Conferencias

## Introduction

1. The history of Casimiro Ferrari and Tadeo Pavez is detailed in chapter 5.

2. Rosetti, *Informe*. See interlude 3 for more on Emilio Rosetti.

3. Marín Vicuña, *Los Hermanos Clark*, 230–32. For the history of the Trans-Andean railroad or Transandine Railway, see, Lacoste, *El Ferrocarril Trasandino*. The English name for the railroad was the Transandine Railway. For consistency with the rest of the narrative, I use the term "Trans-Andean railroad."

4. Unitarians were proponents of a centralized nation-state and early nineteenth-century liberalism. They were opponents of the Federalists, who tended to control the country from the 1830s to the early 1850s. While the term "Unitarian" continued to be used popularly into the 1860s, despite the dissolution of the party officially, I avoid the term and prefer "liberal" instead as a way to emphasize connections with the emerging order. To broaden the term beyond party politics and because of changing names, I do not capitalize it. This is an attempt as much at simplification of changing political identifiers and parties as at deemphasizing the partisan stakes and language that have dominated interpretations of the period. On the use of Unitarian in the latter part of this period, see de la Fuente, *Children of Facundo*, 25. For the history of and divides between Unitarians and Federalists, particularly in the first years of independence, see N. Shumway, *Invention of Argentina*, 47–111. For a sample of classic works on state formation in Argentina, see Halperín Donghi, *Proyecto y construcción*; Oszlak, *La formación del Estado argentino*; Rock, *State Building and Political Movements*; Adelman, *Republic of Capital*. Many histories of state formation in Argentina, this one included, are male dominated. For histories that emphasize women's roles in state formation, see Anzorena, "La participación de las mujeres"; Kerr, *Sex, Skulls, and Citizens*.

5. For a synthesis of this literature, see Sabato, *Republics of the New World*. In particular, see the bibliographies for a comprehensive list of works on this period. For the case of Argentina in particular, see Bragoni and Míguez, *Un nuevo orden político*.

6. Sabato, *Republics of the New World*, 197–99.

7. Sanders, "Vanguard of the Atlantic World," 121–24. For a recent treatment of the economic history of that era, see Kuntz Ficker, *First Export Era Revisited*.

8. Palermo, "Elite técnica y estado liberal"; Salerno, "Los ingenieros"; Lucena, "Imagining Nation, Envisioning Progress"; Safford, *Ideal of the Practical*; Guajardo Soto, *Tecnología, Estado y ferrocarriles*; Dimas, *Poisoned Eden*; Miller, *Republics of Knowledge*.

9. For an important articulation of this dynamic between deterritorialization under capitalism and territorialization under the nation-state and how it related, in the case of Patagonia, to a dual sovereignty, of capitalism and the state, see Harambour Ross, *Soberanías fronterizas*, 34. By conservative liberal order I refer to the marriage of different elite factions and the elimination of alternative political currents. For the case of Argentina and a succinct evaluation of conservative liberalism in the second half of the nineteenth century, see Darío Roldán, "La Cuestión liberal," 279.

10. I draw on David Harvey's articulation of two tripartite divisions of space: absolute, relative, and relational, as well as experienced, conceptualized, and lived. The latter three draw on Henri Lefebvre's spatial practices, representations of space, and representational spaces. Harvey, "Space as a Keyword," 281–82; Lefebvre, *Production of Space*, 33.

11. For collections of works on these spaces in different moments in history, see Bandieri, *Cruzando la cordillera*; Núñez, Sánchez, and Arenas, *Fronteras en movimiento*.

12. For an emphasis on nonimperial spaces, see Ferrari et al., "Pilgrimage, Mountain Worshiping"; Gambier, "Los grupos cazadores-recolectores." For Tawantinsuyu, see García, "Cronología de la anexión"; Garrido, "Rethinking Imperial Infrastructure"; Cornejo, "Sobre la cronología." For the Spanish Empire (not including those listed below), see Lacoste, "El arriero y el transporte terrestre"; Paz, "World Mules Made."

13. Mandrini and Ortelli, "Repensando viejos problemas"; Villalobos R., *Los pehuenches en la vida fronteriza*; Jones, "Warfare, Reorganization, and Readaptation"; Gascón, *Naturaleza e imperio*; Valenzuela-Márquez, "La cordillera de los Andes."

14. For histories that emphasize the early nineteenth century, see Conti, "Circuitos mercantiles y redes de comerciantes"; Crow, "Troubled Negotiations"; Marimán Quemenado, "La República y los Mapuche"; Zarley, "Between the *Lof* and the Liberators"; Varela and Manara, "Montoneros fronterizos." For histories that emphasize the mid-nineteenth century, see Langer, "Desarrollo económico y contrabando"; Davies Lenoble, "La resistencia de la ganadería"; Pinto Rodríguez, *La formación del Estado*; Herr, *Contested Nation*. For histories that emphasize the late nineteenth and early twentieth centuries, see Vezub, *Valentín Saygüeque*; de Jong, "Armado y desarmado"; Bello, *Nampülkafe*; Escolar, "El sueño de la razón"; Larson, *Conquest of the Desert*; Harambour Ross, *Soberanías Fronterizas*; Picone, "Legitimizing and Resisting Spatial Violence." For a broad conceptualization of Greater Trans-Andean regional history, see Bandieri, "La historia en perspectiva regional," 20–26.

15. I do not regularly use Mapuche terms such as "Wallmapu" and "Puelmapu" for geograpahy (the latter refers to the land east of the Andes, including southern Mendoza). When I do, it is as a reference to the area and not divisions between Indigenous-controlled territories and nation-states in the nineteenth century. For an understanding of Mapuche epistemology, including spatial and territorial conceptions, see, Ñanculef, *Tayiñ mapuche kimün*.

16. Escolar, "La república perdida de Santos Guayama"; Davies Lenoble, "La emergencia de los indios gauchos."

17. There is a rich bibliography of works that centered the provinces and dynamics beyond partisan conflicts. See, e.g., de la Fuente, *Children of Facundo*; Bragoni and Míguez, *Un nuevo orden político*; Escolar, "La república perdida de Santos Guayama"; Blumenthal, *Exile and Nation Formation*; Davies Lenoble, "La emergencia de los indios gauchos."

18. This book does not make direct contributions to debates on the history of Chile. However, by linking support of Argentine rebels to northern Chile, where rebellions surged in the 1850s, it points to questions surrounding the persistence of rebelliousness in Chile even though the 1860s are often seen as a period of political consolidation and the coming together of liberal and conservative factions. For those rebellions and political consolidation afterward, see Fernández Abara, *Regionalismo, liberalismo y rebelión*; Blumenthal, "Milicias y ciudadanía de residencia"; Collier, *Chile*, 249–51; Zeitlin, *Civil Wars in Chile*; Vitale, *Las guerras civiles*.

19. Torpey, *Invention of the Passport*, 5.

20. For this period, see Schvarzer and Gómez, *La primera gran empresa*; Palermo, "Del Parlamento al Ministerio de Obras Públicas"; López, *Ferrocarriles, deuda y crisis*; Fleming, *Regional Development*; Lewis, *British Railways in Argentina*; Scalabrini Ortiz, *Historia de los ferrocarriles argentinos*.

21. Lewis, *British Railways in Argentina*, 6. For track by 1900, see Argentina, Ministerio de Obras Públicas, Dirección General de Ferrocarriles, *Estadística de los ferrocarriles*, 22:396.

22. "Alternative geographies," see Bassi, *Aqueous Territory*, 204. Any strict categorization of "alternative geography" scholarship should be seen as arbitrary. However, to provide one arbitrary categorization, one can think of four different spatial foundations for these geographies: transnational, transimperial, Indigenous, and environmental. Of course, the great overlap among these geographies makes compartmentalizing them difficult, but the point here is to emphasize the foundations of studies of alternative geographies. The following is a list of examples not cited elsewhere in this introduction. For transimperial geographies, see Erbig, *Where Caciques and Mapmakers Met*; Bassi, "Beyond Compartmentalized Atlantics"; Landers, *Atlantic Creoles*; Gould, "Entangled Histories, Entangled Worlds." For transnational geographies, see Freitas, *Iguazu Falls and National Parks*; Savala, *Beyond Patriotic Phobias*; Truett, *Fugitive Landscapes*; Muller, *Cuban Émigrés and Independence*. For Indigenous geographies, see Boza, *La frontera indígena de la Gran Talamanca*; Langer, "Eastern Andean Frontier"; Escolar, *Los indios montoneros*. For environmental geographies, see Crawford, *Last Turtlemen*; Radding, *Landscapes of Power and Identity*.

23. For a compelling take on routes and territory, see Bello, *Nampülkafe*, 36–39. See also Zarley, "Rutas de poder," 115; Roller, *Amazonian Routes*, 206–9. For influential works informing my understanding of space and mobility, see Carter, *Road to Botany Bay*; Cresswell, *Place*, 62–85; Cresswell, *On the Move*, 25–56; Massey, *For Space*.

24. On the concept of lived geographies, see Núñez and Benwell, "Comprendiendo el espacio"; de Certeau, *Practice of Everyday Life*.

25. On the meaningfulness of and problems with borderlands histories' production of narrative multiplicity, I draw from Harambour Ross, "Fronteras nacionales, Estados coloniales"; Hämäläinen and Truett, "On Borderlands"; Adelman and Aron, "From Borderlands to Borders."

26. Undermining the nation-state as the analytical unit of analysis has undermined the dialectical method in at least two ways. On the one hand, dialectics is made more difficult by losing a stable social unit. On the other hand, the internal-external spatial divide has also been made difficult to sustain by transnational and borderlands critiques. For an example of the importance of dialectics and the internal-external divide in historical theories, see Cardoso, "Consumption of Dependency Theory," 12–15. In addition, Patrick Wolfe notes the centrality of this internal-external divide in his work on imperialism. Wolfe, "History and Imperialism," 389–97.

27. In particular, I draw on Carlos Sempat Assadourian's conceptualization of "economic space." See Assadourian, *El Sistema de la economía colonial*. See also Langer, "Espacios coloniales." For an application of Assadourian for understanding historical geographies beyond the "Peruvian economic space" and that speak to the Trans-Andean in particular, see Bandieri, "La noción de 'espacio económico.'" Histories of the Caribbean and Atlantic World have been influential on my thinking of economic borderlands for their emphasis on microhistorical methods within the context of such economic spaces as the Atlantic and Carribean. In particular, this has influenced how I conceive of mobility as such histories follow people in space to demonstrate the relations among economic space, contested spaces of imperial (and national) control, and people's understanding of their place within those spaces and histories. For some of the conceptualizations of "microhistories set in motion" and other mobile histories of the Caribbean and Atlantic, see Bassi, *Aqueous Territory*, 6–11; R. Scott, "Microhistory Set in Motion"; Putnam, "To Study the Fragments/Whole."

28. Though by no means an exhaustive list, a history of mid-nineteenth-century economic borderlands in Latin America would include northern Mexico, Yucatán and Belize, Nicaragua and Panama as bioceanic corridors, Talamanca, the Dominican Republic and Haiti, the broader Caribbean, the Andean heartland between Bolivia and Peru, and the Greater Trans-Andean between Argentina and Chile, which has been discussed earlier in this introduction. For some works in addition to those already cited on the Greater Trans-Andean that help reveal the place of those economic borderlands in the mid-nineteenth century, see Terrazas y Basante, "Ganado, armas y cautivos"; Torget, *Seeds of Empire*; Reséndez, *Changing National Identities*; Cerutti and González Quiroga, "Guerra y comercio"; Caso Barrera and Aliphat Fernández, "De antiguos territorios coloniales"; Dutt, "Business as Usual"; Boza, "Diplomacia, comercio y poder"; Lasso, *Erased*, 26–31; Gobat, *Empire by Invitation*; Eller, *We Dream Together*; Chambers, "From One Patria"; Langer, "Desarrollo económico y contrabando." For understanding economic borderlands, ports are fundamental. In the case of the Trans-Andean, the port of Valparaíso was central and demands that historians draw out the connections between western Argentina and the history of a Pacific world in the mid-nineteenth century. For the integration of the Pacific world in this period, see Hellyer, "West, the East, and the Insular Middle"; Igler, "Diseased Goods."

29. This notion of the railroad being the Trans-Andean made durable is drawn from Bruno Latour and his idea that "technology is society made durable." See Latour, "Technology Is Society Made Durable."

30. For the capital-surplus disposal problem as part of capitalism's tendency toward overaccumulation and overproduction, see Harvey, "Right to the City," 24–26. Broadly, I take much inspiration from Marxist geography and theories of space. See Smith, *Uneven Development*; Harvey, *Spaces of Global Capitalism*; Harvey, *Limits to Capital*, esp. 413–23; Lefebvre, *Production of Space*.

31. I draw on Chandra Mukerji's concept of "logistics," although her understanding is not particular to the nineteenth century. Mukerji, "Territorial State," 402–24. Bruno Latour has also informed my understanding of power in relation to the nonhuman world and networks.

32. I mean this in the way that space is broadly "social," and constitutive of and by both modes of production, political power, and social practices. See Lefebvre, *Production of Space*, 73; Lefebvre, "Space and State," 224–29.

33. In the case of Argentina, Juan Bautista Alberdi, the framer of the Argentine Constitution of 1853, celebrated the railroad as a panacea, writing, "The railroad innovates, reforms, and changes the most difficult things without decrees or uprisings." Alberdi, *Organización política y económica*, 48. In other contexts, the railroad has been portrayed as an agent of radical change in Latin America, such as in Gabriel García Márquez's Macondo. For the development of technology as a concept in the United States, which not infrequently centered on infrastructure and the railroad in particular, see L. Marx, *"Technology."*

34. In some ways, my examination of the railroad as the region made durable and as a globally circulating project is in dialogue with Sebastian Conrad's understanding of global history. He states, "Global historians need to remember that global connections are preceded by conditions and that it is essential to thoroughly understand these conditions before they can hope to understand the connections themselves. Exchange, in other words, may be a surface phenomenon that gives evidence of the basic structural transformations that made the exchange possible in the first place." Conrad, *What Is Global History?*, 69–70.

35. Though by no means a strict methodology, this dynamic reflects a larger method present but never explicitly explained throughout the book. It relies on the objectification of mobility and subjecting it to dialectics, which sets up the analysis of an internal contradiction, between mobility's existence in itself (that is to say as transportation, pure movement, or a change in location) and how that existence became socially recognized (through property, work, and nationality papers, etc.). Again, this is more of a useful framework than a strict method for thinking about how to write a history of mobility.

36. Salvatore, *Wandering Paysanos*, 426–27.

## Chapter 1

1. García, "Cronología de la anexión," 2; García, "Intensificación económica y complejidad," 163.

2. Fifer, "Andes Crossing," 36; Ots, Cahiza, and Gascón, "Articulaciones del corredor," 88–89.

3. Assadourian, *Sistema de la economía colonial*; Moutoukias, "Power, Corruption, and Commerce."

4. On the negotiated and transimperial construction of the Río de la Plata in this period, see Prado, *Edge of Empire*.

5. Lacoste, "Viticultura y política internacional," 173.

6. For those different connections, see Lacoste, "Carretas y transporte terrestre"; Lacoste, "El tropero y el origen"; Lacoste, "El arriero y el transporte terrestre"; Valenzuela-Márquez, "La cordillera de los Andes"; Molina, "Circuitos mercantiles."

7. For postindependence political systems and experimentation, see N. Shumway, *Invention of Argentina*, 81–111; Crow, "Troubled Negotiations"; Marimán Quemenado, "La República y los Mapuche."

8. For the rise and establishment of Rosas and Federalism in the country, see Halperín Donghi, *Argentina*, 301–54.

9. For the politics of this period, see Bransboin, *Mendoza federal*; Lacoste, "Viticultura y política internacional."

10. Rock, *State Building and Political Movements*, 11–30. See also Rock, "Argentina under Mitre."

11. For Chilean state formation, see Collier, *Chile*; Jocelyn-Holt Letelier, *El peso de la noche*; Salazar, *Construcción de Estado en Chile*; Herr, *Contested Nation*.

12. Collier, *Chile*, 249–51.

13. Richard-Jorba, *Poder, economía y espacio*, 24.

14. Lacoste, "Viticultura y política internacional," 164.

15. Lacoste, "Viticultura y política internacional," 172–75.

16. Lacoste, "Viticultura y política internacional," 165.

17. Cavieres Figueroa, *Comercio chileno y comerciantes ingleses*, 106.

18. On the trade agreement, see Chile, *Sesiones de los cuerpos lejislativos*, vol. 24, session 36, no. 199, 5 October 1835, 181.

19. Bransboin, *Mendoza federal*, 164–71. See also Saraví, "Consideraciones acerca del tratado"; Segreti, "Mendoza y la política porteña"; Segreti, "Contribución al estudio del convenio," 255–71.

20. Bransboin, *Mendoza federal*, 170–83; Segreti, "El comercio con Chile."

21. Lacoste, "El Paso Pehuenche," 159. Mendocino is the denonym for someone from Mendoza.

22. Chile, *Sesiones de los cuerpos lejislativos*, vol. 34, session 27, 16 August 1844, 276, 278.

23. For some congressional debates on the suspension of trade after it was decreed, see Chile, *Sesiones de los cuerpos lejislativos*, vol. 34, session 27, 16 August 1844, 276; Chile, *Sesiones de los cuerpos lejislativos*, vol. 32, session 33, no. 280, 23 August 1843, 357; Chile, *Sesiones de los cuerpos lejislativos*, vol. 30, session 5, no. 49, 13 June 1842, 50. For debates in the press regarding the suspension of trade and the importance of Trans-Andean commerce to Chile, see "Comercio de transito por cordillera," *El Mercurio* (Valparaíso), 16 September 1845, 2; "Comercio Trasandino," *El Mercurio* (Valparaíso), 22 September 1845, 2; "Comercio trasandino," *El Mercurio* (Valparaíso), 24 September 1845, 2; untitled, *El Mercurio* (Valparaíso), 3 October 1845, 2; untitled, *El Mercurio* (Valparaíso), 12 December 1845, 2. The articles in *El Mercurio* were in direct response to a series of articles published in *El Tiempo*, which were in support of restrictive policies on Trans-Andean trade.

24. "Comercio Trasandino," *El Mercurio* (Valparaíso), 22 September 1845, 3.

25. Vicuña Mackenna, *Páginas de mi diario*, 439.

26. Vicuña Mackenna, *Páginas de mi diario*, 435–37.

27. Vicuña Mackenna, *Páginas de mi diario*, 438.

28. Vicuña Mackenna, *Páginas de mi diario*, 438.

29. Richard-Jorba, *Poder, economía y espacio*, 49–52.

30. For alfalfa producers, see Richard-Jorba, *Poder, economía y espacio*, 78.

31. On the different actors involved in commercialization and financing, see Richard-Jorba, *Poder, economía y espacio*, 82–94.

32. Bauer, *Chilean Rural Society*, 62–69; Bengoa, *Historia rural de Chile central*, 1:129–32, 158–59.

33. On cattle prices, see Bauer, *Chilean Rural Society*, 77; Bengoa, *Historia rural de Chile central*, 1:148–49.

34. Bengoa, *Historia rural de Chile central*, 1:156.

35. The role of Argentina in supplying Chilean markets with cattle and their products was acknowledged as early as the 1840s when free trade debates emerged in the context of a trade embargo on products coming from the eastern side of the Andes. See "Comercio Trasandino," *El Mercurio* (Valparaíso), 22 September 1845, 3. Three of the most important imports coming from Mendoza were cattle, tallow, and soap.

36. Davies Lenoble, "La resistencia de la ganadería," 344–46.

37. Davies Lenoble, "La resistencia de la ganadería," 349–55.

38. Molina, "Circuitos mercantiles"; Davies Lenoble, "La resistencia de la ganadería."

39. Davies Lenoble, "La resistencia de la ganadería," 372.

40. Richard-Jorba, *Poder, economía y espacio*, 65.

41. Belich, *Replenishing the Earth*, 311–14.

42. Hellyer, "West, the East, and the Insular Middle"; Igler, "Diseased Goods."

43. For recent work covering the effects of this fever, see Gobat, *Empire by Invitation*; Aguirre, *Mobility and Modernity*.

44. Tutino, "Americas in the Rise of Industrial Capitalism," 32.

45. Llorca-Jaña and Navarrete-Montalvo, "El rol de Chile," 24.

46. Cavieres Figueroa, *Comercio chileno y comerciantes ingleses*, 189. See also Evans and Saunders, "World of Copper."

47. Richard-Jorba, *Poder, economía y espacio*, 30.

48. Vergara Llano, "El cuero," 80.

49. In 1870, Coquimbo exported 2,172 *cueros vacunos*. Tornero, *Chile ilustrado*, 266. In 1870, 9,472 oxen were exported to Chile from San Juan province. Often, oxen went to Coquimbo and Copiapó. Igarzábal, *Provincia de San Juan*, 291, 388–91.

50. Richard-Jorba, *Poder, economía y espacio*, 30n55. For examples of Californians in Mendoza, see census entry for Clara Castro, 1869, Junín, "Argentina, censo nacional, 1869," *FamilySearch*, accessed 2 March 2021, www.familysearch.org/ark:/61903/3:1:S3HT-6XMS-X43, FSL microfilm 686887. For the Chile-California connection in this period, see Melillo, *Strangers on Familiar Soil*, 33–91.

51. *Sud-América: Política i Comercio* (Santiago), vol. 1, no. 5, 24 February 1851, 129–30.

52. *Sud-América: Política i Comercio* (Santiago), vol. 1, no. 5, 24 February 1851, 132–33.

53. *Sud-América: Política i Comercio* (Santiago), vol. 1, no. 5, 24 February 1851, 133.

54. "Vias comerciales, Chile," *Sud-América: Política i Comercio* (Santiago), vol. 1, no. 1, 24 January 1851, 4.

55. "Vias comerciales, Chile," 4–5.

56. Félix Frías to Mariano Varela, 7 August 1869, Santiago, folios 19v–20r, "Chile. Negociacion relativa al tratado de comercio. Convencion de extradicion. Convencion postal," folder 13, box 8, TC, AHCA.

57. Frías to Varela, 7 August 1869, folio 18r.

58. Frías to Varela, 7 August 1869, folios 19v–20r.

59. This is for 1823. Morales, "El mundo del trabajo," 6.

60. In the early 1840s, for example, there were approximately 400 Chileans counted. See Bransboin, *Mendoza federal*, 175. Although they were probably undercounted, it is very likely that the Chilean population was still in decline. One indicator is marriage records. Over the course of the 1830s, there was a steep decline in foreign men (who were generally Chilean) in marriage records. See Cremaschi de Petra, "Aspectos socio-demográficos de Mendoza," 247–48.

61. The aggregate census puts the number of Chileans at 5,774, representing 8.8 percent of the provincial population. Argentina, Comisión Directiva del Censo, *Primer censo*, 350. However, my own hand count of the census rolls puts the number at 6,024 (9.2 percent). This difference has some effect on my analysis of Chileans in Mendoza because I rely on the aggregate census numbers to understand different proportions of Chileans in Mendocino society, especially professions. However, even accounting for that difference, my analysis of the disproportionality of Chileans as peons, peasant farmers, merchants, and textile workers in Mendoza remains true. This is especially and importantly the case for peons. For all Chilean profession numbers, see table A.3.

62. For San Juan and total Chileans in Argentina (10,882), see Argentina, Comisión Directiva del Censo, *Primer censo*, 388–89, 628.

63. Chile, Oficina Central de Estadística, *Censo jeneral*, 306, 371.

64. Escolar, *Los dones étnicos*, 113.

65. Comadrán Ruiz, *Evolución demográfica Argentina*, 52; Michieli, *Antigua historia de Cuyo*, 55.

66. Escolar, *Los indios montoneros*, 93.

67. Escolar, *Los dones étnicos*, 115.

68. On the reforms of the 1850s in Chile and the centrality of Valparaíso, see Cavieres Figueroa, *Comercio chileno y comerciantes ingleses*, 111–27. On the development of finance in Mendoza and its connections with Valparaíso, see Bragoni, "Mercados, monedas y crédito," 65–69. Of course, this is not to deny connections with other places in Argentina.

69. Richard-Jorba, *Poder, economía y espacio*, 84–86, 167.

70. There were 98 Chilean *comerciantes* in Mendoza, representing 13.6 percent of the merchants in the province. For total number of merchants in the province (721), see Argentina, Comisión Directiva del Censo, *Primer censo*, 357.

71. Vicuña Mackenna, *Páginas de mi diario*, 435–37.

72. Richard-Jorba, *Poder, economía y espacio*, 175–77. For the development of national politics in the context of exile, see Blumenthal, *Exile and Nation Formation*. For the consolidation of power in the province through the Civit family (Francisco Civit was one of those exiles in Chile), see Bragoni, "Un linaje de notables."

73. Bauer, *Chilean Rural Society*, 13–16; Salazar, *Labradores, peones y proletarios*, 37–48; Bengoa, *Historia rural de Chile central*, 1:87–89.

74. Salazar, *Labradores, peones y proletarios*, 158–73. For changes in the landowning class, see Llorca-Jaña, Robles Ortiz, Navarrete-Montalvo, and Araya Valenzuela, "La agricultura y la élite agraria chilena."

75. Salazar, *Labradores, peones y proletarios*, 151–52, 174.

76. On the timing of labor shortages and mechanization, see Robles-Ortiz, "Mechanisation in the Periphery," 201–3. For migrations to the north (as well as to Mendoza), see Vicuña Mackenna, *Páginas de mi diario*, 438. For a historical perspective on the labor migrations to the mining districts, see Salazar, *Labradores, peones y proletarios*, 177–222.

77. Molina, "Circuitos mercantiles."

78. Davies Lenoble, "La resistencia de la ganadería," 349.

79. Davies Lenoble, "La resistencia de la ganadería," 367.

80. Davies Lenoble, "La resistencia de la ganadería," 346–49.

81. Of all departments in Mendoza, Luján and Tupungato report the geographical origins of Chileans most consistently.

82. Barbuto, "'Hacer de cada tribu un pueblo,'" 46n1, summarizing Ratto, "Una experiencia fronteriza exitosa."

83. Davies Lenoble, "La resistencia de la ganadería," 368 (emphasis added).

84. Argentina, Comisión Directiva del Censo, *Primer censo*, 337. For the place of Indigenous people in national census counts in the nineteenth century, see Otero, *Estadística y nación*, 341–50.

85. There exists evidence that at least some people listed as "Chilean" were or were related to "indios amigos," as commonly understood, although not necessarily part of this migration. For example, José Antonio Cumiñan, a twenty-two-year-old "Chilean" *gañán*, lived in San Carlos Department. Census entry for José Antonio Cumiñan, 1869, San Carlos, "Argentina, censo nacional, 1869," *FamilySearch*, accessed 23 February 2024, www.familysearch.org/ark:/61903/3:1:S3HY-6QP9-ZC6, FSL microfilm 0686890. Although his relations are not clear, the Cumiñan name can be traced to "indios amigos" around San Rafael and San Carlos in the early nineteenth century. See Francisco Inalikang, "Carta

al Gobernador Intendente de la Provincia, San Rafael, sin fecha," in Pavez Ojeda, *Cartas mapuche*, 163–64. In other cases Chileans do not have the kinds of last names sometimes identified as Indigenous for Tupungato and San Carlos Departments, the main departments of the Uco Valley (Peletay, Pocoyán, or Cabiltuna, for example). See Molina, "Los tentáculos de la justicia," 187n68.

86. Argentina, Comisión Directiva del Censo, *Primer censo*, 64–75, 118–25, 158–65, 202–8, 246–53, 282–86, 318–22, 356–61, 394–97, 430–34, 468–73, 506–12, 548–54, 584–88, 632–33. Mendoza's peon population was 13.3 percent of its total. The next highest provinces were all in the east: Entre Ríos (13.2 percent), Buenos Aires (11.9 percent), and Santa Fe (11.5 percent). The average for the country was 9.4 percent. Therefore, Mendoza stands out in the interior for its very high peon population.

87. There were 1,940 Chilean peons in Mendoza, representing 22.3 percent of the total peons in the province (8,699) and 32.2 percent of the total Chilean population.

88. For an explanation of the terms *peón* and *gañán* in the context of Mendoza, see Molina, "Los tentáculos de la justicia," 171n31.

89. For Salvatore's definition of the "country peon class" and analysis of their economic activities, see Salvatore, *Wandering Paysanos*, 1, 25–94. For workers in Mendoza during the second half of the nineteenth century into the early twentieth century, see Richard-Jorba, *Empresarios ricos, trabajadores pobres*, 129–85. For labor in La Rioja in this period, see de la Fuente, *Children of Facundo*, 63–66.

90. Debt, peonage, and the labor relations of the rural lower class have been extensively debated. For the Argentine example and comparisons to other places in Latin America, see Mayo, "Estancia y peonaje," 609–16; Campi and Richard-Jorba, "Un ejercicio de historia regional comparada," 100–107. See also Salvatore, *Wandering Paysanos*, 68–79.

91. Salvatore, *Wandering Paysanos*, 161–294; Salvatore, "Crimes of Poor *Paysanos*."

92. Based on a review of Resguardo records. See files 3, 6, folder 390; files 1, 14, 23, folder 389, both in Sección Hacienda, EI, AHM. Review of this data yields this rough formula, total peons (P) is equal to 20 heads of cattle per peon (c) ($.05*c$) plus 1 peon per every 15 *quintales* (q) ($.066*q$), or $P = .05c + .066q$. Trade statistics, specifically from 1854, provide the data to estimate the number of peons (not individual laborers because one can cross more than once per season) needed to handle the traffic in a year. In 1854, 41,406 heads of cattle crossed, and among the highest trafficked commodities, 11,018 *quintales* crossed. Thus, $P = (.05*41,406) + (.066*11,018)$, or $2,070 + 734$, or 2,804 peons. Chile, Oficina Central de Estadística, *Estadística comercial [. . .] primer semestre del año 1854*, 64; Chile, Oficina Central de Estadística, *Estadística comercial [. . .] segundo semestre del año 1854*, 72. For a longer explanation of the formula, Harvey, "Prepositional Geographies," 56n41. The formula is also supported as a decent rough estimate by separate crossing data from San Juan in 1870. Igarzábal, *Provincia de San Juan*, 384–91.

93. For example, see Declaración de José Díaz, 2 June 1866, Mendoza; Declaración de Miguel Navarro, 6 June 1866, Mendoza, folios 5r-v, 6v-7v, file 11, folder N1, SJC, EI, AHM. See also Igarzábal, *La Provincia de San Juan*, 302. The criminal cases reviewed in chapter 3 routinely support the reality that the peon-boss relationship was less absolute than the provincial state would have wanted.

94. For what some of that work might have looked like, see Richard-Jorba, *Poder, economía y espacio*, 51–53, 67–73.

95. Robles-Ortiz, "Mechanisation in the Periphery," 201.

96. Chilean women made up 6.5 percent of the female population in Mendoza but 11.1 percent (732) of the total textile worker population (6,577), including 13.6 percent (369) of weavers and spinners (2,718). Argentina, Comisión Directiva del Censo, *Primer censo*, 357–58.

97. Lacoste and Lacoste Adunka, "Chamantos, ponchos y balandres," 100.

98. Llorca-Jaña, "Reappraisal of Mapuche Textile Production," 103.

99. Lacoste and Lacoste Adunka, "Chamantos, ponchos y balandres," 101.

100. Lacoste and Lacoste Adunka, "Chamantos, ponchos y balandres," 113.

101. Guy, "Oro Blanco," 471.

102. Chilean *labradores* (331) made up 21.7 percent of the total labrador (1,525) population in the province. Chilean *agricultores* (82) made up 15.4 percent of the total agricultor (534) population in the province, with an important number (45) in San Carlos Department. Argentina, Comisión Directiva del Censo, *Primer censo*, 358. Chilean numbers are from table A.3. I use the term "peasant farmer" despite its lack of nuance because my analysis is about the broad experiences of Chileans with relationships to land and because of my interest in the fluidity of categories at the margins, particularly between peon and other categories, present in census records within families or in criminal records, such as analyzed in chapter 3.

103. The total number of Chileans labradores in the East Zone (Junín, La Paz, and San Martín Departments) and Uco Valley (201) represented 60.7 percent of the total Chilean labrador population. The total number of Chilean agricultores in those areas (50) represented 61 percent of the total Chilean agricultor population. Land relationships, whether tenancy or ownership, are not always clearly marked in the census, but based on categories in the census, contemporaneous observations, and secondary literature, it is clear that both ownership and tenancy were part of the Chilean peasant farmer experience. For contemporaneous commentary on Chilean *inquilinos* in Mendoza, see Vicuña Mackenna, *Páginas de mi diario*, 438. For renters, classifications of them, and obligations, as well as understanding of agricultores as "small-property owners," see Richard-Jorba, *Poder, economía y espacio*, 57, 69–71, 79–84, 221n387.

104. Bragoni, "Recuperación y desigualdad económica," 228. The vast majority of land was devoted to alfalfa, see Richard-Jorba, *Poder, economía y espacio*, 47.

105. For different breakdowns in different departments of Mendoza, see Bragoni, "Recuperación y desigualdad económica," 229, 231, 234, 236–37.

106. Molina, "Los tentáculos de la justicia," 187.

107. For example, in San Carlos Department, Pablo Toro, a sixty-two-year-old agricultor, and Agustina Martínez, a fifty-nine-year-old tejendera, had three children, Ignes, José, and Isidora, all in their twenties, listed as "tejendera," "peón," and "peona," respectively. Census entries for Pablo Toro, Augstina Martínez, Ignes Toro, José Toro, and Isidora Toro, 1869, San Carlos, "Argentina, censo nacional, 1869," *FamilySearch*, accessed 23 February 2024, www.familysearch.org/ark:/61903/3:1:S3HY-6QP9-HWM, FSL microfilm 0686890.

108. This includes Departments 1 and 2, Guaymallén, Luján, Maipú, San Vicente, and Mendoza Ciudad. For my understanding of departmental groupings in Mendoza, see Richard-Jorba, *Poder, economía y espacio*, 95. Female migration to Latin America tended to be below 35 percent for the nineteenth and early twentieth centuries. For migration patterns in Latin America in this period, see Gabaccia and Zanoni, "Transitions in Gender Ratios," 207.

## Interlude 1

1. La Compañía del Telégrafo Trasandino, *Estatutos*, 15–21.
2. La Compañía del Telégrafo Trasandino, *Estatutos*, 19.
3. Caimari, "News from around the World," 614.
4. La Compañía del Telégrafo Trasandino, *Estatutos*, 18.
5. Caimari, "News from around the World," 615.
6. Caimari, "News from around the World," 628.
7. Caimari, "News from around the World," 631, 635.
8. Marín Vicuña, *Los Hermanos Clark*, 43–47.
9. Blumenthal, *Exile and Nation Formation*, 3. For a recent treatment of Mariquita Sánchez, see J. Shumway, *Woman, a Man, a Nation*. For a review of Alberdi's thoughts and debates in this period, see N. Shumway, *Invention of Argentina*, 168–86.
10. Blumenthal, *Exile and Nation Formation*, 127–69.
11. Marín Vicuña, *Los Hermanos Clark*, 47–48.
12. Morales Ocaranza, *Historia del Huasco*, 228.
13. Valenzuela, "Chilean Copper Smelting Industry," 511.
14. Mayo, "Development of British Interests," 369, 388.
15. Valenzuela, "Chilean Copper Smelting Industry," 511–12.
16. Marín Vicuña, *Los Hermanos Clark*, 36–39.
17. See Mayo, "Development of British Interests"; Llorca-Jaña, "Shaping Globalization."
18. Marín Vicuña, *Los Hermanos Clark*, 46, 49.
19. Duncan, "William Wheelright [sic] and Early Steam Navigation," 277. See also Clarke, "Development of a Pioneering Steamship Line."
20. Martland, "Trade, Progress, and Patriotism," 61.
21. Mayo, "Joshua Waddington and the Anglo Chilean Connection," 201. For more on the Valparaíso-Santiago line, see Thomson and Angerstein, *Historia del ferrocarril en Chile*, 36–40.
22. Mayo, "Joshua Waddington and the Anglo Chilean Connection," 199–200.
23. La Compañía del Telégrafo Trasandino, *Estatutos*, 48.
24. Mayo, "Joshua Waddington and the Anglo Chilean Connection," 213–14.
25. Latour, "Technology Is Society Made Durable."
26. I draw from Henri Lefebvre to make sense of global space, even though it is not necessarily here that he is talking about it. In considering space at once as "whole and fragmentary" (homogenizing and heterogenous), Lefebvre asks us to think "of a computer science that can dominate space in such a fashion that a computer . . . can assemble an indeterminate mass of information relating to a given physical or social space and process it at a single location." Lefebvre, *Production of Space*, 355.

## Chapter 2

1. Comandancia del 2° Batallón de Guardias Nacionales to Ministro de Estado, 7 April 1868, Villa de San Vicente, folio 2r, file 6, folder L2, SJC, EI, AHM.
2. Comandancia del 2° Batallón de Guardias Nacionales to Ministro de Estado, 7 April 1868, folio 2r.

3. For example, Tutino, *Making a New World*, 490–91; Blanchard, *Under the Flag of Freedom*; Illanes O., *Chile des-centrado*, 15–25.

4. For some of those struggles, see Escolar, "La república perdida de Santos Guayama"; Sabato, *Republics of the New World*; del Castillo, *Crafting a Republic for the World*; Sanders, *Vanguard of the Atlantic World*; Macías, *Armas y política en la Argentina*; Wood, *Society of Equality*; de la Fuente, *Children of Facundo*.

5. For an updated approach to this period in Argentina, see Elena, "Spinsters, Gamblers, and Friedrich Engels." On conservative liberalism in Mexico, see Charles Hale, *Transformation of Liberalism*. For the export era, see Kuntz Ficker, *First Export Era Revisited*.

6. On transnational migrations in different places, see Savala, "Ports of Transnational Labor Organizing"; Pinto Vallejos, Valdivia Ortiz de Zárate, and Artaza Barrios, "Patria y clase"; Purcell, *¡Muchos extranjeros para mi gusto!*, 171–98; Moya, "Italians in Buenos Aires's Anarchist Movement"; R. Edwards, *Carceral Ecology*, 84–104; Baer, "FACA and the FAI"; Shaffer, "Contesting Internationalists." For a rethinking of transnationalism and labor activism, see Craib, "Sedentary Anarchists." For immigration in and to Latin America and the Americas broadly, see Bailey and Míguez, *Mass Migration*; Moya, "Continent of Immigrants"; Fink, *Workers across the Americas*.

7. For more on "boundaries of civic inclusion," see Bryce, "Citizenship and Ethnicity," 23. See also Baily, *Immigrants in the Lands of Promise*, 191–200; Moya, *Cousins and Strangers*, 277–305.

8. Strain, *Cordillera and Pampa*, 115.

9. Molina, "Los tentáculos de la justicia," 171–72, 176; Morales, "El mundo del trabajo," 5–10.

10. Morales, "El mundo del trabajo," 9–10; Molina, "Los tentáculos de la justicia," 173–74.

11. Based on several demographic studies of Mendoza for the early nineteenth century, I use counts and terms as loose approximations and as they appear in the secondary sources. See Morales, "El mundo del trabajo," 6; Molina, "Los tentáculos de la justicia," 170–80; Comadrán Ruiz, *Evolución demográfica Argentina*, 113.

12. The persistence of race-mixing in Mendoza is evident in marriage records up to 1840, which still used racial categories. See Cremaschi de Petra, "Aspectos socio-demográficos de Mendoza," 251–53. There are several ways to approach Chilean migrants' influence on the demographics of Mendoza. First, the 1813 census provides demographic data, although importantly not of Santiago. The nonwhite population varied between 15 and 55 percent, depending on the place, with the north (Copiapó and Coquimbo) being less white than others. One important exception is the province of Curicó, in the south of the country, which categorized almost half its population as nonwhite. Although the Argentine national census of 1869 does not provide consistent data on where Chileans came from in Chile, in the 14.5 percent of cases in which census takers did, about half came from "Santiago" and "Curicó," with 10 percent from Curicó and 40 percent from Santiago. Based on a face-value reading of these figures, it would be difficult to assert that Chilean migrations substantially changed the racial and ethnic demographics of Mendoza one way or the other, although it is more likely that Chilean migrations represented a slight whitening of the countryside than the reverse. See Silva Castro, *Censo de 1813*. Of course, there are issues complicating such a reading. A straightforward reading of racial and ethnic categories ignores the social constructedness of those categories, the changes in statistical norms and unreliability of

counts and classifications, and the malleability of categories of race and ethnicity (and nationality, as this chapter shows) in different contexts. For histories of demographics in Chile and Latin America more broadly, see Estefane Jaramillo, "'Un alto en el camino para saber cuántos somos'"; Vinson, Before Mestizaje.

13. Roig, Concepto de trabajo en Mendoza, 5–12.

14. Salvatore, "Labor Control and Discrimination," 65; Roig, El concepto de trabajo en Mendoza, 4.

15. Provincia de Mendoza, art. 6, "Decreto gubernativo sobre servicio de peones, adicional al Reglamento de Policía" (16 August 1855), in Ahumada, Código de las leyes, 302.

16. For the history of these categories and forms of community from the colonial period, see Herzog, Defining Nations.

17. Sabato, Republics of the New World, 94–99.

18. Salvatore, Wandering Paysanos, 97; Sabato, Republics of the New World, 94.

19. Macías and Sabato, "Estado, política y uso de la fuerza," 73. For how changes in the armed forces affected politics in the 1860s elsewhere in Argentina, see Macías, "Violencia y política facciosa." For broad attempts at changes in the armed forces at this time, see Sabato, Republics of the New World, 194–96.

20. Intendente [?] de Atacama to Ministro de Relaciones Exteriores, 27 June 1855, Copiapó, no. 794, vol. 37, MREL, ANH.

21. For examples of these processes in decades prior in Chile and Argentina, see Blumenthal, "Milicias y ciudadanía de residencia"; Bransboin, Mendoza federal, 171–83.

22. Andrews, Afro-Argentines of Buenos Aires, 114–15.

23. Morales, "Identificaciones de plebeyos de color," 151.

24. Morales, "Identificaciones de plebeyos de color," 140–49. For a postindependence context, see Salvatore, Wandering Paysanos, 262–324.

25. Beattie, "Measures of Manhood," 240–44.

26. For a nuanced analysis of these statistical processes in the first three national censuses in Argentina, see Otero, Estadística y nación, 341–76.

27. Andrews, Afro-Argentines of Buenos Aires, 93.

28. Estefane Jaramillo, "'Un alto en el camino para saber cuántos somos,'" 55–58. For race and nation in a later period, see Walsh, "Chilean Exception."

29. For those contexts in Mendoza, see Escolar, "Huarpe Archives in the Argentine Desert"; Davies Lenoble, "La resistencia de la ganadería"; Gabriel Morales and Caballero, "Abolición de la esclavitud en Mendoza."

30. Briones and Delrio, "'Conquest of the Desert,'" 52–54; Lazzari, "Aboriginal Recognition, Freedom, and Phantoms," 62.

31. For example, see Escolar, Los dones étnicos, 41–43.

32. Pinto Vallejos, Valdivia Ortiz de Zárate, and Artaza Barrios, "Patria y clase," 276–78.

33. Pinto Vallejos, Valdivia Ortiz de Zárate, and Artaza Barrios, "Patria y clase," 309–12.

34. Beckman, "Creolization of Imperial Reason"; Crow, "From Araucanian Warriors to Mapuche Terrorists," 79–81; Tinsman, "Rebel Coolies."

35. Purcell, ¡Muchos extranjeros para mi gusto!, 21, 82–100.

36. DeLaney, "Immigration, Identity, and Nationalism in Argentina," 93–94. See also Bryce, "Undesirable Britons," 247–73.

37. Richard-Jorba, Empresarios ricos, trabajadores pobres, 168–73.

38. Nasatir, "Chileans in California," 52–70; Pinto Vallejos, *Trabajos y rebeldías en la pampa salitrera*, 64–80; Bengoa, *Historia rural de Chile central*, 1:269–74. For how Chilean and Peruvian workers overcame these divides at times, see Savala, *Beyond Patriotic Phobias*.

39. For resistance to the state in different contexts, see Salvatore, *Wandering Paysanos*, 50–55; Salvatore, "Crimes of Poor *Paysanos*."

40. Escolar, "Subjetividad y estatalidad," 147–48.

41. Bello, *Derecho internacional*, 1:141.

42. Bello, *Derecho internacional*, 1:141.

43. Miguel de los Santos to Ministro de Relaciones Exteriores, 30 March 1859, folio 203r, no. 24, vol. 105, MREL, ANH.

44. Although I do not have a copy of the article, its existence was not in question, according to the correspondences exchanged at the time. The article was published 29 March 1860 in *El Constitucional*, no. 2169. Miguel de los Santos (Cónsul de Chile en Mendoza) to Nicasio Marín (Ministro General de Gobierno en Mendoza), 29 March 1860, Mendoza, in Argentina, Ministro de Estado, Departamento de Relaciones Esteriores, *Memoria [. . .] 1860*, 103. See also Blumenthal, *Exile and Nation Formation*, 195.

45. Santos to Marín, 29 March 1860, in Argentina, Ministro de Estado, Departamento de Relaciones Esteriores, *Memoria [. . .] 1860*, 104.

46. Nicasio Marín to Miguel de los Santos, 30 March 1860, Mendoza, in Argentina, Ministro de Estado, Departamento de Relaciones Esteriores, *Memoria [. . .] 1860*, 105.

47. Miguel de los Santos to Nicasio Marín, 7 April 1860, Mendoza, in Argentina, Ministro de Estado, Departamento de Relaciones Esteriores, *Memoria [. . .] 1860*, 91.

48. Santos to Marín, 7 April 1860, Mendoza, in Argentina, Ministro de Estado, Departamento de Relaciones Esteriores, *Memoria [. . .] 1860*, 92.

49. Emilio de Alvear (Ministerio de Relaciones Exteriores) to Gobernador de la Provincia de Mendoza, 21 April 1860, Paraná, in Argentina, Ministro de Estado, Departamento de Relaciones Esteriores, *Memoria [. . .] 1860*, 111–12.

50. Blumenthal, *Exile and Nation Formation*, 175–78. For José de la Cruz Zenteno in the rebellion of 1851, see Castro Valdebenito, "Aconcagüinos en la historia de Chile," 281–82.

51. "El fiscal acusa," 24 January 1853, Mendoza, folios 9v–10r, file 1, folder B3, SJC, EI, AHM. For an example of his work as a defensor, see file 16, folder M3, SJC, EI, AHM (folios related to him in file 16, folder M3 are unnumbered and stuck in between the pages of the case, out of order).

52. For José de la Cruz Zenteno's first and last correspondences, see José de la Cruz Zenteno to Ministro de Estado de Relaciones Exteriores de Chile, 23 December 1864, Mendoza, folio 165r–v, vol. 120, MREL, ANH; Zenteno to Ministro de Gobierno de la Provincia de Mendoza, 22 October 1867, Mendoza, folio 29r, file 60, folder 708, SE, EI, AHM.

53. For policies developed in France at the time, see Weil, "French State," 114–32.

54. For consular reactions elsewhere, see Pinto Vallejos, *Trabajos y rebeldías en la pampa salitrera*, 64–80.

55. Zenteno to Ministro de Estado de Relaciones Exteriores de Chile, 23 December 1864, folio 165r–v.

56. José de la Cruz Zenteno to Ministro Plenipotenciario de Chile cerca del Gobierno de la Confederación Argentina (copy), 3 March 1865, Mendoza, folios 63r–64r, no. 19, vol. 130, MREL, ANH.

57. José Victorino Lastarria to José de la Cruz Zenteno (copy), 18 March 1865, Buenos Aires, folio 69r, vol. 130, MREL, ANH.

58. Declaración de José Francisco Castillo, 15 March 1865, Mendoza; Declaración de Guillermo Morales, 15 March 1865, Mendoza; Declaración de Felipe Pescara, 16 March 1865, Mendoza, all in folios 8r–9r, file 10, folder 451, Sección Sumarios Civiles y Militares, EI, AHM.

59. Declaración de Pedro Gonzales, 10 March 1865, Mendoza, folio 7v, file 10, folder 451, Sección Sumarios Civiles y Militares, EI, AHM.

60. Declaración de Gonzales, 10 March 1865, folio 7v. Juan Godoy accepted the position of Canciller de Consulado en Mendoza in 1858. See Godoy to Ministerio de Relaciones Exteriores de Chile, 9 April 1858, Mendoza, folio 125r, vol. 92, MREL, ANH. For lack of national identification in prior decades, see Blumenthal, "Milicias y ciudadanía de residencia," 102.

61. José de la Cruz Zenteno to Ministerio de Gobierno de la Provincia de Mendoza, 6 March 1865, Mendoza, folio 5r, no. 20, file 32, folder 708, SE, EI, AHM. Juan Gonzales is listed as number 768, registered on 20 July 1861. Declaración de Gonzales, 10 March 1865, folio 7v.

62. For the consulate's request for his birth certificate, see José de la Cruz Zenteno to Ministro de Relaciones Exteriores de Chile, 7 March 1865, Mendoza, folio 66r–v, no. 21, vol. 130, MREL, ANH.

63. For the result of the province's case, see Franklin Villanueva, 27 March 1865, Mendoza, folio 10r, file 10, folder 451, Sección Sumarios Civiles y Militares, EI, AHM.

64. José de la Cruz Zenteno to Ministro de Gobierno de la Provincia de Mendoza, 23 March 1865, Mendoza, folio 10r, file 32, folder 708, SE, EI, AHM (emphasis added).

65. Zenteno to the Ministro de Gobierno de la Provincia de Mendoza, 23 March 1865, folio 10r.

66. For statistics on the Chilean populations in different places in Mendoza and San Juan provinces, see Argentina, Comisión Directiva del Censo, *Primer censo*, 350–51, 388–89. In total, 12 percent of "Chileans" lived in the provincial capitals of San Juan and Mendoza.

67. Antero Barriga to Ministro de Gobierno de Chile en el Departamento de Relaciones Exteriores, 31 July 1863, San Juan, folios 287r–289r, vol. 117, MREL, ANH.

68. José de la Cruz Zenteno to Ministro de Relaciones Exteriores, 31 March 1865, Mendoza, folios 80v–81r, no. 36, vol. 130; Antero Barriga to Ministerio de Relaciones Exteriores de Chile, 15 December 1863, San Juan, folio 303r, vol. 117, both in MREL, ANH.

69. It is possible to think of this as "ID-paper fetishism"; see Gordillo, "Crucible of Citizenship," 162–76. For a broad history of identification, see Caplan and Torpey, *Documenting Individual Identity*.

70. Whigham and Potthast, "Paraguayan Rosetta Stone," 185. For the War of the Triple Alliance, see Garavaglia and Fradkin, *150 años de la Guerra de la Triple Alianza*; Whigham, *Paraguayan War*. For different reactions in the provinces, see Bragoni, "Cuyo después de Pavón" 42; de la Fuente, *Children of Facundo*, 169–71.

71. José de la Cruz Zenteno to Ministro de Relaciones Exteriores de Chile, 31 May 1865, Mendoza, folio 96r, no. 46, vol. 130, MREL, ANH.

72. Chileans also volunteered. See José de la Cruz Zenteno to Ministro de Relaciones Exteriores de Chile, 31 May, 15 June 1865, Mendoza, folios 96r–v, 106r, nos. 46, 53, vol. 130, MREL, ANH.

73. Zenteno to Ministro de Relaciones Exteriores de Chile, 31 May 1865, folio 96r.

74. Although full registration records do not exist, the data that do exist point to a significant increase in rates of registration at the beginning of Argentina's entrance into the War of the Triple Alliance—from 1.9 per day between 20 May 1863 and 5 June 1865 to 3.3 per day between 5 June 1865 and 15 July 1865. For registration numbers from 1858 to 1865, see Juan Godoy to Ministro de Gobierno de la Provincia de Mendoza, 3 March 1863, Mendoza, folio 1r, no. 11, file 24 (Martín Valenzuela is listed as having boleta number 101, registered on 2 October 1858); Zenteno to Ministro de Gobierno de la Provincia de Mendoza, 6 March 1865, folio 5r (Juan Gonzales is listed as number 768, registered on 20 July 1861); Zenteno to Ministro de Gobierno de la Provincia de Mendoza, 17, 23 October 1865, Mendoza, folios 35r, 37r, nos. 89, 96, file 39 (Pedro Trejo was registered as 2462 on 20 May 1863; Baldomero Naveas was listed as number 3863, registered on 5 June 1865); Zenteno to Ministro de Gobierno de la Provincia de Mendoza, 15 July 1865, Mendoza, folio 22r, no. 61, file 36 (Manuel Gonzales, registered as number 3992, specific date unknown), all in folder 708, SE, EI, AHM.

75. State officials harbored concerns about people lying about their nationality for some time. See Bransboin, *Mendoza federal*, 175.

76. Blumenthal, "Milicias y ciudadanía de residencia," 107–8.

77. Franklin Villanueva to Cónsul de Chile en Mendoza (copy), 9 June 1865, Mendoza, folio 103r–v; Zenteno to Ministro de Relaciones Exteriores de Chile, 30 June 1865, Mendoza, folio 111r–v, no. 57, both in vol. 130, MREL, ANH.

78. Comandancia del 2° Batallón de Guardias Nacionales to Ministro de Estado, 7 April 1868, folio 2r.

79. On the subdelegados, see Molina, "Los funcionarios subalternos de justicia"; Sanjurjo de Driollet, "Las continuidades en el gobierno." For the case, see José de la Cruz Zenteno to Ramón Flores (Teniente Coronel), 27 February 1865, Mendoza, folio 87r–v, no. 16, vol. 130, MREL, ANH.

80. José de la Cruz Zenteno to Ramón Flores (Teniente Coronel), 27 February 1865, Mendoza, folio 87r–v, no. 16, vol. 130, MREL, ANH.

81. Sisto Nuñes, Informe, 24 March 1865, San Carlos, folio 90v, vol. 130, MREL, ANH.

82. Luis Molina to Gregorio Beéche, 30 November 1862, Mendoza, folio 1r, no. 1; Beéche to Manuel A. Tocornal, 8 December 1862, Valparaíso, folio 2r–v, no. 2; Tocornal to Beéche, 11 December 1862, Santiago, folio 3r, no. 3, all in Cónsul General Argentino en Chile, "Habla de una nota del Gob [Gobierno] de Mendoza, relativa al temor de una invasión de los argentinos emigrados en Chile e indica se solicite de este Gob [Gobierno] la mayor vigilancia y agrega otras referencias," folder 2, box 39, SDC, AHCA. For the rebellion, see Bragoni, "Cuyo después de Pavón," 36–42. Authorities on both sides of the mountains worked to prevent this invasion. For Argentine-Chilean relations more broadly at the time, see Lacoste, "Las guerras Hispanoamericana."

83. Ministro de Gobierno to Cónsul de Chile en Mendoza, 8 April 1863, Mendoza, folios 4r–5v, no. 4, book 19, Copiadores, EI, AHM.

84. Ministro de Gobierno to Cónsul de Chile in Mendoza, 8 April 1863, folios 4r–5v.

85. José S. Contreras to Ministro de Relaciones Exteriores, 31 October 1864, Mendoza, folio 158r, no. 31, vol. 120, MREL, ANH.

86. The law on punishment for not having papers: Provincia de Mendoza, art. 10, "Decreto gubernativo sobre servicio de peones, adicional al Reglamento de Policía" (16 August 1855), in Ahumada, *Código de las leyes*, 302.

87. José de la Cruz Zenteno to Ministro de Gobierno de la Provincia de Mendoza, 21 December 1866, Mendoza, folio 17r, no. 106, file 51, folder 708, SE, EI, AHM. See also José de la Cruz Zenteno to Ministro de Gobierno de la Provincia de Mendoza, 1 March 1867, Mendoza, folio 3r, no. 21, file 54, folder 708, SE, EI, AHM.

88. Zenteno to Ministro de Relaciones Exteriores de Chile, 31 May 1865, folio 96r.

89. Contreras to Ministro de Relaciones Exteriores de Chile, 31 October 1864, folio 158v.

90. José de la Cruz Zenteno to Ministro General de Gobierno de la Provincia (copy), 8 June 1865, Mendoza, folio 102r, no. 50, vol. 130, MREL, ANH.

91. Nicanor Zenteno to Ministro de Gobierno de la Provincia de Mendoza, 4 June 1869, Mendoza, folio 6v, file 74, folder 708, SE, EI, AHM.

92. This may have been happening earlier, too. Bransboin, *Mendoza federal*, 174–83.

93. Richard-Jorba, *Empresarios ricos, trabajadores pobres*, 143.

94. José de la Cruz Zenteno to Ministro de Relaciones Exteriores de Chile, 22 March, 15 June 1865, Mendoza, folios 70v–71r, 106r, nos. 26, 53, vol. 130, MREL, ANH.

## Interlude 2

1. "Clark & Co. to Exmo. Sr. D. Aníbal Pinto," 27.
2. "Clark & Co. to Exmo. Sr. D. Aníbal Pinto," 27–29.
3. Lacoste, *Ferrocarril Trasandino*, 92.
4. Henderson, "Transandine Railway," 168.
5. For the development of transpacific communications technologies, see Steel, "Re-routing Empire?"
6. This is based on James Belich's timeline of Anglo-settler migrations. For a concise presentation, see Belich, "Exploding Wests."
7. Belich, *Replenishing the Earth*, 358.
8. Belich, *Replenishing the Earth*, 362.
9. The term is popularly attributed to the editor of the journal in which the article appeared, *United States Magazine and Democratic Review*, but the author seems to have been Jane McManus Storm. Citing Linda Hudson, *Mistress of Manifest Destiny* from Gobat, *Empire by Invitation*, 298n14. For recent work on the Mexican-American War, see Guardino, *Dead March*.
10. Belich, *Replenishing the Earth*, 82.
11. Belich, *Replenishing the Earth*, 341.
12. Cronon, *Nature's Metropolis*, 60–70.
13. Belich, *Replenishing the Earth*, 335–36.
14. Belich, *Replenishing the Earth*, 335.
15. For a recent example of this comparison, see Brudney, "Manifest Destiny."
16. Castro, *Estudio sobre los ferrocarriles sud-americanos*, 534.
17. Hellyer, "West, the East, and the Insular Middle."
18. Dolin, *Leviathan*, 211–47; Evans and Saunders, "World of Copper"; Irigoin, "End of a Silver Era"; Steel, "Re-routing Empire?"
19. Schmidt-Nowara, *Empire and Antislavery*, 78–123.
20. Carter and Bates, "Empire and Locality," 51–73.
21. Sell, "Asian Indentured Labor," 21.

22. Hopkins, *Ruling the Savage Periphery*, 21.

23. Matsuda, *Pacific Worlds*, 219–20.

24. Maude, *Slavers in Paradise*; Yun, *Coolie Speaks*, 6–7. For continuities in the slave trade within Latin America at this time, see Echeverri, "Esclavitud y tráfico de esclavos."

25. For examples of responses of labor to wars of independence and their immediate aftermath, see Tutino, *Founding Capitalism in the Bajío*, 490–91; Blanchard, *Under the Flag of Freedom*, 114–26; Illanes O., *Chile des-centrado*, 15–25; Fick, "From Slave Colony to Black Nation," 160.

## Chapter 3

1. This basic information comes from his initial declaration, Declaración de José María Rojas, 13 November 1869, San Carlos, folio 1v, file 20, folder R4, SJC, EI, AHM. For when "peón" is added, see Confesión de José María Rojas, 15 February 1870, Mendoza, folio 21v, file 20, folder R4, SJC, EI, AHM.

2. Their daughter was three years old and listed as Argentine, indicating she had been born there. Census entry for Delfina Rojas, 1869, San Carlos, "Argentina, censo nacional, 1869," *FamilySearch*, accessed 14 February 2019, www.familysearch.org/ark:/61903/3:1:S3HY-6QP9-H8D, FSL microfilm 686890. *Note:* although I consulted records online, microfilm numbers are listed for all *FamilySearch* records to provide a physical location for the source. Original census schedules sourced from Comisión Directiva del Censo, Archivo General de la Nación, Buenos Aires.

3. Declaración de Rojas, 13 November 1869, folio 2v.

4. Declaración de Rojas, 13 November 1869, folio 2v.

5. Declaración de Rojas, 13 November 1869, folio 1v.

6. Although this chapter is not a history of crime but rather a history done through it, the topics of crime and rural disorder have received much attention. For a sample of scholarship on the Argentine case, see Molina, "Circuitos mercantiles, circulación de personas"; Fradkin, *El poder y la vara*; Slatta, "Rural Criminality and Social Conflict"; Agüero, "Formas de continuidad del orden jurídico"; Salvatore, *Wandering Paysanos*, 197–231; Comadrán Ruíz, "Notas para una historia"; Gascón, "Formas de control."

7. Sanjurjo de Driollet, *La organización político-administrativa*, 25–35; Molina, "Los tentáculos de la justicia," 160–64.

8. Romero, *Latinoamérica*, 176. For some of these spatial projects, see Craib, *Cartographic Mexico*; Appelbaum, *Mapping the Country of Regions*; del Castillo, *Crafting a Republic for the New World*. In a different sense, see also Chiaramonte, "'¿Provincias o Estados?'"; Agüero, "'¿Provincias o Estados?'"

9. Marigliano, "Aportes para el estudio de la legislación," 111–12, 126. For *estancia* regulation, see Provincia de Mendoza, Sala de Representantes, "Reglamento de estancias" (11 July 1834), in Ahumada, *Código de las leyes*, 87–89; Provincia de Mendoza, Sala de Representantes, "Honorable resolución, aprobando el Reglamento de Estancias" (9 October 1845), in Ahumada, *Código de las leyes*, 162–65. Although seemingly contrary to the notion that extensive landed property should define categories like hacendados, the use of animals to circumscribe class in Mendoza made sense because the availability of land was not a pressing problem. Indeed, the laws take far more measures to regulate animal

property than landed property. There is no way to do justice to the extensive literature on the hacienda in Latin American historiography. For a good starting point, see Van Young, *Writing Mexican History*, 21–52.

10. Escolar, *Los indios montoneros*, 93.

11. Provincia de Mendoza, Poder Ejecutivo, "Decreto gubernativo, sobre los animales desconocidos del territorio de las Lagunas, y reglamentando el modo de recojer, señalar y marcar" (4 August 1830), in Ahumada, *Código de las leyes*, 68–70.

12. Escolar, "Huarpe Archives in the Argentine Desert," 462–76.

13. Provincia de Mendoza, Sala de Representantes, art. 1, secs. 1–3, "Reglamento de estancias" (11 July 1834), in Ahumada, *Código de las leyes*, 87. For the place of the subdelegado in the livestock economy, see Sanjurjo de Driollet, *La organización político-administrativa*, 63–72.

14. Sanjurjo de Driollet, "Las continuidades en el gobierno," 450–52; Sanjurjo de Driollet, *La organización político-administrativa*, 48–56.

15. Molina, "Tras la construcción del orden provincial," 98. For the thesis that disorder was the reason for the military commissions, see Acevedo, *Orígenes de la organización judicial*, 78, 83–93. On military commissions as indicative of executive control over the judicial, see Molina, "Tras la construcción del orden provincial," 91–97. On the justice system broadly in Mendoza in this period, see Bransboin, *Mendoza federal*, 69–96.

16. Molina, "Tras la construcción del orden provincial," 88.

17. Molina, "Tras la construcción del orden provincial," 105.

18. Provincia de Mendoza, Sala de Representantes, art. 16, "Ley, reglamentando los procedimientos de la Comision Militar, en los delitos de hurtos y robos, y prescribiendo sus penas" (7 May 1845), in Ahumada, *Código de las leyes*, 157. For all other theft, values of stolen effects dictated punishment, which further demonstrates how the military commissions did not engage in the quality of culpability, but rather the direct relationship to punishability. See arts. 11–16.

19. Salvatore, *Wandering Paysanos*, 250.

20. For example, Sumario, 6 April 1853, Mendoza, folio 1r, file 28, folder M5, SJC, EI, AHM. For examples of exile as punishment, see file 15, folder T2; file 7, folder M3; file 6, folder S4; file 13, folder M3; file 4, folder T2, all in SJC, EI, AHM.

21. Agüero and Rosso, "Codifying the Criminal Law in Argentina."

22. Provincia de Mendoza, Presidencia del Honorable Junta de R. R. de la Provincia, "Honorable resolución, prohibiendo la pena de azotes" (1 October 1853), in Ahumada, *Código de las leyes*, 271.

23. Salvatore, "Death and Liberalism."

24. Sanjurjo de Driollet, "Las continuidades en el gobierno," 459–60.

25. Based on my analysis of criminal cases listed in table B.1.

26. Confesión de Rojas, 15 February 1870, folio 22r.

27. Census entry for Dominga Ponse, 1869, San Carlos, "Argentina, censo nacional, 1869," *FamilySearch*, accessed 14 February 2019, www.familysearch.org/ark:/61903/3:1:S3HY-6QP9-DDR, FSL microfilm 0686890.

28. Census entry for Dominga Ponse. Costurera was the second most common profession in rural Mendoza for men or women after peón, see Argentina, Comisión Directiva del Censo, *Primer censo*, 356–61. For how in the nineteenth century "female occupations" such as sewing were "understood as an extension of domestic duties" see K. Zimmerman,

"Pertaining to the Female Sex," 47. For the changing occupations of women in Argentine censuses, see Guy, "Women, Peonage, and Industrialization," 71–72.

29. Lacoste, "Wine and Women," 367.

30. For example, Declaración de María de los Ángeles Castillo, 13 March 1864, Mendoza, folio 4v, file 24, folder G4, SJC, EI, AHM. In a slightly different way, see also Declaración de Sebastiana Arze, 10 September 1869, San Carlos, folios 2v–3r, file 20, folder L3, SJC, EI, AHM.

31. Declaración de José María Pérez, 30 January 1846, Mendoza, folio 3v, file 17, folder 449, Sumarios Civiles y Militares, EI, AHM; Declaración de Lucas Torres, 17 September 1846, Mendoza; Declaración de Isabel Rojas, 17 September 1846, Mendoza, folios 3v, 6r, file 8, folder T2; Declaración de Josefa Arias, 10 February 1859, Mendoza, folios 3r–4r, file 24, folder S4, last three in SJC, EI, AHM.

32. Much of this was discussed in chapter 1.

33. Baptism entry for Dominga Eulogia Ponze, 4 August 1824, Río Cuarto, Catedral Inmaculada Concepción, "Argentina, Córdoba, registros parroquiales, 1557–1974," *FamilySearch*, accessed 2 October 2020, www.familysearch.org/ark:/61903/3:1:S3HT-DR4S-1GR, FSL microfilm 763315.

34. E. Edwards, *Hiding in Plain Sight*.

35. On censuses in Buenos Aires, e.g., see Andrews, *Afro-Argentines of Buenos Aires*, 66–83.

36. Juan A. Gelly y Obes to Señor Gobernador de la Provincia de Mendoza, 6 June 1863, Argentina, Ministro de Estado, Departamento de Guerra y Marina, *Memoria [. . .] 1864*, 94–95. For Irusta on the frontier, see Davies Lenoble, "Resistencia de la ganadería," 369.

37. K. Zimmerman, "Pertaining to the Female Sex," 52. For a comprehensive take on women's property rights in the nineteenth century, see Deere and León, "Liberalism and Married Women's Property Rights." More specifically for Argentina and changing legal status of women, see Guy, "Lower-Class Families, Women, and the Law."

38. Careo José María Rojas and Juan de Dios Arahuna, 24 [?] January 1869, Mendoza [?], folio 19r, file 20, folder R4, SJC, EI, AHM. I use the more familiar word "pasture" instead of "paddock."

39. Sáez, *Límites i posesiones*, 119.

40. Richard-Jorba, *Poder, economía y espacio*, 97.

41. One of the greatest populizers of this division was Domingo Faustino Sarmiento. See Escolar, *Los dones étnicos*, 129–36; N. Shumway, *Invention of Argentina*, 141.

42. Escolar and Saldi, "Making the Indigenous Desert."

43. Declaración de Aniceto Maona, 14 May 1862, San Juan, folio 4v, file 11, folder M1, SJC, EI, AHM. Obviously, this figure must not be taken as absolute as it is based on a singular declaration and cannot factor in the variability in prices based on different geographical and seasonal contexts.

44. For these figures: 10–30 pesos for a mule (disputed in the interrogation), Declaración de Manuel Fuensalida, 19 November 1869, Mendoza [?], folio 4r, file 20, folder R4; 5–12 pesos per mule (price dispute in the interrogations), Declaración de Santiago Medina, 25 November 1869, Mendoza, folios 13v–14r, file 20, folder L3; 12 pesos for a mule, Declaración de Miguel Navarro, 26 [?] April 1866, Mendoza [?], folio 2r–v, file 11, folder N1; 18 pesos for a horse, Declaración de José Serapio Suárez, 12 June 1862, Mendoza, folio 8v, file 19, folder S6; 7 pesos for a mule, Carlos Videla (Policía de Mendoza) to Juez del Crimen,

10 June 1872, Mendoza, folio 1r, file 14, folder CH1; 6 pesos for a mare, Declaración de Juan Mercedes López, 13 December 1858, Mendoza, folio 4r, file 10, folder G1; 5–6 pesos each for a horse and two mules, Sumario, 5 January 1853, folio 1r, file 25, folder H1; 1 peso for a horse, Sumario, 25 March 1853, folio 1r, file 6, folder M3; 12.25 pesos for a horse, Declaración de Juan Silva, 17 February 1852, Mendoza, folio 3r, file 22, folder S1; 6 pesos for a horse, Sumario, 1 April 1853, Mendoza, folio 1v, file 24, folder S1; 5 pesos each for two horses, Declaración de Jesús Lagos, 11 February 1859, Mendoza, folio 5r, file 24, folder S4; 12 pesos for a horse, Declaración de Melchor Troncoso, 15 June 1858, Mendoza, folio 3v, file 24, folder T2, all in SJC, EI, AHM. In San Juan, horses were valued at approximately 15 pesos, mares at 9 pesos, and mules at 26 pesos. Adolfo Sanchez, Juan Covos, Eusebio Zapata, n.d., n.p., folios 246r–250r, "Departamento del Albardón. Nominas de los rovos han echos los invasores desde el 5 de Enero hasta el 8 de Abril"; Lorenzo Jofre, Juan Agustín Castro Gatices, 12 June 1867, San Juan, 251r–260r, "Departamento de Concepción. Razon de los vecinos que han sufrido robos y saqueos desde el cinco de Enero, hasta el siete de Abril, presente año 1867 por las fuerzas invasoras a esta Provincia"; Antero Barriga (Chilean Consulate in San Juan), 11 January 1867, San Juan, 288r–289v, "Razon de los reclamos de nales. [nacionales] chilenos, entablado despues de la ocupacion por las fuerzas del Coronel de Ejército Don Juan de Dios Videla hasta la fecha" (copy); Antero Barriga (Chilean Consulate in San Juan), 15 January 1867[?], San Juan, 291r-v, "Reclamos de nacionales chilenos por despojos i tropelias por las tropas al mando del Coronel Don Juan de Dios Videla" (copy), all in book 318, box 154, FG, AHSJ. Note on currency throughout the book: all currencies are given as they appear in documents, including unspecified pesos. For more on the history of Argentine currency, see Quintero Ramos, *History of Money and Banking*.

45. Obviously, it is difficult to calculate with certainty the wages of rural workers in the mid-nineteenth century. Nevertheless, some triangulation of anecdotal evidence suggests that approximately 4 pesos per month is a reasonable starting point. In 1859, José Gallardo was paid 4 pesos per month "to go to San Luis" province and work, Declaración de José Gallardo, 11 January 1859, Mendoza, 14v–15r, file 10, folder G1, SJC, EI, AHM. In 1865, Cruz Galdames was paid 4 pesos per month for tending to pastures, José de la Cruz Zenteno to Lieutenant Colonel Ramón Flores, 27 February 1865, Mendoza, folio 87r-v, vol. 130, MREL, ANH. Rodolfo Richard-Jorba estimates that in the 1840s and 1850s monthly wages were about 5 pesos per month and by the 1870s rural wages may have been 4–6 reales per day (more in the south of the province). Richard-Jorba, *Empresarios ricos, trabajadores pobres*, 153n373, 162.

46. Cruz Galdames was paid four pesos per month as wages but also given wheat and meat rations to accompany his wages. Zenteno to Flores, 27 February 1865, folio 87r-v.

47. For example, Cruz Galdames was not paid for over two years of work. Zenteno to Flores, 27 February 1865, folio 87r-v.

48. Donato Guevara (Subdelegacía de San Carlos) to Juez de Crimen de la Provincia, 9 November 1869, San Carlos, folio 7r-v, file 20, folder L3, SJC, EI, AHM.

49. Declaración de Santiago Medina, 25 November 1869, Mendoza, folio 14r, file 20, folder L3, SJC, EI, AHM.

50. Declaración de Medina, 25 November 1869, folio 14r.

51. José de la Cruz Zenteno to Ministro de Gobierno, 2 July 1866, Mendoza, folio 8r, no. 63, file 47, folder 708, SE, EI, AHM.

52. Most travel narratives written in the nineteenth century describe the post house system in varying detail, from the basic issues of distances and dangers to the social norms of hospitality at post houses. See, e.g., Brand, *Journal of a Voyage to Peru*, 38–40, 280–83, 332–35.

53. Chikhachev, *Trip across the Pampas*, 33, 55.

54. Mansilla, *Visit to the Ranquel Indians*, 368.

55. Mansilla, *Visit to the Ranquel Indians*, 369.

56. Mansilla, *Visit to the Ranquel Indians*, 368.

57. In his study, Schivelbusch points to both the monotony of railroad travel and the fatigue caused by mechanical jostling. Schivelbusch, *Railway Journey*, 65–66, 114, 117.

58. For the "everyday," see Lefebvre, *Critique of Everyday Life*, 1:97. For other conceptions of everyday life that inform this chapter, see Braudel, *Civilization and Capitalism*, 1:23–24, 28–29, 415–35; J. Scott, *Weapons of the Weak*; J. Scott, *Art of Not Being Governed*; de Certeau, *Practice of Everyday Life*.

59. Lefebvre, *Critique of Everyday Life*, 1:95.

60. See, e.g., Adelman, *Republic of Capital*.

61. Drawing on Marx's definition of technology as what "reveals the active relation of man to nature, the direct process of the production of his life, and thereby it also lays bare the process of the production of the social relations of his life, and of the mental conceptions that flow from those relations." K. Marx, *Capital*, 1:493n4.

62. Star, "Ethnography of Infrastructure," 382. For works in science and technology studies that have informed my interpretation of breakdowns, see Latour, *Science in Action*; Gieryn, *Cultural Boundaries of Science*. For mobility and everyday technologies, see Mavhunga, *Transient Workspaces*; Arnold and DeWald, "Everyday Technology in South and Southeast Asia"; Edgerton, "Innovation, Technology, or History."

63. Declaración de Cipriano (sometimes referred to as Sipriano) Cabieres, 29 November 1869, Mendoza, folio 6r, file 20, folder R4, SJC, EI, AHM.

64. Census entry for Cipriano Cabieres, 1869, Departamento Primero y Segundo, *FamilySearch*, "Argentina, censo nacional, 1869," accessed 2 February 2019, www.familysearch.org/ark:/61903/3:1:S3HY-6SQ9-VMW, FSL microfilm 685907.

65. Baptism entry for Fabián del Carmen Cabieres, 22 February 1868, San Carlos, San Carlos Borromeo, "Argentina, Mendoza, registros parroquiales, 1665-1975," *FamilySearch*, accessed 2 February 2019, www.familysearch.org/ark:/61903/3:1:939X-HJSS-K8, FSL microfilm 1110402.

66. For example, nearby were Alfonso Monteavaro from Spain and Alejandro Luis Ruilar from France. Census entries for Alfonso Monteavaro and Alejandro Luis Ruilar, 1869, Departamento Primero y Segundo, "Argentina, censo nacional, 1869," *FamilySearch*, accessed 2 February 2019, www.familysearch.org/ark:/61903/3:1:S3HY-6SQ9-J6N, FSL microfilm 685907.

67. Declaración de José Dolores Fuensalida, 30 December 1869, San Carlos; Declaración de Baldomero Roco, 7 January 1870, San Carlos; Confesión de Rojas, 15 February 1870, folios 9r, 12r, 21v–22r, file 20, folder R4, SJC, EI, AHM.

68. Declaración de José María Rojas, 7 December 1869, Mendoza; Confesión de Rojas, 15 February 1870, folios 7v–8r, 21v–22r, file 20, folder R4, SJC, EI, AHM.

69. Denuncia de Vicente Molina, 11 November 1869, San Carlos, folio 1r, file 20, folder R4, SJC, EI, AHM.

70. Subdelegacía de San Carlos, 11 November 1869, San Carlos; Declaración de José María Rojas, 13 November 1869, San Carlos, folio 1r–v, file 20, folder R4, SJC, EI, AHM.

71. The relation with José Dolores Fuensalida is not clarified. Nor is it certain if he was the same Manuel Fuensalida (or Fuenzalida) who was a follower of Francisco Clavero during his rebellion several years earlier. See Bragoni, "Cuyo después de Pavón," 39.

72. Careo José María Rojas and Sipriano Cabieres, 14 January 1870, Mendoza, folio 20r–v, file 20, folder R4, SJC, EI, AHM.

73. Declaración de Cabieres, 29 November 1869, folio 6r–v.

74. Rojas and Cabieres, 14 January 1870, folio 20r–v.

75. For example, "Libro 4° f. 172" (written at the top), 30 March 1855, Mendoza, folio 1r, file 5, folder G4; Declaración de José Antonio Maldonado, 19 September 1855, Mendoza, folio 8r, file 23, folder T2; "Libro 5° f. 84 bta" (written at the top), 6 March 1857, Mendoza, folio 1, file 10, folder M3; Declaración de Carme Lucero, 8 February 1859, Mendoza, folio 20r, file 10, folder G1, all in SJC, EI, AHM.

76. In many instances, houses appear as sites for lodging and mobility reproduction for itinerant laborers. For example, Declaración de José Gallardo, 16 November 1858, Mendoza, folio 2r–v, file 10, folder G1; Joaquín Villanueva (Policía de Mendoza) to Juez del Crimen, 12 May 1866, Mendoza, folio 13r–v, file 9, folder R5, both in SJC, EI, AHM. To say that laborers lodged in houses is a seemingly obvious statement. However, important here is how certain houses could become places for safe lodging while itinerant. In the last case cited this was the case with Joaquín Quiros, who was known for having "accommodated in his house unknown people," a suspicious activity.

77. For works that detail different aspects of pulperías, see Mayo, *Pulperos y pulperías de Buenos Aires*.

78. Slatta, "Comparative Frontier Social Life"; Slatta, "Pulperías and Contraband Capitalism."

79. Carrera, "Esplendor y ocaso de las pulperías porteñas"; H. Silva, "Pulperías, tendejones, sastres y zapateros."

80. Lacoste, "Wine and Women," 379.

81. Augé, *Non-places*, vii–viii.

82. Black, "Spaces of Capital," 355–57.

83. Bragoni, "Recuperación y desigualdad económica," 228, 235. For housing, class, ethnicity, and race in earlier periods, see Morales, "El mundo del trabajo," 10–15. See also Molina, "Los tentáculos de la justicia," 172.

84. Bragoni, "Recuperación y desigualdad económica," 229–32.

85. Aside from the place of weavers, seamstresses, and spinners in Chilean communities already discussed, there were 43 Chilean cobblers (*zapateros* and *boteros*) out of 355 total in the province. Cobblers are not in table A.3, but figures are based on the same analysis. For cobblers in the province, see Argentina, Comisión Directiva del Censo, *Primer censo*, 361.

86. For the varied experiences and economic activities of peons, as well as peasant farmers, in the context of Buenos Aires, see Salvatore, *Wandering Paysanos*, 50–58, 68–76.

87. Besides Rojas's case, there are many cases in which houses appear as sites for commercial exchange (not always of horses and mules). For example, Sumario [?], 5 January 1853, Mendoza [?], folio 1v, file 25, folder H1; Sumario [?], 1 April 1853, Mendoza, folio 1v, file 24, folder S1; Declaración de Juan Silva, 17 February 1852, folio 3r–v, file 22, folder S1;

Declaración de Melchor Troncoso, 15 June 1858, folio 3r–v, file 24, folder T2; Declaración de Santiago Alcaras, 12 January 1859, Mendoza, folios 16v–17r, file 10, folder G1; Lorenzo Lescano to Jefe de Policía, 29 February 1862, Cuartel no. 4 del Departamento 1º de Campaña, Mendoza, folio 4r–v, file 19, folder S6; Careo Francisco Lucero and Rumaldo Pérez, 25 November 1869, Mendoza, folio 13r, file 20, folder L3, all in SJC, EI, AHM. Of course, it should be noted that in some cases it is clear that house indicates a place of business. The overlap between the two should not be surprising and is, in fact, part of the argument that everyday economic exchanges and "private" life shared the same spaces, making the relationships among spaces of social life, economic exchange, and labor constitutive of expansive spaces of mobility and the construction of its social character.

88. For an example of a reference to already established social ties facilitating trust in exchange relationships, see Declaración de Santiago Alcaras, 27 December 1858, Mendoza, folios 13v–14r, file 19, folder G1, SJC, EI, AHM.

89. Sumario [?], 1 April 1853, folio 1v. The question of backing or securing an exchange is related to broad senses of trust and truth through social bonds. In a context in which property was not always expressed through marks and written certifications, having witnesses who were trusted by local officials was important. In that sense, buying and selling animals fell into the realm of witnesses. To buy and sell in front of people was a way of creating trust and was a central concern of the state when an exchange was in dispute.

90. An important note is that the question was generally about knowing the suspect, who was almost invariably a man, hence why I use the masculine pronoun.

91. Confesión de Juan de Dios Romero, 11 May 1866, Mendoza [?], folio 10r, file 9, folder R4, SJC, EI, AHM.

92. Declaración de Segundo Corvalán, 19 June 1858, Mendoza, folio 5r–v, file 24, folder T2, SJC, EI, AHM.

93. For the judicial powers of *decuriones*, *comisarios*, and *subdelegados de villas*, see Province of Mendoza, chapters 1, 2, 8, "Reglamento de administración de justicia en la Provincia de Mendoza" (1 August 1834), in Ahumada, *Código de las leyes*, 92–93, 97–98; Molina, "Los funcionarios subalternos de justicia"; Sanjurjo de Driollet, "Las continuidades en el gobierno"; Acevedo, *Orígenes de la organización judicial*, 65.

94. Sanjurjo de Driollet, "Las continuidades en el gobierno."

95. The installation of the first military commission attributed the prevalence of criminality in part to the "little care of the Comisarios and Decuriones." Provincia de Mendoza, "Decreto gubernativo, estableciendo una comision militar que juzgue los delitos de robos y alevosía" (13 July 1831), in Ahumada, *Código de las leyes*, 76. In 1853 legislation blamed the prevalence of rustling "in great part, for not giving a strict and severe observance to the current dispositions that are preventative of that type of crime by those in charge of closely safeguarding their compliance." Provincia de Mendoza, Poder Ejecutivo, "Decreto gubernativo, prescribiendo los requisitos para la estraccion de animales fuera de la Provincia" (11 November 1853), in Ahumada, *Código de las leyes*, 273–74. In a regulation concerning water and irrigation, the legislature inserted an article to remind the subdelegados not to allow "outsiders without jobs to take refuge" in their districts. Provincia de Mendoza, Poder Ejecutivo, art. 11, "Decreto gubernativo, reglamentando el ramo de aguas en la Villa de San Martín" (13 January 1837), in Ahumada, *Código de las leyes*, 126. That article was not necessarily a new obligation. A regulation on policing of 1828 already required local

officials to ensure the identity and lodging of outside individuals. Provincia de Mendoza, Junta de Representantes, arts. 49, 57, "Reglamento de policía" (18 March 1828), in Ahumada, *Código de las leyes*, 57.

96. Declaración de Rojas, 7 December 1869, folio 7v.

97. Navarro, 12 January 1870, Mendoza, folio 11r–v, file 20, folder R4; Meiseno Calderón (Subdelegacía de la Villa de San Carlos) to Juez del Crimen de la Probincia, 21 January 1870, San Carlos, folio 15r, file 20, folder R4, both in SJC, EI, AHM.

98. For example, in one case, Sebastiana Arze gave testimony about animals found at her "house." Her husband, Benito Arias, was named as the possessor of the house in the previous testimony ("casa de Benito Arias"), but he was not there and she was brought in to give testimony instead. Declaración de Arze, 10 September 1869, folios 2v–3r. In criminal cases, in general, men are often listed as owners or renters of houses ("casa de"). This follows other records that tend to list men as heads of households. For example, in the early nineteenth century, censuses listed men as the "jefe de familia" (family head) in the majority of cases, but not all. See Morales, "El mundo del trabajo," 10. In another case, the suspicions raised by a man housing a suspect contrasted with the same man in a woman's house. The man housed the suspect leading to suspicions that he was involved with the theft. In the case of the woman who housed José Zenteno, there were no suspicions raised about her. For suspicions about the man, see Joaquín Villanueva (Policía de Mendoza) to Juez del Crimen, 25 June 1864, Mendoza, folio 1r, file 17, folder Z1, SJC, EI, AHM. For references to the woman, see Declaración de José Zenteno, 27 June 1864, Mendoza, and Declaración de José Figueroa, n.d. June 1864, Mendoza, folios 2v–3r, file 17, folder Z1, SJC, EI, AHM.

99. When giving testimony women were owners or potential buyers of animals or pastures, "concubines," mothers of suspects, or wives of husbands who did not give testimony.

100. The average number of declarations under the military commissions was 1.5 per case, with a maximum of five. See table B.1 for the cases analyzed for these figures.

101. File 3, folder R4; file 25, folder R3; file 12, folder C2; file 9, folder R1; file 7, folder S4; file 25, folder M5; file 5, folder M3, all in SJC, EI, AHM.

102. This is based on a comprehensive review of the only preserved files on verbal declarations from the period. Files 10, 11, 12, folder L4, SJC, EI, AHM.

103. E.g., Ignacio Videla (Comisaría del 3º Departamento) to José Benito Rodríguez, 28 January 1850, Mendoza; Presidencia de la Comisión Militar, 30 January 1850, Mendoza, folios 6v–7v, file 13, folder L4, SJC, EI, AHM.

104. Provincia de Mendoza, La Sala de Representantes de Mendoza, art. 5, "Ley, reglamentando los procedimientos de la Comision Militar, en los delitos de hurtos y robos, y prescribiendo sus penas" (7 May 1845), in Ahumada, *Código de las leyes*, 155–56.

105. File 3, folder R4; file 25, folder R3; file 28, folder P2; file 28, folder M3; file 7, folder S4; file 12, folder G4; file 5, folder M5; file 6, folder S4; file 22, folder S1, all in SJC, EI, AHM. See also file 17, folder 449, Sección Militar, EI, AHM.

106. File 25, folder R3; file 12, folder C2; file 15, folder T2; file 9, folder R1; file 8, folder T2; file 5, folder M3, all in SJC, EI, AHM. There were no patterns for justifications of being in possession of stolen horses or mules.

107. For examples of when the military commission decided to ignore a potential lead or when attempts to follow up by calling up witnesses or potential suspects failed, see Melitón Arroyo (Comisaría de la Ciudad) to Jefe de Policía de la Provincia, 18 February

1846, Mendoza, folio 1r, file 18, folder P2; Declaración de Juan Sevilla, 7 May 1847, Mendoza, folio 2v, file 6, folder S4; León Correas (Juzgado de Letras) to Presidente de la Comisión Militar, 30 July 1844, Mendoza, folio 1v, file 25, folder M5, all in SJC, EI, AHM.

108. Donato Guevara, 11 November 1869, San Carlos, folio 1r, file 20, folder R4, SJC, EI, AHM.

109. Donato Guevara to Juez de Crimen, 24 November 1869, San Carlos, folio 5r, file 20, folder R4, SJC, EI, AHM.

110. Declaración de Juan de Dios Arahuna, 24 January 1870, Mendoza, folio 17v, file 20, folder R4, SJC, EI, AHM.

111. For the processes that led to changes in rural labor relations and connections between this time period and rural violence, see Salazar, *Labradores, peones y proletarios*; Lozoya López, *Delincuentes, bandoleros y montoneros*.

112. Tomás Aspee to Juez de Primera Instancia de Putaendo, 19 December 1874, San Antonio, folios 4r, 6r, folder 10, box 589, Fondo Juzgado del Crimen de Putaendo, ANH.

113. For state/nonstate spaces, see J. Scott, *Art of Not Being Governed*.

114. This kind of conversation can be seen in related ways in other studies of borderlands and frontiers. See, among many other works, Harambour Ross, *Soberanías fronterizas*; Truett, *Fugitive Landscapes*; Radding, *Landscapes of Power and Identity*, 295–326.

115. Confesión de Rojas, 15 Feburary 1870, folios 21v–22r; Confesión de Juan de Dios Arahuna, 15 February 1870, Mendoza, folios 23v–24r, file 20, folder R4, SJC, EI, AHM.

116. Confesión de Rojas, 15 February 1870, folios 21v–22r.

117. Juez del Crimen, 25 February 1870, Mendoza, folio 25v, file 20, folder R4, SJC, EI, AHM.

118. P. Salas, Defensa, n.d., n.p., folio 26r–v, file 20, folder R4, SJC, EI, AHM.

119. Between 1858, the year in which the first case involving being hired as a defense, and 1872, half of the cases contained some form of this defense. See file 10, folder G1; file 24, folder S4; file 13, folder M3; file 11, folder M1; file 17, folder Z1; file 9, folder R5; file 11, folder N1; file 20, folder R4; file 20, folder L3, all in SJC, EI, AHM. Obviously, this defense looked very different from case to case. Occasionally, the hiring relationship was ambiguous or only used by one suspect to differentiate himself from the other suspects.

120. Declaración de Rumaldo Pérez, 2–[?] November 1869, Mendoza, folio 9r, file 20, folder, L3, SJC, EI, AHM (emphasis added).

121. Espinola (Policía de San Juan) to Inspector General de Policía de la Provincia de Mendoza, 3 May 1866, San Juan, folio 1r, no. 381, file 9, folder R5, SJC, EI, AHM.

122. Claudio Bravo, Defensa, n.d., n.p., folio 27r–v, file 9, folder R5, SJC, EI, AHM.

123. Declaración de Juan Antonio Hubilla, n.d. [possibly 5 January 1853], n.p., folio 1v, file 25, folder H1, SJC, EI, AHM.

124. Declaración de Fermín Coria, n.d. [possibly 5 January 1853], n.p., folio 2v, file 25, folder H1, SJC, EI, AHM.

125. In the 1850s, cases began referring periodically to a particular kind of trade: people coming from Chile to buy animals in Mendoza. For references to this profession, see file 25, folder H1; file 24, folder S4, SJC, EI, AHM. Also, for further reference to mountain-crossing people in Mendoza, see file 3, folder B1, SJC, EI, AHM.

126. Provincia de Mendoza, Poder Ejecutivo, "Decreto gubernativo, prescribiendo los requisitos para la estraccion de animales fuera de la Provincia" (11 November 1853), in Ahumada, *Código de las leyes*, 274.

127. Provincia de Mendoza, Poder Ejecutivo, 11 November 1853, "Decreto gubernativo," in Ahumada, *Código de las leyes*, 273–74.

128. Declaración de Fuensalida, 30 December 1869, folio 9r.

129. Declaración de Roco, 7 January 1870, folios 12r–13r.

130. Sumario de testigos, 7 January 1870, San Carlos, folio 10r–v, file 20, folder R4, SJC, EI, AHM.

131. M. Calderón (Subdelegacía de San Carlos), 26 January 1870, San Carlos, folio 21r, file 20, folder R4, SJC, EI, AHM.

132. I do not analyze these cases through the lens of banditry. However, for a classic overview of the question of banditry, including the place of "elite-bandit alliances" in banditry, see Joseph, "On the Trail."

## Interlude 3

1. For Emilio Rosetti's entrance into the University of Buenos Aires in the context of liberal reforms, see Halperín Donghi, *Historia de la Universidad de Buenos Aires*, 73–74.

2. Halperín Donghi, *Historia de la Universidad de Buenos Aires*, 74.

3. The first generation of students received their degrees in 1870. For a convenient list of engineering students who received a degree from the University of Buenos Aires from 1870 to 1887, see Universidad de Buenos Aires, *Anales de la Universidad de Buenos Aires*, 1:424. Cámara de Diputados, "Sesión del 1° de mayo de 1870," in Provincia de Buenos Aires, *Diario de sesiones [. . .] 1870–1871*, 59–60. Specifically, the law of 18 November 1868 authorized studies of a Trans-Andean, or interoceanic, railroad.

4. For the development of engineers as a technical elite in nineteenth-century Latin America, see Palermo, "Del Parlamento al Ministerio"; Palermo, "Elite técnica y estado liberal"; Salerno, *Los comienzos del Estado empresario*; Lucena, "Imagining Nation, Envisioning Progress"; Valderrama et al., "Engineering Education and the Identities of Engineers," 814–18; Guajardo Soto, *Tecnología, Estado y ferrocarriles*, 25–27; Lucena, "De Criollos a Mexicanos," 275–80; Safford, *Ideal of the Practical*.

5. Emilio Rosetti's biography can be found in his own writings—namely, Rosetti, *I viaggi e le memorie di Emilio Rosetti*. His archive also has a website, www.fondazionerosetti.it. For the context of engineers in Italy during unification, see Bocquet, "Engineers and the Nation in Italy," 233–36. For the municipal context of Italy, see De Pieri, "Nineteenth-Century Municipal Engineers."

6. Aside from an inference of this focus based on the choice of thesis topics by his students, this was more or less directly stated in Luis Huergo's thesis: "Among the varied cases that have served as topics for studies done in these four years, we have considered one of those that should call our attention preferentially, is that of the means of communication." Huergo, *Tesis*, 3. In my own investigations, their theses are not available at the Facultad de Ingeniería at Universidad de Buenos Aires (UBA), the Archivo de la UBA, or the Centro Argentino de Ingenieros. The original copies of Carlos Olivera's and Guillermo Villanueva's theses are at the Biblioteca Nacional de Argentina, in Buenos Aires, along with a published copy of Huergo's thesis.

7. For work on the early years, see Schvarzer and Gómez, *La primera gran empresa*. See also Lewis, *British Railways*, 5–45.

8. Argentina, Ministerio de Obras Públicas, Dirección General de Ferrocarriles, *Estadística de los ferrocarriles*, 22:396.

9. Argentina, Ministerio de Obras Públicas, Dirección General de Ferrocarriles, *Estadística de los ferrocarriles*, 22:396.

10. For some developments in this period, see Lewis, *British Railways*, 29–32.

11. For the full debate in the Cámara de Diputados, see Provincia de Buenos Aires, *Diario de sesiones [. . .] 1868*, 327¼–340. (Pages with fractions appear in order no different than whole numbers.)

12. Provincia de Buenos Aires, Cámara de Diputados, *Diario de sesiones [. . .] 1868*, 332.

13. Provincia de Buenos Aires, Cámara de Diputados, *Diario de sesiones [. . .] 1868*, 330.

14. Provincia de Buenos Aires, Cámara de Diputados, *Diario de sesiones [. . .] 1868*, 330.

15. Provincia de Buenos Aires, Cámara de Diputados, *Diario de sesiones [. . .] 1868*, 328½. See art. 9.

16. Rosetti, *Informe*, 15.

17. Bengoa, *Historia del pueblo mapuche*, 251–86.

18. For an introduction to the Conquest of the Desert, see Larson, *Conquest of the Desert*.

19. For an analysis of the railroad as a civilizing technology, see Canaparo, "Marconi and other Artifices," 245–46.

20. N. Shumway, *Invention of Argentina*, 250–62.

21. Rosetti, *Informe*, 11.

22. Rosetti, *Informe*, 8.

23. Rosetti, *Informe*, 7.

24. Rosetti, *Informe*, 7.

25. Rosetti, *Informe*, 9.

26. Davies Lenoble, "La resistencia de la ganadería," 346.

27. Davies Lenoble, "La resistencia de la ganadería," 360.

28. Davies Lenoble, "La resistencia de la ganadería," 349.

29. Davies Lenoble, "La resistencia de la ganadería," 359.

30. For example, Juan Llerena (Oficial 1° Ministerio General de Gobierno) to Domingo Corvalan (Resguardo del Planchón), 26 November 1849, Mendoza, file 10, folder 390, Sección Hacienda, EI, AHM.

31. Davies Lenoble, "La resistencia de la ganadería," 359. For rebel invasion via the Planchón Pass, see, e.g., Gregorio Beéche (Consulado General de Argentina) to Ministro de Relaciones Exteriores de la República Argentina, 23 [?] November 1867, Santiago, box 41, SDC, AHCA. The folder is red and titled only "CHILE," containing primarily this letter.

32. Andermann, *Optic of the State*, 174, 177–78, 181.

33. Radding, *Landscapes of Power and Identity*, 297–320; Truett, *Fugitive Landscapes*, 13–15.

34. Rosetti, *Informe*, 4. Navarrete was a "vaqueano [sic] de la Cordillera," or mountain guide, sometimes associated with gauchos or Indigenous people of an area who were experts in navigating geography. Irrespective of Navarrete's ethnic identity, his expertise in navigating mountain passes was undoubtedly linked to the Pehuenche.

35. Based on my reading of Andrew Sartori's understanding of reification in *Bengal in Global Concept History*, 26–67.

36. Rosetti, *Informe*, 7.

37. Escolar, "El sueño de la razón," 95–102.

38. K. Marx, *Grundrisse*, 524.

39. Rosetti, *Informe*, 15.

40. Escolar, "El sueño de la razón," 101–7; Alonso, "Politics of Space," 382–84.

41. See, e.g., Rodriguez, *Civilizing Argentina*, 177–99; Craib, *Cry of the Renegade*, 14–31; Savala, *Beyond Patriotic Phobias*, 59–136.

42. For a recent history of this crossing, see Ossa Santa Cruz, "Army of the Andes."

43. Hernández, *El gaucho Martín Fierro*, 69–78. Ludmer, *Gaucho Genre*, 69n56.

44. Ludmer, *Gaucho Genre*, 69–77.

45. Ludmer, *Gaucho Genre*, 66–67.

46. Ludmer, *Gaucho Genre*, 76.

47. For a recent treatment of the gaucho, see Adamovsky, *El gaucho indómito*.

48. Sartori, *Bengal in Global Concept History*, 51.

## Chapter 4

1. For an overview of definitions and approaches to Argentine caudillismo, see Goldman and Salvatore, "Introducción," in *Caudillismos rioplatenses*, 8–18. For a classic work on caudillismo, see Lynch, *Caudillos in Spanish America*. For a later period, see Chasteen, *Heroes on Horseback*. For the historiographical tradition studying caudillismo in Argentina, see Buchbinder, "Caudillos y caudillismo." For the development of the concept in nineteenth-century Argentina, see Svampa, "La dialéctica entre lo nuevo y lo viejo."

2. Lynch, *Argentine Dictator*, 124–25. The other figure most often associated with caudillismo and the supposedly nation-defining struggle between "civilization and barbarism" was Facundo Quiroga, particularly as conceptualized by Domingo Faustino Sarmiento. For an analysis of the origins of Sarmiento's image of Facundo and the opposition between "civilization and barbarism," see de la Fuente, "'Civilización y barbarie.'"

3. Lynch, *Caudillos in Spanish America*, 184.

4. Goldman and Salvatore, "Introducción," in *Caudillismos rioplatenses*, 14.

5. This chapter is not an attempt to enter into debates on caudillismo. If anything, by framing Nicolás Naranjo as a caudillo and shifting the focus to how rebellions operated as economic activities, it attempts to decouple the overly tight links between these rebellions and the mystique of the caudillo.

6. For important state-building processes and conflicts of this period, see Bragoni and Míguez, "De la periferia al centro"; Halperín Donghi, *Proyecto y construcción*; Rock, *State Building and Political Movements*, 14–36; de la Fuente, *Children of Facundo*, 164–87.

7. Sommariva, *Historia de las intervenciones*, 251–61; Bragoni, "Cuyo después de Pavón," 42–44; Rosa, *La guerra del Paraguay*, 258–60.

8. For works rethinking caudillismo, see Adelman, *Republic of Capital*, 110–40; de la Fuente, *Children of Facundo*; Goldman and Salvatore, *Caudillismos rioplatenses*.

9. For recent work on the economic history of this period, see Kuntz Ficker, *First Export Era Revisited*.

10. De la Fuente, *Children of Facundo*, 13.

11. Davies Lenoble, "La emergencia de los indios gauchos"; Escolar, "La república perdida de Santos Guayama"; de la Fuente, *Children of Facundo*.

12. The place of Chile and Chileans in the civil conflicts of the 1860s, and particularly the Revolución de los Colorados, has been examined before. Though insightful, those

studies have tended to focus on the geopolitics of the conflicts, whereas mine focuses on the regional economy's place in them. See, e.g., Lacoste, "Las guerras hispanomaericana," 137–41.

13. Sixto Fonsalida, Juan Manuel Aguilar, Salvador Cruz, Benedicto Correa to Gregorio Beéche (Encargado de Negocios de la República Argentina) (copy), 14 February 1867, Valparaíso, folio 3r, Legación Argentina en Chile, "Reclamo de unos viajeros de ganado desde San Juan hasta el Huasco y Coppó, por perjuicios sufridos a consecuencia de malos tratos de autoridades chilenas," folder 4bis, box 41, SDC, AHCA.

14. They also mention two other financers, Apolinario Soto and Marcos González. Fonsalida, Aguilar, Cruz, Correa to Beéche, 14 February 1867, folio 3v. This is not the first mention of Naranjo in the history of the rebellion; he has received a few sparse mentions, although they have not necessarily come from the sources used in this chapter. Most mentions appear to have their origins in an article written by César Reyes in 1916. See Reyes, "Felipe Varela y la batalla de Bargas," 170. Another reference comes from Rodolfo Ortega Peña and Eduardo Luis Duhalde, who refer to Naranjo as a representative of mining interests, particularly those of William Wheelwright, in La Rioja province. Those interests, according to them, demonstrated exploitation of the province's natural wealth, which Varela recognized. See Ortega Peña and Duhalde, *Felipe Varela*, 86, 157.

15. El Juez de Sección, 6 December 1867, San Juan, folder 7bis, box 41, SDC, AHCA. *Note:* folder 7bis has no cover and begins with "San Juan, Diciembre 6, 1867, El Juez de Seccion, Remite en copia algunos antecedentes que pueden servir para esclarecer la conducta de autoridades de la República de Chile relativa a la invasión del Caudillo Varela." Consulado de Chile en San Juan, 28 February 1867, San Juan, no. 2, "Reclamo de Don Gavino Monda por cuatrocientos seis cabezas de ganado vacuno que Don Fabián Martínez le tomó en su tránsito para Coquimbo" (copy), vol. 462, Fondo Intendencia de Coquimbo, ANH.

16. Nicolás Naranjo to Coronel Felipe Varela (copy), 5 March 1867, Vallenar, in El Juez de Sección, 6 December 1867, San Juan, folios 3–4r, folder 7bis, box 41, SDC, AHCA. Folio numbers reflect order in which pages appear as they are not numbered.

17. Naranjo to Varela, 5 March 1867, folio 6r.

18. Naranjo to Varela, 5 March 1867, folio 6r.

19. Naranjo to Varela, 5 March 1867, folio 5r.

20. From 1849 to 1857, Naranjo was part of several petitions for rights to veins or defunct mines in Atacama province. For a sample, see folio 71r–v, no. 128, vol. 108; folio 42r–v, no. 94A, vol. 69; folio 26r–v, no. 48, vol. 72; folio 145r–v, no. 359, vol. 83; folios 117v–118r, no 222A, vol. 78; folio 145r–v, no. 359, vol. 83; folios 1v–2r, no. 2, vol. 89; folio 38r–v, no. 86, vol. 98; folio 111r–v, no. 243, vol. 103; folios 147v–148r, no. 103, vol. 121; folio 26r, no. 33B, vol. 124, all in Notariales de Copiapó, Archivo Nacional de la Administración, Santiago. For a description of cateadores and their place in the mining sector's development, see Vicuña Mackenna, *El Libro de la Plata*, 175–88.

21. Nazer Ahumada, *José Tomás Urmeneta*, 114–16.

22. For a sample of Naranjo's economic activity, see folios 3r–v, 4v–5r, 15r–v, nos. 4, 7, 24, vol. 9; folios 10r–v, 11v, nos. 16, 17, vol. 38, both in Notariales de Vallenar, Archivo Nacional de la Administración, Santiago. See also folios 14r–15r, no. 13, vol. 27, Notariales de Freirina, Archivo Nacional de la Administración, Santiago.

23. For a biographical narrative of the conditions that mining entrepreneurs faced and the choices they could make in response to them, see Nazer Ahumada, *José Tomás Urmeneta*.

24. For Naranjo's experiences with the uncertainties of the mining industry in his dealings with José Tomás Urmeneta, an important mining entrepreneur and businessman in nineteenth-century Chile, see Nazer Ahumada, *José Tomás Urmeneta*, 114–16. Also, his frequent appearances in civil litigation in the 1860s demonstrate some of the difficulties and economic conflicts he faced during his ascent in that very decade. For a fairly complete sample of references to those cases, see *Gaceta de los Tribunales* (Santiago), "900: Don Nicolas Naranjo contra don José Anotnio Montt, sobre internacion de mina," vol. 20, no. 988, 15 June 1861, 566–67; "524: Don Prudencio Martinez con don Nicolas Naranjo, sobre cobro de pesos," vol. 21, no. 1027, 15 March 1862, 219–20; "582: Don Francisco Montau con don Nicolas Naranjo, sobre cobro de pesos," vol. 21, no. 1028, 29 March 1862, 237; "1873: Don Francisco Montau con don Nicolas Naranjo, sobre cobro de pesos," vol. 21, no. 1055, 27 September 1862, 708; "235: Doña Ramona Pizarro con don Nicolas Naranjo, sobre nulidad de una escritura," vol. 21, no. 1074, 7 February 1863, 91–92; "1876: Don Bernardo Iribarren con don Nicolas Naranjo, sobre cobro de pesos," vol. 21, no. 1107, 26 September 1863, 713; "230: Don Bernardo Iribarren con don Nicolas Naranjo, sobre abono de minerales," vol. 21, no. 1127, 13 February 1864, 100–101; "891: Don José Ramon Becerra con don Nicolas Naranjo, por cobro de pesos," vol. 21, no. 1141, 21 May 1864, 331–32; "1800: Doña Ramona Pizarro con don Nicolas Naranjo, sobre nulidad de una escritura," vol. 21, no. 1159, 24 September 1864, 654; "986: Don Nicolas Naranjo con don José Antonio Montt, sobre internacion," vol. 22, no. 1196, 10 June 1865, 413; "2038: Don Nicolas Naranjo con don Gabino Bolados, sobre cobro de pesos," vol. 22, no. 1215, 28 October 1865, 827; "2422: Doña Ramona Pizarro con don Nicolas Naranjo, sobre nulidad de una escritura," vol. 22, no. 1223, 16 December 1865, 992.

25. For the details of the system of payment and repayment, see Naranjo to Varela, 5 March 1867, 1r–6r.

26. Salazar, *Mercaderes, empresarios y capitalistas*, 506–24. To say that habilitación was the credit system that supported mining is a gross oversimplification. There were many different forms of credit particular to mining, which evolved over time. For a description of those systems and their historical evolutions, see Illanes O., *Chile des-centrado*, 161–79.

27. Nearly every witness testimony from the criminal case in San Juan attested to this practice. See testimonies given in file that begins with Ministerio de Gobierno de San Juan to Subdelegado del Gobierno de la Villa de Jáchal (copy), 5 June 1867, San Juan, folios 5r–14r, folder 7bis, box 41, SDC, AHCA. Furthermore, Naranjo's accounting used sales of cattle to discount from Varela's debt. See Naranjo to Varela, 5 March 1867, folios 1r–6r.

28. E.g., Naranjo to Varela, 5 March 1867, folios 1r, 6r.

29. For example, in one case, oxen sold for thirty-five pesos per head in November 1865. In the same case court-appointed appraisers valued oxen in October 1866 at forty-five pesos per head. Rojo and Tarnassi, "Causa CCXXXIV: Don Francisco Cortés Cumplido, con Felipe Santiago Legiuzamon, sobre cumplimiento de una sentencia y liquidación de daños y perjuicios," in *Fallos de la Suprema Corte*, 4:412–36. Citizen claims of stolen property after the rebellion included prices of animals stolen. The average price of oxen was thirty pesos per head. Adolfo Sanchez, Juan Covos, Eusebio Zapata, n.d., n.p., folios 246r–250r, "Departamento del Albardón. Nominas de los rovos han echos los invasores desde el 5 de Enero hasta el 8 de Abril"; Lorenzo Jofre, Juan Agustín Castro Gatices, 12 June 1867, San Juan, 251r–260r, "Departamento de Concepción. Razon de los vecinos que han sufrido robos y saqueos desde el cinco de Enero, hasta el siete de Abril, presente

año 1867 por las fuerzas invasoras a esta Provincia"; Antero Barriga (Chilean Consulate in San Juan), 11 January 1867, San Juan, 288r–289v, "Razon de los reclamos de nales. [nacionales] chilenos, entablado despues de la ocupacion por las fuerzas del Coronel de Ejército Don Juan de Dios Videla hasta la fecha" (copy); Antero Barriga (Chilean Consulate in San Juan), 15 January 1867[?], San Juan, 291r–v, "Reclamos de nacionales chilenos por despojos i tropelias por las tropas al mando del Coronel Don Juan de Dios Videla" (copy), all in book 318, box 154, FG, AHSJ.

30. The Argentine foreign representatives in Chile reported Varela's invasion plans to the Chilean Ministry of Foreign Affairs on 28 December 1866, based on reports received from the Argentine consulate in Copiapó. Gregorio Beéche (Legación Argentina en Chile) to Ministro de Relaciones Esteriores del Gobierno de Chile, 28 December 1867 [sic, 1866], Valparaíso, published in Argentina, Ministro de Estado, Departamento de Relaciones Exteriores, *Memoria [. . .] 1868*, annex G (República de Chile), no. 2, "Correspondencia cambiada entre la Legacion Argentina y el Gobierno de Chile relativa á la invasion armada, efectuada sobre el territorio de la República por refugiados argentinos," 118–19. The official chronology of the invasion produced by the Argentine government can be found published in this *Memoria*.

31. Fonsalida, Aguilar, Cruz, Correa to Beéche, 14 February 1867, folio 1r; Francisco José María Vega to Martín Rodríguez, 12 December 1866, Tudcum, folio 32r–v, both in book 318, box 154, FG, AHSJ.

32. Gaspar Brabo to Ministro de Gobierno, 13, 17 December 1866, Jáchal; Martín Rodríguez to Ministro de Gobierno, 20 December 1866, Jáchal; M. Furque [?] (El Comandante en Jefe de las fuerzas expedicionarias) to Camillo Rojo (Gobernador de la Provincia), 20 December 1866, Jáchal; Juan José Segundo Fonseca (El Juez de Paz y Comisario de Policía de la Iglesia), 20 December 1866; Gregorio Beéche (Legación Argentina en Chile) to Gobernador de la Provincia de San Juan, 29 December 1866, Valparaíso; Wenceslao Paunero (Comisionado Nacional y Comandante en Jefe del Ejército del Interior) to Gobernador de la Provincia de San Juan, 31 December 1866, Cuartel General en marcha, San Luis, folios 37r–v, 47v–48r, 59r, 61r, 64r, 80r–81r, 100r, all in book 318, box 154, FG, AHSJ.

33. Ramón Ferreira (Legación Argentina en Chile), 1 July 1867, Valparaíso, folio 3r, "Se comunica al Encargado de Negocios en Chile la toma de San Juan por fuerzas reboltosas y de las evoluciones del Montonero Juan Saá para impeder el paso de las fuerzas del General Paunero. Se encarece reclamo del Gobierno Chileno las medidas que aconsejan los deberes de amistad y buena vecindad para que desarme é interne a los revoltosos que de nuevo penetrasen en territorio chileno," folder 11, box 41, SDC, AHCA.

34. For mention of the Tránsito River in cattle banditry involving Varela, see "265: Don José Luis Sariego con Don Slavador Godoi, sobre derecho a unos animals vacunos," *Gaceta de los Tribunales* (Santiago), vol. 27, no. 1390, 27 February 1869, 155. On the Huascoaltinos, see José Bengoa, *La memoria olvidada*, 256–60; Molina Otarola, "Pueblo de Indio Huasco Alto," 43.

35. Fonsalida, Aguilar, Cruz, Correa to Beéche, 14 February 1867, folio 1v.

36. Fonsalida, Aguilar, Cruz, Correa to Beéche, 14 February 1867, folios 1v–2r.

37. Based on the sales confirmed in Naranjo's accounting, at least 500 cattle, totaling 12,000 pesos, were sold on behalf of Naranjo. The high estimate of 4,000 comes from Pedro José Cordero's testimony. Naranjo to Varela, 5 March 1867, folio 1r. For the high estimates, see Declaración de Pedro José Cordero, 4 July 1867, San Juan, part of a file that

begins with Ministerio de Gobierno de San Juan to Subdelegado del Gobierno de la Villa de Jáchal (copy), 5 June 1867, San Juan, folio 13r (out of order, between folios 9 and 10), folder 7bis, box 41, SDC, AHCA. *Note:* pagination begins with Ministerio de Gobierno de San Juan to Subdelegado del Gobierno de la Villa de Jáchal and the file includes copies of notary records and testimonies, which all appear as one long copy.

38. For 1870, San Juan exported 9,975 head of cattle to Chile, of which 9,472 were oxen (95 percent). San Juan also exported 8,922 mules to Chile but in that same period imported 6,468 mules from Chile. When counting the mules imported back to San Juan from Chile, the net export of mules to Chile was 2,454. It is not certain how much of that mule traffic involved mountain transport or how many mules were sold in Chile, but it is clear that all oxen stayed in Chile or at least did not come back to San Juan from Chile. In fact, the oxen trade was almost exclusively to Chile: of the 10,528 oxen exported from San Juan to Chile or other provinces in Argentina, 9,472 went to Chile (90 percent). Conversely, San Juan exported 30,902 mules to Chile and other provinces, but only 8,922 went to Chile (29 percent). Igarzábal, *La Provincia de San Juan*, 388–91.

39. MacGregor, *Commercial Tariffs and Regulations*, 270–71.

40. US House of Representatives, 33rd Cong., 1st Sess., Exec. Doc. no. 121, *U.S. Naval Astronomical Expedition to the Southern Hemisphere*, 1:276.

41. In *El Libro de la Plata*, 166–68, Vicuña Mackenna refers to popular representations of mining and miners, one of them includes these lines, possibly indicating miners' diets:

> Él aguanta una semana
> Y un mes, dos meses y ciento
> Trabajando una labor
> Porotos con sal comiendo
> Sin beber más que agua pura
> Y durmiendo sobre el suelo
>
> (He endures a week
> And a month, two, and a hundred more
> Toiling away
> Eating salted beans
> With nothing more than water to drink
> And sleeping on the floor)

Although he was commenting on a different region and earlier period than the one under examination, Charles Darwin also noted how miners' diets did not include a great deal of meat and were based on "boiled beans and bread," in "Beagle Diary," 167–68. With all of that being said, cattle may have been supplied to growing commercial and smelting centers in such places as Copiapó, Huasco, and La Serena for (luxury) consumption.

42. MacGregor, *Commercial Tariffs and Regulations*, 270–71.

43. Pederson, *Mining Industry*, 110–11. See also Tornero, *Chile ilustrado*, 463.

44. Pederson, *Mining Industry*, 122–25.

45. Valenzuela, "Chilean Copper Smelting Industry."

46. Pederson, *Mining Industry*, 213–20.

47. Pederson, *Mining Industry*, 215.

48. For a summary of the case, see "2233: Contra don Nicolas Naranjo, por resistencias a las autoridades," *Gaceta de los Tribunales* (Santiago), vol. 13, no. 645, 23 December 1854, 5573–74.

49. Manuel Uriondo to Juez del Crimen, Querella, n.d., n.p., folio 2r, folder 42, box 112, Fondo Judicial Criminal de Copiapó, ANH. Naranjo was not the first administrator to do something like that for that mine. See Francisco Cortés to Don Bernardino Codecido, 13 June 1850, Tres Puntas, folio 1r, folder 42, box 112, Fondo Judicial Criminal de Copiapó, ANH.

50. Uriondo to Juez del Crimen, Querella, n.d., folio 1r–v.

51. Antero Barriga (Consulado de Chile en San Juan) to Álvaro Covarrúbias (Ministro de Relaciones Exteriores de Chile), 19 January 1867, San Juan, folios 153v–154v, no. 41, Cónsules de la Confederación Argentina (1867), vol. 36, Fondo Argentino, Archivo de la Cancillería de Chile, Santiago. In Mendoza, the Chilean consulate received petitions during the rebellion from Chileans complaining about troops expropriating cattle, sometimes without giving any "receipt" for the animals. How often expropriations were at the orders of military commanders, however, is not certain. See José de la Cruz Zenteno (Consulado de Chile en Mendoza) to Ministerio de Gobierno, 8 December 1866, Mendoza, folio 15, no. 100, file 50, folder 708, SE, EI, AHM.

52. These figures come from two departments, Albardón and Concepción. Sanchez, Covos, Zapata, n.d., folios 246r–250r; Jofre, Castro Gatices, 12 June 1867, folios 251r–260r; Barriga, 11 January 1867, folios 288r–289v; Barriga, 15 January 1867 [?], folio 291r–v.

53. Sanchez, Covos, Zapata, n.d., folio 246r–v.

54. Ministro de Gobierno to Cónsul de Chile en Mendoza, 8 April 1863, Mendoza, folios 4r–5v, no. 4, book 19, Copiadores, EI, AHM.

55. For an example of this practice, see "1587: Don Francisco T. Coll con don Eujenio Figueroa i compartes, sobre reivindicacion de unos bueyes," *Gaceta de los Tribunales* (Santiago), vol. 26, no. 1365, 5 September 1868, 697. De la Fuente points to the "hierarchical organization" of expropriations and the material motivations, including work, for participants in rebellion. De la Fuente, *Children of Facundo*, 94–100.

56. For this labor dispute, see Andrés C. Riveras (Subdelegación de Gobierno) to Ignacio Flores (Gobernador de la Provincia), 11 January 1867, Comandancia de Armas de la Villa de Jáchal, folios 279r–280r, book 318, box 154, FG, AHSJ.

57. Felipe Varela (Jefe expedicionario del Norte) to Gobernador de la Provincia, 9 March 1867, Jáchal, folio 87r–v, book 323, box 157, FG AHSJ, FG.

58. Fonsalida, Aguilar, Cruz, Correa to Beéche, 14 February 1867, folio 3v.

59. Felipe Varela a Fabián Martínez, 6 March 1867, Villa de Jáchal, Venta [?], part of a file that begins with Ministerio de Gobierno de San Juan to Subdelegado del Gobierno de la Villa de Jáchal, 5 June 1867, San Juan (copy), folio 2r, folder 7bis, box 41, SDC, AHCA.

60. Felipe Varela a Fabián Martínez, 6 March 1867, folio 1r–v.

61. Declaración de Pedro José Cordero, 4 July 1867, folio 13v (out of order, between folios 9 and 10).

62. Argentine officials complained about this problem of jurisdiction. In one instance, the Argentine consul in Copiapó explained to the chargé d'affaires in Chile, Gregorio Beéche, that the court in La Serena declared that crimes committed in Argentina were not "indictable" in Chile. Gervasio Baz to Gregorio Beéche, 17 October 1867, Copiapó, folio 2r, no. 2, Cónsul General Argentino en Chile, "Adjunta copia de tres cartas de caracter privado relativas a los emigrados argentinos," no folder number, box 41, SDC, AHCA.

63. "1587," 695.
64. "1587," 697.
65. "1587," 697.
66. The twelve commercial actors were Juan de Dios Herrera (32 cows), Gabriel Rodríguez (41 cows), Rosario Raigada (400–500 cattle), Felipe Ormaechea (60 oxen with Felipe Leguizamón), Quintin Ríos (90 oxen), Fidel Ocampo (60 oxen), Felipe Leguizamón (60 oxen with Felipe Ormaechea), N. Garay (unknown quantity), Féliz Meléndez (unknown quantity), Valentín González (200+ oxen), Eujenio Figueroa (purchased from Valentín González), and Lucio Carrasco (purchased from Valentín González). For references to González, Carrasco, and Figueroa, see "1587," 695–97. For references to Herrera, Rodríguez, Raigada, Ormaechea, Ríos, Ocampo, Leguizamón, Garay, and Meléndez, see declarations of Juan Manuel Aguilar, Gaspar Bravo, Honorio Basualdo, José María Suárez, and Pedro José Cordero in the document that begins with Ministerio de Gobierno de San Juan to Subdelagdo de Gobierno de la Villa de Jáchal, 5 June 1867, folios 6r–12r. For an additional reference to Ríos, see "589: Contra Elias Gutierrez i otros, por robo de ganados i otras especies," *Gaceta de los Tribunales* (Santiago), vol. 26, 11 April 1868, no. 1344, 253–54.

67. My description and the categories I use are simplifications and do not capture some nuances. While they are derived in part from Rafael Igarzábal's account of cattle trading cited below, for a complete analysis in Mendoza, see also Richard-Jorba, *Poder, economía y espacio*, 73–94.

68. Igarzábal, *La Provincia de San Juan*, 300–303. The arriero was skilled not only in the physical aspects of mobility but also in the institutional ones. At least in Mendoza, arrieros were often charged with dealing with customs posts in the mountains and carrying the documents necessary to pass through them. For the case of Mendoza, see Resguardo documents in folders 389, 390, 391, Sección Hacienda, EI, AHM.

69. Schmidtmeyer, *Travels into Chile, over the Andes*, 225; Brand, *Journal of a Voyage to Peru*, 150. This characterization of arrieros continued throughout the nineteenth century, see Crawford, *Across the Pampas and the Andes*, 201–2; Fitz Gerald, *Highest Andes*, 17–21.

70. Ministerio de Gobierno de San Juan to Subdelegado de Gobierno de la Villa de Jáchal, 5 June 1867, folio 10r.

71. Igarzábal, *Provincia de San Juan*, 299–302.

72. Igarzábal, *Provincia de San Juan*, 384–87.

73. Converso, *Lenta formación de capitales*, 51–52.

74. Igarzábal, *Provincia de San Juan*, 301.

75. Querella, n.d., n.p., folio 1v, folder 49, box 112, Fondo Judicial Criminal de Copiapó, ANH.

76. Naranjo was accused of not going into exile. See "3354: Contra don Nicolas Naranjo, por quebrantamiento de condena," *Gaceta de los Tribunales* (Santiago), vol. 14, no. 711, 29 March 1856, 6579–80.

77. Nazer Ahumada, *José Tomás Urmeneta*, 114–16.

78. The majority of these interactions can be seen in the notarial records of Vallenar, vols. 36–38, for this period.

79. Jorge Montt to Diputado de Minas, n.d., n.p., folios 9v–11v, folder 26, box 30, Fondo Judicial Civil de Freirina, ANH.

80. Chile, Oficina Central de Estadística, *Anuario estadístico*, 3:421.

81. Varios ciudadanos, Protesta, 16 May 1864, folio 105v, no. 80, vol. 37, Notarios de Vallenar, Archivo Nacional de la Administración, Santiago.

82. Varios ciudadanos, Protesta, 16 May 1864, folio 105v. For part of Prado's history with the Cámara de Diputados, see Anuario estadístico [. . .] 1868 i 1869, 271–77.

83. For Francisco Antonio Silva as judge in the case, see Varios ciudadanos, Protesta, 16 May 1864, folio 108r. For Prado's post, see Anuario estadístico [. . .] 1868 i 1869, 273.

84. "409: Contra don Nicolas Naranjo, por conato de motin," Gaceta de los Tribunales (Santiago), vol. 23, no. 1231, 10 February 1866, 205.

85. Alvaro Covarrúbias (Ministro del Interior) to Pedro Olate (Intendente de Atacama), 9 October 1865, Santiago, sec. 1, no. 50, vol. 302, Fondo Intendencia de Atacama, ANH.

86. "Situacion imponente," El Copiapino (Copiapó, Chile), 10 September 1865, 1.

87. "Carestíal," El Constituyente (Copiapó, Chile), 30 September 1865, 1.

88. "Motín en Chañaral," El Constituyente (Copiapó, Chile), 30 September 1865, 3.

89. "Huasco," El Constituyente (Copiapó, Chile), 25 October 1865, 1.

90. "Huasco," El Constituyente (Copiapó, Chile), 27 October 1865, 2.

91. "Huasco," El Constituyente (Copiapó, Chile), 4 October 1865, 1.

92. A. Ismael Gárate (Departamento de Vallenar), 30 June 1869, Vallenar, "Nómina de los Tenientes Gobernadores i Gobernadores que ha tenido el departamento de Vallenar desde el año de 1817 hasta el año actual de 1869," vol. 240, Fondo Intendencia de Atacama, ANH.

93. They arrived 22 January 1867, and Silva served until 18 January 1867. Fonsalida, Aguilar, Cruz, Correa to Beéche, 14 February 1867, folio 2r. For a list of governors, see Ismael Gárate, 30 June 1869, "Nómina de los Tenientes Gobernadores." He later became intendente of Atacama. See Chile, Anuario estadístico . . . 1868 i 1869, 258.

94. Fonsalida, Aguilar, Cruz, Correa to Beéche, 14 February 1867, folio 2r–v.

95. Declaración de José María Suárez, 17 June 1867, Jáchal and Declaración de Pedro 4 July 1867, San Juan part of the file that begins with Ministerio de Gobierno de San Juan to Subdelegado de Gobierno de la Villa de Jáchal, 5 June 1867, folios 9r, 11r, 13v (out of order, between folios 9 and 10).

96. Tensions over accusations of Chilean participation in the invasion were perhaps the most intense and widely documented issue discussed between Argentine and Chilean officials. The primary focus of this debate was Vallenar and whether certain officials in the Vallenar government were supporting the rebels' invasion and the extent to which officials from Vallenar lied about the presence of certain rebels in their jurisdiction in the days leading up to the invasion. The dispute is too extensive to cite comprehensively here, nor is the debate itself the central focus of this chapter. However, a few sources are worth consulting to gain an understanding of at least the Argentine government's perspective on the conflict. To begin, the department of foreign affair's Memoria from 1868 detailed the debate through transcribed records. Specifically, see Argentina, Ministro de Estado, Departamento de Relaciones Exteriores, Memoria [. . .] 1868, annex G (República de Chile), no. 5, "Reclamacion de la Legacion chilena sobre los términos de un decreto del Gobierno Argentino relativo á la invasion efectuada al territorio de la República desde el territorio chileno," 196–203. For archival copies and originals of these documents, along with documents not included in the Memoria, see Ferreira, 1 July 1867, Valparaíso, "Se comunica al Encargado de Negocios en Chile la toma de San Juan."

97. Declaración de Pedro José Cordero, 4 July 1867, folio 13r (out of order, between folios 9 and 10).

98. "1015: Don José Ormachea con don Felipe S. Leguizamon, sobre cobro de pesos," *Gaceta de los Tribunales* (Santiago), vol. 26, 12 June 1869, no. 1405, 467–69.

99. The claims listed represented the highest and lowest claims of the case. Rojo and Tarnassi, "Causa CCXXXIV," 418–21.

100. For the above claims, Cortés and Leguizamón were basing their figures on the original price of the cattle (35 pesos per head) for 197 or 198 head (6,895 or 6,930 pesos in total). Rojo and Tarnassi, "Causa CCXXXIV," 419–21.

101. Rojo and Tarnassi, "Causa CCXXXIV," 421–22.

102. Rojo and Tarnassi, "Causa CCXXXIV," 421.

103. Rojo and Tarnassi, "Causa CCXXXIV," 422, 428–29.

104. Rojo and Tarnassi, "Causa CCXXXIV," 422–23.

105. Rojo and Tarnassi, "Causa CCXXXIV," 424.

106. Rojo and Tarnassi, "Causa CCXXXIV," 434–36.

107. Adelman, *Republic of Capital*, 111–13.

108. Martínez Estrada, *Sarmiento*, 184.

## Interlude 4

1. Titus S., *Monografía de los ferrocarriles*, 109. According to Titus, William Wheelwright commissioned Nicolás Naranjo in 1864, too. But according to Wheelwright, he had commissioned Naranjo previously, likely in or around 1854. Wheelwright, "Proposed Railway Route," 155.

2. Wheelwright, "Proposed Railway Route," 155–62.

3. Serje de la Ossa, "Fronteras y periferias," 34.

4. Watts, "Securing Oil," 215–16.

5. Bengoa, *La memoria olvidada*, 91.

6. Molina Otarola, "Pueblo de Indio Huasco Alto," 43. For the distribution of land in later periods involving southern Chile, see Picone, "Legitimizing and Resisting Spatial Violence," 61–63; Harambour Ross, *Soberanías Fronterizas*, 159–66.

7. See, e.g., Craib, *Cartographic Mexico*, 98–115.

8. Watts, "Securing Oil," 217.

9. For a more nuanced conceptualization of the "sovereignty of capital" and "state sovereignty" together, see Harambour Ross, *Soberanías fronterizas*, 29–34.

10. I find David Harvey's theorization of the role of land markets in the perpetuation of capitalism particularly helpful. Harvey, *Limits to Capital*, 367–71.

11. Gobat, *Empire by Invitation*, 6.

12. Gobat, *Empire by Invitation*, 206–7.

13. May, "Young American Males and Filibustering," 882.

14. For a somewhat different sense of infrastructural power, see Mann, "Autonomous Power of the State."

15. P. Edwards, "Infrastructure and Modernity," 184.

16. Mukerji, "Territorial State," 404.

17. Kuntz Ficker, *Historia mínima de la expansión ferroviaria*, 345–53.

18. For public debt in Argentina during the 1880s and its relation to infrastructure projects, see Marichal, *Century of Debt Crisis*, 128–29.

19. Lewis, *British Railways*, 22.

20. Outside of Latin America, see Carroll, *Science, Culture, and State Formation*; Pritchard, "From Hydroimperialism to Hydrocapitalism."

21. Dimas, *Poisoned Eden*, 202.

22. Mitchell, *Carbon Democracy*, 21–27; Palermo, "En nombre del hogar proletario," 586–87.

23. Mitchell, *Rule of Experts*, 312n77. For engineering and infrastructure in Latin America, see Miller, *Republics of Knowledge*, 181–97.

24. Chastain and Lorek, "Introduction," in *Itineraries of Expertise*, 5. For a national context of the same period, see Hecht, *Radiance of France*.

## Chapter 5

1. Declaración de Pedro Espinosa (copy), 7 December 1869, Uspallata, folio 290v, Cónsules en la Confederación Argentina (1869), vol. 36, Fondo Argentino, Archivo de la Cancillería de Chile, Santiago.

2. Declaración de Tomás Jameson, 5 January 1870, San Felipe, folios 2r–3r, Sección San Felipe y Santa Rosa de Los Andes, "Copia del sumario instruido contra los autores del salteo cometido en la Cordillera por D. Casimiro Ferrari i otros," vol. 94, MREL, ANH. *Note:* there are no folio numbers for the case, so folios are numbered as they appear.

3. Declaración de Jameson, 5 January 1870, folio 3r.

4. Declaración de Pedro Antonio Espinosa y Juan José Gómez, 7 December 1869, Uspallata, folio 11r, file 27, folder F1, SJC, EI, AHM.

5. Declaración de Justo Laureano Lucero, 5 January 1870, San Felipe, folio 4r, Sección San Felipe y Santa Rosa de Los Andes, "Copia del sumario instruido contra los autores del salteo cometido en la Cordillera por D. Casimiro Ferrari i otros," vol. 94, MREL, ANH. For reference to his uncle being Manuel Chirino, see Declaración de Espinosa y Gómez, 7 December 1869, folio 11v.

6. For reference to how all three were killed, see Declaración de Diego Ponce, 5 January 1870, San Felipe, folio 20r, Sección San Felipe y Santa Rosa de Los Andes, "Copia del sumario instruido contra los autores del salteo cometido en la Cordillera por D. Casimiro Ferrari i otros," vol. 94, MREL, ANH.

7. For the estimate of the silver's worth, see Declaración de Pedro García, 10 December 1869, Mendoza, folio 4v, file 27, folder F1, SJC, EI, AHM. Unspecified peso.

8. Declaración de Jameson, 5 January 1870, folio 3r–v.

9. Declaración de Pedro García and Manuel Betoño, 5 December 1869, Uspallata, folio 6r–v, file 27, folder F1, SJC, EI, AHM.

10. Tomás Jameson to Guillermo Jameson, 23 January 1862, Jáchal, no. 12, folder 5, William James Collection, Gray Herbarium Library, Harvard University's Botany Libraries, Cambridge, MA.

11. Guillermo Jameson to Dr. Guillermo Jameson, 25 April 1863, Jáchal, no. 3, folder 15, William James Collection, Gray Herbarium Library, Harvard University's Botany Libraries, Cambridge, MA.

12. Jameson to Dr. Jameson, 25 April 1863.

13. Guillermo Jameson to Dr. Guillermo Jameson, 14 February 1869, Jáchal, no. 10, folder 15, William James Collection, Gray Herbarium Library, Harvard University's Botany Libraries, Cambridge, MA.

14. I have no direct information on the reason for this particular trip. As late as January 1868, however, Tomás Jameson and Desiderio Bravo both were listed as "consignatarios" (consignees) for Emilio Moyano. Desiderio Bravo is listed for 2 January and Jameson y Compañía are listed for 23 January. Rafael Perú (Consulado General de la República Argentina) to Ministro de Relaciones Exteriores de la República Argentina, 23 January 1868, Valparaíso, folio 2r–v, folder 1, box 42, SDC, AHCA. *Note:* aside from red "1" on the front and "Caja no. 134" stamped across the top, the cover of folder 1 is blank. First page begins, "Valparaíso Enero 23 1868, Consul Grl."

15. Declaración de García and Betoño, 5 December 1869, folio 6r–v.

16. Declaración de Jameson, 5 January 1870, folio 2r–v.

17. For the three people who heard about the attacks from Pedro García and Manuel Betoño, see folios 8r, 36v, 39r, file 27, folder F1, SJC, EI, AHM. For the person who found out from Pepe León, see Declaración de García and Betoño, 5 December 1869, folio 7r.

18. Declaración de García and Betoño, 5 December 1869, folio 6r–v.

19. Declaración de Jameson, 5 January 1870, folio 2r–v.

20. Casimiro Ferrari had been in Argentina since some point in the mid-1830s. He arrived in Mendoza at some point in the 1850s, likely 1856 or 1857. José de la Cruz Dávila, 29 September 1857, Mendoza, Loreto, box 30 (1856/1861), Informaciones matrimoniales parroquia Matriz de Mendoza, Archivo del Arzobispado de Mendoza, Mendoza, Argentina. I thank Luis Caballero, who generously provided me with all of Ferrari's biographical records from the Archivo del Arzobispado de Mendoza.

21. Ferrari was named administrator of the Hospital San Antonio on 24 December 1857. Inspector de Hospital to Ministro General de Gobierno, 24 December 1857, Mendoza, folio 9r, file 23, folder 82, Sección Gobierno, EI, AHM. The last document from him as administrator was in November 1859, file 40, folder 82, Sección Gobierno, EI, AHM. The first mention of a different administrator, Manuel Pedernera, was in late September 1860, "Presupuesto de gastos y entradas habidas en el hospital San Antonio por el mes de setiembre," 3 October 1860, Mendoza, file 44, folder 82, Sección Gobierno, EI, AHM. It should be noted that the *Registro oficial* of the province shows no record of Pedernera's appointment, despite it being customary to publish administrative appointments in the *Registro oficial*. In that case, Pedernera may have been acting administrator or been appointed at the end of 1859. Provincia de Mendoza, *Registro oficial*.

22. Juana Guillerma Ferrari was born on 15 June 1858 and baptized a month later on 15 July 1858. Bautismo de Juana Guillerma Ferrari, 15 July 1858, Mendoza, folio 167v, no. 26 (1856/1860), Libro bautismos parroquia Matriz de Mendoza, Archivo del Arzobispado de Mendoza, Mendoza, Argentina.

23. Wenceslao Díaz estimates that 3,000 of the city's 8,678 inhabitants survived. Díaz, *Apuntes sobre el terremoto de Mendoza*, 31; Schávelzon, *Historia de un terremoto*.

24. The only reference that I have found to his family after the earthquake comes from the murder case. Félix Frías, the Argentine state representative in Chile, sent a message to the governor of Mendoza, informing him, "The whereabouts are still unknown of Ferrari,

who has his family in this city [Santiago]." Félix Frías to Nicolás A. Villanueva, 23 December 1869, Santiago, folio 5r, file 42, folder 707, SE, EI, AHM.

25. Deposition [?] Casimiro Ferrari, [2 September 1861?], [Mendoza?], folio 1r, file 10, folder F44, Sección Judicial Civil, EI, AHM.

26. Deposition [?] Ferrari, [2 September 1861?], folio 2r.

27. Deposition [?] Ferrari, [2 September 1861?], folio 2r.

28. José María [?] Belomo (Juez de Letras), 12 September 1861, Mendoza, folio 3r, file 10, folder F44, Sección Judicial Civil, EI, AHM.

29. Provincia de Mendoza, *Registro oficial*, 319–21.

30. Casimiro Ferrari (Comandancia Militar del Departamento de Tupungato) to Ministro General de Gobierno, 20 December 1866, Tupungato, folio 32r–v, file 80, folder 505, Sección Militar, EI, AHM.

31. For Ferrari's services in Mendoza as comandante, see Casimiro Ferrari, 18 March 1867, Mendoza, folio 2r, folder 1, Cónsul de Chile en Mendoza, "Solicita la libertad de varios individuos chilenos que se hallan sirviendo forzadamente en el ejército," Cónsul de Chile 1867, box 41, SDC, AHCA. For his role as secretario militar under Rodríguez, see El Director de la Guerra, 29 March 1867, Villa de la Paz, folio 139r, book 323, box 157, FG, AHSJ.

32. The comandante del Resguardo del Río Colorado, Pedro Antonio Herrera Valenzuela, appeared to have an amicable relationship with Ferrari, based on the frequency with which he passed by the outpost. It was close enough that Herrera Valenzuela defended Ferrari only weeks before when a request for his arrest was sent to him by the governor of Los Andes. Declaración de Pedro Antonio Herrera Valenzuela, 13 December 1869, San Felipe, folios 10v–11v, Sección San Felipe y Santa Rosa de Los Andes, "Copia del sumario instruido contra los autores del salteo cometido en la Cordillera por D. Casimiro Ferrari i otros," vol. 94, MREL, ANH. The guard at the same outpost claimed that Ferrari's "servant" was named Pavez but could not identify him, Declaración de Wenceslao Jiménez, 13 December 1869, San Felipe, folio 12v, Sección San Felipe y Santa Rosa de Los Andes, "Copia del sumario instruido contra los autores del salteo cometido en la Cordillera por D. Casimiro Ferrari i otros," vol. 94, MREL, ANH.

33. José de la Cruz Zenteno (Consulado de Chile en Mendoza) to Señor Secretario Militar del Exmo Director de Guerra, 16 March 1867, Mendoza, folio 1r, no. 25, Cónsul de Chile en Mendoza, "Solicita la libertad de varios individuos chilenos que se hallan sirviendo forzadamente en el ejército," Cónsul de Chile 1867, folder 1, box 41, SDC, AHCA.

34. El Fiscal Acusa, n.d., n.p, folios 25v–26v, file 9, folder R5, SJC, EI, AHM; Videla Correas, 4 July 1867, Mendoza, folios 27r–28v, file 9, folder R5, SJC, EI, AHM.

35. Zenteno (Consulado de Chile en Mendoza) to Secretario Militar, 16 March 1867, folio 1r.

36. Ferrari, 18 March 1867, folio 2r.

37. Declaración de García and Betoño, 5 December 1869, folio 6r.

38. Declaración de Tomás Gallardo, 5 December 1869, Uspallata; Declaración de Andrés Canaves, 5 December 1869, Uspallata; Declaración de Juan Olavarría, 5 December 1869, Uspallata, folios 7r–8r, file 27, folder F1, SJC, EI, AHM.

39. Cicerón Lemos to Anacleto Gil (Administrador de Rentas Nacionales), 5 December 1869, Resguardo de Uspallata; Nicolás Villanueva to Ministro de Gobierno, 7 December 1869, Mendoza, folios 10r, 24r–v, file 27, folder F1, SJC, EI, AHM.

40. Lemos to Gil, 5 December 1869, folio 24r-v.

41. Witnesses in Uspallata only made two references to Domingo Pastén and Tomás Farías, only one of which occurred before Cicerón Lemos sent news to San Juan. See Declaración de Gallardo, 5 December 1869, Declaración de Olavarría, 6 December 1869, folios 7r–8r.

42. Ramón González to Juez, 9 December 1869, San Juan, folio 29r, file 27, folder F1, SJC, EI, AHM.

43. González to Juez, 9 December 1869, folio 29r-v.

44. Specifically, the administrator of rentas nacionales suspected Pedro García of having some involvement in the case, although that connection never manifested in subsequent testimonies. For his suspicions, see Nicolás Villanueva to Ministro de Gobierno, 9 December 1869, Mendoza, folio 14r, file 27, folder F1, SJC, EI, AHM.

45. The case ended up revolving mostly around Santos Lobos and Francisca Zapata. For the portion of the case related to Lobos and Zapata, see folios 36r–60r, file 27, folder F1, SJC, EI, AHM.

46. N. A. Villanueva to Félix Frías (Ministro Plenipotenciario de la República Argentina cerca del Gobierno de Chile), 9 December 1869, Mendoza, 46–48, book 34, Copiadores, EI, AHM.

47. Gregorio Beéche (Consulado General de la República Argentina) to Luis Molina (Gobernador de la Provincia de Mendoza), 10, 18, 31 January 1862, Valparaíso, folios, 2r-v, 6r-v, 12r-v, file 17, folder 707, SE, EI, AHM.

48. Beéche to Molina, 10 January 1862, folio 2v.

49. According to the response by Alcade, Beéche requested extradition on 11 January: Manuel Alcalde to Gregorio Beéche, 14 January 1862, Santiago, folio 3r, Cónsul General Argentino en Chile, "Acompaña copia de la correspondencia que ha tenido con el Sor Ministro de RE de Chile sobre los reos Saá, Nazar, Clavero, etc.," folder 6, box 39, SDC, AHCA.

50. Alcalde reminded Beéche twice of the need for documentation. Alcalde to Beéche, 14, 15 January 1862, folios 3r, 4r.

51. Gregorio Beéche to Bartolomé Mitre, 18 January 1862, Valparaíso, folio 5r-v, Cónsul General Argentino en Chile, "Acompaña copia de la correspondencia que ha tenido con el Sor Ministro de RE de Chile sobre los reos Saá, Nazar, Clavero, etc.," folder 6, box 39, SDC, AHCA; Beéche to Luis Molina, 18 January 1862, folio 6r-v. This period between the Battle of Pavón and Mitre's election represents a transitional moment. I refer to the government in Buenos Aires under Mitre as the national government, with the understanding that the process of national reorganization was incipient at the moment.

52. Gregorio Beéche to Manuel Alcalde (copy), 17 February 1862, Valparaíso, folio 15r, file 17, folder 707, SE, EI, AHM.

53. Martín Cano to Gregorio Beéche (copy), 25 January 1862, Santa Rosa de Los Andes, file 20, folder 707, SE, EI, AHM.

54. Gregorio Beéche to Manuel A. Tocornal, 13 April 1863, Valparaíso, folio 3v, no. 1, Cónsul General en Chile, "Comunicaciones relativas á la solicitud del Gobierno de esa República no permitiendo la internacion de ganados que esta efectuando Clavero," folder 14, box 39, SDC, AHCA. See also Beéche to Tocornal, 16 April 1863, Valparaíso, folio 7r, Cónsul General en Chile, "Comunicaciones relativas á la solicitud del Gobierno de esa República no permitiendo la internacion de ganados que esta efectuando Clavero," folder 14, box 39, SDC, AHCA.

55. On the secret trips to Mendoza, see Gregorio Beéche to Luis Molina, 29 April 1862, Valparaíso, folio 34r–35r, file 17, folder 707, SE, EI, AHM. On abusing Chilean hospitality, see Beéche to Manuel Alcalde, 25 April 1862, Valparaíso, folio 1r, no. 1, Cónsul General Argentino en Chile, "Remite copias de la correspondencia tenida con el Sor Ministro de Rs [Relaciones] Exteriores de aquel país para que los argentinos emigrados en aquella República sean alejados de las fronteras de Chile por ser una constante amenaza para la Rep. Argtina [República Argentina] y habla también de los fondos colectados en Chile a beneficio de los desgraciados de Mendoza," folder 5, box 39, SDC, AHCA.

56. Beéche to Mitre, 18 January 1862, folio 5r–v.

57. Manuel Alcalde to Gregorio Beéche, 30 April 1862, Santiago, folio 7v, Cónsul General Argentino en Chile, "Remite copias de la correspondencia tenida con el Sor Ministro de Rs [Relaciones] Exteriores de aquel país para que los argentinos emigrados en aquella República sean alejados de las fronteras de Chile por ser una constante amenaza para la Rep. Argtina [República Argentina] y habla también de los fondos colectados en Chile a beneficio de los desgraciados de Mendoza," folder 5, box 39, SDC, AHCA.

58. Alcalde to Beéche, 30 April 1862, folio 7v.

59. Beéche to Mitre, 18 January 1862, folio 5r–v; Beéche to Mitre, 28 April, 14 May 1862, Valparaíso, folios 5r, 12r–v, Cónsul General Argentino en Chile, "Remite copias de la correspondencia tenida con el Sor Ministro de Rs [Relaciones] Exteriores de aquel país para que los argentinos emigrados en aquella República sean alejados de las fronteras de Chile por ser una constante amenaza para la Rep. Argtina [República Argentina] y habla también de los fondos colectados en Chile a beneficio de los desgraciados de Mendoza," folder 5, box 39, SDC, AHCA.

60. Rufino de Elizalde (Ministro de Relaciones Exteriores) to Gregorio Beéche, 25 August 1862, Buenos Aires, folio 4r, Cónsul General Argentino en Chile, "Acompaña copia de una nota del Vicecónsul en Santa Rosa de los Andes comunicandole algunas noticias sobre los prófugos argentinos y remite una nómina de ellos," folder 9, box 39, SDC, AHCA.

61. Luis Molina to Gregorio Beéche, 30 November 1862, Mendoza, folio 1r, no. 1, Cónsul General Argentino en Chile, "Habla de una nota del Gob [Gobierno] de Mendoza, relativa al temor de una invasión de los argentinos emigrados en Chile e indica se solicite de este Gob [Gobierno] la mayor vigilancia y agrega otras referencias," folder 2, box 39, SDC, AHCA.

62. Unsigned [Rufino de Elizalde] to Luis Molina, 10 January 1863, Buenos Aires [?], folio 8r (*note:* the response from 6 February 1863 by Mendoza indicates that the note is a draft from the Ministro de Relaciones Exteriores, sent from Buenos Aires); de Elizalde to Gregorio Beéche, 7 January 1863, Buenos Aires [?], folio 5v, both in Cónsul General Argentino en Chile, "Habla de una nota del Gob [Gobierno] de Mendoza, relativa al temor de una invasión de los argentinos emigrados en Chile e indica se solicite de este Gob [Gobierno] la mayor vigilancia y agrega otras referencias," folder 2, box 39, SDC, AHCA.

63. The shortest time for an exchange between Mendoza and Buenos Aires was twelve days. See Luis Molina to Rufino Jacinto de Elizalde (Ministro de Relaciones Exteriores de la República Argentina), 15 April 1863, Mendoza; de Elizalde to Molina, 27 April 1863, Buenos Aires, both in Cónsul General en Chile, "Comunicaciones relativas á la solicitud del Gobierno de esa República no permitiendo la internacion de ganados que esta efectuando Clavero," folder 14, box 39, SDC, AHCA. The shortest time for an exchange between Valparaíso and Buenos Aires was twenty-eight days. See Gregorio Beéche to de Elizalde, 13 December 1862, Valparaíso; de Elizalde to Beéche, 10 January 1863, Buenos

Aires, both in Cónsul General Argentino en Chile, "Habla de una nota del Gob [Gobierno] de Mendoza, relativa al temor de una invasión de los argentinos emigrados en Chile e indica se solicite de este Gob [Gobierno] la mayor vigilancia y agrega otras referencias," folder 2, box 39, SDC, AHCA.

64. Molina to Beéche, 30 November 1862, folio 1r; Beéche to Manuel Alcalde, 8 December 1862, Valparaíso, Cónsul General Argentino en Chile, "Habla de una nota del Gob [Gobierno] de Mendoza, relativa al temor de una invasión de los argentinos emigrados en Chile e indica se solicite de este Gob [Gobierno] la mayor vigilancia y agrega otras referencias," folder 2, box 39, SDC, AHCA. Domingo Faustino Sarmiento noted in 1851 that mail between Mendoza and Santiago could take ten days. *Sud-América: Política i Comercio* (Santiago), vol. 1, no. 5, 24 February 1851, 136. The time between Mendoza and Santa Rosa de Los Andes, effectively, the time to cross the mountains, was approximately four days, depending on the conditions. See Mulhall and Mulhall, *Handbook of the River Plate*, 101.

65. "Instrucciones para SE el Sor Enviado Extraordinario y Ministro Plenipotenciario de la República Argentina en la República de Chile Don Félix Frías," 30 January 1869, Buenos Aires, folder 12, box 42, SDC. The cover on folder 12 is otherwise blank with "Caja no. 141" stamped across the top. Inside begins, "Buenos Aires Enero 30 1869."

66. Félix Frías to Mariano Varela (Ministro de Relaciones Exteriores de la República Argentina), 9 July 1869, Santiago, folio 2r, "Expediente 7. Convención de extradición," folder 10, box 8, TC, AHCA.

67. The reality is that this may have been far more about the internalization of that separation and the need to project it than the need to convince the Chileans. In fact, one could easily speculate that the Chileans were very aware of the Argentines' attempts to create a framing of the problem that would satisfy international norms of exile and extradition. For that matter, the Chilean government may have been in agreement with the Argentine government about policing the border in a way that did not embroil Chile in its neighbor's civil conflicts. For example, the minister of foreign affairs in Chile had been explicit about the importance of the extradition treaty in "making the responsibility of criminals effective in order to give to commerce the safety that it needs in its increasing development." Miguel Luis Amunátegui to Félix Frías, 23 December 1869, Santiago, folio 17r, "Expediente 7. Convención de extradición," folder 10, box 8, TC, AHCA. The development of a term such as *malhechores* as a way to threaten extradition of political rebels is covered in the text. In effect, developing a way of handling the rebels through decoupling them from their politics was not just a discursive delegitimation but also a way of ensuring that the Chileans would not have to risk inviting attacks from the rebels. This need would seem even more pertinent if one remembers that Chilean citizens and even state officials were assisting the rebels. As the rebel safe havens were the same places that were at the center of civil conflict in Chile during the 1850s (Copiapó, Curicó, and Aconcagua), it comes as no surprise that the Chilean government was uninterested in rekindling civil conflict within its borders. The solution, therefore, was to allow the Argentines to develop a language and method for diminishing the rebel threat in exile, which, in turn, would reduce the internal threats to Chile.

68. "Banditry" as a term has a lot of intellectual baggage. In this context, it is related to what might be thought of as highway robbery.

69. Frías to Varela, 9 July 1869, folio 1v.

70. Félix Frías to Mariano Varela, 9 June 1869, Santiago, folio 1v, box 42, SDC, AHCA. *Note:* this note and several others between Félix Frías and Mariano Varela are in box 42 as loose letters. One set is held together by a rusty paper clip, but there are several other letters that are scattered throughout the box. Most of them speak to the treaty negotiations, as well as to the case of Casimiro Ferrari.

71. Félix Frías to Mariano Varela, 30 December 1869, Santiago, folio 2r, box 42, SDC, AHCA. See note 70 in this chapter on locating this letter.

72. Frías to Varela, 9 July 1869, art. 5, "Convención de Extradición la República Argentina y la República de Chile," folio 6v.

73. Félix Frías to Mariano Varela, 11 December 1869, Santiago, folios 15r–16r, "Expediente 7. Convención de extradición," folder 10, box 8, TC, AHCA.

74. Félix Frías to Cónsul Argentino en . . . (Circular), 16 July 1870, Santiago, folio 33v, "Expediente 7. Convención de extradición," folder 10, box 8, TC, AHCA.

75. Frías to Varela, 9 July 1869, folio 2r.

76. Félix Frías to Carlos Tejedor (Ministro de Relaciones Exteriores de la República Argentina), 28 October 1870, Santiago, folio 1v, no. 144, folder 6, box 42, SDC, AHCA. *Note:* folder 6 has a blank front cover with "Caja no. 143" stamped across the top. Inside begins, "Mendoza, Diciembre 9 de 1869, El Gobierno de la Provincia."

77. For the treaty language approved by representatives of Argentina and Chile, see "Convención de Extradicion entre la República Argentina y la República de Chile," folios 5r–8r, "Expediente 7. Convención de extradición," folder 10, box 8, TC, AHCA. See also the note from Frías on its approval between the representatives, Frías to Varela, 9 July 1869, folios 1r–2v. For the approval of the treaty by the Argentine Congress, see Argentina, *Registro nacional de la República Argentina*, 8:283–84; for the problems experienced in the Chilean Congress, see Félix Frías to Ministro de Relaciones Exteriores de Argentina, 11 December 1869, Santiago, folio 15r, "Expediente 7. Convención de extradición," folder 10, box 8, TC, AHCA.

78. Félix Frías to Miguel Luis Amunátegui (Ministro de Relaciones Exteriores de Chile), 17 December 1869, Santiago, folio 1v, folder 6, box 42, SDC, AHCA; Circular a los Consulados Argentinos en Chile, 16 July 1870, Santiago, folios 33r–34r, "Expediente 7. Convención de extradición," folder 10, box 8, TC, AHCA.

79. Villanueva to Frías, 9 December 1869, 47.

80. Villanueva to Frías, 9 December 1869, 47.

81. E. S. Garcia to Cónsul de Chile en Mendoza, 10 December 1869, Mendoza, 52, book 34, Copiadores, EI, AHM.

82. Félix Frías to Miguel Luis Amunátegui (Ministro de Relaciones Exteriores de Chile) (copy), 23 December 1869, Santiago, folio 1v, folder 6, box 42, SDC, AHCA.

83. Frías to Amunátegui, 17 December 1869, folio 1v.

84. Miguel Luis Amunátegui to Félix Frías (Ministro Plenipotenciario de Argentina en Chile) (copy), 30 December 1869, Santiago, folio 1r, folder 6, box 42, SDC, AHCA.

85. "Sobre establecimiento de un correo semanal para la carrera de Chile," 4 October 1824, no. 1755, in Argentina, *Registro oficial de la República Argentina*, 2:65–66; Vicuña Mackenna, *Pájinas de mi diario*, 442.

86. "La correspondencia," *El Mercurio* (Valparaíso), 1 March 1839, 2.

87. *Sud-América: Política i Comercio* (Santiago), vol. 1, no. 5, 24 February 1851, 136.

88. The most prolific historian on the subject of the history of communications in Argentina is Walter B. L. Bose. For his most concise summary of the mail system in Argentina up to the 1860s, see Bose, "Historia de las comunicaciones," 579–86.

89. Gregorio Beéche to Luis Molina, 3 March 1862, Valparaíso folio 12v, file 17, folder 707, SE, EI, AHM.

90. Gregorio Beéche to Luis Molina, 31 January 1862, Valparaíso, folio 12r, file 17, folder 707, SE, EI, AHM.

91. Adriano Gómez (Ministro de Gobierno) to Consulado Chileno en Mendoza, 8 April 1863, Mendoza, folios 3r–3v, no. 3, book 19, Copiadores, EI, AHM.

92. José de la Cruz Zenteno to Ministro de Relaciones Exteriores, 31 March 1865, Mendoza, folios 80v–81r, no. 36, vol. 130, MREL, ANH.

93. Richard-Jorba, *Poder, economía y espacio*, 88–89. See also "614: Señores Ovalle Hermanos con la sucesion de don Benjamin Sanchez, sobre liquidacion de cuentas," *Gaceta de los Tribunales* (Santiago), vol. 35, no. 1738, 6 May 1876, 294–300.

94. There is a question whether the business "Ovalle Hermanos" with which Benjamín Sánchez was doing business was the same "Ovalle Hermanos" as the one doing business in the north. Benjamín Vicuña Mackenna refers to a mining entrepreneur in the north named Pastor Ovalle, which is the same name as the head of the "Ovalle Hermanos" doing business with Sánchez. Although it is still possible that they are two different businesses, it is likely that Pastor Ovalle's "Ovalle Hermanos" is the same in both instances. See Vicuña Mackenna, *El libro del cobre*, 293–94.

95. Félix Frías to Miguel Luis Amunátegui (copy), 7 January 1870, Santiago, folder 6, box 42, SDC, AHCA.

96. José M. del Carril to Gobernador de Mendoza, 11 December 1869, San Juan, file 105, folder 686, Sección Provincias, EI, AHM.

97. Gregorio Beéche (Consulado General de la República Argentina en Chile), "Razon de los manifiestos visados en este Consulado por mercaderias despachadas en transito para las Aduanas Argentinas que se espresan desde Octubre 1 de 1866 hasta la fecha," 14 May 1867, Valparaíso, Legación Argentina en Chile, "Instrucciones dadas al E. de N. [Encargado de Negocios] Argentino en Chile para que reclame de aquel Gobierno las penas que se deben imponer a los sublevados contra las autoridades de la Nacion, y sobre venta de objetos robados," folder 4, box 41, SDC, AHCA. Chilean exporter in Valparaíso Emilio Moyano was Bravo's main Chilean contact.

98. Desiderio Bravo, 18 January 1867, San Juan, folio 315r; Bravo to los Señores Ministros del Exmo Gobierno, 21 January 1867, San Juan, folio 323r; Bravo to Oficial Mayor de la Secretaria de Gobierno, 5, 19 February 1867, San Juan, folios 374r, 389r, all in book 318, box 154, FG, AHSJ.

99. Bravo to los Señores Ministros del Exmo Gobierno, 21 January 1867, folio 323r.

100. Rojo and Tarnassi, "Causa XCVIII: Criminal, contra D. Cárlos Leon, D. Desiderio Bravo, D. Julian Aguiar, D. Remigio Ferrer y D. José M. Zavalla, por delito de rebelion," in *Fallos de la Suprema Corte*, 6:144–47.

101. Gregorio Beéche to Ministro de Relaciones Exteriores de Chile, "Nómina de los realizados argentinos autores i complices de la rebelión ejecutada en las provincias argentina de Mendoza, San Juan i San Luis," 28 April 1867, Valparaíso, Legación Argentina en Chile, "Avisa la entrega de armas de los revoltosos pide instrucciones," folder 11bis, box 41, SDC, AHCA.

102. For an analysis of this case, see E. Zimmerman, "En tiempos de rebelión," 262–64. For the original decree on this issue from Mendoza, see Wenceslao Paunero, Decree, 23 April 1867, Mendoza, folio 10r–v, file 6, folder 505, Sección Militar, EI, AHM.

103. Rojo and Tarnassi, "Causa XXII: El Fisco Nacional, con varios comerciantes de San Juan, sobre derechos de importación pagados á los rebeldes, durante su dominio," in *Fallos de la Suprema Corte*, 5:155–56.

104. Rojo and Tarnassi, "Causa XXII," 165–67.

105. This timeline comes from the dates of when the prosecution made its sentencing recommendation. The first case happened in August 1867, and the second case was in January 1868. Rojo and Tarnassi, "Causa XXII," 159; Rojo and Tarnassi, "Causa XCVIII," 145.

106. Rojo and Tarnassi, "Causa XCVIII," 150–52.

107. Rojo and Tarnassi, "Causa XCVIII," 153–55.

108. Perú to Ministro de Relaciones Exteriores de la República Argentina, 23 January 1868, folio 2r–v.

109. M. del Carril to Gobernador de Mendoza, 11 December 1869.

110. Wenceslao Paunero (Comisionado Nacional y Comandante en Gefe del Ejército del Interior) to Julián Martínez (Ministro de Guerra y Marina), 2 July 1867, Cuartel General, San Juan, in Argentina, Ministro de Estado, Departamento de Guerra y Marina, *Memoria [. . .] 1868*, annex B (Operaciones del Ejército del Interior), 86.

111. On the unconstitutionality of execution, see art. 18 of the Argentine Constitution of 1853, in Argentina, *Constitución de la Nación Argentina*, 30.

112. On leniency, see E. Zimmerman, "Tiempos de rebelión," 259, 271–72.

113. Extensive sentencing examples are available in Rojo and Tarnassi, *Fallos de la Suprema Corte*, vols. 4–7.

114. Rojo and Tarnassi, "Causa XCVIII," 153–55.

115. For a broader analysis of sentencing practices, see E. Zimmerman, "En tiempos de rebelión," 255.

116. Miguel Luis Amunátegui to Corte Suprema de Justicia (copy), 12 March 1870, Santiago, folio 1r–v, folder 6, box 42, SDC, AHCA.

117. Frías to Tejedor, 28 October 1870, folio 1v.

118. For Chile, see Intendencia de Aconcagua to Gobernador de Los Andes, 8 August 1868, San Felipe, no. 375, vol. 67, Fondo Gobernación de Los Andes, ANH. For Mendoza, see file 28, folder P1, SJC, AHM.

119. "894: Sumario para averiguar los autores del salteo hecho en la cordillera," *Gaceta de los Tribunales* (Santiago), vol. 30, no. 1528, 16 September 1871, 517; Félix Frías to Carlos Tejedor (Ministro de Relaciones Exteriores de Argentina), 23 March 1871, Santiago, folio 1r, folder 6, box 42, SDC, AHCA.

120. For Guayama's program and context, see Escolar, "La república perdida."

121. Félix Frías to Belisario Prats (Ministro de Relaciones Exteriores de Chile), 18 July 1871, Quillota, folio 1r–v, Legación Argentina en Chile, "Sobre las depredaciones cometidas por Ayala, Pérez y Juan Saa, quien exportó armas de Chile para esta República," folder 24, box 42, SDC, AHCA. *Note:* folder 24 has a red cover.

122. Horacio Iglesia (Cónsul Argentino en los Andes) to Félix Frías, 13 April 1872, Santa Rosa de Los Andes, file 57, folder 707, SE, EI, AHM.

123. Arístides Villanueva (Gobernador de Mendoza) to Carlos Tejedor (Ministro de Relaciones Exteriores de de la Nación), 22 April 1872, Mendoza, folder 7, box 44, SDC,

AHCA; and Escolar, *Los indios montoneros*, 179–80. *Note:* folder 7 is blank with "Caja no. 163" stamped across the top. Inside begins, "Villa María, Abril 15 1872, El Gobernador de la Provincia de Sn Juan."

124. Escolar, *Los indios montoneros*, 181.

125. Escolar, *Los indios montoneros*, 183.

126. Villanueva to Tejedor (copy), 22 April 1872.

127. Horacio Iglesia to Félix Frías (copy), 13 April 1872, Santa Rosa de Los Andes, folder 7, box 44, SDC, AHCA.

128. Valentín Videla (Gobernador de San Juan) to Ministro de Relaciones Exteriores de la Nación, 15, 16 April 1872, San Juan, folder 7, box 44, SDC, AHCA.

129. Ministerio de Relaciones Exteriores de Argentina to Félix Frías, 17 April 1872, Buenos Aires, folder 7, box 44, SDC, AHCA.

130. Iglesias to Frías (copy), 13 April 1872.

131. Félix Frías to Adolfo Ibáñez (Ministro de Relaciones Exteriores de la República de Chile) (copy), 16 April 1872, Santiago, folder 7, box 44, SDC, AHCA.

132. Adolfo Ibáñez to Félix Frías (copy), 18 April 1872, Santiago, folder 7, box 44, SDC, AHCA.

133. On arrests, see Félix Frías to Adolfo Ibáñez (copy), 19 April 1872, Santiago, folder 7, box 44, SDC AHCA. On posses in Aconcagua beforehand, see Iglesias to Frías, 13 April 1872.

134. Arístides Villanueva to Ministro de Relaciones Exteriores de la Nación, 22, 23 April 1872, Mendoza, folder 7, box 44, SDC, AHCA.

135. Félix Frías to Adolfo Ibáñez (copy), 24 April 1872, Santiago, folder 7, box 44, SDC, AHCA.

136. Adolfo Ibáñez to Señor Enviado Estraordinario Ministro Plenipotenciario de la República Argentina, 19 May 1872, Santiago, folder 7, box 44, SDC, AHCA. Frías responded to the note of 15 April 1872 from Buenos Aires: Frías to Carlos Tejedor, 27 May 1872, Santiago; Decree, 19 May 1872, Santiago, both in folder 7, box 44, SDC, AHCA. See also news clipping that contains the series of court decisions on the case from 17 May 1872.

137. Félix Frías to Carlos Tejedor, 29 January 1873, Santiago, folder 7, box 44, SDC, AHCA.

138. Reggini, *Sarmiento y las telecomunicaciones*, 159.

139. Diego Escolar, *Los indios montoneros*, 178–84.

## Interlude 5

1. For the biography of the Clark brothers, see Marín Vicuña, *Los Hermanos Clark*.

2. For the meeting, see Henderson, "Transandine Railway," 151–212.

3. Form A/4376/136, 6 February 1879, balloted for 4 March 1879, Archive of the Institute of Civil Engineers, London.

4. "Sobre construccion de Ferro-Carriles en la República," art. 2, sec. 2; art. 5, sec. 2, 5 November 1872, in Argentina, *Rejistro oficial de la República Argentina*, 6:343.

5. Lewis, *British Railways*, 29–32, 97–123. For the role of local merchant networks in promoting early railroad construction, see Lewis, "Britain, the Argentine and Informal Empire," 108–11.

6. The growth in the public works sector was enormous in this period, as evidenced by the growth in the proportion of the budget taken up by the Ministry of the Interior,

which was responsible before the creation of the Ministry of Public Works for railroad construction. For Argentina's budgets, see Cortés Conde, *Dinero, deuda y crisis*, apps. 1–5.

7. Cassis, *Capitals of Capital*, 41–61.

8. Marín Vicuña, *Los Hermanos Clark*, 121.

9. "Contrato para la construcción de dos vías-férreas de las cinco á que se refiere la Ley de 5 de Noviembre de 1872, con las modificaciones introducidas por la Ley de 18 de Setiembre de 1877," art. 14, 19 March 1878, in Argentina, *Registro oficial de la República Argentina*, 17:51.

10. Argentina, Senado de la Nación, *Diario de sesiones de la Cámara de Senadores, periodo de 1877*, 13 September 1877, 729.

11. Though not specific, Santiago Marín Vicuña claims that the renegotiated concession was necessary for the financiers in London. Marín Vicuña, *Hermanos Clark*, 26.

12. Argentina, Ministerio del Interior, Administración del Ferro-Carril Andino, *Memoria del Ferro-carril Andino por el año 1883*, 47; and *Memoria del Ferro-carril Andino por los años 1884 y 1885*, 53.

13. Regalsky, *Mercados, inversores y élites*, 181–84.

14. Marichal, *Century of Debt Crisis*, 28, 243–49, apps. A–B; Kuntz Ficker, *Historia mínima de la expansión ferroviaria*, 345–53, app.

15. Marichal, *Century of Debt Crisis*, 247, app. B.

16. Böhm-Bawerk, *Capital and Interest*, 1.

17. This acceleration in economic growth, concentrated in western Europe, and its causes have been fundamental problems for many economists and economic historians. For an important treatment of this problem and its different solutions, see Pomerantz, *Great Divergence*.

18. K. Marx, *Grundrisse*, 524.

19. I thank Suman Seth for explaining this to me.

20. None of this is to say that finance capital originated in the nineteenth century. See Murphy, *Origins of English Financial Markets*.

21. *Sud-América: Política i Comercio* (Santiago), vol. 1, no. 5, 24 February 1851, 132–33.

22. Bragoni, "Recuperación y desigualdad económica," 211. For late-century developments and the wine industry, see Fleming, *Regional Development and Transportation in Argentina*; Richard-Jorba, *Empresarios ricos, trabajadores pobres*.

23. Argentina, Ministerio del Interior (Ministro Eduardo Wilde), *Memoria presentada al Honorable Congreso Nacional en el año 1887*, 214–15.

24. Argentine Great Western Railway Company, Limited, "Memorandum of Association," 29 April 1887, art. 3, sec. (a), p. 3, Registered 8185, 29 April 1887, 31/36158/24345CNL23691/1, Board of Trade, The National Archives, Richmond, UK.

25. "Contract between Juan Eduardo Clark and the Argentine Great Western Railway Company Limited," 26 May 1887, arts. 6, 19, pp. 4–8, Registered 10950, 9 June 1887, 31/36158/24345/3, Board of Trade, The National Archives, Richmond, UK.

26. Chile, Cámara de Senadores, 12 May 1887, folio 1r–v, no. 250, vol. 152, Fondo Ministerio de Industria y Obras Públicas, ANH.

27. Trollope, *Way We Live Now*, 74.

28. K. Marx, *Capital*, 3:599. For Victorian literature and finance capital, see Alexander, "Saving Time," 208–17. For infrastructure's peculiar temporality, see Mitchell, "Infrastructures Work on Time."

29. Martínez Estrada, *X-Ray of the Pampa*, 71.

30. For Du Mont's interests in the Argentine Great Western, see Argentine Great Western Railway Company, Limited, "Agreement," 30 June 1887, Registered 12365, 7 July 1887, 31/36158/24345/6; and "Summary of Capital and Shares," 14 January 1891, Registered 1726, 21 January 1891, 31/36158/24345/12, both in Board of Trade, The National Archives, Richmond, UK.

31. Skinner, *Mining Manual for 1888*, 567.

32. López, *Ferrocarriles, deuda y crisis*, 450, 472–77; Lewis, *British Railways*, 125–27, 133–45.

33. Palermo, "Elite técnica y estado liberal."

34. I have elaborated on this elsewhere; see Harvey, "Engineering Value."

35. This is not intended to be an absolute; pasturage may have been one of the things that came closest to necessitating a physical point in space type of border. In addition, national and colonial states had embarked on projects to draw exact borders in different contexts. See, e.g., Erbig, *Where Caciques and Mapmakers Met*. These different projects should probably be understood not as a sustained or transhistorical ideological project by the state but rather as always first a material necessity.

36. The importance of ground rent to this explanation should not be lost. For works that have informed my understanding of these issues, see Coronil, *Magical State*, 30–62; Harvey, *Limits to Capital*, 330–72. These guarantees were not necessarily the only way of attracting investment, and their importance has been scrutinized. See Lewis, "Financing of Railway Development."

# BIBLIOGRAPHY

## Primary Sources

### ARCHIVES AND LIBRARIES

Archive of the Institute of Civil Engineers, London
Archivo de la Cancillería de Chile, Santiago
Archivo del Arzobispado de Mendoza, Mendoza, Argentina
Archivo General de la Nación, Buenos Aires
Archivo Histórico de la Cancillería Argentina, Buenos Aires
Archivo Histórico de Mendoza, Mendoza, Argentina
Archivo Histórico de San Juan, San Juan, Argentina
Archivo Nacional de la Administración, Santiago
Archivo Nacional Histórico, Santiago
Biblioteca del Archivo General de la Nación, Buenos Aires
Biblioteca Nacional de Argentina, Buenos Aires
Biblioteca Nacional de Chile, Santiago
Biblioteca Pública General San Martín, Mendoza, Argentina
FamilySearch Library (digital archive)
Gray Herbarium Library, Harvard University's Botany Libraries, Cambridge, Massachusetts
The National Archives, Richmond, United Kingdom

NEWSPAPERS

*El Constituyente* (Copiapó, Chile)
*El Copiapino* (Copiapó, Chile)
*El Mercurio* (Valparaíso)
*Gaceta de los Tribunales* (Santiago)
*Sud-América: Política i Comercio* (Santiago)

GOVERNMENT PUBLICATIONS

*Argentina*

Argentina. *Constitución de la Nación Argentina*. Paraná: Imprenta Nacional, 1860.
———. *Registro nacional de la República Argentina*. Vol. 7, *Primer semestre, año de 1868*. Buenos Aires: Imprenta del Comercio del Plata, 1868.
———. *Registro nacional de la República Argentina*. Vol. 8, *Año de 1869*. Buenos Aires: Imprenta Argentina de El Nacional, 1869.
———. *Registro oficial de la República Argentina*. Vol. 17, *Año de 1878*. Buenos Aires: Imprenta de La Tribuna, 1879.
———. *Registro oficial de la República Argentina que comprende los documentos espedidos desde 1810 hasta 1873*. Vol. 2, *1822–1852*. Buenos Aires: La República, 1880.
———. *Rejistro oficial de la República Argentina que comprende los documentos espedidos desde 1810 hasta 1873*. Vol. 6, *1870 á 1873*. Buenos Aires: Imprenta Especial de Obras La República, 1884.
Argentina. Comisión Directiva del Censo. *Primer censo de la República Argentina, verificado en los días 15, 16 y 17 de Setiembre de 1869*. Buenos Aires: Imprenta de Porvenir, 1872.
Argentina. Ministerio del Interior. Administración del Ferro-Carril Andino. *Memoria del Ferro-Carril Andino por el año de 1883*. Buenos Aires: Martin Biedma, 1884.
———. *Memoria del Ferro-Carril Andino por los años 1884 y 1885*. Buenos Aires: Martin Biedma, 1886.
Argentina. Ministerio de Obras Públicas. Dirección General de Ferrocarriles. *Estadística de los ferrocarriles en explotación*. Vol. 22, *año 1913*. Buenos Aires: Ministerio de Obras Públicas, 1916.
Argentina. Ministro de Estado. Departamento de Guerra y Marina. *Memoria presentada por el ministro de estado en el Departamento de Guerra y Marina al Congreso Nacional de 1864*. Buenos Aires: n.p., n.d.
———. *Memoria presentada por el ministro de estado en el Departamento de Guerra y Marina al Congreso Nacional en 1868*. Buenos Aires: Imprenta del Plata, 1868.
Argentina. Ministro de Estado. Departamento de Relaciones Esteriores. *Memoria presentada por el ministro secretario de estado en el Departamento de Relaciones Esteriores al Congreso Legislativo Federal*. Buenos Aires: n.p., 1860.
Argentina. Ministro de Estado. Departamento de Relaciones Exteriores. *Memoria presentada por el ministro de estado en el Departamento de Relaciones Exteriores al Congreso Nacional en 1868*. Buenos Aires: Imprenta del Comercio del Plata, 1868.
Argentina. Ministro del Interior. *Memoria presentada al Honorable Congreso Nacional en el año 1887 por el ministro del interior doctor Don Eduardo Wilde*. Buenos Aires: Imprenta de La Tribuna Nacional, 1887.

Argentina. Senado de la Nación. *Diario de sesiones de la Cámara de Diputados del año 1863.* Vol. 1. Buenos Aires: Imprenta del Siglo, 1865.

———. *Diario de sesiones de la Cámara de Senadores, periodo de 1877.* Buenos Aires: El Comercio, 1905.

Provincia de Buenos Aires. Cámara de Diputados. *Diario de sesiones de la Cámara de Diputados de la Provincia de Buenos Aires, 1868.* Buenos Aires: Imprenta de La Tribuna, 1871.

———. *Diario de sesiones de la Cámara de Diputados de la Provincia de Buenos Aires, 1870–1871.* Buenos Aires: Sociedad Anónima, 1874.

Provincia de Mendoza. *Registro oficial de la Provincia de Mendoza que comprende los años 1860, 1861, 1862, 1863 i 1864.* Buenos Aires: Imprenta de Pablo E. Coni, 1877.

## Chile

Chile. *Anuario estadístico.* Vol. 3. Santiago: Imprenta Nacional, 1861.

———. *Anuario estadístico.* Vol. 5. Santiago: Imprenta Nacional, 1863.

———. *Anuario estadístico de la República de Chile, correspondiente a los años de 1868 i 1869.* Santiago: Imprenta Nacional, 1870.

———. *Sesiones de los cuerpos lejislativos de la República 1811 a 1845.* Edited by Valentín Letelier. Vol. 24, *1835–1839.* Santiago: Imprenta Cervantes, 1902.

———. *Sesiones de los cuerpos lejislativos de la República 1811 a 1845.* Edited by Valentín Letelier. Vol. 30, *Cámara de Diputados (1841).* Santiago: Imprenta Cervantes, n.d.

———. *Sesiones de los cuerpos lejislativos de la República 1811 a 1845.* Edited by Valentín Letelier. Vol. 32, *Cámara de Diputados (1843).* Santiago: Imprenta Cervantes, 1908.

———. *Sesiones de los cuerpos lejislativos de la República 1811 a 1845.* Edited by Valentín Letelier. Vol. 34, *Cámara de Diputados (1844).* Santiago: Imprenta Cervantes, 1908.

Chile. Oficina Central de Estadística. *Censo jeneral de la República de Chile levantado el 19 de abril de 1865.* Santiago: Imprenta Nacional, 1866.

———. *Estadística comercial de la República de Chile correspondiente al año de 1846.* Valparaíso: Imprenta Europea, 1848.

———. *Estadística comercial de la República de Chile correspondiente al año de 1847.* Valparaíso: Imprenta Europea, 1848.

———. *Estadística comercial de la República de Chile correspondiente al primer trimestre del año 1850.* Valparaíso: Imprenta y Librería del Mercurio, 1850.

———. *Estadística comercial de la República de Chile correspondiente al segundo trimestre del año 1850.* Valparaíso: Imprenta y Librería del Mercurio, 1850.

———. *Estadística comercial de la República de Chile correspondiente al tercer trimestre del año 1850.* Valparaíso: Imprenta y Librería del Mercurio, 1851.

———. *Estadística comercial de la República de Chile correspondiente al primer semestre del año 1852.* Valparaíso: Imprenta del Diario, 1852.

———. *Estadística comercial de la República de Chile correspondiente al segundo semestre del año 1852.* Valparaíso: Imprenta del Diario, 1853.

———. *Estadística comercial de la República de Chile correspondiente al primer semestre del año 1853.* Valparaíso: Imprenta del Diario, 1854.

———. *Estadística comercial de la República de Chile correspondiente al segundo semestre del año 1853.* Valparaíso: Imprenta del Diario, 1854.

―――. *Estadística comercial de la República de Chile correspondiente al primer semestre del año 1854.* Valparaíso: Imprenta y Librería del Mercurio, 1854.

―――. *Estadística comercial de la República de Chile correspondiente al segundo semestre del año 1854.* Valparaíso: Imprenta del Diario, 1855.

―――. *Estadística comercial de la República de Chile correspondiente al segundo semestre del año 1855.* Valparaíso: Imprenta del Diario, 1856.

## United States

US House of Representatives. 33rd Cong., 1st Sess., Exec. doc., No. 121. *The U.S. Naval Astronomical Expedition to the Southern Hemisphere, during the Years 1849–'50–'51–'52.* Edited by J. M. Gilliss. Vol. 1, *Chile: Its Geography, Climate, Earthquakes, Government, Social Condition, Mineral and Agricultural Resources, Commerce, &c, &c.* Washington, DC: A. O. P. Nicholson, 1855.

### PUBLISHED SOURCES

Ahumada, Manuel de. *Código de las leyes, decretos y acuerdos que sobre administración de justicia se ha dictado la provincia de Mendoza.* Mendoza, Argentina: Imprenta de El Constitucional, 1860.

Alberdi, Juan Bautista. *Organización política y económica de la Confederación Argentina.* Besançon, France: Imprenta de José Jacquin, 1856.

Bello, Andrés. *Derecho internacional.* Vol. 1, *Principios de derecho internacional y escritos complementarios.* Caracas: Ministerio de Educación, 1954.

Brand, Lieut. Charles R. N. *Journal of a Voyage to Peru: A Passage across the Cordillera of the Andes, in the Winter of 1827, Performed on Foot in the Snow; and a Journey across the Pampas.* London: Henry Colburn, 1828.

Castro, Juan José. *Estudio sobre los ferrocarriles sud-americanos y las grandes líneas internacionales publicado bajo los auspicios del Ministerio de Fomento de la República O. del Uruguay y enviado á la Exposición Universal de Chicago.* Montevideo: La Nación, 1893.

Centro Argentino de Ingenieros. *Historia de la ingeniería argentina.* Buenos Aires: Centro Argentino de Ingenieros, 1981.

Chikhachev, Platon Alexandrovich. *A Trip across the Pampas of Buenos Aires (1836–1837).* Translated by Jack Weiner. Lawrence: University of Kansas, Occasional Publications No. 8, Center of Latin American Studies, 1967.

"Clark & Co. to Exmo. Sr. D. Aníbal Pinto, Presidente de la República, Valparaíso, 23 April 1877." In *El ferro-carril trasandino interoceánico entre Buenos Aires y Valparaíso: algunos datos sobre el estado actual de la empresa.* Buenos Aires: Imprenta de La Nación, 1877.

Darwin, Charles. "The Beagle Diary: 'A Peculiar Race of Men.'" In *The Chile Reader: History, Culture, Politics,* edited by Elizabeth Quay Hutchison, Thomas Miller Klubock, Nara B. Milanich, and Peter Winn, 167–71. Durham, NC: Duke University Press, 2013.

Fitz Gerald, E. A. *The Highest Andes: A Record of the First Ascent of Aconcagua and Tupungato in Argentina, and the Exploration of the Surrounding Valleys.* London: Methuen, 1899.

Henderson, Brodie Haldane. "The Transandine Railway (Paper No. 4068)." In *Minutes of the Proceedings of the Institution of Civil Engineers; with Other Selected and Abstracted*

*Papers*. Vol. 195, edited by J. H. T. Tudsbery, 151–212. London: The Institution [of Civil Engineers], 1914.

Hernández, José. *El gaucho Martín Fierro*. Buenos Aires: Imprenta de La Pampa, 1872.

Huergo, Luis. *Tesis presentada y sostenida por D. Luis Huergo para optar al grado de injeniero en la facultad de ciencias exactas de la Universidad de Buenos Aires, año 1870*. Buenos Aires: Americana, 1870.

Igarzábal, Rafael S. *La Provincia de San Juan en la Exposición de Córdoba: geografía y estadística*. Buenos Aires: Sociedad Anónima, 1874.

La Compañía del Telégrafo Trasandino. *Estatutos*. Valparaíso: El Mercurio, 1871.

MacGregor, John. *Commercial Tariffs and Regulations of the Several States of Europe and America, Together with the Commercial Treaties between England and Foreign Countries, Parts XVII, XVIII, and XIX, Spanish American Republics*. London: Charles Whiting, 1847.

Mansilla, Lucio V. *A Visit to the Ranquel Indians*. Translated by Eva Gillies. Lincoln: University of Nebraska Press, 1997.

Mulhall, Michael George, and Edward T. Mulhall. *Handbook of the River Plate; comprising Buenos Ayres, the Upper Provinces, Banda Oriental, and Paraguay*. Vol. 1. Buenos Aires: Standard Printing-Office, 1869.

Rojo, Nemecio, and Antonio Tarnassi. *Fallos de la Suprema Corte de justicia nacional con la relación de sus respectivas causas*. Vols. 4–7. Buenos Aires: Imprenta de Pablo E. Coni, 1869–71.

Rosetti, Emilio. *Informe sobre la practicabilidad de un ferro-carril trasandino en dirección al paso llamado del Planchón en el sur de la provincia de Mendoza*. Buenos Aires: Imprenta del Siglo, 1870.

Sáez, Manuel Antonio. *Limites i posesiones de la provincia de Mendoza, con una espocicion del derecho provincial en la cuestion Territorios Nacionales*. Santiago: Imprenta de la República de Jacinto Nuñez, 1873.

Sarmiento, Domingo F. *Civilización i barbarie. Vida de Juan Facundo Quiroga*. Santiago: Imprenta del Progreso, 1845.

Schmidtmeyer, Peter. *Travels into Chile, over the Andes, in the Years 1820 and 1821, with Some Sketches of the Production and Agriculture; Mines and Metallurgy; Inhabitants, History, and Other Features, of America; Particularly of Chile, and Arauco*. London: McDowall, 1824.

Senillosa, Felipe. *Memoria sobre los pesos y medidas*. La Plata, Argentina: Archivo Histórico de la Provincia de Buenos Aires "Dr. Ricardo Levene," 2003.

Silva Castro, Raúl. *Censo de 1813*. Santiago: Imprenta Chile, 1953.

Skinner, Walter R. *The Mining Manual for 1888, Containing Full Particulars of Mining Companies, and of All Those Registered from June, 1887, Together with a List of Mining Directors*. London: n.p., [1888].

Strain, Lieutenant Isaac G., USN. *Cordillera and Pampa, Mountain and Plain: Sketches of a Journey in Chili, and the Argentine Provinces, in 1849*. New York: Horace H. Moore, 1853.

Tornero, Recaredo S. *Chile ilustrado: guía descriptivo del territorio de Chile, de las capitales de provincia i de los puertos principales*. Valparaíso: Librerías i Ajencias del Mercurio, 1872.

Universidad de Buenos Aires. *Anales de la Universidad de Buenos Aires*. Vol. 1. Buenos Aires: Imprenta de Martin Biedma, 1888.

Vicuña Mackenna, Benjamín. *El libro de la Plata.* Buenos Aires: Francisco de Aguirre, 1978.

———. *El libro del cobre i del carbón de piedra en Chile.* Santiago: Imprenta Cervantes, 1883.

———. *Páginas de mi diario durante tres años de viajes: 1853, 1854, 1855.* Santiago: Imprenta del Ferrocarril, 1856.

Villanueva, Guillermo. "Tesis presentada en la Universidad de Buenos Aires para obtar [sic] al grado de Ingeniero, examinado en octubre 20, 1870." Undergraduate thesis, Universidad de Buenos Aires, 1870.

Wheelwright, William. "Proposed Railway Route across the Andes, from Caldera in Chile to Rosario on the Parana, via Cordova; with Report of Mr. E. A. Flint's Survey." *Journal of the Royal Geographical Society* 31 (1861): 155–62.

## Secondary Sources

Acevedo, Edberto Oscar. *Orígenes de la organización judicial de la Provincia de Mendoza.* Buenos Aires: Fundación para la Educación, la Ciencia y la Cultura, 1979.

Adamovsky, Ezequiel. *El gaucho indómito: de Martín Fierro a Perón, el emblema imposible de una nación desgarrada.* Buenos Aires: Siglo Veintiuno, 2019.

Adelman, Jeremy. *Republic of Capital: Buenos Aires and the Legal Transformation of the Atlantic World.* Stanford, CA: Stanford University Press, 1999.

Adelman, Jeremy, and Stephen Aron. "From Borderlands to Borders: Empires, Nation-States, and the Peoples in between in North American History." *American Historical Review* 104, no. 3 (1999): 814–41.

Agüero, Alejandro. "Formas de continuidad del orden jurídico: algunas reflexiones a partir de la justicia criminal de Córdoba (Argentina), primera mitad del siglo XIX." *Nuevo Mundo, Mundos Nuevos,* no. 10 (2010). http://journals.openedition.org/nuevomundo/59352.

———. "'¿Provincias o Estados?' El concepto de provincia y el primer constitucionalismo provincial rioplatense; un enfoque ius-histórico." *Revista de Historia Americana y Argentina* 54, no. 1 (2019): 137–75.

Agüero, Alejandro, and Matías Rosso. "Codifying the Criminal Law in Argentina: Provincial and National Codification in the Genesis of the First Penal Code." In *The Western Codification of Criminal Law,* edited by Aniceto Masferrer, 297–322. Cham, Switzerland: Springer International, 2018.

Aguirre, Robert D. *Mobility and Modernity: Panama in the Nineteenth-Century Anglo-American Imagination.* Columbus: Ohio State University Press, 2017.

Alexander, Sarah C. "Saving Time: Nineteenth-Century Time Travel and the Temporal Logic of Late Capitalism." *Victorian Studies* 60, no. 2 (2018): 208–17.

Alonso, Ana María. "The Politics of Space, Time and Substance: State Formation, Nationalism and Ethnicity." *Annual Review of Anthropology* 23 (1994): 379–405.

Andermann, Jens. *The Optic of the State: Visuality and Power in Argentina and Brazil.* Pittsburgh, PA: University of Pittsburgh Press, 2007.

Andrews, George Reid. *The Afro-Argentines of Buenos Aires, 1800–1900.* Madison: University of Wisconsin Press, 1980.

Anzorena, Claudia. "La participación de las mujeres en el proceso de formación del Estado Nacional en Argentina de finales del siglo XIX: reflexiones desde una perspectiva de género." *Revista Iberoamericana de Educación* 45, no. 2 (2008): 1–13.

Appelbaum, Nancy. *Mapping the Country of Regions: The Chorographic Commission of Nineteenth-Century Colombia*. Chapel Hill: University of North Carolina Press, 2016.

Arnold, David, and Erich DeWald. "Everyday Technology in South and Southeast Asia: An Introduction." *Modern Asian Studies* 46, no. 1 (2012): 1–17.

Assadourian, Carlos Sempat. *El sistema de la economía colonial: mercado interno, regiones y espacio económico*. Lima: Instituto de Estudios Peruanos, 1982.

Augé, Marc. *Non-places: An Introduction to Supermodernity*. Translated by John Howe. 2nd ed. New York: Verso, 2008.

Baer, James. "The FACA and the FAI: Argentine Anarchists and the Revolution in Spain, 1930–1939." In *In Defiance of Boundaries: Anarchism in Latin American History*, edited by Geoffroy de Laforcade and Kirwin Shaffer, 95–114. Gainesville: University of Florida Press, 2015.

Baily, Samuel L. *Immigrants in the Lands of Promise: Italians in Buenos Aires and New York City, 1870–1914*. Ithaca, NY: Cornell University Press, 1999.

Baily, Samuel L., and Eduardo José Míguez. *Mass Migration to Modern Latin America*. Lanham, MD: Rowan and Littlefield, 2003.

Bandieri, Susana, ed. *Cruzando la cordillera . . . : la frontera argentino-chilena como espacio social*. Neuquén, Argentina: Centro de Estudios de Historia Regional, 2001.

———. "La historia en perspectiva regional: aportes conceptuales y avances empíricos." *Revista de Historia Americana y Argentina* 52, no. 1 (2017): 11–30.

———. "La noción de 'espacio económico' en Carlos Sempat Assadourian y sus posibilidades de uso en historias regionales de lugares y tiempos diferentes." *Revista Estudios del ISHiR* 2, no. 4 (2012): 27–42.

Barbuto, Lorena. "'Hacer de cada tribu un pueblo . . .': los indios amigos y la tierra en la frontera sur bonaerense (1860-1870)." *Diálogo Andino*, no. 68 (2022): 46–61.

Bassi, Ernesto. *An Aqueous Territory: Sailor Geographies and New Granada's Transimperial Greater Caribbean World*. Durham, NC: Duke University Press, 2016.

———. "Beyond Compartmentalized Atlantics: A Case for Embracing the Atlantic from Spanish American Shores." *History Compass* 12, no. 9 (2014): 704–16.

Bauer, Arnold J. *Chilean Rural Society from the Spanish Conquest to 1930*. Cambridge: Cambridge University Press, 1975.

Beattie, Peter M. "Measures of Manhood: Honor, Enlisted Army Service, and Slavery's Decline in Brazil, 1850–1890." In *Changing Men and Masculinities in Latin America*, edited by Matthew C. Gutmann, 233–55. Durham, NC: Duke University Press, 2003.

Beckman, Ericka. "The Creolization of Imperial Reason: Chilean State Racism in the War of the Pacific." *Journal of Latin American Cultural Studies* 18, no. 1 (2009): 73–90.

Belich, James. "Exploding Wests: Boom and Bust in Nineteenth-Century Settler Societies." In *Natural Experiments in History*, edited by Jared Diamond and James A. Robinson, 53–87. Cambridge, MA: Belknap Press of Harvard University Press, 2011.

———. *Replenishing the Earth: The Settler Revolution and the Rise of the Angloworld*. New York: Oxford University Press, 2009.

Bello, Álvaro. *Nampülkafe: el viaje de los mapuches de la Araucanía a las pampas argentinas. Territorio, política y cultura en los siglos XIX y XX*. Temuco, Chile: Ediciones Universidad Católica de Temuco, 2011.
Bengoa, José. *Historia del pueblo mapuche (siglo XIX y XX)*. Santiago: LOM, 2000.
———. *Historia rural de Chile central*. Vol. 1, *La construcción del Valle Central de Chile*. Santiago: LOM, 2015.
———, ed. *La memoria olvidada: historia de los pueblos indígenas de Chile*. Santiago: Publicaciones del Bicentenario, 2004.
Black, Iain S. "Spaces of Capital: Bank Office Building in the City of London, 1830–1870." *Journal of Historical Geography* 26, no. 3 (2000): 351–75.
Blanc, Jacob, and Federico Freitas, eds. *Big Water: The Making of the Borderlands between Brazil, Argentina, and Paraguay*. Tucson: University of Arizona Press, 2020.
Blanchard, Peter. *Fearful Vassals: Urban Elite Loyalty in the Viceroyalty of the Río de la Plata, 1776–1810*. Pittsburgh, PA: University of Pittsburgh Press, 2020.
———. *Under the Flag of Freedom: Slave Soldiers and the Wars of Independence in Spanish South America*. Pittsburgh, PA: University of Pittsburgh Press, 2006.
Blumenthal, Edward. *Exile and Nation Formation in Argentina and Chile, 1810–1862*. Cham, Switzerland: Palgrave Macmillan, 2019.
———. "Milicias y ciudadanía de residencia: la revolución chilena de 1851 en perspectiva transnacional." *Illes i Imperis*, no. 17 (2015): 91–112.
Bocquet, Denis. "Engineers and the Nation in Italy (1750–1922): Local Traditions and Different Conceptions of Unity and Modernity." *History and Technology* 23, no. 3 (2007): 227–40.
Böhm-Bawerk, Eugen von. *Capital and Interest: A Critical History of Economical Theory*. New York: Brentano's, 1922.
Bose, Walter B. L. "Historia de las comunicaciones." In *Historia argentina contemporánea, 1862–1930*. Vol. 3, *Historia económica*. Buenos Aires: El Ateneo, 1966.
Boza, Alejandra. "Diplomacia, comercio y poder en una zona de frontera: el asesinato de un rey indígena en Talamanca, actual Costa Rica, 1870–1872." *Historia Crítica*, no. 82 (2021): 107–28.
———. *La frontera indígena de la Gran Talamanca: 1840–1930*. Cartago, Costa Rica: ET, EUCR, EUNED, EUNA, 2014.
Bragoni, Beatriz. "Cuyo después de Pavón: consenso, rebelión y orden político, 1861–1874." In *Un nuevo orden político: provincias y Estado nacional, 1852–1880*, edited by Beatriz Bragoni and Eduardo Míguez, 29–60. Buenos Aires: Biblos, 2010.
———. "Mercados, monedas y crédito a la luz del funcionamiento de una entidad bancaria (Mendoza, 1866–1879)." *Desarrollo Económico* 45, no. 177 (2005): 55–74.
———. "Recuperación y desigualdad económica en el interior rural argentino del siglo XIX: Un examen sobre la composición y distribución de la riqueza en la campaña de Mendoza a través de fuentes fiscales (1866)." *América Latina en la Historia Económica*, no. 35 (2011): 209–44.
———. "Un linaje de notables del interior argentino en el proceso de unificación política: los Civit de Mendoza." *Entrepasados: Revista de Historia* 16, no. 31 (2007): 13–34.
Bragoni, Beatriz, and Eduardo Míguez. "De la periferia al centro: la formación de un sistema político nacional, 1852–1880." In *Un nuevo orden político: provincias y Estado*

*nacional, 1852–1880*, edited by Beatriz Bragoni and Eduardo Míguez, 9–28. Buenos Aires: Biblos, 2010.

Bransboin, Hernán. *Mendoza federal: entre la autonomía provincial y el poder de Juan Manuel de Rosas*. Buenos Aires: Prometeo, 2014.

Braudel, Fernand. *Civilization and Capitalism, 15th–18th Century*. Vol. 1, *The Structures of Everyday Life*. Translated by Siân Reynolds. Berkeley: University of California Press, 1992.

———. *The Mediterranean and the Mediterranean World in the Age of Philip II*. Translated by Siân Reynolds. New York: Harper & Row, 1972.

Briones, Claudia N., and Walter M. Delrio. "The 'Conquest of the Desert' as a Trope and Enactment of Argentina's Manifest Destiny." In *Manifest Destinies and Indigenous Peoples*, edited by David Maybury-Lewis, Theodore Macdonald, and Biorn Maybury-Lewis, 51–84. Cambridge, MA: Harvard University, David Rockefeller Center for Latin American Studies, 2009.

Brudney, Edward. "Manifest Destiny, the Frontier, and 'El Indio' in Argentina's Conquista del Desierto." *Journal of Global South Studies* 36, no. 1 (2019): 116–44.

Bryce, Benjamin. "Citizenship and Ethnicity: Social Welfare and Paternalism in Buenos Aires, 1880–1930." In *Making Citizens in Argentina*, edited by Benjamin Bryce and David M. K. Sheinin, 21–42. Pittsburgh, PA: University of Pittsburgh Press, 2017.

———. "Undesirable Britons: South Asian Migration and the Making of a White Argentina." *Hispanic American Historical Review* 99, no. 2 (2019): 247–73.

Buchbinder, Pablo. "Caudillos y caudillismo: una perspectiva historiográfica." In *Caudillismos rioplatenses: nuevas miradas a un viejo problema*, edited by Noemí Goldman and Ricardo Salvatore, 31–50. Buenos Aires: Eudeba, 1998.

Caimari, Lila. "News from around the World: The Newspapers of Buenos Aires in the Age of the Submarine Cable, 1866–1900." *Hispanic American Historical Review* 96, no. 4 (2016): 607–40.

Campi, Daniel, and Rodolfo Richard-Jorba. "Un ejercicio de historia regional comparada: Coacción y mercado de trabajo: Tucumán y Mendoza en el horizonte latinoamericano (segunda mitad del siglo XIX)." *História Econômica & História de Empresas* 4, no. 2 (2001): 97–130.

Canaparo, Claudio. "Marconi and Other Artifices: Long-Range Technology and the Conquest of the Desert." In *Images of Power: Iconography, Culture, and State in Latin America*, edited by Jens Andermann and William Rowe, 241–54. New York: Berghahn Books, 2006.

Cañizares-Esguerra, Jorge. "Entangled Histories: Borderland Historiographies in New Clothes?" *American Historical Review* 112, no. 3 (June 2007): 787–99.

Caplan, Jane, and John Torpey, eds. *Documenting Individual Identity: The Development of State Practices in the Modern World*. Princeton, NJ: Princeton University Press, 2001.

Cardoso, Fernando Henrique. "The Consumption of Dependency Theory in the United States." *Latin American Research Review* 12, no. 3 (1977): 7–24.

Carrera, Julián. "Esplendor y ocaso de las pulperías porteñas: El comercio menudo en la ciudad de Buenos Aires, 1810–1870." *Anuario del Instituto de Historia Argentina*, no. 12 (2012): 173–98.

Carroll, Patrick. *Science, Culture, and State Formation*. Berkeley: University of California Press, 2006.

Carter, Marina, and Crispin Bates. "Empire and Locality: A Global Dimension to the 1857 Indian Uprising." *Journal of Global History* 5, no. 1 (March 2010): 51–73.

Carter, Paul. *The Road to Botany Bay: An Exploration of Landscape and History*. Minneapolis: University of Minnesota Press, 2010.

Caso Barrera, Laura, and Mario M. Aliphat Fernández. "De antiguos territorios coloniales a nuevas fronteras republicanas: la Guerra de Castas y los límites del suroeste de México, 1821–1893." *Historia Crítica*, no. 59 (2016): 81–100.

Cassis, Youssef. *Capitals of Capital: A History of International Financial Centres, 1780–2005*. Translated by Jacqueline Collier. New York: Cambridge University Press, 2006.

Castro Valdebenito, Hugo. "Aconcagüinos en la historia de Chile: carta de Pedro Antonio Ramírez a Benjamín Vicuña Mackenna sobre el motín popular de San Felipe del 14 de octubre de 1851." *Historia y Sociedad* 36 (January–June 2019): 271–86.

Cavieres Figueroa, Eduardo. *Comercio chileno y comerciantes ingleses, 1820–1880: un ciclo de historia económica*. Valparaíso: Universidad Católica de Valparaíso, 1988.

Cerutti, Mario, and Miguel González Quiroga. "Guerra y comercio en torno al Río Bravo (1855–1867). Línea fronteriza, espacio económico común." *Historia Mexicana* 40, no. 2 (1990): 217–97.

Chambers, Sarah C. "From One Patria, Two Nations in the Andean Heartland." In *New Countries: Capitalism, Revolutions, and Nations in the Americas, 1750–1870*, edited by John Tutino, 316–49. Durham, NC: Duke University Press, 2016.

Chastain, Andra B., and Timothy W. Lorek. "Introduction." In *Itineraries of Expertise: Science, Technology, and the Environment in Latin America's Long Cold War*, edited by Andra B. Chastain and Timothy W. Lorek, 3–28. Pittsburgh, PA: University of Pittsburgh Press, 2020.

Chasteen, John Charles. *Heroes on Horseback: A Life and Times of the Last Gaucho Caudillos*. Albuquerque: University of New Mexico Press, 1995.

Chiaramonte, José Carlos. "'¿Provincias o Estados?' Los orígenes del federalismo rioplatense." In *Las revoluciones hispánicas: independencias americanas y liberalismo español*, edited by François-Xavier Guerra, 167–205. Madrid: Complutense, 1995.

Clarke, David J. "The Development of a Pioneering Steamship Line: William Wheelwright and the Origins of the Pacific Steam Navigation Company." *International Journal of Maritime History* 20, no. 1 (2008): 221–50.

Collier, Simon. *Chile: The Making of a Republic, 1830–1865: Politics and Ideas*. New York: Cambridge University Press, 2003.

Comadrán Ruíz, Jorge. *Evolución demográfica Argentina durante el período hispano (1535–1810)*. Buenos Aires: Editorial Universitaria de Buenos Aires, 1969.

———. "Notas para una historia de la delincuencia y la criminalidad en Mendoza, 1840–1854." *Revista de historia americana y argentina*, no. 29–30 (1990–91): 349–87.

Conrad, Sebastian. *What Is Global History?* Princeton, NJ: Princeton University Press, 2016.

Conti, Viviana E. "Circuitos mercantiles y redes de comerciantes del espacio surandino entre la Colonia y la Independencia." In *La historia argentina en perspectiva local y regional: nuevas miradas para viejos problemas*. Vol. 1, coordinated by Susana Bandieri and Sandra Fernández. Buenos Aires: Teseo, 2017.

Converso, Félix E. *La lenta formación de capitales: familias, comercio y poder en Córdoba, 1850–1880*. Córdoba, Argentina: Junta Provincial de Historia de Córdoba, 1993.

Cornejo, Luis. "Sobre la cronología del inicio de la imposición cuzqueña en Chile." *Estudios Atacameños*, no. 47 (2014): 101–16.

Coronil, Fernando. *The Magical State: Nature, Money, and Modernity in Venezuela*. Chicago: University of Chicago Press, 1997.

Cortés Conde, Roberto. *Dinero, deuda y crisis: evolución fiscal y monetaria en la Argentina*. Buenos Aires: Sudamericana/Instituto Torcuato Di Tella, 1989.

Craib, Raymond B. *Cartographic Mexico: A History of State Fixations and Fugitive Landscapes*. Durham, NC: Duke University Press, 2004.

———. *The Cry of the Renegade: Politics and Poetry in Interwar Chile*. New York: Oxford University Press, 2016.

———. "Sedentary Anarchists." In *Reassessing the Transnational Turn: Scales of Analysis in Anarchist and Syndicalist Studies*, edited by Constance Bantman and Bert Altena, 139–56. Oakland, CA: PM Press, 2017.

Crawford, Sharika D. *The Last Turtlemen of the Caribbean: Waterscapes of Labor, Conservation, and Boundary Making*. Chapel Hill: University of North Carolina Press, 2020.

Cremaschi de Petra, Martha. "Aspectos socio-demográficos de Mendoza entre 1800 y 1840 a través de registros parroquiales (libros de matrimonios)." *Revista de Historia Americana y Argentina* 15, no. 29–30 (1989): 235–54.

Cresswell, Tim. *On the Move: Mobility in the Modern Western World*. New York: Routledge, 2006.

———. *Place: An Introduction*. 2nd ed. Malden, MA: Wiley Blackwell, 2015.

Cronon, William. *Nature's Metropolis: Chicago and the Great West*. New York: W. W. Norton, 1991.

Crow, Joanna. "From Araucanian Warriors to Mapuche Terrorists: Contesting Discourses of Gender, Race, and Nation in Modern Chile (1810–2010)." *Journal of Iberian and Latin American Studies* 20, no. 1 (2014): 75–101.

———. "Troubled Negotiations: The Mapuche and the Chilean State (1818–1830)." *Bulletin of Latin American Research* 36, no. 3 (2017): 285–98.

Davies Lenoble, Geraldine. "La emergencia de los indios gauchos: montoneras federales, malones y expediciones provinciales en la frontera sur de Córdoba y de la región de Cuyo durante la década de 1860." *Revista de Indias* 82, no. 284 (2022): 137–68.

———. "La resistencia de la ganadería: Los pehuenches en la economía regional de Cuyo y la cordillera (1840–1870)." *Historia* 52, no. 2 (July–December 2019): 341–72.

de Certeau, Michel. *The Practice of Everyday Life*. Translated by Steven F. Rendall. Berkeley: University of California Press, 1988.

Deere, Carmen Diana, and Magdalena León. "Liberalism and Married Women's Property Rights in Nineteenth-Century Latin America." *Hispanic American Historical Review* 85, no. 4 (November 2005): 627–78.

de Jong, Ingrid. "Armado y desarmado de una confederación: el liderazgo de Calfucurá en el período de la organización nacional." *Quinta Sol*, no. 13 (2009): 11–45.

de la Fuente, Ariel. *Children of Facundo: Caudillo and Gaucho Insurgency during the Argentine State-Formation Process (La Rioja, 1853–1870)*. Durham, NC: Duke University Press, 2000.

———. "'Civilización y barbarie': fuentes para una nueva explicación del *Facundo*." *Boletín del Instituto de Historia Argentina y Americana "Dr. Emilio Ravignani,"* no. 44 (2016): 135–79.

DeLaney, Jeane. "Immigration, Identity, and Nationalism in Argentina, 1850–1950." In *Immigration and National Identities in Latin America*, edited by Nicola Foote and Michael Goebel, 91–114. Gainesville: University of Florida Press, 2014.

del Castillo, Lina. *Crafting a Republic for the New World: Scientific, Geographic, and Historiographic Inventions of Colombia*. Lincoln: University of Nebraska Press, 2018.

De Pieri, Filippo. "Nineteenth-Century Municipal Engineers in Turin: Technical Bureaucracies in the Networks of Local Power." In *Municipal Services and Employees in the Modern City: New Historic Approaches*, edited by Michèle Dagenais, Irene Maver, and Pierre-Yves Saunier, 31–46. Aldershot, UK: Ashgate, 2003.

Díaz, Wenceslao. *Apuntes sobre el terremoto de Mendoza (20 de Marzo de 1861)*. Santiago: Cervantes, 1907.

Dimas, Carlos. *Poisoned Eden: Cholera Epidemics, State-Building, and the Problem of Public Health in Tucumán, Argentina, 1865–1908*. Lincoln: University of Nebraska Press, 2022.

Dolin, Eric Jay. *Leviathan: The History of American Whaling*. New York: W. W. Norton, 2007.

Duncan, Roland E. "William Wheelright [sic] and Early Steam Navigation in the Pacific: 1820–1840." *Americas* 32, no. 2 (October 1975): 257–81.

Dutt, Rajeshwari. "Business as Usual: Maya and Merchants on Yucatán-Belize Border at the Onset of the Caste War." *Americas* 74, no. 2 (April 2017): 201–26.

Echeverri, Marcela. "Esclavitud y tráfico de esclavos en el pacífico suramericano durante la era de la abolición." *Historia Mexicana* 69, no. 2 (2019): 627–91.

———. *Indian and Slave Royalists in the Age of Revolution: Reform, Revolution, and Royalism in the Northern Andes, 1780–1825*. Cambridge: Cambridge University Press, 2016.

Edgerton, David. "Innovation, Technology, or History: What Is the Historiography of Technology About?" *Technology and Culture* 51, no. 3 (July 2010): 680–97.

Edwards, Erika Denise. *Hiding in Plain Sight: Black Women, the Law, and the Making of a White Argentine Republic*. Tuscaloosa: University of Alabama Press, 2020.

Edwards, Paul N. "Infrastructure and Modernity: Force, Time, and Social Organization in the History of Sociotechnical Systems." In *Modernity and Technology*, edited by Thomas J. Misa, Brey Philip, and Andrew Feenberg, 185–226. Cambridge, MA: MIT Press, 2003.

Edwards, Ryan C. *A Carceral Ecology: Ushuaia and the History of Landscape and Punishment in Argentina*. Berkeley: University of California Press, 2021.

Elena, Eduardo. "Spinsters, Gamblers, and Friedrich Engels: The Social Worlds of Money and Expansionism in Argentina, 1860s–1900s." *Hispanic American Historical Review* 102, no. 1 (February 2022): 61–94.

Eller, Anne. *We Dream Together: Dominican Independence, Haiti, and the Fight for Caribbean Freedom*. Durham, NC: Duke University Press, 2016.

Erbig, Jeffrey Alan, Jr. *Where Caciques and Mapmakers Met: Border Making in Eighteenth-Century South America*. Chapel Hill: University of North Carolina Press, 2020.

Escolar, Diego. "El sueño de la razón y los monstruos de la nación: la naturalización de la cordillera de Los Andes en la articulación estatal-nacional argentino-chilena." In *Fronteras en movimiento e imaginarios geográficos: la cordillera de Los Andes como espacialidad sociocultural*, edited by Andrés Núñez, Rafael Sánchez, and Federico Arenas V., 89–110. Santiago: RIL, 2013.

———. "Huarpe Archives in the Argentine Desert: Indigenous Claims and State Construction in Nineteenth-Century Mendoza." *Hispanic American Historical Review* 93, no. 3 (2013): 451–86.

———. "La república perdida de Santos Guayama. Demandas indígenas y rebeliones montoneras en Argentina, siglo XIX." *Estudios Atacameños*, no. 57 (2018): 141–60.

———. *Los dones étnicos de la nación: identidades huarpe y modos de producción de soberanía en la Argentina*. Buenos Aires: Prometeo, 2007.

———. *Los indios montoneros: un desierto rebelde para la nación Argentina (Guanacache, siglos XVIII–XX)*. Buenos Aires: Prometeo Libros, 2021.

———. "Subjetividad y estatalidad: usos del pasado y pertenencias indígenas en Calingasta." In *Cruzando la cordillera. . . : la frontera argentino-chilena como espacio social*, edited by Susana Bandieri, 141–66. Neuquén, Argentina: Centro de Estudios de Historia Regional/Universidad del Comahue, 2001.

Escolar, Diego, and Leticia Saldi. "Making the Indigenous Desert from the European Oasis: The Ethnopolitics of Water in Mendoza, Argentina." *Journal of Latin American Studies* 49, no. 2 (May 2017): 269–97.

Estefane Jaramillo, Andrés. "'*Un alto en el camino para saber cuántos somos . . .*'. Los censos de población y la construcción de lealtades nacionales, Chile, siglo XIX." *Historia* 37, no. 1 (January–June 2004): 33–59.

Evans, Chris, and Olivia Saunders. "A World of Copper: Globalizing the Industrial Revolution, 1830–1870." *Journal of Global History* 10, no. 1 (March 2015): 3–26.

Fernández Abara, Joaquín. *Regionalismo, liberalismo y rebelión: Copiapó en la Guerra Civil de 1859*. Santiago: RIL, 2016.

Ferrari, Alejandro A., Félix A. Acuto, Iván Leibowicz, Joaquín Izaguirre, and Cristian Jacob. "Pilgrimage, Mountain Worshiping, and Human–Non-human Entities' Interactions in the South Andes: A Case Study from the North Calchaquí Valley (Salta, Argentina)." *Journal of Anthropological Archaeology*, no. 61 (2021): 1–17.

Fick, Carolyn. "From Slave Colony to Black Nation: Haiti's Revolutionary Inversion." In *New Nations: Capitalism, Revolutions, and Nations in the Americas, 1750–1870*, edited by John Tutino, 138–74. Durham, NC: Duke University Press, 2016.

Fifer, J. Valerie. "Andes Crossing: Old Tracks and New Opportunities at the Uspallata Pass." *Yearbook: Conference of Latin Americanist Geographers* 20 (1994): 35–48.

Fink, Leon, ed. *Workers across the Americas: The Transnational Turn in Labor History*. New York: Oxford University Press, 2011.

Fleming, William J. *Regional Development and Transportation in Argentina: Mendoza and the Gran Oeste Argentino Railroad, 1885–1914*. New York: Garland, 1987.

Fradkin, Raúl, ed. *El poder y la vara: estudios sobre la justicia y la construcción del Estado en el Buenos Aires rural*. Buenos Aires: Prometeo, 2007.

Freitas, Frederico. *Iguazu Falls and National Parks at the Brazil-Argentina Border*. New York: Cambridge University Press, 2021.

Gabaccia, Donna, and Elizabeth Zanoni. "Transitions in Gender Ratios among International Migrants, 1820–1930." *Social Science History* 36, no. 2 (Summer 2012): 197–221.

Gambier, Mariano. "Los grupos cazadores-recolectores del extremo sudeste de los Andes Meridionales." *Revista Chungara*, no. 16/17 (October 1986): 119–24.

Garavaglia, Juan Carlos, and Raúl Osvaldo Fradkin, eds. *A 150 años de la Guerra de la Triple Alianza contra el Paraguay*. Buenos Aires: Prometeo, 2016.

García, Alejandro. "Cronología de la anexión incaica de Mendoza (frontera sudoriental del Tawantinsuyu)." *Revista TEFROS* 19, no. 1 (January–June 2021): 10–33.

———. "Intensificación económica y complejidad sociopolítica huarpe (centro-norte de Mendoza)." *Intersecciones en Antropología* 18, no. 2 (2017): 157–67.

Garrido, Francisco. "Rethinking Imperial Infrastructure: A Bottom-Up Perspective on the Inca Road." *Journal of Anthropological Archaeology* 43 (2016): 94–109.

Gascón, Margarita. "Formas de control y de conflicto social durante el siglo XIX en una comunidad periférica: notas sobre Mendoza (1820–1870)." *Cuadernos de Historia Regional* 5, no. 14 (1989): 62–95.

———. *Naturaleza e imperio: Araucanía, Patagonia, Pampas, 1598–1740*. Buenos Aires: Dunken, 2007.

Gieryn, Thomas. *Cultural Boundaries of Science: Credibility on the Line*. Chicago: University of Chicago Press, 1999.

Gobat, Michel. *Empire by Invitation: William Walker and Manifest Destiny in Central America*. Cambridge, MA: Harvard University Press, 2018.

Goldman, Noemí, and Ricardo Salvatore. "Introducción." In *Caudillismos rioplatenses: nuevas miradas a un viejo problema*, edited by Noemí Goldman and Ricardo Salvatore, 7–30. Buenos Aires: Eudeba, 1998.

Gordillo, Gastón. "The Crucible of Citizenship: ID-Paper Fetishism in the Argentinean Chaco." *American Ethnologist* 33, no. 2 (2006): 162–76.

Gould, Eliga H. "Entangled Histories, Entangled Worlds: The English-Speaking Atlantic as a Spanish Periphery." *American Historical Review* 112, no. 3 (June 2007): 764–86.

Grinberg, Keila. "Emancipación y guerra en el Río de la Plata, 1840–1865: hacia una historia social de las relaciones internacionales." *Historia Mexicana* 69, no. 2 (2019): 693–742.

Guajardo Soto, Guillermo. *Tecnología, Estado y ferrocarriles en Chile, 1850–1950*. Mexico City: Universidad Nacional Autónoma de México, 2007.

Guardino, Peter. *The Dead March: A History of the Mexican-American War*. Cambridge, MA: Harvard University Press, 2017.

———. *Peasants, Politics, and the Formation of Mexico's National State, Guerrero, 1800–1857*. Stanford, CA: Stanford University Press, 1996.

Gulliver, Katrina. "Finding a Pacific World." *Journal of World History* 22, no. 1 (March 2011): 83–100.

Guy, Donna J. "Lower-Class Families, Women, and the Law in Nineteenth-Century Argentina." *Journal of Family History* 10, no. 3 (1985): 318–31.

———. "Oro Blanco: Cotton, Technology, and Family Labor in Nineteenth-Century Argentina." *Americas* 49, no. 4 (April 1993): 457–78.

———. *Sex and Danger in Buenos Aires: Prostitution, Family, and Nation in Argentina*. Lincoln: University of Nebraska Press, 1990.

———. "Women, Peonage, and Industrialization: Argentina, 1810–1914." *Latin American Research Review* 16, no. 3 (1981): 65–89.

Hale, Charles. *The Transformation of Liberalism in Late Nineteenth-Century Mexico*. Princeton, NJ: Princeton University Press, 1990.

Halperín Donghi, Tulio. *Argentina: de la revolución de la independencia a la confederación rosista*. Buenos Aires: Paidós, 1993.

———. *Historia de la Universidad de Buenos Aires*. Buenos Aires: Editorial Universitaria de Buenos Aires, 1962.

———. *Proyecto y construcción de una nación (1846–1880)*. Buenos Aires: Emecé, 2007.

Hämäläinen, Pekka, and Samuel Truett. "On Borderlands." *Journal of American History* 98, no. 2 (September 2011): 338–61.

Harambour Ross, Alberto. "Fronteras nacionales, Estados coloniales. ¿Para una historia plurinacional de América Latina?" *Historia Crítica*, no. 82 (2021): 3–27.

———. *Soberanías fronterizas: Estados y capital en la colonización de Patagonia (Argentina and Chile, 1830–1922)*. Valdivia: Ediciones Universidad Austral de Chile, 2019.

Harvey, David. *The Limits to Capital*. New York: Verso, 2018.

———. "The Right to the City." *New Left Review* 53 (September–October 2008): 23–40.

———. "Space as a Keyword." In *David Harvey: A Critical Reader*, edited by Noel Castree and Derek Gregory, 270–93. Malden, MA: Blackwell, 2006.

———. *Spaces of Global Capitalism: Towards a Theory of Uneven Geographical Development*. New York: Verso, 2006.

Harvey, Kyle E. "'Because That's What His Consul Had Ordered': The Chilean Consulate as a Labor Institution in Mendoza, Argentina (1859–1869)." *Historia Crítica*, no. 80 (April–June 2021): 81–102.

———. "Engineering Value: The Transandine Railway and the 'Techno-Capital' State in Chile at the End of the Nineteenth Century." *Journal of Latin American Studies* 52, no. 4 (November 2020): 711–33.

———. "Prepositional Geographies: Rebellion, Railroads, and the Transandean, 1830s–1910s." PhD diss., Cornell University, 2019.

Hecht, Gabrielle. *The Radiance of France: Nuclear Power and National Identity after World War II*. Cambridge, MA: MIT Press, 1998.

Hellyer, Robert. "The West, the East, and the Insular Middle: Trading Systems, Demand, and Labour in the Integration of the Pacific." *Journal of Global History*, no. 8 (2013): 391–413.

Herr, Pilar M. *Contested Nation: The Mapuche, Bandits, and State Formation in Nineteenth-Century Chile*. Albuquerque: University of New Mexico Press, 2019.

Herzog, Tamar. *Defining Nations: Immigrants and Citizens in Early Modern Spain and Spanish America*. New Haven: Yale University Press, 2003.

Hobsbawm, Eric. *The Age of Capital: 1848–1875*. New York: Charles Scribner's Sons, 1975.

Hopkins, Benjamin D. *Ruling the Savage Periphery: Frontier Governance and the Making of the Modern State*. Cambridge, MA: Harvard University Press, 2020.

Hutchison, Elizabeth Quay, Thomas Miller Klubock, Nara B. Milanich, and Peter Winn, eds. *The Chile Reader: History, Culture, Politics*. Durham, NC: Duke University Press, 2013.

Igler, David. "Diseased Goods: Global Exchanges in the Eastern Pacific Basin, 1770–1850." *American Historical Review* 109, no. 3 (2004): 693–719.

Illanes O., María Angélica. *Chile des-centrado: formación socio-cultural republicana y transición capitalista (1810–1910)*. Santiago: LOM, 2003.

Irigoin, Alejandra. "The End of a Silver Era: The Consequences of the Breakdown of the Spanish Peso Standard in China and the United States, 1780s–1850s." *Journal of World History* 20, no. 2 (2009): 207–43.

Izechksohn, Vitor. *Slavery and War in the Americas: Race, Citizenship, and State Building in the United States and Brazil, 1861–1870*. Charlottesville: University of Virginia Press, 2014.

Jocelyn-Holt Letelier, Alfredo. *El peso de la noche: nuestra frágil fortaleza histórica*. Buenos Aires: Ariel, 1997.

Jones, Kristine L. "Warfare, Reorganization, and Readaptation at the Margins of Spanish Rule: The Southern Margin (1573–1882)." In *The Cambridge History of the Native Peoples of the Americas*. Vol. 3, *South America, Part 2*, edited by Frank Salomon and Stuart B. Schwartz, 138–87. New York: Cambridge University Press, 1999.

Joseph, Gilbert M. "On the Trail of Latin American Bandits: A Reexamination of Peasant Resistance." *Latin American Research Review* 25, no. 3 (1990): 7–53.

Joseph, Gilbert M., and Daniel Nugent, eds. *Everyday Forms of State Formation: Revolution and the Negotiation of Rule in Modern Mexico*. Durham, NC: Duke University Press, 1994.

Kerr, Ashley Elizabeth. *Sex, Skulls, and Citizens: Gender and Racial Science in Argentina (1860–1910)*. Nashville, TN: Vanderbilt University Press, 2020.

Kocka, Jürgen. "Comparison and Beyond." *History and Theory* 42, no. 1 (February 2003): 39–44.

Kuntz Ficker, Sandra, ed. *First Export Era Revisited: Reassessing Its Contribution to Latin American Economies*. Cham, Switzerland: Palgrave Macmillan, 2017.

———. *Historia mínima de la expansión ferroviaria en América Latina*. Mexico City: El Colegio de México, 2015.

Lacoste, Pablo. "Carretas y transporte terrestre biocéanico: la ruta Buenos Aires-Mendoza en el siglo XVIII." *Estudios Ibero-Americanos* 31, no. 1 (2005): 7–34.

———. "El arriero y el transporte terrestre en el Cono Sur (Mendoza, 1780–1800)." *Revista de Indias* 68, no. 244 (2008): 35–68.

———. *El Ferrocarril Trasandino y el desarrollo de los Andes Centrales argentino-chilenos, 1872–2013*. Santiago: IDEA, 2013.

———. "El Paso Pehuenche y su aporte al desarrollo regional (1658–1846)." *Universum* 33, no. 1 (2018): 143–63.

———. "El tropero y el origen de la burguesía en el Cono Sur (Mendoza, siglo XVIII)." *Estudios Ibero-Americanos* 31, no. 2 (December 2005): 177–205.

———. "Las guerras hispanoamericana y de la Triple Alianza, la Revolución de los Colorados y su impacto en las relaciones entre Argentina y Chile." *Historia* 29, no. 1 (1995–96): 125–58.

———. "The Rise and Secularization of Viticulture in Mendoza: The Godoy Family Contribution, 1700–1831." *Americas* 63, no. 3 (January 2007): 385–407.

———. "Viticultura y política internacional: el intento de reincorporar a Mendoza y San Juan a Chile (1820–1835)." *Historia* 38, no. 1 (2005): 155–76.

———. "Wine and Women: Grape Growers and *Pulperas* in Mendoza, 1561–1852." *Hispanic American Historical Review* 88, no. 3 (August 2008): 361–91.

Lacoste, Pablo, and Michelle Malén Lacoste Adunka. "Chamantos, ponchos y balandres en Colchagua y Rancagua (siglos XVII–XIX)." *Estudios Atacameños*, no. 57 (2018): 97–118.

Landers, Jane. *Atlantic Creoles in the Age of Revolutions*. Cambridge, MA: Harvard University Press, 2010.

Langer, Erick D. "Desarrollo económico y contrabando de plata en el siglo XIX (Andes centromeridionales)." *Diálogo Andino*, no. 66 (2021): 313–24.

———. "The Eastern Andean Frontier (Bolivia and Argentina) and Latin America Frontiers: Comparative Contexts (19th and 20th Centuries)." *Americas* 59, no. 1 (July 2002): 33–63.

———. "Espacios coloniales y economías nacionales: Bolivia y el Norte Argentino (1810–1930)." *Siglo XIX: Revista de Historia* 2, no. 4 (July–December 1987): 135–60.

Larson, Carolyne R., ed. *The Conquest of the Desert: Argentina's Indigenous Peoples and the Battle for History*. Albuquerque: University of New Mexico Press, 2020.

Lasso, Marixa. *Erased: The Untold Story of the Panama Canal*. Cambridge, MA: Harvard University Press, 2019.

Latour, Bruno. *Science in Action: How to Follow Scientists and Engineers through Society*. Cambridge, MA: Harvard University Press, 1988.

———. "Technology Is Society Made Durable." In *A Sociology of Monsters: Essays on Power, Technology and Domination*, edited by John Law, 103–31. New York: Routledge, 1991.

Lazzari, Axel. "Aboriginal Recognition, Freedom, and Phantoms: The Vanishing of the Ranquel and the Return of the Rankülche in La Pampa." *Journal of Latin American Anthropology* 8, no. 3 (2003): 59–83.

Lefebvre, Henri. *Critique of Everyday Life*. Vol. 1, *Introduction*. Translated by John Moore. New York: Verso, 2008.

———. *The Production of Space*. Translated by Donald Nicholson-Smith. Malden, MA: Blackwell, 1991.

———. "Space and the State (1978)." In *State, Space, World: Selected Essays*, edited by Neil Brenner and Stuart Elden, 223–53. Translated by Gerald Moore, Neil Brenner, and Stuart Elden. Minneapolis: University of Minnesota Press, 2009.

Lewis, Colin M. "Britain, the Argentine and Informal Empire: Rethinking the Role of Railway Companies." In *Informal Empire in Latin America: Culture, Commerce and Capital*, edited by Matthew Brown, 99–123. Malden, MA: Blackwell, 2008.

———. *British Railways in Argentina, 1857–1914: A Case Study of Foreign Investment*. London: Athlone, 1983.

———. "The Financing of Railway Development in Latin America, 1850–1914." *Iberoamerikanisches Archiv* 9, no. 3/4 (1983): 255–78.

Linebaugh, Peter, and Marcus Rediker. *The Many-Headed Hydra: Sailors, Slaves, Commoners, and the Hidden History of the Revolutionary Atlantic*. Boston: Beacon, 2000.

Llorca-Jaña, Manuel. "A Reappraisal of Mapuche Textile Production and Sheep Raising during the Nineteenth Century." *Historia* 47, no. 1 (2014): 91–111.

———. "Shaping Globalization: London's Merchant Bankers in the Early Nineteenth Century." *Business History Review*, no. 88 (Autumn 2014): 469–95.

Llorca-Jaña, Manuel, and Juan Navarrete-Montalvo. "El rol de Chile en la primera globalización del cobre, 1700–1840." *Revista de Historia y Geografía*, no. 42 (2020): 15–44.

Llorca-Jaña, Manuel, Claudio Robles Ortiz, Juan Navarrete-Montalvo, and Roberto Araya Valenzuela. "La agricultura y la élite agraria chilena a través de los catastros agrícolas, c. 1830–1855." *Historia* 50, no. 2 (July–December 2017): 597–639.

López, Mario Justo. *Ferrocarriles, deuda y crisis: historia de los ferrocarriles en la Argentina, 1887–1896*. Buenos Aires: Belgrano, 2000.

Lozoya López, Ivette. *Delincuentes, bandoleros y montoneros: violencia social en el espacio rural chileno (1850–1870)*. Santiago: LOM, 2014.

Lucena, Juan C. "De *Criollos a Mexicanos*: Engineers' Identity and the Construction of Mexico." *History and Technology* 23, no. 3 (2007): 275–88.

———. "Imagining Nation, Envisioning Progress: Emperor, Agricultural Elites, and Imperial Ministers in Search of Engineers in 19th Century Brazil." *Engineering Studies* 1, no. 3 (2009): 191–216.

Ludmer, Josefina. *The Gaucho Genre: A Treatise on the Motherland*. Translated by Molly Weigel. Durham, NC: Duke University Press, 2002.

Lynch, John. *Argentine Dictator: Juan Manuel de Rosas, 1829–1852*. New York: Oxford University Press, 1981.

———. *Caudillos in Spanish America, 1800–1850*. New York: Oxford University Press, 1992.

Macías, Flavia. *Armas y política en la Argentina: Tucumán, siglo XIX*. Madrid: Consejo Superior de Investigaciones Científicas, 2014.

———. "Violencia y política facciosa en el norte argentino: Tucumán en la década de 1860." *Boletín Americanista*, no. 57 (2007): 15–34.

Macías, Flavia, and Hilda Sabato. "La Guardia Nacional: Estado, política y uso de la fuerza en la Argentina de la segunda mitad del siglo XIX." *PolHis* 6, no. 11 (2013): 70–81.

Malanima, Paolo. "Energy Crisis and Growth, 1650–1850: The European Deviation in a Comparative Perspective." *Journal of Global History*, no. 1 (2006): 101–21.

Mallon, Florencia E. *Peasant and Nation: The Making of Postcolonial Mexico and Peru*. Berkeley: University of California Press, 1995.

Mandrini, Raúl J., and Sara Ortelli. "Repensando viejos problemas: observaciones sobre la araucanización de las pampas." *RUNA, Archivo para las Ciencias del Hombre* 22, no. 1 (1995): 135–50.

Mann, Michael. "The Autonomous Power of the State: Its Origins, Mechanisms, and Results." *European Journal of Sociology* 25, no. 2 (1984): 185–213.

Marichal, Carlos. *A Century of Debt Crises in Latin America: From Independence to the Great Depression*. Princeton, NJ: Princeton University Press, 1989.

Marigliano, Cicilia. "Aportes para el estudio de la legislación ganadera en Mendoza." *Revista de Historia del Derecho*, no. 13 (1985): 107–27.

Marimán Quemenado, Pablo. "La República y los Mapuche: 1819–1828." In *Ta iñ fijke xipa rakizuameluwün. Historia, colonialismo y resistencia desde el páis Mapuche*, edited by Héctor Nahuelpán Moreno, Herson Huinca Piutrin, Pablo Mariman Quemenado, Luis Carcamo-Huechante, Maribel Mora Curriao, José Quidel Lincoleo, Enrique Antileo Baeza et al., 63–87. Temuco, Chile: Comunidad de Historia Mapuche, 2012.

Marín Vicuña, Santiago. *Los Hermanos Clark*. Santiago: Establecimientos Gráficos "Balcells & Co.," 1929.

Martínez Estrada, Ezequiel. *Sarmiento. Meditaciones sarmientinas. Los invariantes históricos en el Facundo*. Buenos Aires: Beatriz Viterbo, 2001.

———. *X-Ray of the Pampa*. Translated by Alain Swietlicki. Austin: University of Texas Press, 1971.

Martland, Samuel J. "Trade, Progress, and Patriotism: Defining Valparaíso, Chile, 1818–1875." *Journal of Urban History* 35, no. 1 (November 2008): 53–74.

Marx, Karl. *Capital: A Critique of Political Economy*. Vol. 1, *The Process and Production of Capital*. Translated by David Fernbach, with an introduction by Ernest Mandel. New York: Penguin Classics, 1992.

———. *Capital: A Critique of Political Economy*. Vol. 3, *The Process of Capitalist Production as a Whole*. Translated by David Fernbach, with an introduction by Ernest Mandel. New York: Penguin Books, 1991.

———. *Grundrisse: Foundations of the Critique of Political Economy*. Translated by Martin Nicolaus, with notes by Ben Fowkes. New York: Penguin Books, 1993.

Marx, Leo. "*Technology*: The Emergence of a Hazardous Concept." *Technology and Culture* 51, no. 3 (July 2010): 561–77.

Massey, Doreen. *For Space*. London: SAGE, 2005.

Matsuda, Matt. *Pacific Worlds: A History of Seas, Peoples, and Cultures*. New York: Cambridge University Press, 2012.

Maude, H. E. *Slavers in Paradise: The Peruvian Slave Trade in Polynesia, 1862–1864*. Stanford, CA: Stanford University Press, 1981.

Mavhunga, Clapperton Chakanetsa. *Transient Workspaces: Technologies of Everyday Innovation in Zimbabwe*. Cambridge, MA: MIT Press, 2014.

May, Robert E. "Young American Males and Filibustering in the Age of Manifest Destiny: The United States Army as a Cultural Mirror." *Journal of American History* 78, no. 3 (December 1991): 857–86.

Mayo, Carlos. "Estancia y peonaje en la región pampeana en la segunda mitad del siglo XVIII." *Desarrollo Económico* 23, no. 92 (January–March 1984): 609–16.

———, ed. *Pulperos y pulperías de Buenos Aires, 1740–1830*. Mar del Plata, Argentina: Universidad de Mar del Plata, 1996.

Mayo, John. "The Development of British Interests in Chile's Norte Chico in the Early Nineteenth Century." *Americas* 57, no. 3 (January 2001): 363–94.

———. "Joshua Waddington and the Anglo Chilean Connection." *Boletín de la Academia Chilena de la Historia* 71, no. 114 (2005): 189–216.

Melillo, Edward Dallam. *Strangers on Familiar Soil: Rediscovering the Chile-California Connection*. New Haven, CT: Yale University Press, 2015.

Michieli, Catalina Teresa. *Antigua historia de Cuyo*. San Juan, Argentina: Ansilta, 1994.

Miller, Nicola. *Republics of Knowledge: Nations of the Future in Latin America*. Princeton, NJ: Princeton University Press, 2020.

Mintz, Sydney W. *Sweetness and Power: The Place of Sugar in Modern History*. New York: Penguin Books, 1986.

Mitchell, Timothy. *Carbon Democracy: Political Power in the Age of Oil*. New York: Verso, 2011.

———. "Infrastructures Work on Time." *New Silk Roads*, January 2020, www.e-flux.com/architecture/new-silk-roads/312596/infrastructures-work-on-time/.

———. *Rule of Experts: Egypt, Techno-Politics, and Modernity*. Berkeley: University of California Press, 2002.

Molina, Eugenia. "Circuitos mercantiles, circulación de personas y criminalidad en la configuración de espacios políticos: Valle de Uco (Mendoza, Río de la Plata), primera mitad del siglo XIX." *Revista Complutense de Historia de América*, no. 43 (2017): 153–78.

———. "Los funcionarios subalternos de justicia en Mendoza, 1820–1852: entre el control comunitario y el disciplinamiento social." *Nuevo Mundo, Mundos Nuevos*, no. 23 (2010). http://journals.openedition.org/nuevomundo/59353.

———. "Los tentáculos de la justicia: equipamiento institucional para gobernar la campaña y la frontera a fines del período colonial, Mendoza, 1780–1810." In *Fronteras y periferias en arqueología e historia*, edited by Margarita Gascón and María José Ots, 159–94. Buenos Aires: Dunken, 2013.

———. "Tras la construcción del orden provincial: las comisiones militares de justicia en Mendoza, 1831 y 1852." In *La justicia y las formas de la autoridad. Organización política y justicias locales en territorios de frontera. El Río de la Plata, Córdoba, Cuyo y Tucumán, siglos XVII a XIX*, edited by Darío Barriera, 83–105. Rosario, Argentina: Red Columnaria/ISHIR/CONICET, 2010.

Molina Otarola, Raúl. "Pueblo de Indio Huasco Alto: lugar de memoria y fantasmas de la etnicidad." In *Memorias sujetadas: hacia una lectura crítica y situada de los procesos de memorialización*, compiled by Soledad Biasatti and Gonzalo Compañy, 35–52. Madrid: JAS Arquelogía, 2014.

Morales, Orlando Gabriel. "El mundo del trabajo libre y esclavo en la campana cuyana luego de la Guerra de Independencia Argentina (Mendoza, 1823)." *Mundo Agrario* 22, no. 50 (2021): e167.

———. "Identificaciones de plebeyos de color militarizados durante la revolución de la independencia en el Río de la Plata: Cuyo, 1810–1816." *Estudios Sociales* 53 (July–December 2017): 127–54.

Morales, Orlando Gabriel, and Luis César Caballero. "Abolición de la esclavitud en Mendoza, 1853: liberación y trayectorias sociales de los últimos esclavizados." *Anuario del Instituto de Historia Argentina* 22, no. 2 (2022): e173.

Moutoukias, Zacarías. "Power, Corruption, and Commerce: The Making of the Local Administrative Structure in Seventeenth-Century Buenos Aires." *Hispanic American Historical Review* 68, no. 4 (November 1988): 771–801.

Moya, José. "A Continent of Immigrants: Postcolonial Shifts in the Western Hemisphere." *Hispanic American Historical Review* 86, no. 1 (February 2006): 1–28.

———. *Cousins and Strangers: Spanish Immigrants in Buenos Aires, 1850–1930*. Berkeley: University of California Press, 1998.

———. "Italians in Buenos Aires's Anarchist Movement: Gender Ideology and Women's Participation, 1890–1910." In *Women, Gender, and Transnational Lives: Italian Workers of the World*, edited by Donna R. Gabaccia and Franca Iacovetta, 189–216. Toronto: University of Toronto Press, 2002.

Mukerji, Chandra. *Territorial Ambitions and the Gardens of Versailles*. New York: Cambridge University Press, 1997.

———. "The Territorial State as a Figured World of Power: Strategics, Logistics, and Impersonal Rule." *Sociological Theory* 28, no. 4 (2010): 402–24.

Muller, Dalia Antonia. *Cuban Émigrés and Independence in the Nineteenth-Century Gulf World*. Chapel Hill: University of North Carolina Press, 2017.

Murphy, Anne L. *The Origins of English Financial Markets: Investments and Speculation before the South Sea Bubble*. New York: Cambridge University Press, 2009.

Ñanculef Huaiquinao, Juan. *Tayiñ mapuche kimün. Epistemología mapuche. Sabiduría y conocimiento*. Santiago: Universidad de Chile, 2016.

Nasatir, Abraham P. "Chileans in California during the Gold Rush Period and the Establishment of the Chilean Consulate." *California Historical Quarterly* 53, no. 1 (Spring 1974): 52–70.

Nazer Ahumada, Ricardo. *José Tomás Urmeneta: un empresario del siglo XIX*. Santiago: Dirección de Bibliotecas, Archivos y Museos, 1994.

Nobbs-Thiessen, Ben. *Landscape of Migration: Mobility and Environmental Change on Bolivia's Tropical Frontier, 1952 to the Present*. Chapel Hill: University of North Carolina Press, 2020.

Núñez, Andrés, and Matthew C. Benwell. "Comprendiendo el espacio desde otras escalas: la geografía del habitar como geo-grafía y geo-política cotidiana." *Revista Austral de Ciencias Sociales*, no. 37 (2019): 161–66.

Núñez, Andrés, Rafael Sánchez, and Federico Arenas V., eds. *Fronteras en movimiento e imaginarios geográficos. La cordillera de los Andes como espacialidad sociocultural*. Santiago: RIL, 2013.

Ocaranza, Morales, and Luis Joaquín. *Historia del Huasco*. Valparaíso: Librería del Mercurio, 1896.

Ortega Peña, Rodolfo, and Eduardo Luis Duhalde. *Felipe Varela contra el Imperio Británico (las masas de la Unión Americana enfrentan a las potencias europeas)*. Buenos Aires: Sudestada, 1966.

Ossa Santa Cruz, Juan Luis. "The Army of the Andes: Chilean and Rioplatense Politics in an Age of Military Organisation, 1814–1817." *Journal of Latin American Studies* 46, no. 1 (February 2014): 29–58.

Oszlak, Oscar. *La formación del Estado argentino*. Buenos Aires: Belgrano, 1982.

Otero, Hernán. *Estadística y nación. Una historia conceptual del pensamiento censal de la Argentina moderna, 1869–1914*. Buenos Aires: Prometeo, 2006.

Ots, María José, Pablo Cahiza, and Margarita Gascón. "Articulaciones del corredor trasandino meridional: el río Tunuyán en el valle de Uco, Mendoza, Argentina." *Revista de Historia Americana y Argentina* 50, no. 1 (2015): 81–105.

Palermo, Silvana Alejandra. "Del Parlamento al Ministerio de Obras Públicas: la construcción de los Ferrocariles del Estado en Argentina, 1862–1916." *Desarrollo Económico* 46, no. 182 (2006): 215–43.

———. "Elite técnica y estado liberal: la creación de una administración moderna en los Ferrocarriles del Estado (1870–1910)." *Estudios Sociales*, no. 30 (2006): 9–41.

———. "*En nombre del hogar proletario*: Engendering the 1917 Great Railroad Strike in Argentina." *Hispanic American Historical Review* 93, no. 4 (2013): 585–620.

Pavez Ojeda, Jorge, comp. *Cartas mapuche: siglo XIX*. Santiago: CoLibris y Ocho Libros, 2008.

Paz, Gustavo L. "The World Mules Made: Mule Trade in the Colonial Rio de la Plata." In *The Rio de la Plata from Colony to Nations: Commerce, Society, and Politics*, edited by Fabrício Prado, Viviana L. Grieco, and Alex Boruki, 53–76. Cham, Switzerland: Palgrave Macmillan, 2021.

Pederson, Leland R. *The Mining Industry of the Norte Chico, Chile*. Berkeley: University of California Press, 1965.

Piccato, Pablo. *City of Suspects: Crime in Mexico City, 1900–1931*. Durham, NC: Duke University Press, 2001.

Picone, María de los Ángeles. "Legitimizing and Resisting Spatial Violence in Southern Chile (1890s–1910s)." *Historia Crítica*, no. 82 (2021): 55–78.

Pinto Rodríguez, Jorge. *La formación del Estado y la nación, y el pueblo mapuche. De la inclusión a la exclusión*. Santiago: Dirección de Bibliotecas, Archivos y Museos, 2003.

Pinto Vallejos, Julio. *Trabajos y rebeldías en la pampa salitrera*. Santiago: Editorial de la Universidad de Santiago de Chile, 1998.

Pinto Vallejos, Julio, Verónica Valdivia Ortiz de Zárate, and Pablo Artaza Barrios. "Patria y clase en los albores de la identidad pampina (1860–1890)." *Historia* 36 (2003): 275–332.

Pomerantz, Kenneth. *The Great Divergence: China, Europe, and the Making of the Modern World*. Princeton, NJ: Princeton University Press, 2000.

Prado, Fabrício. *Edge of Empire: Atlantic Networks and Revolution in Bourbon Río de la Plata*. Oakland: University of California Press, 2015.

Pritchard, Sara. "From Hydroimperialism to Hydrocapitalism: 'French' Hydraulics in France, North Africa, and Beyond." *Social Studies of Science* 42, no. 4 (August 2012): 591–615.

Purcell, Fernando. *¡Muchos extranjeros para mi gusto! Mexicanos, chilenos e irlandeses en la construcción de California, 1848–1880*. Santiago: Fondo de Cultura Económica Chile, 2016.

Putnam, Lara. "To Study the Fragments/Whole: Microhistory and the Atlantic World." *Journal of Social History* 39, no. 3 (2006): 615–30.

Quintero Ramos, Ángel M. *A History of Money and Banking in Argentina*. Río Piedras: University of Puerto Rico, 1965.

Radding, Cynthia. *Landscapes of Power and Identity: Comparative Histories in the Sonoran Desert and the Forests of Amazonia from Colony to Republic*. Durham, NC: Duke University Press, 2005.

Ratto, Silvia. "Una experiencia fronteriza exitosa: el negocio pacífico de indios en la Provincia de Buenos Aires (1829–1852)." *Revista de Indias* 63, no. 227 (2003): 191–222.

Regalsky, Andrés Martín. *Mercados, inversores y élites. Las inversiones francesas en la Argentina, 1880–1914*. Buenos Aires: Editorial de la Universidad Nacional de Tres de Febrero, 2002.

Reggini, Horacio C. *Sarmiento y las telecomunicaciones. La obsesión del hilo*. Buenos Aires: Galápago, 1997.

Reséndez, Andrés. *Changing National Identities at the Frontier: Texas and New Mexico, 1800–1850*. New York: Cambridge University Press, 2005.

Reyes, César. "Felipe Varela y la batalla de Bargas (10 de Abril de 1867)." *Revista de Derecho, Historia y Letras* 18, no. 55 (1916): 164–83.

Richard-Jorba, Rodolfo A. *Empresarios ricos, trabajadores pobres. Vitivinicultura y desarrollo capitalista en Mendoza (1850–1918)*. Rosario, Argentina: Prohistoria, 2010.

———. *Poder, economía y espacio en Mendoza, 1850–1900. Del comercio ganadero a la agroindustria vitivinícola*. Mendoza, Argentina: Editorial de la Facultad de Filosofía y Letras de la Universidad Nacional de Cuyo, 1998.

Robles-Ortiz, Claudio. "Mechanisation in the Periphery: The Experience of Chilean Agriculture, c. 1850–1890." *Rural History* 29, no. 2 (2018): 195–216.

Rock, David. "Argentina under Mitre: Porteño Liberalism in the 1860." *Americas* 56, no. 1 (1999): 31–63.

———. *State Building and Political Movements in Argentina, 1860–1916*. Stanford, CA: Stanford University Press, 2002.

Rodriguez, Julia. *Civilizing Argentina: Science, Medicine, and the Modern State*. Chapel Hill: University of North Carolina Press, 2006.

Roig, Arturo Andrés. *El concepto de trabajo en Mendoza durante la segunda mitad del siglo XIX*. Mendoza, Argentina: Imprenta Oficial, 1970.

Roldán, Darío. "La cuestión liberal en la Argentina en el siglo XIX: política, sociedad, representación." In *Un nuevo orden político: provincias y Estado nacional, 1852–1880*, edited by Beatriz Bragoni and Eduardo Míguez, 275–91. Buenos Aires: Biblos, 2010.

Roller, Heather. *Amazonian Routes: Indigenous Mobility and Colonial Communities in Northern Brazil*. Stanford, CA: Stanford University Press, 2014.

Romero, José Luis. *Latinoamérica, las ciudades y las ideas*. Buenos Aires: Siglo Veintiuno, 2011.

Rosa, José María. *La guerra del Paraguay y las montoneras argentinas*. Buenos Aires: A. Peña Lillo, 1964.

Sabato, Hilda. *Republics of the New World: The Revolutionary Political Experiment in Nineteenth-Century Latin America*. Princeton, NJ: Princeton University Press, 2018.

Safford, Frank. *The Ideal of the Practical: Colombia's Struggle to Form a Technical Elite*. Austin: University of Texas Press, 1976.

Salazar, Gabriel. *Construcción de Estado en Chile (1760–1860): democracia de los "pueblos," militarismo ciudadano, golpismo oligárquico*. Santiago: Sudamericana, 2005.

———. *Labradores, peones y proletarios*. Santiago: LOM, 2000.

———. *Mercaderes, empresarios y capitalistas (Chile, siglo XIX)*. Santiago: Sudamericana, 2009.

Salerno, Elena. *Los comienzos del Estado empresario: la Administración General de los Ferrocarriles del Estado (1910–1928)*. Buenos Aires: Imprenta de la Facultad de Ciencias Económicas de la Universidad de Buenos Aires, Centro de Estudios Económicos de la Empresa y el Desarrollo, 2002.

———. "Los ingenieros, la tecnocracia de los Ferrocarriles del Estado." *H-industri@* 9, no. 16 (first semester 2015): 13–34.

Salvatore, Ricardo D. "The Crimes of Poor *Paysanos* in Midnineteenth-Century Buenos Aires." In *Reconstructing Criminality in Latin America*, edited by Carlos A. Aguirre and Robert Buffington, 59–84. Wilmington, DE: Scholarly Resources, 2000.

———. "Death and Liberalism: Capital Punishment after the Fall of Rosas." In *Crime and Punishment in Latin America: Law and Society since Late Colonial Times*, edited by Ricardo D. Salvatore, Carlos Aguirre, and Gilbert M. Joseph, 308–41. Durham, NC: Duke University Press, 2001.

———. "Labor Control and Discrimination: The Contratista System in Mendoza, Argentina, 1880–1920." *Agricultural History* 60, no. 3 (1986): 52–80.

———. *Subalternos, derechos y justicia penal. Ensayos de historia social y cultural Argentina, 1829–1940*. Barcelona: Gedisa, 2013.

———. *Wandering Paysanos: State Order and Subaltern Experience in Buenos Aires during the Rosas Era*. Durham, NC: Duke University Press, 2003.

Sanders, James E. *Contentious Republicans: Popular Politics, Race, and Class in Nineteenth-Century Colombia*. Durham, NC: Duke University Press, 2004.

———. "The Vanguard of the Atlantic World: Contesting Modernity in Nineteenth-Century Latin America." *Latin American Research Review* 46, no. 2 (2011): 104–27.

———. *The Vanguard of the Atlantic World: Creating Modernity, Nation, and Democracy in Nineteenth-Century Latin America*. Durham, NC: Duke University Press, 2014.

Sanjurjo de Driollet, Inés. *La organización político-administrativa de la campaña mendocina en el tránsito del antiguo régimen al orden liberal*. Buenos Aires: Instituto de Investigaciones de Historia del Derecho, 2004.

———. "Las continuidades en el gobierno de la campaña mendocina en el siglo XIX." *Revista de Estudios Histórico-Jurídicos*, no. 26 (2004): 445–68.
Saraví, Mario Guillermo. "Consideraciones acerca del tratado entre Mendoza y Chile (1835)." In *Cuarto congreso nacional y regional de historia Argentina*. Vol. 1. Buenos Aires: Academia Nacional de la Historia, 1979.
Sartori, Andrew. *Bengal in Global Concept History: Culturalism in the Age of Capital*. Chicago: University of Chicago Press, 2008.
Savala, Joshua. *Beyond Patriotic Phobias: Connections, Cooperation, and Solidarity in the Peruvian-Chilean Pacific World*. Oakland: University of California Press, 2022.
———. "Ports of Transnational Labor Organizing: Anarchism along the Peruvian-Chilean Littoral, 1916–1928." *Hispanic American Historical Review* 99, no. 3 (2019): 501–31.
Scalabrini Ortiz, Raúl. *Historia de los ferrocarriles argentinos*. Buenos Aires: Plus Ultra, 1964.
Schaefer, Timo. *Liberalism as Utopia: The Rise and Fall of Legal Rule in Post-colonial Mexico, 1820–1900*. New York: Cambridge University Press, 2017.
Schávelzon, Daniel. *Historia de un terremoto: Mendoza 1861*. Buenos Aires: De los Cuatro Vientos, 2007.
Schivelbusch, Wolfgang. *The Railway Journey: The Industrialization of Time and Space in the Nineteenth Century*. Berkeley: University of California Press, 1986.
Schmidt-Nowara, Christopher. *Empire and Antislavery: Spain, Cuba, and Puerto Rico, 1833–1874*. Pittsburgh: University of Pittsburgh Press, 1999.
Schvarzer, Jorge, and Teresita Gómez. *La primera gran empresa de los argentinos. El Ferrocarril del Oeste (1854–1862)*. Buenos Aires: Fondo de Cultura Económica de Argentina, 2006.
Scott, James C. *The Art of Not Being Governed: An Anarchist History of Southeast Asia*. New Haven, CT: Yale University Press, 2009.
———. *Seeing Like a State: How Certain Schemes to Improve the Human Condition Have Failed*. New Haven, CT: Yale University Press, 1998.
———. *Weapons of the Weak: Everyday Forms of Peasant Resistance*. New Haven, CT: Yale University Press, 1985.
Scott, Rebecca. "Microhistory Set in Motion: A Nineteenth-Century Creole Atlantic Itinerary." In *Empirical Futures: Anthropologists and Historians Engage with the Work of Sidney W. Mintz*, edited by George Baca, Aisha Khan, and Stephan Palmié, 84–111. Chapel Hill: University of North Carolina Press, 2009.
Scott, Rebecca, and Jean Hébrard. *Freedom Papers: An Atlantic Odyssey in the Age of Emancipation*. Cambridge, MA: Harvard University Press, 2012.
Segreti, Carlos S. A. "Contribución al estudio del convenio particular mendocino-chileno de 1835 hasta la muerte del gobernador José Félix Aldao." In *Cuarto congreso nacional y regional de historia argentina*. Vol. 1. Buenos Aires: Academia Nacional de la Historia, 1979.
———."El comercio con Chile y la renuncia del gobernador Pedro Pascual Segura." *Investigaciones y Ensayos* 27 (July–December 1979): 125–61.
———. "Mendoza y la política porteña (1835–1836)." *Investigaciones y Ensayos* 16 (January–June 1974): 177–209.
Sell, Zach. "Asian Indentured Labor in the Age of African American Emancipation." *International Labor and Working-Class History*, no. 91 (Spring 2017): 8–27.

———. *Trouble of the World: Slavery and Empire in the Age of Capital*. Chapel Hill: University of North Carolina Press, 2021.

Serje de la Ossa, Margarita. *El revés de la nación. Territorios salvajes, fronteras y tierras de nadie*. Bogotá: Ediciones Universidad de los Andes, 2005.

———. "Fronteras y periferias en la historia del capitalismo: el caso de América Latina." *Revista de Geografía Norte Grande*, no. 66 (2017): 33–48.

Sexton, Jay. "Steam Transport, Sovereignty, and Empire in North America, circa 1850–1885." *Journal of the Civil War Era* 7, no. 4 (December 2017): 620–47.

Shaffer, Kirwin R. "Contesting Internationalists: Transnational Anarchism, Anti-imperialism and US Expansion in the Caribbean, 1890s–1920s." *Estudios Interdisciplinarios de América Latina y el Caribe* 22, no. 2 (2011): 11–38.

Shumway, Jeffrey. *A Woman, a Man, a Nation: Mariquita Sánchez, Juan Manuel de Rosas, and the Beginnings of Argentina*. Albuquerque: University of New Mexico Press, 2019.

Shumway, Nicolas. *The Invention of Argentina*. Berkeley: University of California Press, 1991.

Sieferle, Rolf Peter. *The Subterranean Forest: Energy Systems and the Industrial Revolution*. Translated by Michael Osmann. Winwick, UK: White Horse Press, 2010.

Silva, Hernán Asdrúbal. "Pulperías, tendejones, sastres y zapateros: Buenos Aires en la primera mitad del siglo XVIII." *Aunario de Estudios Americanos*, no. 26 (1969): 471–506.

Slatta, Richard. "Comparative Frontier Social Life: Western Saloons and Argentine Pulperías." *Great Plains Quarterly* 7, no. 3 (Summer 1987): 155–65.

———. "Pulperías and Contraband Capitalism in Nineteenth-Century Buenos Aires Province." *Americas* 38, no. 3 (January 1982): 347–62.

———. "Rural Criminality and Social Conflict in Nineteenth-Century Buenos Aires Province." *Hispanic American Historical Review* 60, no. 3 (August 1980): 450–72.

Smith, Neil. *Uneven Development: Nature, Capital, and the Production of Space*. Athens: University of Georgia Press, 2008.

Sommariva, Luis H. *Historia de las intervenciones federales en las provincias*. Vol. 1. Buenos Aires: El Ateneo, 1929.

Star, Susan Leigh. "The Ethnography of Infrastructure." *American Behavioral Scientist* 43, no. 3 (1999): 377–91.

Steel, Frances. "Re-routing Empire? Steam-Age Circulations and the Making of an Anglo Pacific, c. 1850–90." *Australian Historical Studies* 46, no. 3 (September 2015): 356–73.

Subrahmanyam, Sanjay. "Connected Histories: Notes towards a Reconfiguration of Early Modern Eurasia." *Modern Asian Studies* 31, no. 3 (July 1997): 735–62.

Svampa, Maristella. "La dialéctica entre lo nuevo y lo viejo: sobre los usos y nociones del caudillismo en la Argentina durante el siglo XIX." In *Caudillismos rioplatenses. Nuevas miradas a un viejo problema*, edited by Noemí Goldman and Ricardo Salvatore, 51–82. Buenos Aires: Eudeba, 1998.

Sweet, James. *Domingos Álvares, African Healing, and the Intellectual History of the Atlantic World*. Chapel Hill: University of North Carolina Press, 2011.

Terrazas y Basante, Marcela. "Ganado, armas y cautivos. Tráfico y comercio ilícito en la frontera norte de México, 1848–1882." *Mexican Studies/Estudios Mexicanos* 35, no. 2 (2019): 171–203.

Thomson, Ian, and Dietrich Angerstein. *Historia del ferrocarril en Chile*. Santiago: Dirección de Bibliotecas, Archivos y Museos, 2000.

Thurner, Mark. *From Two Republics to One Divided: Contradictions of Postcolonial Nation-making in Andean Peru*. Durham, NC: Duke University Press, 1997.
Tinsman, Heidi. "Rebel Coolies, Citizen Warriors, and Sworn Brothers: The Chinese Loyalty Oaths and Alliance with Chile in the War of the Pacific." *Hispanic American Historical Review* 98, no. 3 (August 2018): 439–69.
Titus S., Arturo. *Monografía de los ferrocarriles particulares de Chile*. Valparaíso: Scherrer y Herrman, 1910.
Torget, Andrew J. *Seeds of Empire: Cotton, Slavery, and the Transformation of the Texas Borderlands, 1800–1850*. Chapel Hill: University of North Carolina Press, 2015.
Torpey, John C. *The Invention of the Passport: Surveillance, Citizenship, and the State*. New York: Cambridge University Press, 2000.
Trollope, Anthony. *The Way We Live Now*. London: Wordsworth, 2001.
Truett, Samuel. *Fugitive Landscapes: The Forgotten History of the U.S.-Mexico Borderlands*. New Haven: Yale University Press, 2006.
Tutino, John. "The Americas in the Rise of Industrial Capitalism." In *New Countries: Capitalism, Revolutions, and Nations in the Americas, 1750–1870*, edited by John Tutino, 25–70. Durham, NC: Duke University Press, 2016.
———. *Founding Capitalism in the Bajío and Spanish North America*. Durham, NC: Duke University Press, 2011.
Tyrrell, Ian. "AHR Forum: American Exceptionalism in an Age of International History." *American Historical Review* 96, no. 4 (October 1991): 1031–55.
Valderrama, Andrés, Juan Camargo, Idelman Mejía, Antonio Mejía, Ernesto Lleras, and Antonio García. "Engineering Education and the Identities of Engineers in Colombia, 1887–1972." *Technology and Culture*, no. 50 (October 2009): 811–38.
Valenzuela, Luis. "The Chilean Copper Smelting Industry in the Mid-nineteenth Century: Phases of Expansion and Stagnation, 1834–58." *Journal of Latin American Studies* 24, no. 3 (October 1992): 507–50.
Valenzuela-Márquez, Jaime. "La cordillera de los Andes como espacio de circulaciones y mestizajes: un expediente sobre Chile central y Cuyo a fines del siglo XVIII." *Nuevo Mundo, Mundos Nuevos* (2007). http://journals.openedition.org/nuevomundo/7102.
Van Young, Eric. *Writing Mexican History*. Stanford, CA: Stanford University Press, 2012.
Varela, Gladys A., and Carla G. Manara. "Montoneros fronterizos: pehuenches, españoles y chilenos (1820–1832)." *Revista de Historia*, no. 7 (1997–98): 180–201.
Vergara Llano, Héctor. "El cuero: un insumo básico para la minería chilena del siglo XVIII." In *Episodios de historia minera. Estudios de historia social y económica de la minería chilena, siglos XVIII–XIX*, edited by Julio Pinto Vallejos, 57–95. Santiago: Editorial Universidad de Santiago, 1997.
Vezub, Julio. *Valentín Saygüeque y la "Gobernación Indígena de las Manzanas." Poder y etnicidad en la Patagonia septentrional (1860–1881)*. Buenos Aires: Prometeo, 2009.
Villalobos R., Sergio. *Los pehuenches en la vida fronteriza*. Santiago: Ediciones Universidad Católica de Chile, 1989.
Vinson, Ben, III. *Before Mestizaje: The Frontiers of Race and Caste in Colonial Mexico*. New York: Cambridge University Press, 2017.
Vitale, Luis. *Las guerras civiles de 1851 y 1859 en Chile*. Concepción, Chile: Universidad de Concepción, 1971.

Vurpillat, J. Taylor. "Empire, Industry, and Globalization: Rethinking the Emergence of the Gold Standard in the 19th-Century World." *History Compass* 12, no. 6 (2014): 531–40.

Walsh, Sarah. "The Chilean Exception: Racial Homogeneity, Mestizaje, and Eugenic Nationalism." *Journal of Iberian and Latin American Studies* 25, no. 1 (2019): 105–25.

Watts, Michael J. "Securing Oil: Frontiers, Risk, and Spaces of Accumulated Insecurity." In *Subterranean Estates: Life Worlds of Oil and Gas*, edited by Hannah Appel, Arthur Mason, and Michael Watts, 211–36. Ithaca, NY: Cornell University Press, 2015.

Weil, François. "The French State and Transoceanic Emigration." In *Citizenship and Those Who Leave: The Politics of Emigration and Expatriation*, edited by Nancy L. Green and François Weil, 114–32. Champaign: University of Illinois Press, 2007.

Whigham, Thomas L. *The Paraguayan War: Causes and Early Conduct*. 2nd ed. Calgary, AB: University of Calgary Press, 2018.

Whigham, Thomas L., and Barbara Potthast. "The Paraguayan Rosetta Stone: New Insights into the Demographics of the Paraguayan War, 1864–1870." *Latin American Research Review* 34, no. 1 (1999): 174–86.

White, Richard. *The Middle Ground: Indians, Empires, and Republics in the Great Lakes Region, 1650–1815*. New York: Cambridge University Press, 1991.

———. *The Organic Machine: The Remaking of the Columbia River*. New York: Hill and Wang, 1995.

———. *Railroaded: The Transcontinentals and the Making of Modern America*. New York: W. W. Norton, 2011.

Wolfe, Patrick. "History and Imperialism: A Century of Theory, from Marx to Postcolonialism." *American Historical Review* 102, no. 2 (April 1997): 338–420.

Wood, James A. *The Society of Equality: Popular Republicanism and Democracy in Santiago de Chile, 1818–1851*. Albuquerque: University of New Mexico Press, 2011.

Yun, Lisa. *The Coolie Speaks: Chinese Indentured Laborers and African Slaves in Cuba*. Philadelphia: Temple University Press, 2008.

Zarley, Jesse. "Between the *Lof* and the Liberators: Mapuche Authority in Chile's *Guerra a Muerte* (1819–1825)." *Ethnohistory* 66, no. 1 (January 2019): 117–39.

———. "Rutas de poder: espacio y autoridad interétnica entre la araucanía y el sur mendocino, 1790–1800." *Revista de Historia Americana y Argentina* 50, no. 1 (2015): 107–21.

Zeitlin, Maurice. *The Civil Wars in Chile (or the Bourgeois Revolutions That Never Were)*. Princeton, NJ: Princeton University Press, 1984.

Zimmerman, Eduardo. "En tiempos de rebelión: la justicia federal frente a los levantamientos provinciales, 1860–1880." In *Un nuevo orden político: provincias y Estado nacional, 1852–1880*, edited by Beatriz Bragoni and Eduardo Míguez, 245–73. Buenos Aires: Biblos, 2010.

Zimmerman, Kari. "'As Pertaining to the Female Sex': The Legal and Social Norms of Female Entrepreneurship in Nineteenth-Century Rio de Janeiro." *Hispanic American Historical Review* 96, no. 1 (February 2016): 39–72.

# INDEX

*Page numbers in italics refer to illustrations.*

Aconcagua province, Chile, 134, 204n67, 208n133
Afro-Argentines, 39, 41–42, 62, 69
agricultores. *See* peasant farmers
Alberdi, Juan Bautista, 32, 165n33
Alcalde, Manuel, 122–23, 202n50. *See also* Chile: minister of foreign relations of; exile; extradition
*almacenes. See* pulperías
Alto Verde, 79
Álvares, Cupertino, 70
Anglo-settler boom, 5, 53–54
Arahuna, Juan de Dios, 63, 67, 72, 74, 77, 80. *See also* Chilean migrants
Argentina: consulate general of, 121, 123–25; formation of Trans-Andean and, 3–4; identity construction in, 41–43, 62, 174n26; minister of foreign relations of, 45, 123–24, 134; relations with Chile, 21–22, 100–101, 105, 122–27, 134–35, 195n62, 197n96. *See also* exile; migrants; railroads; rebels; state formation
Argentine Central Railroad, 109. *See also* railroads
Argentine Great Western, 141–42. *See also* railroads
Arias, Josefa, 62. *See also* transport animals: theft of
army, 40
Arroyo, Melitón, 92
Atacama province, Chile, 23, 33, 95, 97, 104, 109
Atlantic world, 14, 20, 55, 164n27
Atuel River, *xvi*, 86
Azufre River, 85

Banegas, Gregorio, 70. *See also* transport animals
*baqueanos*, 23, 87, 189n34
Baring Crisis, 143. *See also* railroads: history of, in Argentina

239

Barrancas, Argentina, 19, 86. *See also* Pehuenches
Battle of Pavón, 2, 83, 202n51
Beéche, Gregorio, 121–24, 128, 195n62. *See also* Argentina: consulate general of
Bello, Andrés, 44–45
Betoño, Manuel, 116–17, 120. *See also* Ferrari, Casimiro: murder and
borderlands, 3, 6–10, 93, 116, 144–45, 147–52, 164nn26–27, 165n28, 187n114. *See also* Trans-Andean
bosses, 26, 51, 58, 70, 78, 102–3, 151, 170n93
Bravo, Desiderio, 115, 129–32, 200n14, 206n97. *See also* rebels: merchants and
Bravo, Marco Antonio, 115, 129. *See also* Ferrari, Casimiro: murder and
British Empire, 14, 53, 55
Buena Esperanza mine, 98
Buenos Aires, xvi; colonial trade and, 14; communication delays with, 123–24, 127, 134–35; infrastructure and, 2, 9, 31, 52–53, 83–84, 141, 151–52; nation-state formation and, 2, 5–6, 9, 15, 22, 82, 87, 124; province of, 9, 15–16, 21, 41; resistance to, 48, 92–94
Buenos Aires Western Railroad, 84
Bulnes Prieto, Manuel, 15

Cabieres, Cipriano, 66–69, 77, 79. *See also* Chilean migrants
*caciques*. *See* lonkos
Calingasta, San Juan, 43, 47
Callejas, Miguel, 104
Canales, Manuel, 78. *See also* Chilean migrants
Carrasco, Lucio, 196n66. *See also* cattle: rebels' expropriation of
Carrizal, Atacama, 94
casas. *See* houses
Catamarca province, Argentina, 97
cattle: as property, 59–60, 78, 105–8, 151; rebels' expropriation of, 10, 94, 96–103, 105, 110, 193n37, 194n51, 196n66; state power and, 59–60, 71–72, 78, 85–86; trade, 3, 10, 14–26 passim, 27, 28–29, 54, 85–86, 102–3, 117, 129, 148, 167n35, 170n92, 194n38
caudillismo. *See* caudillos
caudillos, 21, 91–93, 98, 108, 190n1, 190n5
Cea, José Manuel, 33
Central Valley, Chile, 7, 18, 25, 28, 148. *See also* Chile: agriculture in
Chile: agriculture in, 10, 18–20, 24; Argentine consulate general in, 121, 123–25; cattle markets in, 10, 18–20, 98, 100–102, 105, 168n49, 194n38; exiles in, 1–2, 15–16, 32–33, 50, 88, 92, 119, 124, 169n72; identity construction in, 41–42, 48; migrations from, 23–26, 28–29, 39–40, 46, 57, 67, 173n12; mining in, 10–11, 18, 20, 33, 54, 56, 90, 95, 97–98, 104; minister of foreign relations of, 121–22, 127; Pacific world and, 34–35; railroads to, 84, 87–88, 109, 144, 151–52; rebellions in, 44–45, 163n18, 204n67; relations with Argentina, 21–22, 122, 134–35; relations with Mendoza, 16–17, 122, 169n68; role of, in defining the Trans-Andean, 3–7, 74, 75, 76, 148, 165n28; support of Argentine rebels in, 93–96, 105, 133, 149, 190n12, 192n24, 195n62, 197n96; trade with, 27, 58, 67, 77–80, 117, 129–31, 149; war with Spain, 104–5. *See also* Chilean consulate; Chilean migrants; Trans-Andean
Chilean consulate: conscription and, 11, 37, 47–51, 119, 148–49; consular agents of, 48, 100, 128–29; consuls of, 37, 44–50; identity formation and, 11, 38, 42–43, 49, 78, 148–49; migrants' influence on, 11, 45–46, 148–49; nationality papers and, 43, 46, 48–51, 56–57, 61, 128, 148, 151; Pacific world and, 42–43; power of, in Mendoza, 43–45, 126–27, 148–49; rebellions and, 44–45, 98, 100, 119, 128–29; registry of, 46–48, 51. *See also* Godoy, Juan; Martínez, Fabián; Sánchez, Benjamín; Zenteno, José de la Cruz

Chilean migrants: conscription of, 11, 37, 47–51, 119, 132, 148–49; identity formation of, 11, 39–44, 78; nationality papers for, 43, 46, 48–51, 56–57, 61, 128, 148, 151; number of, in Argentina, 23, 154–56, 168nn60–62; occupations of, 26–29, 171n96, 171nn102–3, 171n107; reasons for migrating of, 24–25; rebels and, 1, 50, 99, 119, 128, 132–33; theft cases and, 61. *See also* Arahuna, Juan de Dios; Cabieres, Cipriano; Canales, Manuel; Chilean consulate: migrants' influence on; Chilean consulate: registry of; Fuensalida, José Dolores; Hubilla, Juan Antonio; Pavez, Tadeo; Reveco, Manuel; Roco, Baldomero; Rojas, José María; Romero, Juan de Dios; Trans-Andean: social aspects
Chincha Islands War, 104
Clark, James, 33–34
Clark, Juan and Mateo: family history of, 11, 30, 32–35, 208n1; origins of Trans-Andean railroad and, 9, 52–53, 56, 109, 135, 137; role of, in financing Trans-Andean railroad, 12, 138–39, 141; telegraph and, 11, 30–32, 35
Clavero, Francisco, 50, 129, 184n71
Colchagua province, Chile, 28
Coll, Francisco Tristán, 101
*comerciantes*. *See* merchants
commerce. *See* Trans-Andean: commerce
Compañía del Telégrafo Trasandino, 31
*complicidad*, defense of, 77–78
Conquest of the Desert, 42, 85–86, 147
Copiapó, Atacama, *xvi*, 21, 96, 98, 100, 105, 109, 168n49, 194n41
Coquimbo province, Chile, 20–21, 168n49
Córdoba province, Argentina, 13, 62, 84, 103, 109, 112, 134
Cornejo, Francisca, 62
Cortés Cumplido, Francisco, 106–7
Corvalán, Segundo, 71
*costureras*, 28, 62, 156, 184n85
Cousiño, Matías, 34

Curicó, Colchagua, *xvi*, 25, 50, 134
Cuyo, Argentina, *xvi*, 3–4, 7, 148, 150, 152; economy of, 13–17, 22; laborers in, 23, 38, 40, 133. *See also*, Mendoza; San Juan; San Luis; Trans-Andean

*defensor de los pobres y menores*, 77–78
Department of Exact Sciences, University of Buenos Aires, 82
Diaguitas, 96, 110
Du Mont, Jérôme, 142–43

Ejército de línea, 40
engineers: education of, 81–83, 188n3; frontiers and, 12, 109–11; global space and, 9, 12, 35; infrastructural power and, 12, 109–11, 113; mining and, 91, 95, 103, 108; mobility and, 10, 81, 150; state formation and, 2–3, 11, 85, 87, 89, 143–44, 152. *See also* Clark, Juan and Mateo; Naranjo, Nicolás; Rosetti, Emilio
Errázuriz, Federico, 134
Errázuriz, Maximiano, 95, 104
Espinosa, Pedro Antonio, 115–17
estancias, 24, 49, 60, 91, 98, 102–3, 179n9
exile: after independence, 15–16, 21, 24, 32–33; of Argentine rebels, 1–2, 7, 11, 92–93, 114, 118–19, 130–32; Chileans in, 44–45, 103, 109; rebel invasions from, 94, 121; surveillance and extradition of rebels in, 122–25, 204n67. *See also* extradition; rebels
extradition, 115, 120–27, 132–37, 149, 202n49, 204n67

Farías, Tomás, 120, 132–33, 202n41
FCA, 139, 141
Federalists, 2, 15, 21, 32, 50, 60–61, 92–93, 118–19, 122, 162n4
Ferrari, Casimiro: biography details of, 118, 200nn20–21, 200n24; extradition of, 126, 132, 135; murder and, 1, 114–17, 120–21, 124, 137, 201n32; as rebel, 1–3, 119–22, 129–31, 133
Ferrari, Juana Guillerma, 118, 200n22

*Index* 241

Ferrocarril Andino (FCA), 139, 141
Ferrocarril Oeste de Buenos Aires, 84
Fierro, Martín, 88–89
Figueroa, Eujenio, 196n66. *See also* cattle: rebels' expropriation of
Frías, Félix, 22, 121, 124–27, 129, 134. *See also* Argentina: consulate general of
frontiers: as concept, 7, 12, 55, 108, 110–11, 187n114; in southern Argentina, 19, 25, 28, 42, 54, 62, 86–87, 129. *See also* borderlands; Indigenous peoples; Planchón Pass
Fuensalida, José Dolores, 67–68, 77, 79–80. *See also* Chilean migrants
Fuensalida, Manuel, 68, 184n71

Galdames, Cruz, 49, 182n45. *See also* Chilean migrants
Gallo, Custodio, 34
gañanes. *See* peons
Garay, N., 196n66. *See also* cattle: rebels' expropriation of
García, Pedro, 116–17, 120
gauchesque poetry, 88–89
global economy, 3, 6, 8, 55, 83, 92, 138, 142, 147
global history, 5, 150, 165
globalization. *See* global economy
global space, 9, 11, 30–32, 35–36, 144, 152, 172n26
Godoy, Francisco Javier, 32–34
Godoy, Juan, 46, 176n60
Gomes, Juan José, 115
Gonzales, Juan, 46–47, 49, 176n61. *See also* Chilean migrants
González, Valentín, 101, 196n66. *See also* cattle: rebels' expropriation of
Goyenechea de Gallo, Candelaria, 34
Grande River valley, 85, 87
Greater Trans-Andean, 3–4, 163n14, 165n28
Guardia Nacional, 40, 46
Guardia Vieja, Aconcagua, 117
Guayama, Santos, 133–35
Guevara, Francisco, 49
Gutiérrez, Juan María, 82

habilitación, 95, 107, 192n26
haciendas, 24, 28, 180n9
Hernández, José, 88–89
Herrera, Juan de Dios, 196n66. *See also* cattle: rebels' expropriation of
*hilanderas*, 28, 156
horses. *See* transport animals
houses, 58, 66–74, 75, 77, 79, 184n76, 185n87, 186n98
Huarpes, 23, 25, 42, 59, 93, 133
Huasco, Atacama, 33–34, 94, 105, 110, 194n41
Huascoaltinos, 96, 110
Hubilla, Juan Antonio, 78. *See also* Chilean migrants

Iglesia, San Juan, 96
Indigenous peoples, xvi, 4, 7, 25, 29, 39, 41–42, 84, 110, 133, 169n84. *See also* Diaguitas; Huarpes; Mapuches; Pehuenches
infrastructure: financing of, 138–39, 152; as global space, 9, 11, 32, 35–36, 143–44, 152; as history made material, 8, 10, 34, 136; state formation and, 3, 8–11, 112–13, 143
invernadas, 18, 28
Irusta, Tomás Aquino, 62

Jáchal, San Juan, xvi, 47–48, 96, 99–100
Jameson, Guillermo, 117
Jameson, Tomás, 114–17, 129, 200n14
Jameson, William, 117
Junín, Mendoza, 21, 29, 171n103

labor: control over, 11, 37–38, 40–41, 43, 48–51, 98–100, 102, 132–33, 149; mobility and, 10–11, 22–24, 26, 40, 49, 57, 62, 81, 88, 147–48, 185n87; regimes, 11, 55–56; as social obligation, 39, 50–51; of trading animals, 78, 80. *See also* peons
laborers. *See* peons
labradores. *See* peasant farmers
Lagunas de Guanacache, Argentina, xvi, 23, 25, 59, 93. *See also* Huarpes
Laguneros, 23, 133. *See also* Huarpes

242  *Index*

Lambert, Charles, 33
Lang, Samuel, 33
La Rioja province, Argentina, 97, 191n14
Leguizamón, Felipe Santiago, 105–8, 196n66
Lemos, Cicerón, 120
León, Carlos, 130
León, Pepe, 117
Lescano, Andrés, 37, 49
liberal global rule, 55, 87, 89, 138
liberalism, 38, 87–88, 93, 108–9, 136, 162n4, 162n9
liberal state making, 5, 81, 85, 125, 162n9; historical transition to, 3, 61, 66, 71, 76, 92–93, 116, 119, 162n4. *See also* Alberdi, Juan Bautista; Mitre, Bartolomé; Sarmiento, Domingo Faustino
Linares, Maule, 25
lonkos, 19, 25, 86

Malargüe, Argentina, 19, 86. *See also* Pehuenches
Mansilla, Lucio V., 65
Mapuches, 4, 28, 42, 163n15
Martínez, Fabián, 48, 100
Masonic Society, 118
Medina, Santiago, 64
Meléndez, Féliz, 196n66. *See also* cattle: rebels' expropriation of
Mendoza province, Argentina: cattle economy in, 14, 18–19, 29, 59–60, 129; migrants in, 1, 17–18, 23–26, 28–29, 37, 39–40, 42–50, 56–58, 67, 99, 128, 147–49; mobility in, 11, 26, 28, 58, 63–64, 66, 69, 80–81, 148–49; Pacific world and, 21, 29, 35, 42–43, 56; railroads in, 84, 139, 141; rebellions in, 92–93, 99, 128–29; relations with Chile, 3–4, 15–17, 32, 44–45, 122, 126–27; relations with national government, 45, 48, 120–24, 128, 132, 134, 141; southern frontier of, 19, 25, 84, 86; state formation in, 58–61, 72–74, 76, 80–81, 148–49; trade with Chile, 3–4, 9, 14–19, 22–23, 53–54, 58, 78–79, 129–30;

viticulture in, 15–16, 32. *See also* Chilean consulate; Chilean migrants; Huarpes; military: commissions
merchants: attacks on, 115–17, 129, 133; capital from, 24; cattle trade and, 18, 117; in mining, 33, 95; mobility and, 58, 62, 64, 67, 79–80, 127–28, 134, 140, 144, 150; participation in rebellions, 12, 116, 129–32; state formation and, 5, 44, 128–32, 135; in Valparaíso, 21, 33–34, 117. *See also* Trans-Andean: commerce
migrants. *See* Anglo-settler boom; Chilean migrants; exile; mobility; peons
military: commissions, 60, 73–74, 75; conscription, 16, 37, 46–48, 50–51; laborers and, 11, 40–41, 43, 50–51, 55, 61, 128, 132, 148; rebels and, 98–99, 102, 119, 131–32. *See also* caudillos; Irusta, Tomás Aquino; Mansilla, Lucio V.
mining: booms, 4, 10, 17–18, 20–21, 33–34, 110; formation of Trans-Andean and, 3–4, 10, 23, 34, 48, 93, 97–98, 129, 142–43, 148; Pacific world and, 13–14, 18–21; rebels and, 12, 90–91, 93, 95, 97–98, 104, 107–8, 149
Mitre, Bartolomé, 2, 15
mobility: everyday, 56, 63–66, 68, 74, 80–81, 148–49; gender and, 28, 62; history and, 7, 9–10, 147–52, 164n27, 166n35; Indigenous peoples and, 4, 23, 164n23; of information, 10, 128, 132, 135–36, 151; labor and, 26, 28, 40, 56, 58, 74, 76, 80–81, 102; property and, 11, 58, 61, 63–66, 76, 80, 148–49, 151; rebels and, 12, 149; state formation and, 4, 6, 10, 58, 61, 71–72, 74, 76, 80–81, 88, 128–29, 132, 135, 148–49; technology, 65–66, 76, 80, 135. *See also* cattle; exile; migrants; railroads; rebels: mobility of; Trans-Andean: commerce
Molina, Vicente, 67–68
Montt, Jorge, 104
Montt, Manuel, 15, 44
Morales, Miguel, 115
mountain passes, *xvi*, 19, 81, 96, 120, 129, 134, 137, 189n34; Pehuenche Pass, 25;

mountain passes (*continued*)
  Planchón Pass, *xvi*, 25, 84, 86, 151; San Francisco Pass, *xvi*, 109; Uspallata Pass, *xvi*, 13, 152
Moyano, Emilio, 117, 200n14, 206n97
mules. *See* transport animals

Naranjo, Nicolás: as caudillo, 91–93, 108, 190n5; economic activities of, 104, 107–8, 191n20, 191n22, 192n24; as engineer, 95, 109–10, 113; support of rebels and, 94–96, 100, 102, 105, 149, 191n14; violence and, 98, 103–4
narratives, historical: as concept, 7, 36, 144, 152; railroads as, 7–8, 10, 88–90, 147, 151–52
Nazar, Laureano, 122
Ngulumapu, 19
Norte Chico, Chile, 4, 7, 17, 148, 151

Ocampo, Fidel, 196n66. *See also* cattle: rebels' expropriation of
O'Higgins, Bernardo, 33
Olascoaga, Manuel, 86
Ormaechea, José, 105, 196n66. *See also* cattle: rebels' expropriation of
Ovalle Hermanos, 129, 206n94

Pacific Steam Navigation Company, 34
Pacific world, 4, 17, 20–21, 29, 35, 42–43, 51, 165n28
paddocks. *See* pastures
Pampas, 4, 14, 19, 23, 25, 65, 93, 102
papeleta de conchabo, 11, 39–40, 49–51, 61, 99
Paraguayan War. *See* War of the Triple Alliance
Paraná River, 109
Pastén, Domingo, 120, 132, 202n41
pastures: cattle trade and, 16, 18–19, 25, 28, 86, 106–7; mobility and, 11, 58, 62–64, 66–68, 72, 74, 75, 151; property and, 63–64, 72, 77, 85–87, 106–7, 151; state formation and, 72, 74
Patagonia, 4, 42, 86, 93, 147, 162n9
patrones. *See* bosses

Pavez, Tadeo, 1–3, 119, 131–33, 201n32. *See also* Chilean migrants
peasant farmers, 29, 69, 168n61, 171nn102–3, 184n86. *See also* Chilean migrants: occupations of
Pehuenche Pass, 25
Pehuenches, 4, 16, 19, 25, 42, 86–87, 93, 189n34
Peñaloza, Ángel Vicente "Chacho," 92–93, 131
peons: conscription of, 48; definition of, 26; identity of, 39–44, 78; labor relations and, 26, 48–51, 55, 57–58, 63, 77–78, 80, 102–3, 151; migration of, 14, 17–18, 24, 29, 57, 148; mobility and, 9, 11, 14, 26, 28, 61–64, 66–70, 147–48, 151, 184n76; rebels and, 50, 99–100, 119, 132; state formation and, 5, 11, 37–38, 44, 46, 50, 71–72, 74, 76, 149; transportation and, 26, 170n92. *See also* Chilean migrants; labor
Pérez, José Joaquín, 15
Pérez, Rumualdo, 78
Pinto, Francisco Antonio, 33
Planchón Pass, *xvi*, 25, 84, 86, 151
Ponce de Irusta, Dominga, 61–62, 64, 66–67, 77, 79–80
Portalian state, 15
potreros. *See* pastures
Prado, Fermín, 90
Prado, Santiago, 104
Prieto Vial, Joaquín, 15
property: animal, 11, 14, 58–61, 72, 76, 149, 180n9, 185n89; mobility and, 11, 58, 63–66, 80, 149, 151–52, 166n35; railroad as, 87, 152; rebels and, 100–101, 103–5, 107–8, 127, 130–31, 192n29
Puelmapu, 163n15
pulperías, 62, 68–69
Putaendo, Aconcagua, 76

Quesada, José B., 105
Quiroga, Facundo, 88, 92–93, 190n2

Raigada, Rosario, 196n66. *See also* cattle: rebels' expropriation of railroads: Andino (FCA), 139, 141; Argentine Central, 109; Argentine Great Western, 141–42; Caldera-Copiapó, 109; global space and, 9–10, 12, 35, 136, 143–44, 152; history made durable and, 7–10, 90, 152; history of, in Argentina, 6, 83, 138–43; interoceanic, 20; Oeste de Buenos Aires, 84; property and, 65, 87, 137–38, 141–42, 152; state formation and, 3, 83, 85, 110, 112–13, 140–41, 144, 147; Trans-Andean, 1–2, 5–9, 11–12, 30–31, 51–54, 56, 81–89, 109, 135–44, 151–52; Valparaíso-Santiago line, 34. *See also* Clark, Juan and Mateo; engineers; global space; infrastructure; Rosetti, Emilio; technology; Trans-Andean: railroad

Rancagua, Santiago, 28

Rawson, Guillermo, 54–55

rebels: cattle and, 96–98, 100–102, 105–6, 196n66; depoliticization of, 120–22, 124, 126, 132; extradition and, 124–26, 132–33, 135, 149; financing of, 93–96, 98, 149; formation of Trans-Andean and, 4–5, 14; laborers and, 1, 50, 98–100, 102, 119–20, 131; merchants and, 126–28, 130–32; mining and, 5, 12, 95, 97, 103, 149; mobility of, 4, 10, 86, 137, 147, 150–51; state formation and, 1–2, 6, 44–45, 92, 116, 119, 122–24, 144, 148–49. *See also* Clavero, Francisco; Ferrari, Casimiro; Guayama, Santos; Martínez, Fabián; Peñaloza, Ángel Vicente "Chacho"; Varela, Felipe

Reveco, Manuel, 78. *See also* Chilean migrants

Revolución de los Colorados, 90, 92, 104, 110, 116, 120, 130, 133, 190n12

Ríos, Quintín, 196n66. *See also* cattle: rebels' expropriation of

Roco, Baldomero, 67, 79. *See also* Chilean migrants

Rodríguez, Cea y Cía, 33

Rodríguez, Gabriel, 196n66. *See also* cattle: rebels' expropriation of

Rojas, Isabel, 62

Rojas, José María, 57–61, 63–64, 66–70, 72, 74, 76–80, 82, 87. *See also* Chilean migrants

Romero, Juan de Dios, 70. *See also* Chilean migrants

Rosario, Santa Fe, *xvi*, 84, 109

Rosas, Juan Manuel de, 15, 21, 91–92, 108

Rosetti, Emilio, 1–3, 81–89, 109

rural stores, 62, 68–69

Salinas, Julián, 70

Salta province, Argentina, 105

San Antonio Hospital, 118, 200n21

San Carlos, Mendoza, *xvi*; cattle trade and, 19, 24, 129; Chilean migrants in, 29, 47, 57, 61, 119, 129, 170n85, 171n102; mobility and, 64, 67–68, 75, 77; state formation in, 72, 74, 78–79

Sánchez, Benjamín, 48, 128–29, 206n94

Sánchez, Mariquita, 32

San Felipe, Aconcagua, 76, 117, 121, 132

San Juan province, Argentina: migrants in, 23, 37, 42–43, 47, 148–49, 168n62; mobility in, 63, 74, 75, 78; as part of Cuyo, 3; railroads in, 139; rebellions in, 92–94, 96, 98, 100–101, 130; relations with national government, 120–21, 134; trade with Chile, 21, 97, 102–3, 105, 117, 129–30, 141, 168n49. *See* Chilean consulate; Chilean migrants; Huarpes

San Luis province, Argentina, 74, 75, 84, 139, 182n45

San Martín, José de, 88–89

San Rafael, Mendoza, *xvi*, 19, 28, 47, 49, 74, 75, 169n85

Santa Rosa de Los Andes, Aconcagua, *xvi*, 27, 76, 122, 134, 204n64

Santiago del Estero province, Argentina, 103

Sarmiento, Domingo Faustino: caudillismo and, 93, 108, 181n41, 190n2; exile of, 32–33, 88; infrastructure and, 83, 134, 137; Trans-Andean commerce and, 21–22, 127–28, 141, 204n64

*sastres*, 69

Sewell, John, 33

*Index* 245

Sewell and Patrickson, 33–34
Silva, Francisco Antonio, 104–5, 197n93
Spanish Empire, 4, 13, 55, 163n12
state formation: alternative paths of, 133; animal property and, 59, 76; borderlands and, 4, 8, 14, 43, 148–49; capitalism and, 3–4, 116, 149; mobility and, 6, 11, 38, 58, 61, 149. *See also* liberal state making
state making, liberal. *See* liberal state making
Strain, Isaac, 39
subdelegacía, 60, 76
*subdelegación. See* subdelegacía
subdelegado, 49, 60–61, 67, 72, 79, 98, 185n95

Talca, Talca, 25, 134
Tawantinsuyu (Inka Empire), 4, 13
technology, 35, 65–66, 76, 87, 90, 140, 151–52, 165n33. *See also* railroads, Trans-Andean: telegraph
*tejedoras*, 28, 156
*tejenderas*, 28, 156
telegraph, 3, 8, 11, 30–32, 34–35, 52, 125, 133–36, 140, 143
Teno River valley, 85
theft. *See* transport animals: theft of
Torres y Quiroga, Tadea, 32–34
Trans-Andean
—commerce: labor relations in, 76, 79–80, 102; Pacific markets, 10, 29; state protections of, 126–27, 129, 131; trade policy, 15–17, 20–22 (*see also* cattle; merchants)
—infrastructure: global space, 5, 32, 35, 136, 143–45, 152; infrastructure, 30, 113, 143; telegraph, 30–32, 34–35 (*see also* Trans-Andean: railroad)
—railroad: concession for, 137–39, 144; construction of, 141, 144; financing of, 12, 138–42; as global space, 11, 35, 51–53, 136, 144–45, 152; as historical narratives, 7–8, 10, 88–90, 147, 151–52; Indigenous peoples and, 54, 84–86; origins of, 5–9, 31, 83–84, 109, 135; studies of, 1–2, 82, 84–88, 109; via Planchón Pass, 54, 82–87; via San Francisco Pass, 109; via Uspallata Pass, 5, 31, 137–42, 144, 152
—social aspects: labor, 26, 39–40, 44; migrations, 23, 29; mobility, 6, 14, 23, 61, 76, 81, 102, 151; subjects, 57–59, 61, 74, 75 (*see also* Chilean migrants)
—spatiohistorical aspects: closure in, 116, 136; definition of, xvi, 3–4; as economic borderland, 7–8, 148–51; formation of, 4–6, 13–14, 34, 56, 76, 80, 82, 151; historical narratives of, 10, 147, 152; Pacific world and, 19–20
—state formation: border governance, 116, 121, 129, 132, 136; economic borderlands and, 148–49; information mobility and, 127; laborers' mobility and, 38, 61, 74, 76, 80; rebellions and, 11, 92–93, 133
Trans-Andean Telegraph Company, 31
*transeúntes*, 40
Tránsito River valley, 96, 110
transport animals: mobility and, 10–11, 58, 63–66, 75, 147, 149–51; state formation and, 11, 59–61, 72–74, 76, 148–49; theft of, 57, 67–68, 74–80, 75, 119; trading of, 62–64, 68–71, 78–79, 149
Trollope, Anthony, 142
Troncoso, Melchor, 71
Tupungato, Mendoza, xvi, 24, 119, 169n81, 170n85

Uco Valley, Argentina, 24, 28–29, 119, 170n85, 171n103
unbuilt environment, 144. *See also* global space; infrastructure
University of Buenos Aires, 2, 82
Urmeneta, José Tomás, 95, 104, 192n24
Uspallata, Mendoza, xvi, 13, 74, 75, 115, 117, 120, 133–34, 152, 202n41

Valenzuela valley, 85
Valle Fértil, San Juan, 47

Vallenar, Atacama, *xvi*, 94, 96, 104–5, 197n96
Valparaíso, Valparaíso, *xvi*; merchants in, 33–34, 117, 129, 206n97; Trans-Andean formation and, 4, 7, 21, 24, 29, 35, 141, 150, 165n28; Trans-Andean infrastructure and, 9, 31, 35, 52–53, 56, 152
Varela, Felipe, 92–95, 99, 100, 104, 105, 108, 110, 124, 131, 191n14
Vargas, Máxima, 118
Varvarco, Argentina, 19, 86. *See also* Pehuenches
Viceroyalty of the Río de la Plata, 14
Vicuña Mackenna, Benjamín, 17, 24, 194n41, 206n94
Villaseca, Toribio, 63, 67, 74, 76–77

Waddington, Joshua, 34
Wallmapu, 4, 14, 28, 163n15
War of the Pacific, 42
War of the Triple Alliance, 37, 41, 50–51, 57, 177n74
war with Paraguay. *See* War of the Triple Alliance
Wheelwright, William, 109, 191n14, 198n1; and Pacific Steam Navigation Company, 34
whiteness, 41–43, 53–55, 62–63, 173n12
work papers, 11, 39–40, 49–51, 61, 99

*zapateros*, 69, 184n85
Zenteno, José de la Cruz, 45–47, 49–51. *See also* Chilean consulate

www.ingramcontent.com/pod-product-compliance
Lightning Source LLC
Chambersburg PA
CBHW021853230426
43671CB00006B/375